PENGUIN BOOKS

MOSTLY MEDITERRANEAN

Paula Wolfert is the author of the James Beard and Julia Child/IACP award-winning *The Cooking of the Eastern Mediterranean, Couscous and Other Good Food from Morocco*, and the Tastemaker Award winner *The Cooking of South-West France*. Her writing has appeared in *Bon Appétit, Connoisseur, Elle, Food & Wine, The New York Times, Pleasures of Cooking*, and *The Traveler*. She lives in San Francisco.

MOSTLY MEDITERRANEAN

More than 200 Recipes from France, Spain, Greece, Morocco, and Sicily

PAULA WOLFERT

PENGUIN BOOKS

PENGUIN BOOKS

Published by the Penguin Group

Penguin Books USA Inc., 375 Hudson Street, New York, New York 10014, U.S.A.

Penguin Books Ltd, 27 Wrights Lane, London W8 5TZ, England

Penguin Books Australia Ltd, Ringwood, Victoria, Australia

Penguin Books Canada Ltd, 10 Alcorn Avenue, Toronto, Ontario, Canada M4V 3B2

Penguin Books (N.Z.) Ltd, 182–190 Wairau Road, Auckland 10, New Zealand

Penguin Books Ltd, Registered Offices: Harmondsworth, Middlesex, England

First published in the United States of America under the title *Paula Wolfert's World of Food*
by Harper & Row, Publishers, Inc. 1988
Published in Penguin Books 1996

10   9   8   7   6   5   4   3   2   1

Portions of this book have appeared in somewhat different form in: *Bon Appétit*; *Connoisseur*;
Cuisine; *Elle*; *Food & Wine*; *Metropolitan Home*; *New York Magazine*; *The New York Times*;
Pleasures of Cooking; and *The Traveler*.

The recipe for Walnut Roll on page 306 is courtesy *House & Garden*.
Copyright © 1958 by The Condé Nast Publications Inc.

LIBRARY OF CONGRESS CATALOG CARD NUMBER: 88-3311
ISBN 0-06-015955-3 (hc.)
ISBN 0 14 02.5769 1 (pbk.)

Printed in the United States of America
Set in Bulmer
Designed by Richard Oriolo

CONTENTS

ACKNOWLEDGMENTS

Many generous people helped with this book, and I hope every one of them will find his or her name, arranged alphabetically below.

With thanks to Antonia Allegra, Colman Andrews, Jean-Marie Arzak, Manuel Balló, Pierre Bardeche, Lidia Bastianich, Alex Bespaloff, Michel Bras, Patricia Brown, Ramón Cabau (deceased), Maggie Cheney, Jacques Chibois, Bernard Clayton, Jr., Aude Clement, Catherine Cocuard, Eliane Comelade-Thibaut, Serge Coulons, André Daguin, Ariane Daguin, Danielle Delpeuch, Adolpho De Martino, Frank Ducate, Alain Dutournier, Jane Freiman, Daniel Fuchs, Paola Gallo, Vittorio Gallo, Ruth Gardner, Georgie Géry, Rudolf Grewe, Pasqualino Giudice, Montse Guillén, André Guillot, Marc Haeberlin, Suzanne Hamlin, Barbara Kafka, Grace Kirschenbaum, Sotiris Kitrialakis, Rick Kot, René Lasserre, Susan Lescher, Maria and Dimitris Lykouresis, Richard Lord, Lorenza de' Medici, Salvatore and Silvana Monasteri, Joseph Montebello, Madame Muruamendiaraz, Leslie Newman, Fiametta di Napoli Olivier, Gianfranco Pagliaricci, Marie-Luisa de Palermo, Jean-Louis Palladin, Ambassador George Papoulias, Dr. André Parcé, Toula Patsoulas, Maricel Persilla, Lulu Peyraud, Warren Picower, Lola Pijoan, Vita Coppola Poma, Tony Schneider, Margaret Simmons, the Sindoni Family, Romano Soltari, Lois Stanton, Jaime Subiros, Jean-Claude Szurdak, Marimar Torres, Lucien Vanel, James Villas, Jan Weimer, Susan Wyler, and Sophia Yannis.

And finally a very special thanks to my dear husband, Bill Bayer.

This book, I hope, stands clearly labeled for what it is—a personal collection, recipes drawn together from my travels and my friends, worked up and refined in my kitchen. My choices here have been selective and subjective, mediated by my taste. I have written and will write only about food I like to cook and eat.

Although my previous books were regional, limited by the geography of their subjects, they, too, were personal, for I never set out to write definitive books about Moroccan cooking, or the cooking of South-West France, or Mediterranean food. In this book I have forsworn the restrictions of national frontiers, drawing together recipes from Catalonia, Sicily, the Ionian islands, Morocco, and various parts of France. But this collection is not, in fact, as eclectic as it may sound. It represents my culinary world, mostly but not exclusively Mediterranean-based, defined, as always, by my taste, my palate.

I have always been drawn to what I call the Mediterranean Myth, the ideal, shared by many, of a robust, simple, and sensual life far from the madding crowds of our competitive North Atlantic culture. I have been drawn too to traditional Mediterranean ingredients: olives, olive oil, garlic, capers, anchovies, honey, lemons and oranges, grapes, and lots of herbs and spices. Foods made with these easy-to-find products are the dishes I prepare most frequently.

A few words, first, about the criteria I applied in selecting the following recipes. When people ask me how I develop recipes, I have to respond: "Traveling, eating, watching, experimenting, and constantly asking myself: 'Do I want to eat this dish again?' " That, I think, is the ultimate test: whether a dish is worth making a second time. Other ways of posing the question: Does this food taste true? Will I yearn for it some evening when I'm hungry? Will I remember it in six months' time? In a year? Five years from now?

I don't think it's enough that a recipe be unique, interesting, odd-ball, previously unpublished, or simply "new." A dish worth repeating has to taste really good. That may, I confess, sound obvious, but in our current culinary scene, it is too often forgotten.

Personally, I love the bistro classics best—beef with carrots, duck with apples, veal with morels, chicken with wine. When I ask myself why I'm so fond of these recipes, I realize it's because they employ ingredients that have traditionally complemented one another and that, when combined, create a flavor different and more pleasing than when served on their own. This collection includes many dishes of this type.

When I develop my recipes I always look for ways to create what I call the Big Taste. While I enjoy eating simple grilled foods, what interests me when I *cook* are dishes with a taste that is fully dimensional.

What do I mean by Big Taste? I mean food that is deeply satisfying, and that appeals to all the senses. I like dishes that leave their flavor with me, whose tastes and aromas I will never forget. This doesn't mean that they have to be fussy or elaborate. I believe a well-made pasta served with a squid-ink sauce has a bigger taste than the seductive "black ravioli" we see on so many menus these days, in which the ink is used as a coloring agent instead of the primary source of flavor.

Another example of a dish with Big Taste is Duck You Can Eat with a Spoon, in which the meat is marinated in *cooked* red wine for a fuller, rounder effect. The cooked duck pieces, soft and succulent, are boned and garnished with rich caramelized baby onions, crisp lardons, mushrooms, and garlic-parsleyed croutons. The sauce resonates with the dark, musky perfume of bitter cocoa and Cognac and is both extraordinary and memorable.

Along with a Big Taste, I also like dishes that have real polish, by which I mean food that is refined in its structure—or, to make an analogy with music, dishes that have perfect pitch.

An example of such a dish is Michel Bras's Cèpe Tart with Walnut Cream, in which a light mixture of prosciutto, cream, and walnuts produces a rich and flavorful background for a layer of wild mushrooms. Every step in the recipe works toward the final result; every nuance has a meaning, and in the end, something sophisticated happens: the dish tastes clean and fresh.

There are other common threads in this book: cooking techniques and products that cut across national and cultural frontiers.

The first of these, a technique, is long, slow cooking, which allows the development of a deep, satisfying taste through the mellowing and interaction of ingredients. Dishes such as my French-inspired Expatriate's Ragout, an Estofat of Beef from Barcelona, and Moroccan Lamb Tagine with Melting Tomatoes and Onions all employ this traditional farm house method.

I am equally intrigued by sophisticated kitchen techniques. To name just a few: low-temperature cooking of selected fish to achieve silky texture and vivid taste; wrapping lean meats and fish in caul fat for constant self-basting; marinating Atlantic fish in seaweed, in preparation for a *bouillabaisse,* to recreate the unique flavor of Mediterranean rockfish.

Another theme that runs through these pages is the attainment of richness without heaviness. Years of eating in restaurants (mostly French) have conditioned us to perceive a dish as rich only if it contains cream or butter. But there are ways to produce food that is equally rich, no less flavorful, and much better for our health. An example is the use of ground almonds as a thickening agent in such disparate dishes as Quail Enrobed in Red Peppers, a specialty of Tarragona in Spain, and Fish Couscous from Trapani in Sicily.

Richness-with-lightness can also be achieved by careful preparation. In this book you will find many techniques for lightening food, such as methods for degreasing cooking liquids and double-blanching beans, and a technique for frying eggplant slices that have first been salted, soaked in milk, and then dredged in flour, so that they come out with crisp exteriors and creamy interiors, absorbing nary a drop of frying oil.

Friends have pointed out to me that many of my dishes are brown. They're right; I love dark, earthy food, sturdy, homey dishes, and you will find many in these pages, ranging from Apples Baked on Cabbage Leaves from Poitou in France, to Beef Stew with Tomatoes and Onions from the Peloponnesian mountains in Greece.

And just as I have always been interested in rustic ingredients (salt cod, squid, rabbit) so too have I had a parallel fascination with sophisticated items such as sea urchins, chestnut honey, and *foie gras*.

Though I have never wished to be faddish with my cooking, it does seem appropriate, as new products such as fresh *foie gras* have become available, to delve into them, explore their possibilities, and set my discoveries down. Just to handle a whole raw *foie gras* for the first time is an extremely exciting and sensual experience.

One of the pleasures of being a food writer is to meet and work with talented people. Among the talented chefs whom I most admire are three Frenchmen: Michel Bras of Laguiole, who has reinterpreted peasant dishes of the Auvergne, raising them to new and luminous heights; Jacques Chibois of Cannes, who has forged a bright and happy style of working with the produce of Provence; and Jean-Louis Palladin, a Gascon transplanted to Washington, D.C., who has applied his dazzling technique and explosive creativity to native American products. I have learned much from each, and have tried to interpret their lessons in these pages.

I have always loved dishes about which a story can be told, a story, perhaps, about why and by whom a particular dish is cooked, or relating something about the place where it is served. When I come to understand the whys and wherefores behind a dish, I feel a friendship, a kinship with the people who cook it. It is this same kind of friendly bridge I hope to create with my readers. If one of these stories can place a dish in context and make it come alive, convey enough of my own enthusiasm so that you will want to cook it yourself, then I will have achieved my goal.

But in the end, with any cookbook, it is the recipes that must be the real revelation. I hope that mine will be understood, prepared, eaten, and enjoyed!

NOTE TO THE COOK

In this book you will find recipes for dishes that I have served to my friends and taught in my cooking classes. All have been tested and retested, not only by me but sometimes, too, in the test kitchens of the various publications in which some of them first appeared.

Though many of these recipes may look long, that does not necessarily mean that they are difficult. I sometimes write expansively in order that the instructions be as precise as possible—especially when I want to share a new technique.

Many of the dishes here can be prepared long in advance of a dinner because this is the way I like to prepare food myself, completing as many steps as possible long before the meal so that cooking is relaxing and I am not harried before I eat.

A NOTE ON ATTRIBUTION

A recipe generally has a source, and we food writers must be scrupulous about assigning credit. I've developed my own way of acknowledging sources, a system that worked well in my last book, and which I have adapted for use here again.

I prefer, whenever possible, to work from primary sources: When I learn a dish I stand next to the person cooking it. I ask a lot of questions and take copious notes. When I use books, they are most often primary source books (see Bibliography), generally written in the language of the country where the dish was originally prepared. When I develop a recipe, I base it on my research, various tastings of the dish, the literature and oral lore that surrounds it, and my own amalgam of methods and techniques, most taught to me by various cooks throughout the years.

If a recipe bears no attribution, then it is my version of a modern or traditional dish belonging legally or morally to no individual—a dish, therefore in the public domain.

If a recipe bears the name of a specific individual in its title, is attributed in my recipe introduction, or ends with the line: "Inspired by a recipe from———," then, in fact, that is just what has occurred: I've taken a recipe taught or inspired by a particular cook and made changes in it. These changes may include any or all of the following: substitution of ingredients more readily available in the United States; simplification of a restaurant dish so it will work in a home kitchen; changes in technique; other improvements that will better serve my readers.

Finally, if a recipe is directly attributed to a published source, then it is copyrighted material used here with permission.

MOSTLY
MEDITERRANEAN

BREADS

The search for great bread: It has been my passion. Whenever I travel I constantly ask people: "Where can I find the best bread around here?" "Who is the best baker?" And nearly always, as soon as I ask, the eyes of my respondent will light up. He or she will utter a name and an address. And then I am off upon the hunt.

I remember one such expedition outside Palermo. I had heard tales of this particular bread even before I got to Sicily. Adolfo, my Sicilian friend in New York, had wanted to phone Salvatore, his friend in Palermo, to ensure I would be able to taste it.

"Too much trouble," I had said. "Surely I can find it on my own."

"You will never find it," Adolfo had declared. "And for a bread such as this no amount of trouble can ever be too much."

Such a passion for food! But I soon discovered that that was a Sicilian trait. So there I was, in the back of Salvatore's tiny car, plunging through the unbelievable traffic of Palermo. A light rain was falling, the window wipers were slapping away, and my new friend and his wife kept turning in their seats to tell me of other Sicilian gastronomic pleasures I must not miss. The swordfish preparations of Messina! The fish couscous of Trapani! The harmonious *stemperata* of Siracusa! Ricotta ice cream! Pasta alla Norma! Pasta con le sarde! A little family restaurant by the railroad station in Bagheria . . .

It was dusk when we finally arrived at a fresh-water spring near the great cathedral town of Monreale in the hills behind Palermo. We made our way through the mist and mud to where people were filling water jugs, then around to a shack where the famous bread was made. The bakers were two women in their eighties wearing aprons and blue hats, their eyes twinkling with pleasure at my arrival.

No, I cannot tell you how to find the place. The only address I have is "Fonta di Veniero beside the Villa Scarlata." And, no, I cannot give you a recipe for this sublime bread with its chewy, wheaty flavor and crisp, shattering crust. Its excellence depends on the special qualities of the local water, the use of lemon and olive woods to heat the oven, and the fact that the ladies knead the dough by hand for forty-five long minutes. But I hope I have conveyed to you a little of my own thrill and passion. Bread is enormously important to me, a wonderful complement to food. Here are three recipes for various breads. I hope you will make and enjoy a Sicilian semolina loaf, a Moroccan bread flavored with anise, and a Catalan crusty round.

Sicilian Semolina Bread

MAKES 2 LOAVES
(freeze the extra loaf)

One of my favorite Sicilian cookbooks, Giuseppe Coria's *Profumi di Sicilia,* describes so many breads, in so many shapes and sizes, that I've thought that a book devoted solely to Sicilian breads might be in order. The shapes range from ordinary circles and arcs to wreaths, ladders, babies, flowers, fruits, and even cornucopias. Nearly every Sicilian town has at least two favorite shapes, one for every day, and another for religious feasts. By far the most attractive form is the bunch of grapes, symbolizing the fertility of the Sicilian soil.

Unlike white-flour Italian bread, Sicilian bread is often made from semolina, which gives it a pale yellow color and a special nutty taste. The color may remind you of brioche, but this bread contains neither eggs nor butter, just a tablespoon of olive oil added for richness and elasticity. I can buy semolina bread sprinkled with sesame seeds at my local supermarket in New York, but if you cannot find it where you live, I offer here a simple recipe. The bread is delicious on its own, or try it in Sicilian dishes such as Pasqualino's Crunchy Bread (page 3); Island of Lipari Spicy Bread Salad (page 10); and Involtini of Swordfish with Capers (page 119).

It is easy to knead this dough in the food processor, using the same finely ground 100 percent semolina (durum) flour required for pasta. (Do not confuse this flour with coarse semolina, which is used to make couscous.) The dough needs three risings for lightness and flavor.

1 *package active dry yeast*

½ *teaspoon sugar*

1 *tablespoon olive oil*

1 *pound (about 2⅔ cups) finely ground semolina flour (1 cup equals 6 ounces)*

12 *ounces (approximately 2 cups) all-purpose unbleached flour*

1 *tablespoon coarse (kosher) salt*

Flour for dusting work surface

1 *tablespoon sesame seeds (optional)*

1. In a large bowl, combine the yeast and sugar with 3 tablespoons of warm water, stirring to dissolve the yeast completely. Add 1¾ cups of water and the olive oil. Gradually stir in the semolina flour, all but ½ cup of the all-purpose flour, and the salt, to make a soft, rather sticky dough. Turn it out onto a lightly floured surface and knead for 10 minutes. (The dough can be halved, each half kneaded in the food-processor workbowl for 1 minute and returned to the work surface.) Knead all the dough together for 1 minute. Transfer the dough to a lightly oiled bowl, turn to coat all surfaces, cover with a kitchen towel, and let it rise at room temperature for 2 hours or until almost tripled in bulk.

2. Punch the dough down, transfer it to a floured work surface (using the remaining ½ cup of flour as necessary) and knead for 1 minute. Return the dough to the bowl, cover

with a towel, and allow a second rise at room temperature for 1 hour or until the dough is doubled in bulk.

3. Punch the dough down, transfer it back to the work surface, and shape it into 2 balls or loaves. Place them on a large baking sheet dusted with flour, cover with the kitchen towel, and let them rise until almost doubled in bulk.

4. When the loaves are almost double in bulk, use a razor blade or sharp knife to make diagonal gashes on top about 3 inches apart. Brush the tops with water and sprinkle with sesame seeds.

5. Preheat the oven to 425° F. Bake the loaves for 30 minutes or until they are hollow-sounding when thumped. Cool on racks.

Pasqualino's Crunchy Bread

Now that you have semolina bread, try this delicious antipasto preparation of flavored bread croutons, served by my friend Pasqualino Giudice in his restaurant Jonica in Siracusa. Thin slices of semolina bread are fried, then seasoned with fine sea salt, fine hot red pepper, and oregano. (Pasqualino fries his bread in Sicilian olive oil, and he uses the highly aromatic wild oregano from Mount Iblei.) These croutons are also delicious with tomato-enriched fish soups.

Fruity extra-virgin olive oil

24 *stale ⅓-inch-thick slices of semolina bread*

Fine sea salt

Cayenne pepper

2 *tablespoons Mediterranean oregano (see note)*

Wine vinegar (optional)

Heat the oil to a depth of ¼ inch in a nonstick skillet. Fry the slices in hot oil, a few at a time, until golden brown on one side, then turn and fry them on the second side. Remove the slices to drain and repeat with the remaining slices. Sprinkle them with salt, cayenne, and oregano while still hot. Allow to cool to room temperature, or serve at once, sprinkled lightly with vinegar, if you wish.

McCormick packages Mediterranean oregano. If unavailable at your local supermarket, see Appendix, page 347, for mail-order source for Greek oregano.

NOTE TO THE COOK

Moroccan Anise-Flavored Bread

MAKES 2
LOAVES

Just as Sicilian semolina bread goes perfectly with many Sicilian dishes, so this dense anise-scented bread is the ideal complement to Moroccan salads and *tagines*. The characteristics of a *tagine* include a succulent, highly seasoned sauce, long, slow, steady cooking, and meat or poultry so well cooked it can easily be eaten with the fingers. Wedges of anise-scented Moroccan bread are used by the Moroccan diner to grasp and then transport the tender meat to his mouth, and to soak up the delicious gravy.

I urge you to make this bread whenever you serve Moroccan food. It is one of the easiest bread recipes I know—it needs only one rising—and it enhances Moroccan food enormously.

1 *package active dry yeast*
¼ *teaspoon sugar*
3½ *cups bread flour*

1 *cup coarse whole-wheat flour, plus 2 tablespoons*
1 *tablespoon salt*
1 *tablespoon anise seeds*

1. Proof the yeast in sugared water. In a large mixing bowl, combine the bread flour, whole-wheat flour, and salt. Add the yeast mixture and enough lukewarm water (about 1½ cups) to form a stiff dough. Knead 15 minutes or until the dough is smooth and elastic. Knead in the anise seeds. Divide the dough in half, shape it into 2 balls, and let them stand 5 minutes. Lightly oil the surface of each ball of dough. Grasp a small part of one ball and begin to roll it around the inside of a wide mixing bowl until smooth. Flatten it into a disk 1 inch thick and 5 to 6 inches in diameter. Repeat with the second ball of dough. Sprinkle a baking sheet with the 2 tablespoons of whole-wheat flour. Place each loaf on the sheet. Cover loosely with a damp towel and let the loaves rise about 2 hours, or until a hole poked in the dough with your fingers remains deeply indented. Prick each loaf deeply 6 or 7 times with a fork to release the gas.

2. Heat the oven to 400° F. Bake the loaves 12 minutes. Reduce the oven temperature to 300° and bake for 40 minutes longer, or until the bottom of the bread sounds hollow when thumped. Remove the loaves from the oven and let cool before slicing into wedges.

Catalan Coarse Country-Style Bread

It was ten o'clock in the morning. I was seated at the coffee bar Kiosco in the La Boqueria, the huge, boisterous, and legendary central market of Barcelona, just off the Ramblas. Behind me great commotion—buying, selling, haggling. Before me, on the counter, an array of Catalan delicacies. Tiny fish, *salmonettas*, lifted straight from the hot oil. Paper-thin slices of mountain ham. A medley of green olives, seven different kinds, including soft *perlas*, small and bitter *arbequinas*, and meaty *sevillanas*, which had been soaked in anchovy water. But the *chef d'oeuvre* of this market breakfast was a platter piled high with *pa amb tomàquet* *—slabs of country bread, wood-fire toasted, then smeared with ripe red tomatoes and drizzled with olive oil.

My host was the late Barcelona gastronome Ramón Cabau, who, with his charming smile and straw hat, looked a bit like Maurice Chevalier. Surveying the richness of the meal, Ramón twirled the handlebars of his mustache, then lifted his glass of Vega Sicilia '78. "To the cuisine of Catalunya, to gastronomy and friendship," he said. "And," he added, nodding toward the *pa amb tomàquet*, "to bread."

In order to make the simple, round dense loaf of bread required for *pa amb tomàquet* you will need to have some starter on hand. (You can make it up to 4 days in advance.) Your only ingredients are yeast, flour, water, and salt. Use only fresh flour, and if your water is chlorinated, use Evian or a similar bottled water. The bread keeps fresh up to 7 days.

Use bread flour or an all-purpose flour with at least 13 percent gluten so that the bread will have the stretch necessary to rise. The sequence of three risings allows this bread to develop body and flavor.

* *Pan y tomate* in Spanish. Catalan dishes are spelled in the Catalan language in this book.

STARTER FOR 1 OR 2 LOAVES

1 *package active dry yeast*	1⅔ *cups warm water*
⅓ *cup warm water (approximately 105° F)*	5½ *cups (approximately) bread flour*
½ *cup bread flour*	1 *tablespoon fine salt*

1. Make the starter at least one day in advance. In a small bowl, mix the yeast with 2 tablespoons of warm water and stir until well dissolved. Stir in the remaining water and the flour, mixing until smooth. Cover the starter with plastic wrap and let it stand at room temperature overnight.

(continued)

2. The day you plan to make the bread, put the starter into a mixing bowl. Add 1⅔ cups water and the bread flour by cupfuls, mixing thoroughly and allowing each cupful of flour to be absorbed before adding the next. (You can use an electric mixer with a dough hook, set on slow.) Add the salt at the end. If the dough is tacky after all the flour has been added, add 1 to 2 tablespoons more flour. Allow the dough to rest 5 minutes before kneading.

3. Knead the dough by hand for 20 minutes, or use an electric mixer, kneading 10 minutes on slow. Turn out and knead by hand for 1 minute to achieve the proper consistency—a smooth, elastic, satiny-soft dough. Place the dough in a lightly oiled mixing bowl; turn to coat all sides, cover it with a cloth, and let it rise in a warm draft-free place, about 1½ hours.

4. Punch the dough down. Turn it onto a lightly floured work surface and knead ½ minute. Return the dough to the bowl and let it rise once more, about 1 hour.

5. Turn the dough out onto the lightly floured work surface, divide it in half, and knead each half about 1 minute. Shape each half into a 6-inch flat round, place on a floured baking sheet, cover, and let it rise in a warm place until doubled in volume, about 1 hour. Use a razor blade or a very thin, sharp knife to make 3 to 4 crisscrossing gashes on tops. Let the loaves stand 15 minutes. Meanwhile preheat the oven to 425° F. Place a shallow baking pan with 1 inch of water on the oven floor. Bake the loaves 30 to 40 minutes until well browned and hollow-sounding when thumped. Immediately remove them to wire racks to cool.

(Pa amb tomàquet)

Wood-Grilled Slices of Bread Rubbed with Fresh Tomato

This famous Catalan specialty, delicious any time of the day, is best prepared during the late summer and early autumn months when the tastiest tomatoes are available. There is no recipe; one simply assembles, but all the ingredients must be perfect.

Cut the Catalan-style bread with a serrated knife into ½-inch slices. Lightly toast the slices in a toaster-oven, or grill them, as they do at Can Juanito, a restaurant in Barcelona, over a fire of hardwood. Slather the toasted slices (on both sides, if desired) with freshly crushed ripe tomatoes. The layer must not be too thin—or too thick—more like a thin, even red sheen. Sprinkle with fine salt. Slowly drizzle a light, golden extra-virgin olive oil on top of one side.

If you like, you can top the bread off with paper-thin slices of Serrano-type cured ham or large, fat fillets of anchovy, preferably imported from l'Escale. You may want to rub some garlic on the bread as well, but I've yet to meet a Catalan gastronome who would approve. Eat with a knife and fork.

BREAD AND OIL

What I am about to describe has no name, at least not, so far as I know, in Greece. (In southern Italy another version is called *bruschetta,* and there are variations in other Mediterranean countries as well.) It is not an exotic ingredient, like truffles or caviar, nor is it a great and mighty "world-class" dish, such as Moroccan *bisteeya* or the *cassoulet* of South-West France. It involves no cooking and no culinary technique; a child can put it together in moments. Like *pa amb tomàquet,* it is nothing more than an assemblage of a few common ingredients, and, oh yes, on the day when I first tasted it I knew it was one of the most delicious things I had ever eaten.

It would be disingenuous not to add that the quality of these ingredients was all-important, as was the place where this snack was eaten, the smell of the air, the slant of the light, the sound of the sea. Suddenly everything I loved about Mediterranean life came together in a perfect moment, and the dish revealed to me the soul of Mediterranean food.

For twenty years I'd been roaming this region in search of recipes, food that appealed to all my senses. So, in the end, where did I find perfection? I'm almost ashamed to admit it: the dish was nothing much more than bread and oil.

But what bread! What oil!

The occasion was a picnic on the Ionian island of Paxos. My husband and I had been staying in Corfu, a beautiful, marvelous place, but the tourist mobs were becoming overwhelming and we longed for something pure. Paxos is relatively unspoiled. Three hours by ferry from Corfu and barely five miles long, the island is really one great orchard of three hundred thousand ancient, gnarled olive trees, a rocky garden of wildflowers, and a utopia of hidden coves, sand and pebble beaches, craggy lookout points, and caves carved out by the sea. The Ionian islands aren't dry like the islands of the Aegean—they are lush, green, Italianate. And on Paxos the air seemed clearer, the water cleaner, the hues of blue and green more intense than on most other Mediterranean paradises we had known.

Our picnic was carefully planned. We bought our bread in the little fishing village of Loggos, a special round loaf reputed to be the best on the island. Our olive oil, purchased in Gaios, was from the first pressing of the Paxos fruit, rich, clear, and golden, bearing a faint overtaste of hazelnut. And in Gaios, too, we hired a fishing boat to prowl the western coast of the island, with its natural rock obelisks and the strange "arch" of Tripito hewn out of its cliffs.

On board we cut our bread into thick slices, which we then left out in the sun to "toast." (A gastronome friend from Crete had given us precise instructions, using a local toasted bread called *frigania.*) We landed at the small beach of Galasio, swam, sunned ourselves, and then set about to assemble our dish. First we sprinkled the pieces of sun-toasted bread with a few drops of water. Next we poured on a generous amount of olive oil and then a light sprinkling of salt. After ten minutes, time enough for the oil to soak into the dried bread, we added slices of perfectly ripened tomatoes and a few thin rings of red onion on the top.

That was all. The dish was made. We ate it. And it was perfect. . . .

CHAPTER 2 *FIRST COURSES*

SEVEN SICILIAN ANTIPASTI

They call it Vucciria, "the voices," and it is one of the great food markets of the Mediterranean, a maze of alleyways in the heart of old Palermo lined with stalls and stands. As you approach you can hear the voices of the city blending into a kind of music, echoing but subdued by the narrow, angled streets.

Then the bounty: Piles of fennel both wild and sweet. Sturdy, thick cardoons. Eggplants in all sizes and hues, from whitish-pink to black. Bronze lobsters, blue mackerel, silver fish flashing in the sun. Pyramids of olives. Strings of garlic. Meats, sausages, and hams hanging from hooks. There are hordes of people, sellers calling out the quality of their produce, buyers haggling over price. Firm cheeses bound with rope. Soft cheeses oozing onto plates. It is a magnificent scene, and it all comes triumphantly together in the square called Piazza Garraffello. Here beneath red awnings fresh swordfish is sold, swordfish both pale cream and white, the swords still attached to the heads pointing proudly at the sky.

Such produce! How I loved it, and how I loved what the Sicilians could do with it. Their cooking is rich, colorful, and highly seasoned, an exciting, pure-tasting cuisine based on wonderful ingredients. Sicilian food seemed to me to be totally original, unlike any other Italian food I had known.

The following seven dishes, served in Sicilian restaurants as "antipasti," are actually *contorni*, vegetable accompaniments to a main dish of meat or fish. Often when I entertain I make anywhere from three to five of them (most can be made early in the day). I may begin the meal with a pasta and go on to a main course of meat or grilled fish, but the *contorni* stay on the table throughout, so each guest can help himself.

Island of Lipari Spicy Bread Salad

SERVES 4

This delicious semolina bread salad, called *pane a caponata,* is from the Aeolian island of Lipari. The extraordinary flavor of lightly toasted semolina gives it a special distinction. I prefer it to the famous Tuscan *panzanella* (a salad of bread, olive oil, and tomato, made with a Tuscan peasant-style saltless loaf) or the Middle Eastern *fattouche* (a bread, olive oil, and mixed-vegetable salad, made with stale toasted Arab bread).

½ *loaf crusty peasant-style Italian bread, preferably semolina bread (page 2), crusts removed, cut into ½-inch cubes (1½ cups)*

2 *red-ripe tomatoes, peeled and cubed (1 cup)*

¼ *cup extra-virgin olive oil (preferably Sicilian)*

6 *scallions (white part only), sliced thin*

2 *tablespoons chopped French cornichons*

2 *teaspoons minced fresh oregano or ½ teaspoon dried, crumbled*

1½ *tablespoons minced flat-leaf parsley*

½ *teaspoon salt*

¾ *teaspoon fine-minced green pickled peppers or hot Italian peperoncini, seeds and membranes removed, or to taste*

Preheat the oven to 300° F. Spread the bread cubes on a baking sheet. Bake for 10 minutes to toast them lightly. Transfer the bread to a medium bowl. Add all the remaining ingredients and toss. Let the salad stand 30 minutes before serving.

NOTES TO THE COOK

This salad is quite peppery. You may want to use it as an accompaniment to paper-thin slices of raw beef.

When tomatoes are red, ripe, and aromatic, peel them with a vegetable peeler. If you drop them into boiling water, you risk cooking them.

Maria Sindoni's Caponatina

Most published recipes for *caponata*—*caponatina* in Palermitano dialect—result in a somewhat heavy dish. Not so this version of Maria Sindoni, who shared her secret with me at the kitchen stove in her restaurant, Azzurro, in New York. Maria emphasized a few points: fry only the eggplant in olive oil; cook each vegetable separately (this way each one retains its natural flavor); and do not mix the vegetables until they have all cooled down (so that each retains its individual texture). The resulting salad is very light.

Caponatina is delicious, but it is not a pretty dish. At Azzurro they serve a portion in a leaf of radicchio, and top it with a big sprig of basil. My friend Fiametta, who lives in Mondello near Palermo, decorates her *caponatina* with a mixture of hard-boiled eggs, lobster, baby octopus, shrimps, and the salted roes of tuna, all chopped up together. Finally, she sprinkles the top with toasted and finely chopped almonds and with the yolks and whites of hard-boiled eggs, fillets of anchovy, capers, and olives.

This *caponatina* is best made 2 to 3 days in advance, giving the dish time to mellow.

2½ to 3 pounds eggplant

Coarse (kosher) salt

½ cup extra-virgin olive oil

1 cup chopped onion

1 cup chopped celery heart, with some leaves

¾ cup homemade tomato sauce (see note)

7 tablespoons red wine vinegar

1 tablespoon sugar, or more to taste

Pinch of hot red-pepper flakes, or to taste

6 pitted green olives, Sicilian or Greek green-cracked, cut into small pieces

1. Peel the eggplant, stem, cut the flesh into 1-inch cubes, and place them in a large colander. Toss the eggplant with salt and let stand for 30 minutes. Rinse well and drain dry.

2. Slowly heat the oil in a small skillet, preferably nonstick. Add the eggplant in small batches and fry over medium-high heat until golden brown on all sides. Transfer the eggplant with a slotted spoon to a colander set over a plate to catch any excess oil.

3. Strain the oil from the skillet, leaving only a film. Add the onions, 1 teaspoon of salt, and 1½ cups water, and cook for 30 minutes. Separately place the celery in a small heavy saucepan with ½ teaspoon salt and water to cover, and cook for 30 minutes. Whenever necessary add a few tablespoons of the simmering celery water to the onions to keep

(continued)

them from burning. When the onions have cooked 30 minutes and most of the water has evaporated, slowly let them turn golden, stirring occasionally. Add the tomato sauce, and cook, stirring, for 1 minute.

4. Drain the celery of excess moisture, and add it to the onions and tomato sauce. Scrape the mixture into a bowl and set it over ice to cool down quickly, stirring frequently. Without rinsing the skillet, add the vinegar and sugar and cook, stirring, until a light reddish-orange color is produced and the mixture has reduced to 3 tablespoons. Scrape it into a small bowl and set it aside. Allow to cool.

5. Combine the eggplant with the onion-celery-tomato mixture, vinegar-sugar mixture, pepper flakes, and olives, stirring carefully. Pack the mixture into a jar, cover tightly, and refrigerate. (*The recipe can be prepared up to this point in advance.* Let the mixture return to room temperature before serving.)

NOTES TO
THE COOK
A recipe for a good homemade tomato sauce is on page 60, or use a top-quality commercial sauce.

Siracusan Baked Onion Slices

This easy and delectable salad is from the city of Siracusa on the eastern or "Greek" side of Sicily. "We are Greek." "We have a Greek mentality." Over and over, talking to Siracusans, I heard this sentiment, which struck home early one morning when I visited their wonderful Tempio Apollo market.

Here I found the same gorgeous eggplants, fish, olives, almonds, cheeses, and herbs that I had seen in all the markets of Sicily. But the atmosphere was remarkable, the pace less frantic. While at the Vucciria market in Palermo the vendors had no time to answer questions, then grew angry when I passed them by, in Siracusa they offered me tastes: a date, an orange, a fresh sea urchin roe on a piece of bread. Their method is seduction, not confrontation. I recognized Greek temperance.

Most cooks who execute this dish bake a whole onion and then slice and dress it with a vinaigrette. In the salad below the onions are sliced first, then slowly baked so that each slice caramelizes to a golden brown and turns meltingly tender. The resulting sweetness is played against the peppery salad dressing.

5 *medium onions, about 1½ pounds*

5 *tablespoons olive oil*

1 *small garlic clove, peeled, halved, green shoot removed and fine-minced*

¼ *teaspoon hot red-pepper flakes, or to taste*

1 *tablespoon chopped parsley*

4 *turns of the pepper mill*

½ *teaspoon red or white wine vinegar*

½ *teaspoon salt*

1. Preheat the oven to 300° F.

2. Trim off one end of each onion and discard. Cut the onions into ⅝-inch-thick slices, leaving the skin on. Discard the other ends. Put the onions on an oiled heavy baking sheet, brush very lightly with olive oil, and bake 1 hour. Turn the slices with a spatula, and continue baking for 30 minutes. The onions should be caramelized but not burned.

3. Using a spatula, transfer the slices to a wide, shallow serving dish. Remove the skin and any dried-out rings. Mix the remaining oil with the garlic, red-pepper flakes, parsley, 2 tablespoons of water, pepper, vinegar, and salt. Spoon the mixture over the onions. Serve at room temperature.

Sweet and Sour Pumpkin

SERVES 4 TO 6

In Palermo this famous dish is called Fegato a Setti Cannoli, a complicated reference to a prepared dish sold in the vicinity of the Garraffello Fountain. The fountain, which stands near the center of the maze of alleys that make up the fabulous Vucciria market, has seven running water spouts, each shaped like a cannoli—thus "seven cannoli." *Fegato* is the word for liver. The story goes that a peddler, who sold only vegetables by the fountain, gave this pumpkin dish its name to suggest to his poor customers that it tasted like meat. And in fact, it does have a liverlike texture!

Sweet and sour pumpkin, with a characteristic taste so popular in Sicily, is an excellent antipasto. Make it early in the day and serve it cold.

2½ *pounds pumpkin, peeled thick, halved, and seeded*	5 *tablespoons mild white wine vinegar (see notes)*
Coarse salt	¾ *teaspoon fine salt*
Virgin olive oil for frying (see notes)	½ *teaspoon freshly ground pepper*
1 *cup thin-sliced onion*	6 *sprigs fresh, aromatic mint*
1½ *teaspoons granulated sugar*	*Additional mint leaves*

1. Cut the pumpkin into ¼-inch-thick slices, then into 2½-by-3¼-inch rectangles. Sprinkle them with coarse salt. Let them stand a few minutes. Blot up most of the excess moisture on the surface (but do not press down), using paper towels.

2. Heat the olive oil in a 9-inch skillet, preferably nonstick, over medium-high heat. Add the pumpkin in batches (do not crowd) and fry until golden brown on both sides, about 5 minutes. Drain on paper towels. Reduce the heat to medium. Pour off all but 4 tablespoons of oil. Add the onions to the skillet. Sprinkle with the sugar. Cook until the onions are soft and golden brown, stirring frequently, about 15 minutes. Add the vinegar and ⅓ cup water. Increase the heat to high and cook the mixture until the liquid is reduced by half, stirring up any browned bits.

3. Mix the salt and pepper and season the slices of pumpkin. Arrange them on a platter. Pour the contents of the skillet over the top. Sprinkle with torn mint leaves. (*The recipe can be prepared to this point up to 1 day in advance.* Cover and refrigerate. Let it return to room temperature before serving.) Garnish with additional fresh mint and serve.

NOTES TO THE COOK   If pumpkins are unavailable, you can substitute butternut squash. Start at the neck end of the squash and cut it into ¼-inch-thick rounds. (Use a mandoline to obtain even slices; or cut directly through the tough skin of the squash with a heavy serrated knife, then use a cookie cutter to remove the flesh.) When you reach the bulb end, cut it in half, remove the seeds and pulp, and slice the flesh into 1-by-¼-inch pieces.

Choose an inexpensive virgin olive oil such as Goya or Ybarra. Oil of this quality (below 1 percent acidity) can heat to 400° F without smoking. Use only enough oil so that the pumpkin slices float on the surface. After cooling the oil, strain it through cheesecloth and reserve it for frying other vegetables later on. (When reusing oil, fry a cinnamon stick in it to make it "sweet.")

Use a good-quality light wine vinegar, or substitute a Japanese rice wine vinegar. Avoid white wine vinegar with more than 6 percent acidity; dilute with water if necessary.

SERVES 6   *Siracusan Baked Olives*

The Sicilian olives traditionally used for this dish are as large as pigeon eggs, very pulpy, and full of flavor, and they exude an extraordinary aroma. Here in the U.S. I use greenish-purple Greek Atalanti or Royal olives, which are large, round, and cracked. When baked, the olives express some of their moisture and become intensely flavorful.

8 *to 10 ounces (drained weight) Greek Royal or Atalanti olives, drained and soaked in several changes of water to remove salt*

⅓ *cup dry white wine*

2 *tablespoons olive oil*

1 *small garlic clove, peeled and cut up*

1 *tablespoon chopped flat-leaf parsley*

2 *teaspoons aged red wine vinegar*

¾ *teaspoon Greek or Sicilian oregano*

⅛ *teaspoon freshly ground pepper*

¼ *teaspoon hot red-pepper flakes (with few seeds) crushed, or ⅛ teaspoon hot red pepper*

Preheat the oven to 375° F. Rinse and drain the olives, place them in a shallow 8- to 9-inch baking dish with the white wine and half the olive oil. Bake the olives, stirring several times, for 40 minutes or until they are glistening and somewhat swollen. Remove them from the oven and prick each with the tines of a fork. In a mortar pound the garlic with the parsley until smooth. Mix with the vinegar, the remaining oil, oregano, pepper, and pepper flakes. Let the olives stand in this mixture for several hours. Roll them in paper towels before serving to remove the excess oil.

Pan-Fried Artichokes

SERVES 4

I didn't have to travel more than two blocks from my Manhattan apartment to learn this Palermitano dish. Azzurro, the traditional Sicilian restaurant where I often go for *pasta con le sarde*, thinly sliced swordfish, and these marvelous pan-fried artichokes is truly a family establishment. Maria Sindoni, the mama, prepares the sauces and *caponatina* each day. Her son Marcello does the grilling and fast sautés at night. Second son, Vittorio, manages the front of the house, and daughter, Mariella, takes reservations and minds the cash register.

Frying artichokes is not unusual, but here the results are extraordinarily light. The artichokes are cooked in oil *and* water; the minute the water has evaporated they are ready. Be sure to use the correct-size pan for the best results. Unlike the previous five antipasti, these should ideally be served warm.

3 *medium-sized fresh artichokes*	½ *teaspoon salt*
lemon, halved	2 *tablespoons chopped fresh parsley*
2½ *tablespoons extra-virgin olive oil*	1¼ *teaspoons mashed garlic*

1. Slice off 1 inch from the top of each artichoke, trim the stem, remove layers of thick leaves until you reach the tender pale yellow-green petals, and trim off all hard green parts around the base and the stem. Rub all cut surfaces with lemon, then soak in cool acidulated water (1 quart of water to the juice of 1 lemon) until the leaves soften and can be splayed easily, about 10 minutes. Spread the inner leaves and use a melon scoop to remove the thistly choke from the center of each artichoke. Return them to soak in acidulated water, cover, and keep refrigerated until you are ready to cook.

2. About 15 minutes before serving, pat the artichokes dry with a kitchen towel. Halve them lengthwise, cut each half into ¼-inch-thick slices and place them in a 9- or 10-inch heavy nonaluminum skillet with the olive oil, ⅓ cup of water, salt, parsley, and garlic. Set the skillet over high heat, tossing, until all the water has evaporated, about 2 minutes. Immediately remove the skillet from the heat to avoid "frying," which would make the garlic turn bitter. Scrape the slightly crunchy artichokes into a serving dish and serve warm.

NOTES TO THE COOK
Choose artichokes weighing about 5½ to 6 ounces. To keep them fresh until ready to clean, submerge them in cold water mixed with a pinch of bicarbonate of soda.

Artichokes may be cleaned 1 to 2 hours before cooking. After cleaning keep them submerged in acidulated water in the refrigerator.

SERVES 2	# Broiled Artichokes with Pecorino Cheese

Globe artichokes are abundant in Sicily, where they are prepared in a number of interesting ways. One of the most delicious and unusual is to grill them, as is done in the town of Bagheria on the northern coast of the island.

In Sicilian homes it's traditional to serve these artichokes at Christmas dinner, after the meat course and before dessert. The artichokes are cooked slowly over embers, or packed between hot flat stones or tiles set over burning coals. Whatever the method, the resulting flavor is unique, smoky and mysterious, not at all like the taste of boiled artichokes. In this version a long cooking under the broiler imparts a comparable flavor. With a dusting of coarsely grated pecorino cheese, rather than the usual adornment of lemon juice, this dish becomes truly memorable. Eat the artichokes just as you would if they were boiled, pulling them apart leaf by leaf, then cutting and eating the heart with a knife and fork.

2 *large globe artichokes*

1½ *lemons*

2 *large garlic cloves, minced fine*

2 *tablespoons chopped flat-leaf parsley*

Coarse (kosher) salt and freshly ground pepper

4 *tablespoons extra-virgin olive oil*

3 *to 4 tablespoons coarsely grated pecorino cheese*

Cruet of extra-virgin olive oil

1. Slice off 1 inch from the top of each artichoke. Use scissors to snip off the spiky tips. Cut the stems to make level bases. (If char-broiling, trim stems to ¾ inch of base.) Remove 3 layers of the thick outer leaves. Trim off all hard green parts around the base. Soak in cool acidulated water (1 quart water to the juice of 1 lemon) until the leaves soften and can be splayed easily, about 10 minutes. Spread the inner leaves and use a melon scoop to remove the thistly choke from the center of each artichoke. Rub the artichokes with lemon juice and return them to the acidulated water. Cover and keep refrigerated until you are ready to cook.

2. About ¾ hour before serving, preheat the broiler. Place the broiler rack about 7 inches away from the heat source.

3. Drain the artichokes. Combine the garlic, parsley, salt, pepper, and 3 tablespoons of the olive oil. Put a small amount of the garlic mixture in the choke area of each artichoke. Distribute small amounts of the mixture between the leaves of the artichokes. Press them to reshape. Roll them in the remaining oil and broil them *slowly,* stem side up, until lightly charred, about 15 to 18 minutes. Turn, baste with some of the expressed oil mixture, and continue broiling 15 to 18 minutes or until the bottoms test tender. Remove and cut each artichoke in half. Serve at once with a sprinkling of coarsely grated cheese. Pass a cruet of olive oil.

TWO MEDITERRANEAN SPREADS

Mediterranean Caviar

MAKES ABOUT 1 ½ CUPS

The following spread, served cool on toasted slices of French bread, is a combination of eggplant caviar and the famous *samfaina* of Catalonia. *Samfaina* is a ratatouille-style garnish of tomatoes, onions, peppers, and eggplant cooked down to a marmalade and used to accompany fish, poultry, and meat. Though its ingredients are classically Mediterranean, a really first-rate *samfaina* is not easy to make. The Catalan food commentator Josef Pla has called it "a dish of optimism." Made properly in autumn, when its component vegetables are in a state of absolute perfection, it becomes a truly great thing—great enough, to paraphrase Pla, to give one optimism about the possibility of perfection on this earth.

1 *eggplant (1¼ pounds) firm, smooth-skinned*

3 *tablespoons extra-virgin olive oil*

1 *medium onion, sliced thin.*

1 *large, fleshy sweet red bell pepper, stemmed, seeded, and cut into small squares*

1 *small green bell pepper, cored, stemmed, seeded, and cut into small cubes*

1 *medium tomato, peeled, seeded, and chopped, or ½ cup drained canned plum tomatoes, seeds discarded*

3 *garlic cloves, minced*

2 *flat anchovy fillets, drained and crushed with a fork*

Salt and freshly ground pepper to taste

1. Preheat the oven to 425° F. Prick the eggplant; brush it with 1 teaspoon of the olive oil, and place it in a baking dish. Bake 40 minutes, turning midway. Place the peppers (red and green) in a baking dish and set in the oven to bake 20 minutes, turning them midway, too.

2. Meanwhile, heat 2 tablespoons of the olive oil over low heat in a heavy skillet; add the onion and 3 tablespoons of water, and cook, stirring, for 10 minutes. Add the tomato and cook until very thick, about 5 minutes. Add the diced peppers and the garlic, and cook over low heat, stirring, until the mixture thickens, about 10 minutes. Fold in the anchovies and cook 1 to 2 minutes. Leave the mixture in the skillet off the heat.

3. Remove the eggplant when it is completely soft and the skin is blistery. Scrape the flesh from the skin (this is very easy if you first split the cooked eggplant lengthwise while still hot, then allow it to cool for 10 minutes under a kitchen towel). Discard any hard seeds and the skin. (See note.)

4. On a wooden work surface, mash the eggplant with a wooden spoon until smooth. At the same time work in the remaining 2 teaspoons of olive oil. Add the eggplant, salt, and pepper to the other vegetables. Fry, constantly stirring, until all the liquid evaporates and there are only oil and vegetables left, about 15 minutes. Stir carefully to avoid scorching but be sure to allow mixture to become somewhat dark in color. Season to taste. Cool, cover, and refrigerate the mixture until you are ready to serve. Return it to room temperature before serving.

However carefully you select them, some eggplants will be extremely bitter. After scraping off the baked skin, taste the flesh; if necessary squeeze the warm pulp through fingers to remove bitter juices.

NOTE TO THE COOK

SERVES 6 TO 8

Marmalade of Spring Greens

In southern Sicily one finds tasty and rather thick, doughy *impanatas* filled with greens and a multitude of other things, including raisins, capers, anchovies, and cheese. When juicy black olives are also added, the result is luscious but much too heavy. I have remedied the heaviness of this dish by eliminating the doughy exterior and turning the mixture into a spread. You can present a plate of the lukewarm marmalade spread on thin rounds of baked or fried bread, or you can sprinkle the covered rounds with cheese, run them under the broiler to glaze, then serve them hot.

Try serving the rounds with drinks, perhaps also with paper-thin slices of very fresh raw swordfish (swordfish *carpaccio).* Season the swordfish with plenty of lemon juice, fruity olive oil, salt, pepper, and Greek or Sicilian oregano.

2 *pounds fresh spinach, escarole, Swiss chard, etc. (see notes)*

Salt

1 *garlic clove, peeled and lightly crushed*

2 *tablespoons olive oil*

4 *flat anchovy fillets, drained and crushed with a fork*

1½ *teaspoons capers, preferably salted, rinsed, and drained*

¼ *cup chopped pitted purple olives (7 or 8 Kalamatas)*

1½ *tablespoons seedless black or yellow raisins, soaked in warm water, drained dry and chopped*

⅛ *teaspoon hot red-pepper flakes, with few seeds, or more to taste*

32 *grilled or fried rounds of Italian or French bread*

⅓ *cup coarsely grated provolone or caciocavallo cheese, optional*

1. Wash the greens until the water runs clear; remove the stems, stalks, and/or tough leaves, and drain. Cook the greens 10 minutes in boiling salted water; drain, refresh in cold

(continued)

water, drain, and squeeze thoroughly. Makes 1 cup. (Or cook them in the microwave: place them in a covered dish with a few tablespoons of water and use full power until they are fully cooked. Drain thoroughly and squeeze dry.)

2. In a small skillet fry the garlic in olive oil until lightly browned; remove the garlic and discard. Add the greens and fry them for 1 minute, stirring. Add the anchovies and capers and cook, stirring, 30 seconds longer. Remove the mixture to a work surface, allow to cool, then chop fine (by hand or "pulse" in a food processor) with the olives, raisins, and pepper flakes. (*The dish can be prepared several hours in advance.* Cover and refrigerate.)

3. Divide the mixture evenly and pile it onto bread rounds. Sprinkle them with cheese and run under the broiler to glaze. Serve warm or at room temperature.

NOTES TO
THE COOK
There are two approaches: you can mix your greens or use just one type. Avoid frozen spinach, which does not have enough taste.

I prefer to cook greens by dropping them by handfuls into lots of boiling salted water (about ½ tablespoon of salt per quart of water), then keeping the water at a full boil throughout. I use about ½ tablespoon of salt per quart of water. According to my friend Jacques Chibois, the greens do not absorb the salt, and the boiling "sears" the leaves so that they hold all their nutrients. A microwave using minimum moisture works just as well.

SIX FIRST-COURSE SALADS

SERVES 3 TO 4

Pulled Parsley Salad with Black Olives

Throughout the Mediterranean area a diner is likely to be greeted with an assortment of refreshing salads at the beginning of a meal: Middle Eastern *mezethes*, Spanish *tapas*, Moroccan *salatits* are only a few of the typical preparations. Many such salads employ parsley, which grows easily and profusely in the warm climates.

Moroccans, for example, season parsley with cumin and paprika. Some Middle Easterners make salads by combining chopped parsley with bulghur, and occasionally add fresh or dried tomatoes and/or mint. Other Middle Easterners mix parsley with a sesame-seed dressing, or with chunks of cheese and olives, or torn mint leaves and paper-thin slices of red onion.

The following parsley salad (a version of which I first tasted in Southern California) is not authentic to any particular national cuisine, but it does have a true Mediterranean spirit. The only component that is not Mediterranean is curly parsley, which I used here rather than the flat-leafed variety because it lends a certain fluffiness when the salad is mounded into a pyramid.

The unique oily texture of Greek Kalamata olives packed in a vinegar brine emphasizes a vinaigrette; when slivered and tossed with greens they produce an especially clean-tasting salad. The grated pecorino is added for sharpness.

You can serve this salad with a garlic-laden roast lamb dish, and a bowl of honey *all-i-oli*.

1 *large bunch very fresh curly parsley*

12 *pitted Kalamata olives*

1½ *tablespoons minced shallots*

¼ *teaspoon Worcestershire*

1½ *tablespoons extra-virgin olive oil*

2 *teaspoons mild vinegar, preferably cider*

Salt and freshly ground pepper to taste

1½ *tablespoons freshly grated pecorino cheese*

1. Wash and spin-dry the parsley. Remove all stems. Tear each parsley tuft into tiny bits, or use a small pair of scissors. You should have about 1½ cups of fluffy parsley flakes. Pit and sliver the olives.

2. At serving time, gently toss all ingredients except cheese in a mixing bowl. Pile them into a mound on a serving plate; sprinkle cheese on top.

Chanterelle and Cheese Croquettes with Mesclun

SERVES 3 TO 4
Makes about 12 croquettes

I own many cookbooks that feature mushroom dishes, but none includes a recipe for a commonly found and utterly delicious chanterelle that pops up during the summer, the fragrant thumb-tack size red chanterelle (*Cantharellus cinnabarius minor*).

For years I had collected these mushrooms along an old logging trail in the oak forest near our house on Martha's Vineyard, then combined them with other large chanterelles in various sautés. It wasn't until Michel Bras taught me this recipe, in which just a handful of mushrooms are needed, that I was able to enjoy them on their own. Here their strong aroma, akin to that of fresh apricots, infuses itself into pancakes—a far more interesting use of their aromatic properties than simply serving them sautéed.

In the Auvergne these croquettes are called *subrics,* a word used generally to describe any mushroom confection bound with flour and eggs. These particular miniature pancakes, partially thickened with Laguiole cheese, Cantal, or (my substitute) Monterey Jack, are extremely light and delicious. You can make up the mixture ahead—it will hold for 3 to 5 hours.

You can, of course, sliver larger chanterelles to make this dish. But since tiny "red nail" chanterelles are so common in many parts of America, if you see them in the woods (and know your way around wild mushrooms) it is well worth the few minutes it will take to gather a handful.

In the central market of the French Riviera city of Cannes, wooden boxes of the tenderest and youngest mixed greens (and violet-reds) are sold as a mélange called *mesclun.* Picked on the hillsides near Mougins, *mesclun* is a study in vivid color, fragile texture, and eclectic flavor (ranging from peppery to delicate), qualities that continually vary, depending on the time of year. *Mesclun* greens are always picked small and never torn into pieces.

The greens that go into making a *mesclun* are no longer unfamiliar in the U.S. If they are unavailable, grow your own (see Appendix, page 343) or substitute an assortment of the small, tender greens offered in local greenmarkets: delicate Bibb, sharp-tasting arugula, tender oak leaf, pungent radicchio, crisp baby romaine, fragile lamb's lettuce, bitter white chicory, sharp-tasting curly endive, peppery watercress, mild Boston lettuce, and hazelnut-tasting escarole. Add a small amount of chive flowers, sage, thyme, or nasturtium flowers, wild mustard greens, purslane, and whatever else is small, tender, and fresh. Only the simplest dressing should be used: a light olive oil with a drop of vinegar or lemon juice. Anything more aggressive will detract from the charm of *mesclun.*

One of the most delicious *mesclun* salads I ever ate was at the bistro Chez Pauline in Paris. A pigeon had been baked in a salt crust for about 30 minutes, removed from its hard salt shell, and served on top of the greens. Its rosy juices became part of the dressing, flavoring and wilting the leaves.

½ cup (1½ ounces) fresh chanterelles

½ cup milk

1¼ cups (1¾ ounces) dried cubed crustless white bread

2 to 3 teaspoons clarified butter

1 large egg, lightly beaten

½ loosely packed cup (1¾ ounces) shredded cheese, Laguiole, Cantal, or Monterey Jack

Salt and freshly ground white pepper

1 teaspoon balsamic wine vinegar, or more to taste

3 tablespoons fruity extra-virgin olive oil

2 fine-chopped shallots

1 small garlic clove, halved and slightly bruised

4 cups (2 ounces) mixed tiny greens (mesclun), or substitute tender greens: arugula, watercress, Bibb, lamb's lettuce, radicchio, white chicory

Freshly ground black pepper

1. To clean tiny chanterelles, simply toss them in a deep sieve and shake vigorously to release surface dirt. Trim the ends and use a water spray to wash quickly; drain and blot dry. Keep them refrigerated until you are ready to use them. For larger chanterelles, brush them with a clean soft paintbrush; rinse them quickly, drain, blot dry, and cut into thin slivers.

2. Pour the milk over the bread and let stand for a few minutes. Press out and discard the milk. The bread should measure about ⅓ cup.

3. Meanwhile, heat 1 teaspoon of the clarified butter in a small nonstick skillet; add the chanterelles and sauté over medium heat until they have expressed all their moisture. Remove them to a side dish.

4. In a mixing bowl using a fork work the bread and egg together until smooth. Add the cheese and blend the mixture until smooth. Fold in the chanterelles. Season with salt and pepper. Keep the mixture covered with plastic wrap until you are ready to cook.

5. In a bowl dissolve ½ teaspoon of salt in the vinegar. Gradually whisk in the oil to make an emulsion. Stir in the shallots and set the dressing aside to allow the flavors to blend. Correct the acidity with sugar if necessary. Rub a salad bowl with the cut clove of garlic.

6. Ten minutes before serving, heat the remaining clarified butter in a large nonstick skillet. Drop the mixture by tablespoons into the skillet and slowly brown on one side, about 5 minutes. Turn, and cook on the other side until golden brown and crisp, about 5 minutes longer.

7. Toss the *mesclun* with the prepared dressing and a fresh grinding of black pepper. Serve with the hot pancakes.

NOTE TO THE COOK

The chanterelles can be sautéed in butter, cooled, covered, and kept frozen until you are ready to use them. Defrost them before adding to the cheese mixture. If you wish to substitute another type of chanterelle, choose the smallest and most aromatic, preferably all the same color. Sniff before purchasing: Aroma-less chanterelles generally have no flavor.

Salade Canaille

SERVES 4 TO 6

According to my French dictionary *canaille* means "riffraff." I use this word to describe one of my favorite salads, a potpourri of ingredients that achieves a flavorful balance of textures, tastes, and smells. It is terribly important to choose greens with a lot of character, so that each type holds its own: peppery arugula and bitter curly white endive, a few torn pieces of sharp radicchio, balanced off with such sweet-tasting greens as lamb's lettuce and Bibb.

I serve this salad with meat or poultry, and have even served it as a main course. With roasted Grated Potato Cakes with Mace, or with pieces of grilled *confit* of duck served lukewarm, it makes a memorable lunch.

½ *teaspoon salt*

1½ *tablespoons mild white wine vinegar*

2½ *tablespoons light salad oil*

1 *tablespoon imported walnut oil*

¼ *teaspoon freshly ground pepper*

4 *to 5 cups mixed greens*

1 *teaspoon fine-chopped chives*

1 *teaspoon fine-chopped parsley*

3 *large basil leaves, rolled and slivered*

1 *teaspoon fine-grated orange rind*

3 *small shallots, peeled and* minced by hand

In a mixing bowl, dissolve the salt in the vinegar; then beat in the oils. Season with pepper. Correct the acidity if necessary. Let the dressing rest while washing and drying the greens. Toss the greens with the vinaigrette, then scatter the herbs, orange rind, and shallots on top. Serve at once on individual plates.

SERVES 4	# Chestnut Salad with Walnuts and Pancetta

For me there are four ingredients worth the trouble to shell: peas, favas, shrimps, and chestnuts.

In late autumn, when the first sweet chestnuts come into the markets, I serve them warm in this delicious country-style green salad from South-West France—a great accompaniment to grilled chicken. Of course, you can buy peeled chestnuts in jars, but the flavor will never be as good.

¾ *to 1 pound fresh chestnuts*

4 *tablespoons unsalted butter*

½ *teaspoon fennel seeds*

6 *to 7 inches of celery rib with leaves*

1 *bay leaf*

3 *to 4 cups mixed greens: torn escarole, chicory, arugula, etc.*

1 *garlic clove, peeled*

Salt and freshly ground pepper

4 *thin slices firm white bread, crusts removed*

4 *ounces pancetta or thick slices of lean bacon*

3 *tablespoons imported walnut oil*

2 *teaspoons aged red wine vinegar*

¼ *cup chopped walnuts*

1. Peel the chestnuts (see notes). Makes about 2 cups.

2. Choose a heavy 8-inch skillet and place in it the chestnuts in one layer. Add 1 tablespoon of the butter, the fennel seeds, celery, bay leaf, and enough water to cover. Cover the skillet and cook very slowly until the chestnuts are tender. Depending on size and age, chestnuts cook in 15 to 45 minutes. Do not shake the skillet lest the chestnuts break. Remove at once if the chestnuts begin to fall apart during this time.

3. Meanwhile, wash the greens thoroughly; drain and wrap them in a kitchen towel. Crush the garlic with salt and set aside. Cut the bread into croutons. Heat 2 tablespoons of the butter in a nonstick skillet. When hot, add the croutons and fry until golden on all sides. Add the garlic and toss for an instant. Remove the croutons to drain on paper towels.

4. When the chestnuts are tender, transfer them with a slotted spoon to a flat plate to dry. Wipe out the skillet. Cut the pancetta or bacon into thin strips crosswise. Makes about ½ cup. Fry it without added fat until almost crisp. Add the remaining tablespoon of butter and the chestnuts, and season with salt and pepper. Gently sauté for 30 seconds or until the chestnuts are glistening. *(The recipe can be prepared up to this point 30 minutes in advance.* Keep the chestnut mixture and the croutons warm in a 275° oven.)

5. Just before serving, make a vinaigrette with the walnut oil, vinegar, salt, and pepper. Mix the greens with the vinaigrette and the walnuts. Then add the chestnuts, being

(continued)

SIX FIRST-COURSE SALADS   25

careful when mixing not to break them. Scatter croutons on top. Serve while the chestnuts are still warm.

NOTES TO THE COOK   Fresh chestnuts in their shells can be packed airtight in plastic bags and kept frozen for up to 3 months. Cooked chestnuts can be refrigerated, covered, and kept for 1 day.

To prepare chestnuts: Make a slit on the flat side of each with a sharp knife. (A chestnut knife is the ideal instrument to slash and peel a chestnut. It has a short, slightly hooked pointed blade set into a 4-inch wooden handle. See Appendix, page 340, for mail-order source.)

Drop the chestnuts into boiling water and cook for 2 to 3 minutes. Remove them with a slotted spoon and keep warm under a thick kitchen towel. One by one cut away the shell and skin together. If the inner skin is difficult to remove, return the chestnuts to the hot water for an instant. If the inner skin still resists, spread the chestnuts out on a baking sheet and place them in a slow oven to dry. Once bone dry they can be rubbed with a coarse cloth.

Lean bacon can be substituted for the pancetta if it is blanched in simmering water for 3 minutes, rinsed, and drained.

Warm Lentil Salad, Auvergne Style

Slate (in shades of green, dark blue, brown) is the color of the wonderful little *lentilles de Puy* from the Auvergne. (See Appendix, page 343, for mail-order source.) They have an extraordinary flavor, which probably derives from the volcanic soil in the area where they are grown. Unlike other lentils, they are very light. They cook quickly without soaking, and they don't become mushy when cooked. I simmer them slowly until they are tender, about 25 to 30 minutes. Toward the end of the cooking I add Cognac, which is a great flavor enhancer. In this recipe the lentils are dressed while still warm in a walnut-oil vinaigrette and studded with large pieces of onion. The onion is removed before serving, leaving a faint hint of its flavor behind. The salad is delicious with sautéed bacon, small sausages, or *confit* of duck.

½ pound (1 cup) French lentilles de Puy	6 tablespoons imported walnut oil
¼ cup Cognac	1 small onion, halved and separated into leaves
VINAIGRETTE	¼ pound sliced bacon or small sausages, or 1 piece of duck confit, fat removed, and sliced thin
2 tablespoons aged red wine vinegar or sherry vinegar	
1 teaspoon Dijon-style mustard	3 tablespoons minced flat-leaf parsley
¾ teaspoon fine salt	Salt and freshly ground pepper
2 tablespoons vegetable or olive oil	¼ pound lamb's lettuce or arugula

1. Pick over and wash the lentils. Put them in a saucepan, cover with water, and bring them slowly to a full boil. Drain. Cover them again with 1 quart of cold water, and bring them back to a boil and skim. Reduce the heat and cook at a simmer for 20 minutes. Add the Cognac and continue to cook for about 10 minutes, or until the lentils are tender. Drain them immediately (discard the liquid) and place them in a deep bowl.

2. Make the vinaigrette dressing by mixing the vinegar, mustard, salt, and oil. Use half to flavor the lentils. Mix well, add the onion pieces, and leave the lentils in a cool place for several hours, stirring from time to time.

3. Just before serving, remove and discard the onion. Fry the bacon, sausages, or confit in a 9-inch skillet until crisp. Discard the fat, add the lentils, and cook gently over moderate heat, stirring, until they are just heated through, about 1 minute. Stir in the parsley and all but 1 tablespoon of the vinaigrette, adjust the seasoning, adding salt, freshly ground pepper, and perhaps a little more vinegar to taste. Mix the greens with the remaining vinaigrette and use them as a garnish.

Mixed Greens with Confit of Duck Gizzards

SERVES 4

"They call us the three little ducks of Paleyrac," Georgette Desffarges told me, grinning, as she poured out glasses of thick walnut wine. "Our family has been serving food here on and off since 1914."

I was deep in the Périgord, on the southern bank of the Dordogne River, just ten kilometers from St. Cyprien, in an outbuilding beside Georgette's house. There was a bar at one end, six tables, family photos on the wall, and a case displaying slippers signed by ballerinas, resident dancers at the summer ballet company in the town. The building had been converted into a private restaurant with no name on its door. I was about to have lunch at what the French call "a precious address."

Red-headed Georgette Desffarges was the boss, a smiling, vivacious woman in her fifties. Her mother, Valentine, ninety-two years old (yes! ninety-two!) did the cooking, along with Georgette's daughter, Janine.

I had ordered a stuffed duck, which Valentine and Janine had cooked slowly the entire morning in a heavy black pot and would serve with sautéed cèpes. But first Georgette gave me a wonderful garlicky mixed salad of garden greens and preserved duck gizzards (*confit;* see recipe below), a loaf of crusty country bread, and an enormous platter of just-picked white asparagus, served in a light walnut-oil vinaigrette—asparagus so warm and sweet it tasted almost like candy. A superbly produced home-cooked meal, pure home cooking of the Périgord. Indeed *une adresse précieuse . . .*

⅔ cup thin-sliced preserved duck gizzards (see next recipe) with 1½ tablespoons fat reserved

Freshly ground black pepper, to taste

4 cups (6 ounces) mixed greens: curly endive (white part only), arugula, Bibb lettuce, etc.

3 to 4 radicchio leaves (optional)

½ teaspoon Dijon-style mustard

2 teaspoons aged red wine vinegar

3 tablespoons imported walnut oil

Salt

½ teaspoon full-bodied red wine

1. Generously sprinkle the gizzards with black pepper, place in a small skillet with the reserved fat, and set aside.

2. Wash the greens and radicchio; drain well and spin dry. Tear them into bite-size pieces. Roll them in paper towels and keep chilled. Mix the mustard, vinegar, and pepper in a wide salad bowl until well combined. Whisk in the walnut oil. Salt to taste.

3. Five minutes before serving, gently fry the sliced gizzards in *confit* fat until barely crisp. Meanwhile, place the chilled greens over the dressing. Pour the contents of the skillet over the greens, add the wine to the skillet to deglaze, pour it over the greens and toss. Serve immediately.

Preserved Duck Gizzards (Confit)

Gizzards from fattened ducks and geese are even better than ordinary gizzards. Transformed into *confit* (salted and preserved in their own fat) they become a luscious, traditional delicacy that gives hearty flavor to soups, bean dishes, and salads.

Your butcher might be persuaded to sell you extra duck gizzards, or you can collect them as you prepare various duck dishes through a season, keeping them frozen until you have about a cup. Every fall I purchase, through mail order, a 2-pound bag of fresh mullard duck gizzards (see Appendix, page 343). At the same time I order enough rendered duck fat so I can cook and store the gizzards properly.

Multiply the seasonings proportionately if you have a larger amount of gizzards (3 teaspoons salt for every pound of gizzards).

5 *ounces fresh duck gizzards (1 cup), trimmed of fat and membranes*	1 *teaspoon chopped shallots*
1 *teaspoon coarse salt*	¼ *teaspoon crushed peppercorns*
2 *teaspoons chopped fresh parsley*	½ *crumbled bay leaf*
½ *teaspoon minced garlic*	¼ *teaspoon dried thyme*
	Rendered duck or goose fat

1. Toss the gizzards with salt and other seasonings. Place them in a covered dish and refrigerate overnight.

2. The following day, rinse the gizzards, wipe them dry, and place them in an earthenware bowl with enough rendered duck and/or goose fat to cover. Cover the bowl with a lid and place it in a preheated 225° F oven to cook about 2½ hours or until the gizzards are fork-tender.

3. Remove the gizzards from the fat. Transfer a small amount of the fat (ladling from the top) into a sterile jar and let it congeal. Place a portion of the gizzards on the fat, then ladle in some more fat, letting it congeal before adding more gizzards. Continue until all gizzards are covered with fat. Cover and refrigerate until you are ready to use them. They keep up to 2 weeks in the fat in the refrigerator. The gizzards can be frozen.

THREE MOROCCAN SALADS

I published more than twenty-five recipes for Moroccan salads in *Couscous and Other Good Food from Morocco,* but there are many more. A good Moroccan cook knows how to turn each and every vegetable, type of olive, piece of fish, bit of wild green, or even crust of bread into an interesting and compatible appetizer-salad. You'll rarely find fewer than four salads when you sit down to eat at the low, round dining table in a Moroccan home. Some will be perfumed with rose or orangeflower water, or heightened with lemon preserved in salt. Others will be headily spiced with cumin, paprika, and cinnamon. Using a wedge of anise-flavored bread as your scoop, you'll taste one after the other, marveling at their variety and their startling effect upon your senses.

Spicy Eggplant and Tomato Salad

SERVES 6

In this recipe—one of the best of the so-called cooked Moroccan salads—eggplant and tomato are cooked down to a jam, which is utterly delicious on slices of Moroccan bread.

2 *pounds firm eggplant*
  Coarse salt
  Olive oil for frying
1 *pound ripe tomatoes, peeled, seeded and chopped or 2 cups drained canned Italian-style tomatoes*
  Pinch of sugar (if tomatoes are acidic)

2 *teaspoons crushed garlic*
  Pinches of cayenne to taste
1 *teaspoon sweet paprika*
¼ *teaspoon ground cumin seed*
  Juice of 1 lemon

Begin 1 day in advance.

1. Remove the top and bottom of each eggplant. Use a one-holed lemon zester to remove 3 or 4 narrow vertical strips of skin from each, leaving the eggplants striped, then cut them into ½-inch slices, Salt the slices and leave them to drain in a nonaluminum colander for at least 1 hour. Rinse, drain, and dry the eggplant.

2. Heat a good quantity of oil in a seasoned black skillet and fry the eggplant slices in batches until golden brown on both sides. Drain them on paper towels. Strain the oil (it can be used for other purposes). Return 3 tablespoons to the skillet and reheat. Add the tomatoes and a pinch of salt, and fry them, stirring often to avoid burning, over medium-low heat for 5 minutes. Add a pinch of sugar if needed.

3. Mash the eggplant with the garlic and spices. Add it to the skillet and cook over very low heat for 20 minutes, stirring occasionally. During this time turn the mixture over and over in the pan so that all the moisture evaporates, and only the oil is left to fry the mixture. It will become very thick and rich in texture. Remove the mixture and fold in the lemon juice. Adjust the seasoning. Keep the salad well covered and refrigerated. Return it to room temperature before serving.

SERVES 4 TO 6	# Red Peppers and Preserved Lemon Peels

Lemons preserved in salt and lemon juice are one of the main flavorings of Moroccan *tagines* and salads. Their unique flavor *cannot* be duplicated by fresh lemons or limes, despite what you may read in other books. Happily, preserved lemons are easy to make. In my Moroccan cookbook I give a recipe that takes one month to mature. I have now developed a quicker version that matures in just a week. See page 32. If you live on the West Coast, where delicious thin-skinned Meyer lemons are available, be sure to use them, as they preserve extremely well.

The glory of adding a few cubes of preserved lemon peel to a salad is the unexpected taste and contrast it provides to such things as red peppers flavored with cumin and paprika; fat and juicy ripe olives with chopped garlic and coriander; and, also, meat and poultry dishes with herbs and spices. Sometimes the lemon peeel is cubed and placed on the table at the beginning of a meal and left there throughout, to be nibbled as an aid to digestion. The memory of the superb flavor stays with you, as in this piquant salad, which is best freshly made. It makes a perfect accompaniment to Moroccan Fried Chicken Breasts.

1 *pound ripe tomatoes (2 large), peeled, seeded, and cut into ¾-inch chunks*

2 *to 3 red bell peppers, roasted, peeled, stemmed, seeded, cut into small pieces (¾ cup)*

3 *tablespoons finely chopped red onion or scallions (white only)*

3 *tablespoons fruity olive oil*

1 *tablespoon fresh lemon juice*

½ *teaspoon ground cumin seed*

½ *teaspoon salt*

   Pinch of sweet paprika

   Pinch of cayenne pepper

4 *wedges preserved lemon (see page 32)*

In a medium glass serving dish, combine the tomatoes and peppers. Add the onion, oil, lemon juice, cumin, salt, paprika, and cayenne, and toss to mix. Cover the mixture and refrigerate for 30 to 60 minutes, until well chilled. Rinse the preserved lemon under running water and cut away and discard the pulp. Cut the peel into ⅛- to ¹⁄₁₆-inch dice. Just before serving, sprinkle the preserved lemon peel over the chilled salad.

Moroccan "Midway" Olive and Preserved Lemon Salad

SERVES 4 TO 6

Moroccan "midway" or ripe olives can be tan, russet, violet, green, or deep purple. Unfortunately they are rarely available in this country. As a substitute I suggest you use the cracked, large, crunchy Greek Atalanti or Royal olives; their fruity flavor plays well against red pepper, cumin, and paprika.

1½ cups Greek Royal or Atalanti olives, rinsed and drained

1 garlic clove, peeled and halved, green shoot removed

Coarse salt

6 leafy sprigs fresh coriander

1 sprig flat-leaf parsley

1 teaspoon sweet paprika

¼ teaspoon cayenne pepper

½ teaspoon fine-ground cumin seed

1½ tablespoons fruity olive oil

2 tablespoons fresh lemon juice

¼ preserved lemon rind (see below), rinsed, drained, and cut into thin slivers

Rinse and drain the olives. Place them in an earthenware bowl and set aside. In a mortar crush the garlic with the salt until puréed. Roughly chop the herbs, add them to the garlic, and crush until pasty. Add the spices, oil, and lemon juice, and pour the mixture over the olives. Mix to coat well and let them stand for 2 to 3 hours before serving. Garnish with preserved lemon.

Seven-Day Preserved Lemons

2 ripe lemons

⅓ cup coarse (kosher) salt

½ cup fresh lemon juice

Olive oil

Scrub the lemons and dry well. Cut each into 8 wedges. Toss them with the salt and place in a ½-pint glass jar with a glass or plastic-coated lid. Pour in the lemon juice. Close the jar tightly and let the lemons ripen at room temperature for 7 days, shaking the jar each day to distribute the salt and juice. To store, add olive oil to cover and refrigerate for up to 6 months.

SERVES 4 TO 6	*Gypsy-Style Small Fish with Currants*

Small fish such as smelts are fried until crisp, then left to cool. The sauce of red and green peppers, tomatoes, and a touch of white wine is flavored with coriander, garlic, and fennel. When cool, it is poured over the fish, enabling the flavors to mingle and mellow.

This recipe is best prepared 1 or 2 days in advance, and served at room temperature.

1 *pound fresh or defrosted smelts, gutted, rinsed, and wiped dry (see note)*

Sea salt

Freshly ground white pepper

5 *tablespoons extra-virgin olive oil*

1 *lemon*

6 *sprigs fresh flat-leaf parsley*

2 *scallions, white part and 3 inches of the green*

¾ *cup dry white wine*

¼ *teaspoon fennel seeds*

1 *garlic clove, lightly crushed,*

1 *teaspoon coriander seeds*

2 *green peppers, peeled, stemmed, seeded, and membranes removed, cut into julienne (1 cup)*

1 *red pepper, peeled, stemmed, seeded, and membranes removed, cut into julienne (⅔ cup)*

⅛ *teaspoon hot red-pepper flakes*

1 *ripe tomato, peeled, seeded, and cubed*

1½ *tablespoons currants, soaked in warm water and drained dry*

1 *cup flour for dredging*

About ⅔ cup vegetable or olive oil for frying

Sprigs of dill for garnish

1. Open up each fish, pull out the central bone, and reserve. Discard the heads. Mix 1½ teaspoons of salt and ⅛ teaspoon of pepper, and season the flesh evenly. Lightly brush the fish with 1 tablespoon of the oil, cover, and refrigerate under plastic wrap until you are ready to fry.

2. Grate the lemon rind to make 1 teaspoon. Squeeze and reserve the juice for step 3. Place half the lemon rind, the reserved bones, parsley, green parts of the scallions, and ½ tablespoon of the olive oil in a small saucepan. Cover and sweat over low heat for 5 minutes to bring up the flavors. Add the wine and cook for 10 minutes; strain and set aside.

3. Meanwhile, slice the white parts of the scallions thin and gently sauté them along with the fennel seeds in the remaining 3½ tablespoons of olive oil in a heavy 10-inch skillet

(continued)

for 2 minutes. Add the garlic, coriander seeds, peppers, pepper flakes, tomato, and currants, and cook, stirring, over high heat for 3 minutes to allow the excess moisture to evaporate. Add the reserved liquid from step 2 and bring the mixture to a boil. Remove the skillet from the heat and cool to lukewarm. Stir in the remaining ½ teaspoon lemon rind and the lemon juice. Season to taste with salt and pepper.

4. Thoroughly dry the fish with paper towels. Dust them lightly with flour, and fry them in hot oil until crisp and golden, about 30 seconds to a side. Drain them on paper toweling. Cool.

5. Arrange the cold fish in a shallow ceramic dish, pour over the cold vegetable garnish, and cover with plastic wrap. Refrigerate for at least 24 hours before serving. Serve at room temperature decorated with sprigs of dill.

NOTE TO THE COOK — Bell-pepper skins are not very digestible, and are unsightly if left on—they begin to curl up. They can be easily removed with a swivel vegetable peeler.

Inspired by a recipe from Alain Dutournier.

Salmon Salad with Bacon Dressing

Here's a quick and easy savory variation on the wonderful old bistro favorite, wilted dandelion and bacon salad. In this recipe thin slices of sautéed salmon are presented on a bed of mixed greens wilted by a sweet-sour dressing enriched with a small amount of bacon fat.

The addition of Cognac to bring out the delicate flavor of the salmon is an idea of my friend, the estimable cook Lois Stanton, who makes her version of this dish with sea scallops.

¾ *pound very fresh salmon fillet, tail end*
   Salt and freshly ground pepper

4 *slices thick bacon, cut crosswise into julienne*

1 *teaspoon crushed garlic*

1 *tablespoon sugar*

4 *teaspoons white wine vinegar*

1½ *tablespoons Cognac*

4 *cups mixed salad greens (escarole, watercress, leaf lettuce, chicory, endive)*

½ *teaspoon vegetable oil*

3 *tablespoons snipped chives*

1. Lay the fillet of salmon skin side down on a work surface. Use a flexible, long thin knife to cut the salmon into eight pieces, each about ⅓ inch thick. Discard the skin. Season the salmon pieces with salt and pepper. Cover and refrigerate until ready to cook.

2. In a small skillet, fry the bacon until crisp. Drain on paper towels. Pour off all but 2 tablespoons fat in the skillet. Add the garlic and cook 30 seconds over low heat, stirring. Add the sugar and the vinegar and bring to a boil. Add the Cognac and continue simmering 30 seconds longer. Remove the skillet from the heat.

3. Divide the salad greens evenly on four individual serving plates.

4. Five minutes before serving, slowly heat a lightly oiled 10-inch nonstick skillet. Meanwhile reheat the dressing and spoon some of the mixture over each serving of the greens. Cook the salmon slices for 30 seconds to a side, or until just cooked. Transfer to the prepared greens. Sprinkle with the remaining dressing. Finally, sprinkle with freshly ground pepper, bacon, and chives.

Fish with Greens and Escabeche Vinaigrette

SERVES 4 TO 6

I like this recipe for the way it employs an unusual combination of textures and tastes. Filleted strips or *goujonettes* of lean fish are fried, then pickled in a tangy marinade. They are served at room temperature with a salad prepared with the same marinade. The moist, chewy fish contrasts with the various bitter and peppery greens, while the tangy sauce brings the dish together. Accompany with a white Bordeaux or a simple Chablis.

THE FISH

¾ *pound boneless, skinless fresh or thawed fish fillets (farmed catfish, snapper, tilefish), cut into 24 thin strips of approximately equal size*

½ *cup floured seasoned with salt and pepper*

½ *cup vegetable oil for frying*

⅓ *cup extra-virgin olive oil*

½ *pound small red onions, sliced*

½ *pound sliced carrots*

⅓ *cup thin-sliced scallions (white part only)*

12 *small garlic cloves, unpeeled*

10 *sprigs fresh thyme*

2 *bay leaves*

5 *sprigs of flat-leaf parsley*

2 *cloves*

8 *juniper berries*

1 *teaspoon black peppercorns*

1 *cup dry white wine*

1 *cup white wine vinegar*

Salt

THE MIXED GREENS (CHOOSE 3)

About 3 cups loosely packed assorted greens: radicchio, arugula, field lettuce, chicory, escarole, or watercress

ESCABECHE VINAIGRETTE

3 *tablespoons of the fish marinade, strained*

½ *tablespoon imported walnut oil*

1 *tablespoon French peanut oil or olive oil*

⅛ *teaspoon freshly ground pepper*

GARNISHES

Sprigs of fresh thyme

1½ *tablespoons mixed chopped fresh herbs; basil, thyme, chives, tarragon*

Grated rind of ½ orange

1 *tablespoon finely sliced scallion (white part only) or shallot*

Prepare the fish according to steps 1 and 2 two days before serving.

1. Rinse the fish, pat it dry, roll in seasoned flour, and fry in hot vegetable oil in a wide skillet until golden on both sides. Remove, drain, and place the fish in a glass,

earthenware, or porcelain serving dish. Discard the oil. Add the olive oil to the skillet and gently sauté the onions, carrots, and scallions until softened but not browned, about 5 minutes. Raise the heat, add the garlic, herbs, and spices and let them sizzle 1 minute, stirring constantly. Add 1 cup of water, white wine, vinegar, and 1 teaspoon of salt and bring to a boil. Simmer, partially covered, over low heat for 25 minutes.

2. Pour the contents of the skillet, still hot, over the fish (to finish the cooking). Allow to cool, then refrigerate the fish for at least 24 hours, turning the pieces in the marinade once or twice.

3. Wash the greens, drain, and pat dry. Tear them into bite-size pieces. Roll them in paper towels and keep chilled until you are ready to serve.

4. One to 2 hours before serving, remove the fish from the refrigerator so it will come to room temperature. Pour off 3 tablespoons of the marinade, and blend the ingredients for the vinaigrette.

5. At serving time, toss the greens with the vinaigrette. Place the salad in a large bowl and scatter the herbs, orange rind, and scallions on top. Serve the fish in a separate dish garnished with sprigs of fresh thyme.

Generally, oily fish (such as sardines, herring, tinker mackerel, or smelts) are used in an escabeche, but in this recipe the leaner fine-fleshed fish work even better.   NOTES TO THE COOK

Use small carrots and small white onions because they will cook in a shorter amount of time and will be more attractive in the sauce. Cut them into thin (⅛-inch) slices. Use the smaller inner cloves of large heads of garlic for the same reasons.

Smoked Salmon with Mixed Melon

This delicate, refined appetizer is similar in concept to the classic melon with prosciutto, exploiting an unexpected affinity by matching the rich texture of salmon to the sweet, refreshing quality of melon and the acidity of grapefruit.

6 *ounces smoked salmon, preferably Scottish or Norwegian, sliced*

2 *cups cranshaw, casaba, or Spanish melon, cut into ¾-inch squares ¼ inch thick*

2 *cups honeydew melon, cut into ¾-inch squares ¼ inch thick*

2 *cups cantaloupe, cut into ¾-inch squares ¼ inch thick*

⅓ *cup cubed grapefruit flesh*

2 *tablespoons freshly squeezed orange juice*

3 *tablespoons freshly squeezed lemon juice*

2 *tablespoons olive oil*

Salt and freshly ground black pepper

1. Cut the smoked-salmon slices into ¾-inch squares. Keep them chilled. In a large bowl, combine the melon squares and grapefruit. Cover and keep chilled.

2. Just before serving, add the salmon to the fruit, along with the fresh juices and oil. Season lightly with salt and generously with pepper. Toss to mix. Serve in individual chilled serving cups.

NOTES TO THE COOK   For this recipe I use as many different kinds of melons as I can find. Since you need only 2 cups each, take advantage of the halved melons sold wrapped in plastic in fruit and vegetable stores; that way you'll be able to choose melons that are ripe. Be sure the seeds are still in the melon—when the seeds are scraped out, the fruit tends to dry out. If purchasing whole melons, sniff the blossom end to be sure there's a sweet, fruity aroma. When peeling melon, remove at least ¼ inch of the hard rind. To store any unused remaining portion: leave the seeds in place, tightly cover with plastic wrap, and keep refrigerated up to 3 days.

For a richer fruit flavor, let the melons steep with the grapefruit for an hour or so before mixing with the salmon.

Anchovy Vinaigrette with Celery and Eggs

It was in Marseilles that I first tasted this famous Corsican combination of celery and hard-cooked eggs, dressed with a delicious anchovy vinaigrette. I have since expanded it to include sliced fennel and boiled baby potatoes cooked in their skins.

6 *salted anchovies, cleaned and filleted, or 12 flat fillets, jarred or canned, either kind soaked in cool, milky water, rinsed, and drained dry*

1 *garlic clove, peeled, halved, green shoot removed, and crushed to a purée*

1 *tablespoon mild wine vinegar*

Freshly ground black pepper

7 *to 8 tablespoons extra-virgin olive oil*

1 *bunch tender celery with tops*

½ *teaspoon salt*

1 *or 2 slices lemon*

1 *bunch dandelions or watercress, washed, trimmed, and dried*

12 *new potatoes, boiled in their jackets*

1 *small fennel bulb, sliced thin*

8 *hard-cooked eggs, peeled while hot, then soaked in icy water for ten minutes, and drained*

1. In a small saucepan over low heat crush the anchovy fillets with a wooden spoon or fork until creamy and smooth (makes about 3 tablespoons). Scrape them into a small bowl or blender jar, add garlic, vinegar, and pepper. Gradually add the olive oil. Let the mixture stand at room temperature for at least 1 hour before serving.

2. Meanwhile, thoroughly wash the celery and scrape away any thick ribs. In a bowl of water containing the salt soak the celery along with the lemon slices for 1 hour.

3. Just before serving, peel and quarter the eggs. Line a serving platter with the greens. Arrange the drained celery, potatoes, and fennel in small clusters on top. Garnish with the eggs. Pass the sauce with a leafy rib of celery (to be used as a whisk whenever necessary).

NOTES TO THE COOK

Salt-cured anchovies, available in Italian or Greek food stores and fine food shops (for mail order see Appendix, page 339), have a better texture than the canned variety, and produce a richer, deeper-tasting sauce. But high-quality oil-packed anchovies in small jars imported from southern Italy are excellent, too.

Soaking times vary for anchovies: 10 minutes is usually sufficient for salted fillets, 2 minutes for jarred. If your fillets are very salty, change the soaking water once or twice.

TWO SALT-COD APPETIZERS

There are three foods that must never be overcooked lest they become tough: eggs, calf's liver, and salt cod.

The longer salt cod is cooked in water, the tougher and stringier it becomes, and overcooked cod is also tasteless and cottony. A well-cooked piece of salt cod is moist and tender, and its taste is succulent, briny, and extremely delicate. Despite its name, when it is properly prepared, it's not really salty at all. (See Appendix for more details, page 339.)

One of the best ways to prepare salt cod involves no cooking at all. The Catalan dish *esqueixada* (pronounced esk-key-shada) is made of uncooked salt cod, olive oil, and fresh tomatoes. Since the fish is salt-cured it need not be cooked in order to be edible, and, in its uncooked form, its taste is subtle and delicious, especially with crisp greens and a chilled rosé wine on a hot summer day.

E*squeixada*   SERVES 4

In this recipe, salt cod is hand-torn into small, plump flakes *(it must never be cut with a knife)* and combined with the grated, frothy flesh of a ripe red tomato. A little grated onion and a sharp edge of vinegar makes this one of the freshest-tasting salads I know. Serve with an assortment of grilled vegetables: halved tomatoes, small eggplants, pimentos, halved baking potatoes, all dressed with a fruity olive oil.

½ *pound salt cod, cut from the thick upper center*	2 *ripe tomatoes, halved crosswise*
¼ *cup extra-virgin fruity olive oil*	*Freshly ground white pepper*
2 *garlic cloves, peeled and lightly crushed*	*Salt to taste*
½ *medium onion*	12 *small black olives, such as Niçoise*
1 *tablespoon red or white wine vinegar*	*Crisp Romaine lettuce leaves*
	Crackers or crusty bread

1. Soak the salt cod in cold water to cover for 1 to 2 days, or until swollen, changing the water at least 4 times.

2. About 1 hour before serving, drain the soaked cod, remove the skin and bones. Tear the cod with your fingers into 6 or 7 small pieces; do not cut with a knife. Shred one piece at a time with your fingers, pulling and tearing the cod into small plump strips, and

discarding any bones or skin. Makes about 1¼ cups. Press the cod between double thicknesses of paper toweling; extract excess moisture. Toss the cod with olive oil and garlic cloves and leave it to macerate for 40 minutes.

3. Grate the onion. Place it in a small sieve and squeeze out excess liquid. In a small bowl, soak the onion in vinegar for 30 minutes.

4. Meanwhile, halve and gently squeeze the tomatoes to remove seeds. Grate tomato halves, cut side facing the coarsest side of a four-sided grater or on a flat shredder. You should be left with just the tomato skin in your hand; discard. Place the pulp in a sieve to drain off excess liquid. Wash, pit, and cut up the olives.

5. Drain the onion, reserving only the vinegar. In a serving bowl combine the vinegar, white pepper, tomato pulp, and 2 to 3 tablespoons of the oil from the cod. Discard the garlic. Drain the cod and reserve the remaining oil for some other purpose. Toss the cod with the tomato mixture; add salt to taste. Let the mixture stand about 10 minutes before serving with the lettuce leaves, crackers, or crisp bread rounds.

Inspired by a recipe from Montse Guillén.

Salt-Cod Fritters

These small, crisp, spicy fritters, made with a yeast batter, are puffier and lighter than if baking powder were employed. If the proper temperature is maintained during frying, very little oil will be absorbed.

Serve with a salad of thin-sliced raw fennel bulb, dressed with oil, lemon slices, and fresh mint leaves.

8 *ounces boneless, skinless salt cod*

2 *teaspoons dry active yeast, or ½ ounce fresh compressed yeast*

½ *cup milk, at room temperature*

1 *tablespoon olive oil*

1 *large egg, lightly beaten*

1 *cup all-purpose flour*

3 *tablespoons chopped coarse flat-leaf parsley*

2 *fresh hot red chili peppers, stemmed, seeds, and membranes removed, finely chopped, or 2 teaspoons hot red-pepper flakes, with few seeds, crushed*

3 *scallions (white and 1-inch green part), chopped fine (3 tablespoons)*

Salt

Freshly ground black pepper

½ *teaspoon dried thyme, crumbled*

1 *garlic clove, halved*

1¾ *cups vegetable oil for frying*

3 *tablespoons clarified butter (see note)*

1. *One day before serving,* rinse the salt cod thoroughly under running water. Cut it into 3 or 4 pieces. Cover with cold water. Refrigerate, changing the water 3 or more times.

2. About 1½ hours before serving, soften the yeast in ¼ cup of warm water in a medium bowl. Combine the milk, 1 tablespoon of oil, and the egg in a small bowl; stir into the yeast mixture. Sift the flour over the mixture, then stir to blend. Let it stand 30 minutes, covered with a light kitchen towel or cheesecloth.

3. Drain the salt cod. Drop it all at once into a deep saucepan of rapidly boiling water (the action should stop the boiling immediately). As soon as the first bubbles reappear, about 1 minute, add ½ cup cool water, simmer for 1 minute, then remove the fish with a slotted spoon to drain and cool. Remove any bones and bits of hard skin; flake the cod coarse. Set it aside.

4. Place the flaked cod, parsley, chilies, scallions, ½ teaspoon of salt, pepper, thyme, and garlic in a mortar or workbowl of a food processor. Grind or pulse until well blended

but not entirely smooth. Stir the cod mixture into the batter until well combined. Use it at once or let stand in a cool place (not the refrigerator) up to 1 hour.

5. Heat the frying oil and clarified butter in a deep nonstick skillet to 370° F. Use a melon-ball scoop to drop the mixture into the hot oil. Work in batches and fry the fritters until crisp and golden on all sides, about 1¼ minutes. Remove them to a double thickness of paper toweling or crumbled brown paper to drain; keep warm in an oven set at the lowest setting while you fry the remaining fritters. Sprinkle them lightly with salt and serve at once.

Clarified butter is added to the vegetable oil to enhance both color and taste. If you wish to use the oil again, clear it as described on page 15. NOTE TO THE COOK

THE CATALAN WAY OF
COOKING ON IRON

Cooking *a la planxa* is a Catalan method of searing food (typically baby squid, sardines, wild mushrooms, kidneys, mussels, quail, rabbit, jumbo shrimp, etc.) on a very hot, lightly oiled flat iron griddle. Food cooked this way has a pure, clean, slightly iron taste, which concentrates its flavor.

While a number of recipes for cooking *a la planxa* follow, most preparations are simple enough not to require instructions.

Young squid need only be dried, simply seared on both sides, then dotted before serving with a small quantity of chopped fresh herbs, coarse salt, and garlic.

Mussels are placed on their sides on the hot griddle. Even as they open slowly and release their briny aroma, they remain juicy and flavorful.

Wild mushrooms (fresh cèpes, shiitakes, chanterelles, etc.) are seared and weighted on both sides, a process that makes them particularly succulent and tasty.

A Mexican *comal*, or a seasoned cast-iron skillet, is ideal for this very simple method of cooking. To season an iron griddle or skillet: wash, rinse, and dry thoroughly. Wipe 2 tablespoons of vegetable oil over the surface. Heat over medium heat until very hot, about 5 minutes. Let cool, wipe the surface dry, and repeat once more. To clean the iron surface, use coarse salt and damp paper towels; never use detergents or a stiff brush. Heat and wipe down with a light coating of oil before cooking.

F*resh Young Squid a la planxa*

SERVES 8

---

8 *very small squid, cleaned, left whole, as directed in Appendix, page 349*

2 *garlic cloves, peeled, halved, green shoot removed, and chopped very fine*

Olive oil

Ten minutes before serving, heat an absolutely clean griddle, *comal* or iron skillet, wipe it down with an oiled cloth, and place the squid pouches on the hot iron, side by side. After 1 minute, add the tentacles. Use tongs to lift each pouch and shake out any excess moisture, and let it dance and boil off on the griddle. Continue cooking ½ minute, turn, and continue ½ minute longer. Place a pinch of chopped garlic and drop of oil on each pouch and set of tentacles and cook ½ minute, or until opaque. Serve at once.

Shrimps
a la planxa

8 *jumbo shrimps, unpeeled*   *Olive oil for the griddle*

  Sea salt   *Lemon quarters*

Starting at the thick end of each shrimp, remove 1-inch of shell and make a 1-inch slit down the exposed flesh. Sprinkle the shrimp with salt and place them on a hot oiled griddle to cook 1 minute. Turn and continue on the second side. Finish cooking the shrimp by placing each on the slit end for 1 minute. Serve with lemon quarter.

Smelts, Sardines, and Small
Mackerel *a la planxa*

8 *small fish, split and central bones*   1 *teaspoon fine-chopped parsley*
  removed   2 *teaspoons olive oil*

½ *teaspoon fine-chopped garlic*

Place the open fish, skin side down, on a hot, oiled griddle and cook for 2 minutes. Place tiny pinches of garlic and parsley and drops of oil on the flesh side of each fish. Turn and finish cooking, about 30 seconds. Serve at once.

Brochettes of Kidneys and Rosemary a la planxa

MAKES 8 OR 9 BROCHETTES

¾ *pound fresh veal or lamb kidneys*

8 *or 9 woody sprigs of fresh rosemary, each about 6-inches long*

2 *thin slices mild-smoked bacon cut into ½-by-¼-inch pieces*

Salt and freshly ground pepper

2 *tablespoons olive oil*

1. To clean the kidneys, remove the membranes and any fat; with a sharp knife, cut the kidneys lengthwise and remove the inner cores. Remove the deeper sections of fat with a pair of small scissors. Cut each kidney half into ½-inch chunks. Makes 32.

2. Strip each rosemary sprig, leaving only a small tuft at the end. Use the leaves for some other purpose. Trim the cut ends of the sprigs into points or use a metal or wooden skewer to pierce each piece of kidney and bacon. Thread 4 kidney pieces alternately with 3 pieces of bacon on each rosemary "skewer." Sprinkle them lightly with pepper and salt. Brush with olive oil. Keep the kidneys refrigerated until you are ready to cook.

3. Ten minutes before serving, slowly heat a griddle until very hot. Wipe the surface lightly with an oiled cloth. Add the brochettes, side by side, and use a weight to press down on them. Sear them for 25 seconds, then turn and finish the cooking, in 30 seconds.

THREE COLD MEAT DISHES

Roulade of Pig's Feet

My Catalan friend Montse Guillén taught me this dish. It can be made in advance and is perfect for adventurous eaters. The pig's feet are slowly poached in an aromatic broth, then boned, stuffed, and rolled into one long cylinder. The cylinder is then wrapped in foil, returned to the still-simmering broth to cook to a congealed state (akin to that of a sausage), allowed to cool, then finally sliced into rounds. I like to serve the slices with a spicy vinaigrette.

4 *pig's feet, split lengthwise*

COURT BOUILLON
4 *fresh coriander sprigs*
  1-inch piece of peeled fresh ginger
1 *onion, halved*
1 *garlic clove*
1 *tablespoons coarse (kosher) salt*

2 *thin carrots, pared*
  Vegetable oil
  Salt and freshly ground pepper
½ *hot red- or green-pepper pod, seeded and membrane removed, diced fine*
2 *tablespoons pinenuts (pignoli), toasted*

VINAIGRETTE
2 *tablespoons reserved cooking liquid*
¼ *cup extra-virgin olive oil*
1 *tablespoon chopped fresh parsley*
¼ *cup fresh lime juice*
3 *scallions (white part only), sliced thin*
1 *tablespoon fresh coriander, without stems, snipped*
½ *hot red- or green-pepper pod, seeded and membrane removed, diced fine*
2 *tablespoons chopped pimento*
  Salt and freshly ground pepper

1. Wash the pig's feet. Wrap pairs in cheesecloth and tie securely. Place in a deep pot. Cover with fresh water; add coriander sprigs, ginger, onion, garlic clove, and salt, and cook for 3 hours or until the pig's feet are very tender. After 2 hours, add the carrots.

2. Remove the pig's feet from the liquid. Set aside the carrots and 2 tablespoons of strained cooking liquid. Bone the pig's feet while still warm. Discard the bones and gristle. Brush a 15-inch-long sheet of aluminum foil with oil. Spread the pig's feet, skin side down, on the sheet of foil. Scatter any loose pieces on top. Season with salt and pepper. Spread

(continued)

the chili dice and pinenuts evenly over the flesh. Cut up the carrot and place down the middle. Using the foil as an aid, roll the pig's feet into a cylinder; wrap tightly. Be sure that the stuffing remains inside. Rewrap tightly in waterproof and heatproof plastic (either seal in boilable pouches or wrap a few times with heatproof wrap). Reheat the cooking liquid, add the roll, and boil 15 minutes. For a fast cooldown, immediately drop the roll into a bowl filled with icy slush. Refrigerate the roll until 4 to 5 hours before serving. *(The roll can be prepared 2 days in advance to this point.)*

3. Two to 3 hours before serving, unwrap the roll. Use a serrated knife to slice it thin. Mix the ingredients for the vinaigrette and spread half the mixture onto a large serving plate. Arrange the slices overlapping, and cover with the remaining vinaigrette. Allow to stand at room temperature.

Calf's Liver with Radish Vinaigrette

It was in Albi, hometown of the painter Henri Toulouse-Lautrec, sometimes called The Florence of France, that I first tasted an unusual and delicious salad of sliced cured pork liver and radishes sautéed and cooled to room temperature.

In rethinking this dish for his restaurant in Laguiole, chef Michel Bras decided to use an unorthodox technique. He vacuum-packed an entire baby calf's liver, then poached it very slowly in barely heated water, his intention being to cook it without allowing it to toughen. The silky texture was extraordinary, the result of precision cooking by an enormously talented and innovative chef. I have adapted his technique so that this remarkable texture can be achieved in a home kitchen. Please be sure you have a dependable candy thermometer to monitor the temperature of the water, and an accurate instant-reading thermometer to measure the internal temperature of the meat.

In Bras's version of this salad, after being cooked to medium-rare, the liver is chilled, sliced very thin, and served with a light and fragrant dressing in which grated radishes become the sharp component of a vinaigrette.

3 to 3¼ pounds young calf's liver, in one piece, preferably baby calf's liver (see notes)

Coarse salt

½ teaspoon freshly ground pepper

½ teaspoon dried thyme

1 bay leaf, crumbled

RADISH ViNAIGRETTE

6 ounces fresh red radishes, washed and trimmed

1½ tablespoons strained fresh lemon juice

½ teaspoon sugar (if radishes are extremely pungent; see note)

1 teaspoon fine salt

⅛ teaspoon white pepper

⅓ cup French peanut oil (huile d'arachide), or fine salad oil

GARNISH

1 pound young tender turnips, with green stems attached

3 tablespoons homemade vinaigrette dressing (2 teaspoons vinegar, 8 teaspoons oil, salt and pepper to taste)

20 large leaves of fresh tarragon, snipped fine

½ teaspoon grated orange rind

Begin preparation 2 days in advance.

1. Have the butcher remove the membrane surrounding the liver, and cut away surface veins and tendons. (You can do it yourself with a thin-bladed knife.) Rinse the liver well under cool running water. Submerge it in a deep bowl of cool water mixed with 2 tablespoons of coarse salt, cover with plastic wrap, and refrigerate for 24 hours, changing the water and salt twice.

(continued)

2. The following day, drain the liver and dry it. Mix coarse salt (1½ teaspoons per pound of liver), pepper, thyme, and crumbled bay leaf and rub them over the liver. Place it in a dry bowl, cover, and refrigerate for about 6 hours.

3. Drain the liver and blot it dry. Pack it into a 1-quart cooking pouch or wrap in several layers of heatproof plastic wrap, press out air, and seal. Fill a deep kettle with enough water to cover the liver. Heat the water to 158° F (70° C), and regulate the heat to keep it constant. Slip in the liver and weight, if necessary, to keep it submerged. Cook for 1½ hours. Liver is perfectly cooked when the internal temperature has reached 148° F (65° C). If undercooked, wrap in a fresh layer of plastic wrap and return it to the kettle to cook 5 minutes longer. Immediately remove the liver from the water, still wrapped in plastic, and cool it down in icy slush. Weight the liver and refrigerate it at least 4 hours before serving. Liver keeps up to 2 days in the refrigerator if wrapped airtight.

4. One hour before serving, make the radish vinaigrette. Grate the radishes in a food processor. Replace the grating blade with the metal blade and chop until fine but still gritty in texture. Transfer the radish to a deep bowl, add lemon juice, sugar if needed, salt, and pepper, and whisk to combine. Slowly whisk in the oil to make an emulsion. (Do not use a food processor for this step or the vinaigrette will be without character.) Makes about 1 cup sauce.

5. Peel and slice the turnips thin lengthwise so that a little of the green stem is attached to each slice. Cook them in boiling salted water until just tender, about 2 minutes. Drain and refresh the turnips in cold water to stop the cooking. Meanwhile, in a small saucepan gently heat 2 tablespoons of the radish mixture with half the tarragon (to enhance its anise flavor) and pour it over the turnips. Toss them and arrange on a serving plate. Sprinkle with orange rind and the remaining tarragon, and adjust the seasoning with salt and pepper.

6. Using a meat slicer or a very sharp, thin, flexible knife, cut the liver slightly on the diagonal (as you would London broil) into very thin slices. Arrange them overlapping on a large serving plate. Season with salt and pepper and spoon the remaining radish vinaigrette over. Serve with the turnips.

NOTES TO
THE COOK

In spring radishes are usually sweet, but in late summer and fall they tend to be extremely pungent, so you may need to add a pinch of sugar to the vinaigrette.

It is not easy to find true baby calf's liver (a whole liver that weighs under 3¼ pounds). (See mail-order source in Appendix, page 339.) I have also tested this recipe using a 3- to 3¼-pound piece cut from a *young* calf's liver weighing about 5 pounds, with excellent results.

Because the taste of liver varies from animal to animal, follow these suggestions when purchasing: Ask for a rosy-hued liver; avoid those that are tan or brown; sniff the liver to assure yourself of its freshness—it should not smell "livery"; and examine its texture—it should not be mushy.

Smoked Tongue Salad with Spring Greens

Tongue intrigues me, perhaps because I cook it only twice a year—once in winter, when I serve it with a rich brown gravy heightened with chopped vegetables and pickles, and again in the spring, when I serve it cool as an early Sunday dinner dish.

In the latter recipe the tongue is first poached in an aromatic broth, then cooled, sliced, and very lightly seasoned with a nut oil dressing. It is served with tender spring greens, such as arugula, dandelion, or watercress. Any one of these greens, tossed with chick-peas, grated radishes, a creamy dressing, and a hint of cumin, will give this salad a slightly Middle Eastern glow.

1 *smoked beef tongue (about 3 pounds)*
   Bouquet garni: parsley sprigs, bay leaf, and thyme sprigs

1 *onion, sliced*

1 *carrot, sliced*

½ *teaspoon peppercorns*

2 *cloves*

6 *tablespoons mayonnaise*

2 *tablespoons mild vinegar, preferably rice wine or cider vinegar*

1½ *cups cooked chick-peas, peeled*

2 *tablespoons chopped shallots (by hand)*

½ *scant teaspoon freshly ground cumin seeds*
   Salt and freshly ground pepper

1 *bunch radishes, trimmed*

2 *bunches tender greens, washed and stemmed*

3 *tablespoons imported fresh hazelnut or walnut oil*

2 *teaspoons chopped parsley*

2 *teaspoons snipped chives*

1. Place the smoked beef tongue in a deep pot. Add enough cold water to cover and bring it to a boil. Add the bouquet garni, onion, carrot, peppercorns, and cloves. Lower the heat, partially cover, and cook at a simmer for 45 minutes a pound, or until tender. Allow the tongue to cool in the cooking liquid. Meanwhile, strain, degrease, and reserve 4 tablespoons of the broth.

2. When the tongue is cool enough to handle, use a sharp knife and a long pronged fork to remove the skin, bones, and gristle from the tongue. Trim away the root end. Cut the tongue into thin even slices (about 30). Place the slices overlapping in a wide bowl, cover with about 3 cups of the cooking liquid to keep the tongue moist. Set aside.

3. Thin the mayonnaise with the 4 tablespoons of cooking liquid and 1 tablespoon of

(continued)

the vinegar. Combine the chick-peas, shallots, cumin, salt, pepper, and the mayonnaise, mixing gently. Store covered in a cool place until you are ready to serve.

4. Twenty minutes before serving, shred the radishes coarse (¼ inch × ¼ inch), using the large shredding disk in a food processor. Sprinkle the radishes lightly with salt. Let stand for 10 to 15 minutes, then drain them and place in a bowl.

5. Add the greens and chick-pea mixture to the bowl, mixing them gently. Arrange in a mound in the center of a large serving dish. Combine the hazelnut or walnut oil and the remaining vinegar in a small bowl, whisking until well combined; season with salt and pepper. Drain the tongue and arrange the slices around the mound of greens and radishes. Brush the tongue with the walnut oil dressing. Scatter over the herbs.

NOTE TO
THE COOK
The wonderful strong and flavorful taste of freshly ground cumin seeds is important to this dish. The supermarket cans of ready-ground are simply not the same. I suggest you buy the whole seeds and grind them as you need them. If using a mortar, press them through a fine sieve before using. A simpler method is to fine-grind them by the teaspoonful in an electric spice mill.

FOUR TERRINES

SERVES 12

Duck Foie Gras Terrine

A classic *foie gras* terrine on the buffet is the height of Christmas luxury. Chilled and sliced, then served cool, pink-beige and delicately veined, *foie gras* literally melts on one's tongue. Richer than butter and cream together, smoother and silkier than any ordinary liver, it provides a flavor that, once tasted, will never be forgotten.

In Gascony *foie gras* is often served in a porcelain terrine along with a serving spoon and a small bowl of hot water. Each person dips his spoon in the water to heat it so it will cut neatly through the liver. He then scoops out a portion and smears it on a slab of grilled coarse French bread.

A more elegant presentation is to slice the *foie gras,* then arrange the slices on a Limoges plate surrounded with chopped aspic and lightly toasted brioche. Slices can be served with a variety of greens, flavored with a walnut-oil vinaigrette or the radish vinaigrette on page 49.

Wine with *foie gras:* Sauternes, the sweet white wine from Bordeaux, is the classic accompaniment. Its sweetness complements the liver's richness, creating a velvet-smooth combination that should be slowly savored. Other sweet white wines, such as Monbazillac from the Périgord or any number of American sweet white wines, will also make a good marriage. Further possibilities include Champagne, a lightly chilled old red Port, or even a light red Bordeaux.

Please note: The preparation and resting times for this terrine are 5 to 7 days, so plan accordingly.

2 *fresh domestic duck* foie gras, *"A"*
 quality (about 1½ pounds each)
 soaked, rinsed, and deveined (see
 Appendix, page 341)

1 *tablespoon fine salt*

1¼ *teaspoons sugar*

¾ *teaspoon finely ground white pepper*

Pinches of freshly grated nutmeg or
 quatre épices

3 *tablespoons duck or veal demiglace or*
 poultry stock reduced to a syrup
 (optional)

3 *tablespoons Armagnac or Cognac*
 (optional)

Flour and water paste (optional)

1. Drain the livers on paper towels and pat dry. In a deep bowl, combine the salt, sugar, white pepper, and nutmeg, Add the livers and rub them all over with the mixture. If desired, sprinkle on the demiglace and/or Armagnac. Cover the liver and refrigerate overnight.

(continued)

2. About 2 hours before cooking, remove the livers from the refrigerator and let them return to room temperature.

3. Preheat the oven to 215° F. Fit one of the large lobes, smooth side down, in a 5-cup earthenware, enameled cast-iron, or porcelain terrine. Flatten it to eliminate air pockets. Place the smaller lobes and any pieces of liver in the middle and top with the remaining large lobe, smooth side up. Press the livers to fit the mold. Put on the lid, seal airtight with a paste made from equal parts of flour and water or cover securely with heatproof plastic wrap and a tight-fitting lid.

4. Place a double layer of newspapers or a folded kitchen towel in the bottom of a roasting pan. Put the sealed terrine on the papers and add warm water to reach halfway up the sides of the terrine. Set in the oven and cook for 55 to 60 minutes. Break the seal and check for doneness. Use a touch test to poke at the liver; as it cooks, it gets softer. It is done when it has a soft, elastic feel to it. Or insert a metal skewer into the thickest part of the *foie gras* for 20 seconds; then test the skewer on your wrist. If the skewer feels warm and the juices spurting from the liver are pink the *foie gras* is cooked. The internal temperature measures just below 130° F on an instant-reading thermometer. The lid does not need to be resealed if the terrine is not done when checked. Return the covered terrine to the waterbath and continue cooking 5 minutes longer. Remove the terrine from the waterbath, place it in a baking dish, or jelly-roll pan, and let cool for 10 minutes. The liver continues to cook as it cools down.

5. Gently push down the *foie gras* with a flat board weighted with cans or a terrine of the same shape, filled with cans, to press out most of the fat and blood. Pour off and reserve the fat; discard the bloody juices (refrigerate if necessary to separate the two). When it is cool, wrap the weighted terrine in plastic wrap and foil and refrigerate for at least 4 hours, or overnight.

6. When the liver is cold, unmold it from the terrine and wipe away any bloody juices from the bottom of the liver. Wash and dry the terrine and return the congealed liver to it. In a small saucepan, melt the reserved fat just until it is liquid. Pour over the liver in the terrine to cover it completely. Wrap it tightly in plastic wrap and aluminum foil and refrigerate for 3 to 5 days before serving to allow the flavors to develop.

7. Serve cool, not chilled. Unmold the liver onto a cutting board; cut with a knife dipped in hot water and dried before cutting each slice. Arrange the slices overlapping on a serving dish or on individual plates. Pass thin slices of warm toasted country bread or brioche.

NOTES TO THE COOK   For detailed notes on purchasing and handling *foie gras*, see the Appendix, page 341.

If using a terrine smaller than 5 cups, save any extra *foie gras* for a quick sauté. (See recipe on page 190.)

The shape of the mold, the density of the liver, and the temperature of the water and the oven will affect the cooking time of *foie gras*. Some oval-shaped terrines require a longer cooking time.

If terrine is made of earthenware or porcelain, a layer of newspaper sheets is not necessary.

Weighting a *foie gras* helps it become a solid mass and brings up fat trapped between its layers.

If there is any leftover *foie gras*, wrap the remainder airtight, first in plastic wrap and then in foil to keep it from discoloring.

Variations: Small Foie Gras Terrine

To make a terrine with a single liver, use a terrine that holds the liver snugly, about 2½ cups. Check the doneness of the liver after 40 minutes. For every pound of raw *foie gras* use seasonings in the following proportions: 1 teaspoon fine salt; ⅓ teaspoon superfine sugar; ¼ scant teaspoon finely ground white pepper. Pinches of grated nutmeg or *quatre épices* can be added to taste.

Foie Gras Terrine Flavored with Sauternes Wine

For a different, sweeter taste, soak the *foie gras* in Sauternes mixed with some coarse salt overnight. Rinse it under cool running water to remove the salt, devein, season with salt, pepper, and sugar, and add 1 glass of fresh Sauternes before cooking. Cook as directed above.

Terrine of Foie Gras Poached in Goose Fat

Foie gras cooked in goose fat has an extraordinary taste that is surprisingly different from that of the preceding cold terrine. Submerged in goose fat the liver cooks evenly, and retains all its flavors. After cooking and cooling, it is packed in a small terrine, enveloped in fat, then left to ripen for a minimum of 5 days. It is excellent plain, but can also be served with a coating of Port-wine jelly.

For this terrine, try to choose a liver in perfect condition, one with as few blood spots as possible.

1½ *teaspoons fine salt*

½ *teaspoon sugar*

⅜ *teaspoon fine-ground white pepper*

Pinch of nutmeg or quatre épices *or mixed spices*

1 *to 1½ pounds fresh domestic duck* foie gras, *"A" quality, soaked, rinsed, and deveined (see Appendix, page 341)*

1½ *tablespoons ruby Port wine*

3½ *to 4½ cups rendered duck or goose fat (for mail-order source, see page 341.)*

1. Mix the salt, sugar, pepper, and nutmeg in a small bowl. Sprinkle the mixture evenly over the *foie gras.* Sprinkle the Port over the *foie gras.*

2. Place the *foie gras* on a square of fine cheesecloth (double the thickness of the cloth if it is coarsely woven). Roll the liver in the cloth and twist the ends to form a compact 7-inch log. Tie the ends with string. Let it stand in a cool place, but not the refrigerator, for 1 to 2 hours.

3. Preheat the oven to 215° F. Heat the fat to 100° and pour ½ inch into a 2-quart heatproof glass loaf pan or terrine. Place the liver in the pan and pour on enough of the remaining fat to completely cover the liver. Place the dish on a baking sheet and cook it in the middle of the oven for 1 hour, or until an instant-reading thermometer registers 125° to 130° F in the center of the liver. The temperature of the fat should rise to and remain around 140° F.

4. Very carefully transfer the liver to a dish to drain. Strain the fat from the pan into a bowl and reserve.

5. Roll the *foie gras* in a kitchen towel and hold it over the bowl of fat. Twist the towel ends to shape the liver and to squeeze out a little more fat. Unwrap the liver and pack it into a 2- or 3-cup terrine or ramekin. Press the liver into the mold with your hands or the back of a large spoon. Let it stand for 2 or 3 hours, until cooled to room temperature.

6. Cover the liver with a ¼-inch-thick layer of the reserved fat; if it has cooled too much, heat it until pourable. When the entire terrine is completely cooled, cover it with plastic wrap and then with aluminum foil to seal well. Refrigerate for 3 to 5 days to allow the flavors to develop before serving.

7. To serve, let the *foie gras* return to room temperature. Scrape off the fat. Unmold, slice, and serve with thin slices of toast. (Or scoop it out with a warm spoon at the table.)

A water bath is not necessary when cooking *foie gras* in fat. If the cooked liver is completely enrobed in fat it will keep 10 days under refrigeration. NOTE TO THE COOK

Jellied Terrine with Provençal Vegetables

SERVES 6

"I always want to keep the taste of my original ingredients . . . to make dishes that are clear and clean," Jean-Louis Palladin, chef at Washington's best restaurant, Jean-Louis in the Watergate Hotel, told me. He was explaining how to make his seductive Provence-inspired terrine of early fall vegetables, studded with sweet garlic cloves and fresh basil leaves. Unlike a lot of chefs whose invented dishes have no basis in traditional cooking, Jean-Louis's create free-form versions of French classics—in this case, ratatouille. Its sensitive intermingling of eggplants, peppers, tomatoes, squash, garlic, and basil produces a sensational terrine. Make no mistake: This is a demanding dish for the home cook, but it is well worth the effort. Accompany with a well-chilled Sauvignon blanc.

2 medium eggplants (each about 14 ounces)

Coarse salt

⅓ pound yellow squash

¾ pound firm zucchini

Fruity extra-virgin olive oil

1 pound (3 medium-size) ripe tomatoes, sliced in rounds

4 large garlic cloves, peeled and sliced thin, green shoot removed

1 pound bell peppers (equal combination of red, yellow, and green), roasted, stemmed, seeded, and cut into strips

10 whole large basil leaves, stemmed

1 cup Reduced Quick Chicken-Flavored Jelly (see recipe, page 59) or substitute a high quality commercial consommé, lukewarm

Garnish: 3 Sauces—tomato, red bell pepper, and yellow bell pepper (see recipes, pages 60 to 61)

Make the terrine up to 2 days before serving.

1. Do not peel the eggplant, but trim off the ends on the diagonal, then continue to cut it on the diagonal into ½-inch-thick slices. Arrange the slices in layers in a colander, sprinkling each with coarse salt. Cover the eggplant with a weight and let stand 45 minutes. Cut the yellow squash and zucchini on the diagonal into ½-inch-thick slices and sprinkle lightly with salt. Spread the slices out and let stand for 30 minutes. Press out moisture with a kitchen towel.

2. Heat at least ½ inch of olive oil in a nonstick skillet until hot. Fry the eggplant, yellow squash, and zucchini in batches until golden brown on both sides. Then fry the tomato slices. Drain each group separately on kitchen towels. Cool completely. Meanwhile, in a small, heavy saucepan, gently cook the garlic slices in 1 tablespoon of oil and 2 tablespoons of water until soft and golden, 10 minutes. Set aside.

3. Line a 4-cup foil loaf pan or plastic or metal mold with a sheet of oiled plastic wrap, letting some of the wrap overlap the rim. Make one layer of half the tomato slices in the prepared mold, then place in it alternating layers of eggplant, yellow squash, zucchini, and assorted peppers. Cover with a layer of fresh basil leaves and the cooked garlic. Repeat the vegetable layers until all ingredients have been used, ending with tomatoes. Pour the lukewarm jelly into the mold, poking holes through the vegetables, then gently press the vegetables to keep them in place. Fold the plastic wrap over the top, cover with aluminum foil, and add a weighted plate. Let the mold stand overnight in the refrigerator.

Make the accompanying sauces (see recipes, pages 60 to 61).

4. Just before serving, invert the terrine onto a platter and peel off the plastic. With a sharp, thin knife, preferably electric, cut the terrine into 6 equal slices. Place 1 slice on each serving plate (if the slice breaks up, simply re-form it by pressing the vegetables together). Garnish with thin ribbons of red-pepper sauce, yellow-pepper sauce, and tomato sauce.

MAKES 1 ¾ CUPS   *Reduced Quick Chicken-Flavored Jelly*

---

3 *pounds chicken carcasses*

3 *pounds veal bones*

1 *garlic clove, halved*

1 *shallot, sliced*

1 *onion, halved and charred under a broiler or over a flame*

2 *tablespoons olive oil*

2 *small ribs celery with greens*

1 *leek with greens, washed well and halved*

½ *turnip, sliced*

2 *carrots, sliced*

1 *tomato, unpeeled and halved*

Bouquet garni: parsley sprigs, bay leaf, and thyme sprigs

2 *egg whites, lightly beaten*

2 *egg shells, crushed*

1 *envelope unflavored gelatin*

1 *teaspoon salt*

½ *teaspoon freshly cracked black peppercorns*

Mostly unattended cooking time: 2 hours

1. Cover the bones with 6 cups of cold water and slowly bring to a boil. Cook, skimming, for 15 minutes. Add the garlic, shallots, and charred onion. Meanwhile, heat the oil in a large skillet and slowly glaze the celery, leek, turnip, and carrots on all sides, about 15 minutes. Add to the pot along with the tomato and herbs. Bring the mixture to a boil and simmer, partly covered, for 1 hour. Strain; degrease thoroughly. Reduce by boiling to 2¾ cups. Set aside ¾ cup for the 3 accompanying sauces.

(continued)

2. Place the remaining 2 cups of reduced stock, egg whites and shells, gelatin, salt, and pepper in a saucepan and bring slowly to a boil, whisking constantly. Reduce the heat and simmer gently until a crust forms on the surface. Strain the liquid through a colander lined with damp cheesecloth and set over a bowl. The colander must not touch the cleared stock below. If the stock is not clear, repeat straining. Makes about 1 cup well-reduced jelly.

Homemade Tomato Sauce

1 *medium white onion, chopped fine*

2 *ounces chopped prosciutto*

2 *tablespoons olive oil*

1 *can (28-ounce) plum tomatoes, seeds removed*

Herb bouquet with parsley, thyme, bay leaf, and celery

½ *cup V8 juice*

½ *cup reserved stock*

Salt, pepper, and pinch of sugar

3 *drops Tabasco*

In a heavy skillet cook the onion and prosciutto in oil until soft but not browned. Add the remaining ingredients and slowly simmer for 20 minutes to blend flavors. Push through the fine blade of a foodmill into a saucepan. Return to heat, boil until it's reduced to a good consistency, and correct the taste. Use at room temperature.

Two Pepper Sauces

1 *red bell pepper, stemmed, seeded, membranes removed, and cut into small pieces*

6 *tablespoons heavy cream*

2 *to 4 tablespoons reserved stock*

1 *yellow bell pepper, stemmed, seeded, membranes removed, and cut into small pieces*

1. Combine the red pepper, 3 tablespoons of the cream, and ¼ cup of water in a heavy saucepan. Cover and cook gently until the pepper is soft, stirring occasionally to prevent burning. Drain, purée the pulp in a food processor with 1 to 2 tablespoons of the stock. Pour into a small bowl and set aside until ready to serve.

2. Repeat step 1 using the yellow bell pepper. Pour into a separate bowl and set aside.

It takes about 2 hours to prepare this terrine, but all the work can be done a day in advance. It keeps several days in the refrigerator.

When quick-frying unfloured thin slices of very moist vegetables (zucchini, yellow squash, tomatoes) it helps to salt them first, in order to draw off some of their moisture. But, if you do this, be sure to dry them out in a slow oven or pat them dry with paper towels before frying.

I like to shallow fry in a nonstick skillet in plenty of oil. When the oil reaches the desired temperature of 375° F, regulate the heat to keep it steady. You'll rarely need to add more oil to the skillet, and you'll find that vegetables cooked this way absorb much *less* oil than those that are cooked in a much smaller quantity.

SERVES 4 TO 6   # Cheese and Walnut "Terrines"

Roquefort and Laguiole are two of the great cheeses of the French South-West. Put them together, as in this recipe, and you will have something truly sublime. Though there is *no* substitute for Roquefort (for this dish, at least, no other blue cheese is acceptable), Cantal or Monterey Jack can be substituted for the Laguiole.

This "terrine" is not unlike a soufflé, except that its lightness and unusual creaminess come from the addition of whipped cream. Serve hot or lukewarm with semisweet white wine.

3 to 3½ ounces Roquefort cheese	Freshly ground white pepper
2 ounces (10 tablespoons) grated walnuts	¼ cup heavy (whipping) cream, chilled
2 egg yolks	3 egg whites
2 tablespoons walnut liqueur, or substitute a nut liqueur such as Nocciole or Frangelico	1 ounce Laguiole cheese, or Cantal, Monterey Jack, or Canadian 9-month-old Cheddar, shredded

1. Preheat the oven to 450° F.

2. Combine the Roquefort, walnuts, egg yolks, and walnut liqueur in the workbowl of a food processor fitted with the metal blade. Process until very smooth. Transfer to a mixing bowl. Butter 4 ¾-cup or 6 ½-cup ramekins, and set aside.

3. In a separate cold metal bowl, using chilled beaters, beat the heavy cream until stiff. Gradually fold it into the cheese-walnut mix. Beat the egg whites until stiff but not

(continued)

dry. Stir one-fourth into the cheese-walnut mixture. Carefully mix in the remaining whites. Spoon a small portion of the mixture into each buttered ramekin, then scatter some shredded cheese on top and cover with the remaining mixture. Fill each ramekin three-quarters full. Sprinkle any remaining shredded cheese on top and place the ramekins in a water bath. Bake 8 to 10 minutes or until the "terrines" are puffed and golden. Remove them from the water bath as soon as they are cooked.

NOTES TO THE COOK If your Roquefort is very salty, use the smaller amount. To keep the walnuts from becoming oily, chop them by hand, with a nut grinder, or with the shredding disk of your food processor.

To avoid overcooking the "terrines," use hot but not boiling water in the water bath.

Inspired by a recipe from Michel Bras.

CHAPTER 3

RICE, PASTA, AND COUSCOUS

Risotto with Solleone Wine

SERVES 2

I learned this extraordinary white-wine risotto from chef Gianfranco Pagliaricci of Le Tre Vaselle, in Torgiano, Italy. The hotel, located in the Umbrian wine country, is owned and operated by the Lungarotti family, producers of some of the best Umbrian wines and olive oils. The risotto is a creamy ivory-colored dish that smells intensely of Parmesan cheese and a dry white fortified wine called Solleone, similar in taste to a fragrant and soft, dry sherry such as Tío Pepe.

As much as I love risottos, I've resisted making them for friends—they take up so much time and last-minute energy. I had been taught that the only way to obtain a properly tender risotto was by slowly swelling the rice with small additions of hot stock, while carefully and constantly stirring. But Gianfranco showed me an easy method of making a small quantity (for 2 or 3 people): use a wide, heavy pan, and add the hot broth in two segments, the second just after the first addition has been absorbed. With his method, the following risotto (and any other risotto) will come out perfectly in less than 20 minutes, with only occasional stirring required.

4 tablespoons unsalted butter, cut into small pieces

1 scant tablespoon chopped onion

¾ cup (5 ounces) small-grain Italian-style rice (Arborio)

¼ cup Solleone wine or dry Sherry, such as Tío Pepe

2¾ cups rich unsalted chicken or meat stock, simmering

4 tablespoons (1 ounce) grated Parmesan cheese

Freshly ground white pepper

Pinch of salt, if necessary

Heat half of the butter in a heavy, wide saucepan, add the onion, and sauté it over medium heat for 1 to 2 minutes, or until golden. Add the rice, stir, and cook over moderate heat 2 minutes, or until the rice is lightly toasted and well coated with butter. Add 2 tablespoons of the wine and allow it to evaporate. Add enough of the stock to cover the rice by ½ inch. Cook, stirring often, until all the liquid is absorbed. Add the remaining stock and cook the rice over medium-high heat, stirring occasionally, until it is cooked, but still slightly firm to the bite and not too dry (total cooking time is about 20 minutes). Remove the pan from the heat; add the remaining wine and butter and the cheese and immediately swirl the pan to create a creamy, well-combined sauce that coats each grain of rice. Taste for seasoning and serve immediately.

| SERVES 6 TO 8 | # Catalan Black Rice with Garlic Mayonnaise |

I'll never forget the famous "black ink" dishes of the Mediterranean: dark, deep-flavored, and velvety risotto made with cuttlefish *(risotto di seppioline)* from Venice; sweet, tender cuttlefish cooked in their own ink with wild bitter greens from the Ionian islands; *daube des muscardins,* a stew of tiny cuttlefish and ink from Martigues, cooked in wine and pungent with the wild herbs of Provence; *arròs negre,* rice, deeply blackened with squid ink, enriched with bits of squid, mussels, and shrimp from the Costa Brava. There is something ineffably sensual about these dishes, sweet and rich and full of the essence of the sea. Even as they temporarily blacken one's mouth they become a permanent gastronomic memory.

Catalan black rice, *arròs negre,* sometimes called "the black paella," is a fascinating dish. Rounds of sausage are buried in the rice along with the shrimp, mussels, and strips of squid. This mixture of land and sea products is typical of Catalan cuisine. Unlike the now-fashionable black ravioli, which looks striking but does not have a particularly exciting taste, rice cooked in an inky sauce actually does develop a distinctive flavor.

I have recently discovered an inexpensive and easy way to make these briny, ebony-colored, and quintessentially Mediterranean sauces, using canned cuttlefish imported from Spain. I extract the ink from the canned cuttlefish to add color and flavor to my black ink dishes, while using the solids to make flavorful stocks. (See Appendix, pages 349 to 350.)

1 *pound fresh or defrosted squid or cuttlefish, cleaned, skinned, and cut into bite-size pieces, ink sacs reserved*

2 *cans* calamares en su tinta, *or substitute 4 grams extract of "Chipiron" (see Appendix, pages 339, 350)*

6 *cups Squid or Cuttlefish Stock, kept simmering (see Appendix, page 350)*

6 *tablespoons extra-virgin olive oil*

¾ *pound fresh pork sausages, blanched 2 minutes in simmering water and cut into 1-inch lengths*

1 *dried hot red pepper*

1 *garlic clove, peeled and crushed*

1 *pound medium-large shrimp, peeled and deveined, shells reserved*

Salt and freshly ground pepper to taste

1½ *cups chopped onion*

¾ *cup peeled, seeded, chopped, and drained tomatoes*

1 *small red bell pepper, cored, seeded, membranes removed, and diced*

3 *tablespoons red wine*

2 *cups raw short-grain rice such as Spanish SOS or Goya Blue Rose*

2 *pounds mussels, well scrubbed and bearded*

*Garlic Mayonnaise (*all-i-oli negat*) (see recipe, page 83)*

1. Early in the day, clean the squid as described in the Appendix (page 339). Cut the squid into bite-size pieces. Rinse and drain well; keep them refrigerated. Carefully place

(continued)

all the ink sacs in a small bowl; crush them with the back of a wooden spoon. Open the tins of *calamares en su tinta*, spoon off the surface oil, wrap the solids in cheesecloth, and squeeze to extract the ink. Add it to the bowl. Makes about ½ cup ink. Cover the ink and keep refrigerated; strain it before using. Use the solids for the stock. If substituting a 4-gram packet of *"Chipiron,"* simply add it along with the wine at the end of step 3.

2. In a deep 12-inch ovenproof skillet or *cazuela*, heat 1 tablespoon of the olive oil and fry the sausages over medium heat until lightly browned, about 5 minutes. Drain the sausages and set them aside. To the same skillet add another tablespoon of oil, the hot pepper, and the garlic, and sauté until the pepper is brown and the garlic is golden, about 5 minutes. Discard the pepper and garlic; reserve the oil in the pan. Add another tablespoon of the oil, the reserved shrimp shells and salt and pepper, and sauté 5 minutes, tossing. (Keep the shrimps refrigerated.) Transfer the shells to the simmering squid stock.

3. To the skillet or *cazuela* add another tablespoon of oil, the onions, and ¼ cup of simmering stock *without any solids*. Cook over moderate heat, stirring, until the liquid has evaporated and the onions begin to turn golden, about 10 minutes. Then add the squid and cook until the water it produces evaporates. Continue to cook, stirring frequently, about 15 minutes, until the squid is golden. Stir in the tomatoes and bell pepper and cook for 2 to 3 minutes. Add the strained ink and wine and the reserved sausages, stir to combine, then remove the mixture from the heat.

4. Strain the simmering stock, discard the solids. Set aside 1 cup. Cool, cover, and refrigerate the remaining stock. Reheat the contents of the skillet, add the reserved cup of strained stock, partially cover, and cook the mixture over medium heat, stirring from time to time, about 15 minutes. The mixture should be thick and the squid very tender. *(The dish can be prepared up to this point in advance.)* Cool, cover, and refrigerate.

5. Thirty minutes before serving, preheat the oven to 300° F. At the same time, gently reheat the squid and sausage mixture in the skillet or *cazuela*. Separately, bring the remaining stock to a boil and keep it at a simmer. Meanwhile, place the mussels and ½ cup of water in a saucepan or skillet, bring them to a boil, cover, and steam until the mussels open. Discard any that do not open. Strain the mussel liquor and add it to the simmering stock. Discard the top shells of the mussels. Keep the mussels moist and warm.

6. Stir the rice into the skillet or *cazuela* with the squid and sausage, then slowly stir in 4 cups of the simmering stock. Bring the mixture to a boil and cook, uncovered, over medium heat, stirring once or twice, for 12 minutes. Cover the skillet tightly with foil and place in the oven for 10 minutes.

7. In a skillet over brisk heat sauté the shrimps in the remaining 2 tablespoons of olive oil until they turn pink, stirring constantly, about 2 minutes. Add the shrimp and mussels to the rice, cover again, and finish cooking in the oven, 5 to 10 minutes longer. Serve directly from the skillet or *cazuela* with an accompanying bowl of garlic mayonnaise.

Note: A *cazuela* is a shallow glazed Spanish earthenware dish. See Appendix (page 339) for mail-order source.

SIX SICILIAN PASTA DISHES

SERVES 4 TO 6 — **P**asta with Wild Fennel and Sardines

If there is one recipe that sums up what is best and most interesting in Sicilian cookery, it is surely pasta with wild fennel and sardines, a dish so subtle, mysterious, and harmonious that I consider it one of the triumphs of the blending of disparate ingredients.

Pasta con le sarde plays the soft texture and saline flavor of Mediterranean sardines against the slightly bitter and pungent taste of wild green fennel from the Sicilian mountains. The play is further enhanced by the addition of sweet dried grapes from the lowland orchards, pinenuts from the forests, and a little saffron (a touch of Moorish Spain), all combined with fine Sicilian olive oil, then presented to the diner against the soothing backdrop of a pasta.

All of Sicily is present in this dish, which dates back to the time of the Arabs. As related by Tommaso d'Alba in *La Cucina Siciliana di Derivazione Araba,* the Arab General Eufemio, having conquered Sicily, and wanting to appease the hunger of his troops, ordered his cooks to put together the best of what the island offered, and then to add a little Arab fantasy—the pinenuts and saffron.

The reason you rarely find this dish served in our Italian or Sicilian restaurants (a situation slowly being remedied) is that some of the ingredients are very difficult to find in the U.S. Having tried many versions I have finally opted for the one below, knowing that some Sicilian purists will be horrified.

If you live in southern California you can pick your own wild fennel (darker, with thinner stalks and a stronger flavor than farm-grown bulb fennel) from spring through autumn, in which case your Pasta con le sarde will be especially authentic, and in New York some fancy New York greengrocers sell it (see notes below for handling fresh wild fennel). But lacking either opportunity you can still create a fine rendition of Pasta con le sarde. During my testing I sampled versions side by side, some cooked with wild fennel, others with assorted combinations of fresh bulb-fennel leaves, dill weed, and fennel seeds. A little dill, I found, brought the dish closer in texture but absolutely *not* closer to taste, color, or aroma to the earthier wild fennel. Adding a few pinches of ground fennel seeds brought my bastardized version near to the original—thus the combination in my recipe.

Finding a reasonable substitute for Sicilian wild fennel was a lot easier than finding a viable substitute for fresh sardines, for except in large cities along the Atlantic Coast they are very difficult to find. (Defrosted smelts, often suggested as a substitute, are much too flabby and tasteless.) And so, with my heart in my hand, I am suggesting an alternative: Portuguese canned sardines that have been packed in olive oil and well drained. (If this substitution displeases you, you can prepare a version

(continued)

called *pasta con le sarde . . . a mare*—"pasta with sardines . . . at sea," the same recipe except without any sardines at all.)

Green as pesto but a little bit more lumpy, this mysterious-tasting sauce doesn't quite cling to pasta. For this reason I like to mix sauce and pasta just before serving, then place them together in a hot oven to settle and to blend. I sprinkle a little olive oil over the pasta just before eating to bring up the flavor. Pasta con le sarde is delicious hot from the oven, lukewarm or cold.

Like most pasta dishes with fish, Pasta con le sarde does not get a topping of cheese, though some Sicilians do sprinkle on toasted breadcrumbs or crushed almonds for added texture.

When you make this pasta, I suggest you follow it with two other interesting Sicilian dishes: an extraordinary roll-up, or *involtini*, of thinly pounded swordfish stuffed with semolina breadcrumbs and capers, accompanied by a fresh tomato salad, and for dessert Ricotta Ice Cream.

2 *cups packed, mixed leaves of fresh bulb fennel and fresh dillweed (bulbs reserved for some other purpose), or 5½ ounces (3 stalks) California wild fennel (see notes)*

Coarse (kosher) salt

2 *tablespoons currants*

1 *piece sun-dried tomato, cut into small bits (optional)*

2 *pinches pulverized saffron in ¼ cup hot water*

6 *tablespoons extra-virgin olive oil*

½ *cup finely chopped onion*

7 *flat fillets of anchovy, drained, rinsed, and chopped*

¼ *teaspoon powdered fennel seed (if using mixed greens)*

A pinch of sugar (if using California wild fennel)

2 *tablespoons pinenuts*

2 *cans (4-ounce) boneless sardines packed in olive oil, preferably Italian, French, or Portuguese, drained, or 12 fresh sardines (see notes)*

Freshly ground pepper

½ *pound hollow spaghetti, maccheroncini, bucatini, or perciatelli*

1. Cook the greens in 3 quarts of salted water until tender, about 15 minutes (10 minutes longer if using wild fennel). Scoop out the greens, drain, and set them aside. Reserve the fennel water for cooking the pasta and moistening the sauce as it cooks.

2. Soak the currants and tomato, if using, in saffron-tinted hot water for 10 minutes.

3. Meanwhile heat the olive oil in a wide, heavy skillet, add the onions and gently cook them until soft and golden. Add the anchovies and crush them well with a fork. Cook for 1 minute and remove the skillet from the heat.

4. When the greens are cool enough to handle, squeeze out the excess moisture, then roughly chop them in a food processor.

5. Add the greens, currants, tomato, if using, and soaking liquid, ground fennel seed *or* sugar, pine nuts, and ½ cup of the reserved fennel cooking water to the skillet. Cook 2 minutes, stirring, over moderate heat to blend the flavors. Add the canned sardines, crushing a few of them into the sauce. If the sauce seems too dry, moisten it with a little of the

fennel water. Adjust the seasoning with salt and pepper and set the sauce aside. Makes about 2 cups. (*The sauce can be prepared to this point in advance.*)

6. Twenty minutes before serving, preheat the oven to 425° F. Bring the reserved water to a boil, add the pasta, and return to a boil; cook until *al dente*. Drain the pasta; transfer it to a baking-serving dish and toss with half the sauce. Spread the remaining sauce on top. Cover it with foil and set in the oven for 5 minutes. Serve very hot. Pass a cruet of olive oil.

NOTES TO THE COOK

Outside southern California, wild fennel can be found in Italian markets around March 19, the day of the feast of Saint Joseph. Wash, drain, and trim away all hard stalks and any tough sprigs.

To prepare ground fennel seeds, simply grind some in a spice mill.

If you find fresh sardines: Cut off the head from each of the fish. Slit each belly lengthwise; turn it over, press down on the backbone to loosen, then turn back the fillets and pull out the bones. Trim the tails. With a paper towel wipe away the guts. Sprinkle the flesh with salt and pepper. Fry fresh sardines with the anchovies, and when half cooked, crush some of them with a fork. After adding the saffron-tinted water simmer the sardines until fully cooked.

Canned *pasta con le sarde* is surprisingly good, one of the few canned sauces I can recommend. (See mail-order source in the Appendix, page 347.) Improve it by sautéing chopped onions in olive oil, then add the canned sardine-fennel mix, and use as above.

Pasta with Anchovies and Toasted Breadcrumbs

SERVES 4

The Sicilian city of Siracusa is a city I could live in. Its people are different from those in the rest of the island. They speak more softly, behave more gently, act, as they like to say, "more Greek." Their profiles look Greek, too, which is no wonder, since in ancient times Siracusa was a Greek city second only in importance to Athens.

There are many fine Greek ruins in the town, including one of the largest and best-preserved Greek theatres. But the special quality of Siracusa is felt most keenly in its old quarter, called Ortygia, which is connected to the new town by a narrow isthmus and a bridge. Here I walked for hours down crooked narrow streets, marveling at the eclectic architecture, Baroque palaces, Gothic and Norman churches, fountains, squares, and planted promenades along the quais. It reminded me a little of Venice without, of course, the canals. Every so often, making my way through the interior labyrinth, I would catch a sight of water flashing in the sun. . . .

There is an excellent restaurant in Siracusa, Jonico. The chef-owner, Pasqualino Giudice, has seriously researched traditional Siracusan cuisine; his food is fine and delicate, soft like the speech of his city. I adore his Spaghetti with Tuna Caviar and Smoked Herring (next recipe), and this dish, Pasta with Anchovies and Toasted Breadcrumbs, is excellent, combining the delicious flavors of pan-toasted breadcrumbs, fleshy imported anchovies, good olive oil, and imported 100 percent durum-wheat semolina pasta.

⅓ cup fruity, green extra-virgin olive oil, preferably Sicilian

1 garlic clove, halved and peeled

2 or 3 pinches hot red-pepper flakes (with few seeds), to taste

10 salted anchovies, filleted, or 20 flat fillets of anchovy, either type soaked in milk 10 minutes, drained and cut small

½ pound thin spaghetti

2 tablespoons roughly chopped fresh flat-leaf parsley

½ cup toasted coarse breadcrumbs, preferably semolina (see note)

1. Heat the olive oil in a heavy skillet, add the garlic, and gently cook over medium heat for 2 minutes, or until golden. Discard the garlic and remove the skillet from the heat. Add the red-pepper flakes and anchovies, and mash to a purée with a wooden spoon. Reheat gently, stirring, for 1 minute to blend the flavors. Remove the pan from the heat before the oil gets too hot. (The sauce can be prepared in advance.)

2. Cook the spaghetti in boiling salted water until *al dente*. While the pasta is cooking transfer 3 tablespoons of the pasta cooking water to the anchovy-oil mixture (in order to stretch the sauce) and reheat carefully. Drain the pasta, then transfer it to the skillet and toss it with the hot sauce. Divide it evenly onto 4 heated dishes, sprinkle with parsley, and serve at once. Pass the breadcrumbs.

The tastiest breadcrumbs are made from day-old Sicilian-style semolina bread. (See page 2 for a recipe if it is unavailable at your local supermarket.) To make ½ cup toasted coarse breadcrumbs: Coarsely grate 6 or 7 chunks of crustless day-old Italian bread. Coat a seasoned skillet, preferably of iron, with 1 tablespoon of olive oil; add the breadcrumbs and stir constantly over medium-high heat until they are golden brown, about 2 minutes. Immediately scrape into a bowl. Do not allow the breadcrumbs to burn. Set aside.

NOTE TO THE COOK

SERVES 6 TO 8 — Spaghetti with Tuna Caviar and Smoked Herring

This is an unusual and complex Siracusan pasta recipe employing an esoteric ingredient called *bottarga* (salted and pressed tuna eggs), the Sicilian "caviar." It's an expensive ingredient, but a little bit goes a long way. When fresh it has a rosy color, but as it dries and hardens it turns reddish brown. In this condition it is sold in the form of slabs that look like thick, miniature, grayish colored oars. In Palermo thin slices of *bottarga* are served with lemon juice, olive oil and thin slices of bread as part of an antipasto. When very dry, it is sold grated. Grated slab *bottarga* is often served over pasta and sometimes over a green salad. In the city of Trapani the *bottarga* is dissolved in water, stirred into olive oil, and then mixed with parsley, basil, and garlic for a simple, robust pasta sauce. The more interesting recipe that follows—another adapted from the Ristorante Jonico—also uses the less-expensive grated *bottarga*. (See Appendix, page 339, for a mail-order source.)

Whole smoked herring is also popular in Sicily. You should avoid canned fillets when preparing this recipe. Instead, look for those imported from Canada, packed in Kriovac or sold whole in fine delicatessens or fish markets (many German delis carry them). You will need the skin, head, and bones for flavoring the sauce, as well as the eggs or milt.

(continued)

2 whole smoked herrings

Milk (optional)

½ cup extra-virgin olive oil, preferably Sicilian

4 large garlic cloves, sliced thin

½ teaspoon hot red-pepper flakes, or to taste

1 ounce (about ⅓ cup) grated bottarga

Juice of 1 lemon

Freshly ground black pepper

1 pound thin spaghetti or linguine fini

⅓ cup roughly chopped flat-leaf parsley leaves

1. Skin and fillet the herring, reserving the heads, skin, bones, and eggs (if female herring) or creamy long milt (if male). See the note below. Rinse the heads under running water. If the fillets are excessively smoky, soak them in milky water for 20 minutes. Drain them, rinse, and pat dry. Break up the eggs with a fork, or cut up the milt into cubes, and set aside.

2. Heat the olive oil in a medium skillet, add the garlic, and cook over medium heat for 30 seconds. Add the skin, bones, heads, trimmings, and pepper flakes, and sauté over low heat for 2 to 3 minutes, or until the garlic turns golden brown. Set the mixture aside, and when slightly cooled, strain it through damp cheesecloth, pressing down on the solids; reserve only the oil. Return it to the skillet.

3. Mix all but 1 tablespoon of the *bottarga* with the eggs or milt and add them to the oil, and reheat gently. Separately, warm the fillets in a covered dish over simmering water; sprinkle them with lemon juice and plenty of black pepper.

4. Cook the pasta in boiling, salted water. Add about 2 tablespoons of the pasta-cooking water to the skillet (to dilute the sauce). Drain the pasta when it tests *al dente*, add it to the skillet, and toss. Add half the parsley, and toss again over low heat for 30 seconds. Arrange the warmed herring pieces over the pasta. Sprinkle with the remaining *bottarga* and parsley, cover, and rush the skillet to the table. Serve directly from the skillet onto heated plates. Pass the peppermill.

NOTE TO THE COOK

To tell the difference between male and female herrings, have the deli man press on the stomach. The stomach of a female herring will feel firmer than that of a male. Both milt and/or eggs are good in this dish. The creamy long milt of the male is considered a great delicacy by Eastern Europeans.

(Pasta alla Norma)

SERVES 6

Pasta with Fried Eggplant, Tomatoes, and Toasted Ricotta Salata Cheese

According to legend, the popular name of this dish can be traced to the 1920s. A famous Sicilian actor, complimenting a cook in Catania on a pasta dish made with tomato, basil, fried eggplant, and grated salted ricotta, said it was "as good as *Norma*"—in Catania the very highest of compliments, since Vincenzo Bellini is a native son of that city, and his opera *Norma* was his masterpiece. Actually the dish is traditional in the small towns that dot the slopes of Mount Etna, with variations served all the way from Modica, on the southeastern tip of the island, up to Messina in the northeast corner.

There are various options to be considered in the preparation of Pasta alla Norma: Should the tomato sauce be thick or thin? Should the ricotta be toasted or not? I have opted for a lighter tomato sauce and for the toasted *ricotta salata*, a mature ricotta treated with salt, popular in Sicily for grating onto pasta dishes. It is available in Italian delicatessens throughout the United States.

6 *to 7 ounces salted ricotta cheese,* ricotta salata, *in one piece*

1 *(2-pound) can stewed Italian-style tomatoes, or 3½ pounds ripe Italian plum tomatoes, washed and gently crushed, cored and seeds removed*

1 *teaspoon chopped garlic*

1 *small piece of dried* pepperoncino *(the size of a pinenut) or ½ teaspoon dried hot-pepper flakes, with few seeds*

2 *tablespoons finely chopped onion*

4 *tablespoons extra-virgin olive oil*

3 *tablespoons shredded fresh basil leaves*

  Small pinches of sugar and baking soda, if necessary to balance the acidity

2 *pounds (4 or 5) small Italian eggplants (see notes for substitution and handling)*

  Coarse salt

  Pure olive oil for frying

  Freshly ground pepper to taste

12 *ounces* penne, mezzani, *spaghetti, or* canestrini

1. Preheat the oven to 400° F.

2. Toast the cheese on a flat baking dish, turning often, until golden brown on all sides, about 20 minutes. Cool it completely, then rub it over the large holes of a four-sided grater. Makes just over 1 cup, loosely packed. Set aside.

3. Meanwhile, gently simmer the tomatoes, their juices, the garlic and the hot pepper in a wide saucepan for 20 minutes or until thickened. In a small skillet cook the onion in 3 tablespoons of the olive oil until just soft but not brown. Add the contents of the skillet to the tomatoes and press through the finest blade of a foodmill. Reheat the sauce, stir in the

(continued)

basil leaves, and correct the seasoning. Add pinches of sugar and baking soda if necessary to balance the acidity. Makes 1½ cups. Set aside.

4. Remove the top of each eggplant and discard. Cut each eggplant lengthwise into ¼-inch-thick slices. You should have about 32 slices. Peel the end slices only. Soak the eggplant in cold salted water for 30 minutes, or until the eggplant leaches brown juices.

5. Rinse the eggplant slices, drain and pat them dry on a kitchen towel. Pour the oil ½ inch deep in an 8- or 9-inch skillet, preferably nonstick. *Slowly* heat it to hot (375° to 390° F) but not smoking. Even heat is easily maintained if you fry a few slices at a time. *(If your oil is hot enough, and you start with a lot of it, you should not have to add more, no matter how many pieces of eggplant you fry.)* Fry the eggplant, turning once, until it is golden on both sides and the peel crackles. Drain it on paper towels. Sprinkle it with freshly ground pepper. Set it aside. *(Up to this point the dish can be made in advance.)*

6. Lower the oven heat to 350° F.

7. Cook the pasta in boiling salted water until cooked but still firm to the bite. Drain the pasta and toss it with almost all of the tomato sauce and half the cheese. Season with freshly ground pepper. Arrange half the pasta in one layer in a baking-serving dish. Cover with half the eggplant slices and a final layer of pasta. Arrange remaining eggplant on top, overlapping, scatter the top with cheese, and drizzle with the remaining tomato sauce and 1 tablespoon olive oil. Put the dish in the oven to reheat for 5 minutes. Serve at once.

NOTES TO
THE COOK
If small eggplants are unavailable, substitute 2 one-pound eggplants. Skins on large eggplants are tougher, so they must be peeled. Halve the larger eggplants crosswise and cut each half into lengthwise slices as directed above.

The method of using salted water (2 tablespoons salt to 1 quart) to soak the eggplants rather than salting layered slices works beautifully to extract bitter juices without oversalting the slices themselves. Soaking will also deter the absorption of oil during frying. The added moisture causes the slices to steam when they hit the hot oil, and a thin film which forms on its surfaces keeps the oil from entering the flesh. Be sure to rinse the eggplant and dry it carefully before using.

When frying use a nonstick skillet, and slowly heat the oil so it will remain stable at the desired temperature. Avoid lowering the heat, or adding more oil while the eggplants are frying, or crowding the skillet, any of which will result in too much absorption of oil, which renders eggplant indigestible.

Linguine with Sea Urchins and Sautéed Artichokes

I love fresh, raw sea urchins served simply in their shells. If you've never tasted them, their flavor will be a revelation. Sea urchins should smell like sweet, fresh seaweed, and their gonads (roe) which you will eat should glisten. The color of the gonads can vary from white-cream to dark orange. You can buy the roe separately (called *uni*) at Oriental fish stores.

I also like sea urchins slightly warmed, which heightens their flavor and aroma. Some cooks make beignets with them, or bake them with quail eggs, or combine them with reductions of cream and fish stock. (Robert Courtine's *Zola at Table* gives a recipe for a soufflé of sea urchins baked right in their shells.) I prefer the warmed roes, slightly crushed, bound with olive oil and a drop of lemon juice. I recall with pleasure a meal on the Ionian island of Zakinthos, when a whole bowl of coral sea-urchin roes and their juices was presented on the table, for dipping into with coarse Greek country bread.

In Siracusa, some of the restaurants serve a thin spaghetti tossed with the roes of sea urchins, olive oil, black pepper, chopped parsley, and a few drops of lemon juice to taste. I have expanded this idea to include artichokes, which go well with sea urchins, and developed the following nonauthentic recipe for our domestic Maine sea urchins—larger and somewhat wilder in taste than the Sicilian variety. Serve the pasta with a cold, dry white wine, such as a Provençal Cassis.

15 *to 20 fresh sea urchins, or 1 cup sea-urchin roe (see note) (See Appendix, page 348, for a mail-order source.)*

2 *medium-sized fresh artichoke bottoms, cut into ¼-inch slices (see page 16)*

3 *tablespoons extra-virgin olive oil*

1½ *teaspoons fine-chopped garlic*

7 *to 8 ounces thin spaghetti*

Sea salt

6 *tablespoons chopped flat-leaf parsley*

¼ *teaspoon freshly ground white pepper*

Juice of ½ lemon

1. To open sea urchins: Use a glove or a folded kitchen towel to hold an urchin. With a pair of small, sharp scissors cut a wide circle around the orifice, remove and discard this part of the shell. Shake the juices into a strainer set over a bowl. Place each shell under cool running water in order to flush out and discard the brown viscera, then use a melon-ball scoop to remove the orange or yellow roe. Keep the fresh roe in the reserved strained juices, and store in a tightly closed jar in the refrigerator for up to 24 hours before serving.

2. Place the prepared artichokes, olive oil, garlic, ½ cup of water, and a pinch of salt in a 10-inch nonaluminum skillet, and cook over high heat, tossing until all the water has evaporated, 2 to 3 minutes. Set the artichokes aside until just before serving.

(continued)

3. Cook the spaghetti in boiling salted water until *al dente*. Meanwhile, drain the sea-urchin roe, reserving ½ cup of the liquid for the sauce. Cut the roe (gonads) into ⅓-inch cubes. Reheat the artichokes in the skillet to sizzling, add the reserved sea-urchin liquid, and remove the skillet from the heat. Swirl the skillet to form a thick sauce. Add the sea-urchin roe, parsley, salt, pepper, and lemon juice to taste. Drain the pasta, transfer it to a bowl, add the sauce, and toss well. Serve hot.

NOTE TO
THE COOK
When buying sea urchins select the heavier ones—they are said to contain the largest roe. To yield enough roe for this pasta, buy about 15. The bristles should remain intact when brushed; if they break off easily the urchins are not fresh. Check that the mouth is tightly closed and *level with the surrounding shell*. Sea urchins that have been out of the water a long time have receding orifices. But, most important, the sea urchin must smell sweet. If you open a sea urchin and find a soft, mushy roe and a sour odor, discard, as the creature is in decay. Unhappily, if one of a lot of sea urchins has gone bad, usually the whole crate will be in the same condition. Occasionally you will find sea-urchin shells that are empty.

Pasta with Squid and Its Ink

SERVES 2 TO 4

The Sicilian town of Noto is absolutely extraordinary. When I first went there I had a sense that I had seen the place before, and, in fact, I had—in Michelangelo Antonioni's famous film of the early sixties, *L'Avventura.* Destroyed by an earthquake in 1693, Noto was rebuilt in pure Sicilian baroque, its public buildings laid out like a stage set. Having later fallen into great decay, it is now being restored. In the late afternoon, when the sun plays upon the faces of its buildings, the stone turns to gold. The worn craggy faces of old men who stand and talk politics before its magnificent baroque façades, are kind of quintessential vision of Sicilian life.

I first ate this dish in Noto, though it is served along the entire eastern coast, or "Greek side" of Sicily. Tiny bits of squid are sautéed, then stewed in a sauce of cuttlefish ink and white wine that has been flavored with olives, garlic, capers, and sun-dried tomatoes. The result is a rich, indeed robust, ebony-colored pasta dish. Because baby cuttlefish are unavailable, I have substituted small squid in the following recipe. With this fish-based pasta sauce Sicilians offer grated pecorino cheese.

1 *pound baby squid, with their ink sacs*

2 *tablespoons extra-virgin olive oil*

¾ *cup chopped onions*

2 *tablespoons chopped sun-dried tomatoes*

½ *teaspoon crushed dried red-pepper flakes*

2 *tablespoons pitted and chopped Greek-style green-cracked olives*

½ *teaspoon chopped capers*

1 *tablespoon minced garlic*

½ *cup dry white wine*

⅓ *cup chopped fresh Italian parsley leaves*

   Salt and freshly ground black pepper

½ *pound thin spaghetti*

½ *cup grated pecorino cheese*

1 *tin* calamares en su tinta, *preferably Goya brand (see Appendix, page 339) (optional)*

1. Early in the day, clean the squid as described in the Appendix, page 349. Cut the squid into bite-size pieces to make about 1½ cups. Rinse them and drain well; keep refrigerated. Carefully place all the long, silvery ink sacs in a small bowl; crush them with a wooden spoon to release the ink, add 2 tablespoons of water, cover, and keep refrigerated until you are ready to use the ink. Strain before using.

2. Heat the oil in a 10-inch skillet over medium heat, and add the onion and ⅓ cup of water. Cook, stirring, until the onion is soft and golden, and the water has completely evaporated. Add the squid, tomatoes, pepper flakes, olives, capers, and garlic. Cook and

(continued)

stir the mixture over medium-high heat until the water produced evaporates and the squid begins to turn golden, about 8 minutes. Add the white wine, parsley, salt and pepper, and simmer, tightly covered, until the squid is tender, about 30 minutes. (*The sauce can be prepared a few hours in advance to this point.* Cool, cover and refrigerate.)

3. Bring a large pot of water to a boil. Add 1 tablespoon of salt and the spaghetti. While the pasta is cooking, reheat the sauce, press the squid ink through a fine sieve into the sauce, and bring it to a boil. Adjust the seasoning. Cook until the pasta is *al dente*; drain, and place it in a warmed bowl. Pour the sauce over and bring the bowl to the table. Toss the pasta and sauce just before serving. Serve with grated cheese.

NOTE TO THE COOK   If you prefer a darker sauce, you will need more ink sacs: rather than buy more squid, substitute a tin of *calamares en su tinta*, spoon off the surface oil, wrap the contents of the tin in cheesecloth, and squeeze the solids to extract the ink. Add it to the reserved ink in step 1. Discard the solids. Or substitute ½ packet of extract of *Chipiron*. (See Appendix, page 350.)

A PASTA DISH FROM FRANCE

Warm *Pasta with Mixed Greens* and *Sautéed Scallops*   SERVES 6 TO 8

Though I love authentic Italian and Sicilian pasta salads (such as cold Pasta con le sarde), I have never been a fan of the ubiquitous, chef-invented "new" pasta salads, especially those made with egg pasta.

Therefore, it was a tremendous surprise when Jacques Chibois, a fine, inventive young chef in Cannes, took me into his kitchen and taught me this absolutely terrific dish of *warm* fettuccine with scallops and shredded wild greens. Egg pasta is delicious enrobed in a creamy tarragon vinaigrette, and here, with the addition of sautéed deep-sea scallops, whose flavor has been brightened with a dash of Sherry vinegar, it reaches exalted heights.

TARRAGON VINAIGRETTE

½ teaspoon coarse salt

¼ teaspoon freshly ground pepper

2 tablespoons fresh lemon juice

1 tablespoon Sherry vinegar

3 tablespoons extra-virgin olive oil, preferably French

3 tablespoons French peanut oil (huile d'arachide) or high-quality salad oil

1 tablespoon chopped fresh tarragon

2 teaspoons chopped fresh chervil (optional)

1½ cups each: arugula, field lettuce (mâche), tender chicory, trimmed, washed, and dried (or 4 cups mesclun, see page 22)

1 small Belgian endive, core cut out, sliced into thin julienne strips 2 to 3 inches long

½ small fresh fennel bulb (without feathery leaves), cut into thin strips (about ⅔ cup)

3 teaspoons grated lemon rind

1 cup Noilly Prat vermouth

½ cup dry white wine

½ cup chopped shallots

⅔ cup heavy cream

Salt and pepper to taste

1 medium ripe tomato, peeled, seeded, and cubed (½ cup)

3 teaspoons chopped fresh tarragon

1 tablespoon unsalted butter

1 tablespoon extra-virgin olive oil

24 deep-sea scallops with tough muscle removed, rinsed and patted dry with paper towels

2 teaspoons sherry vinegar

Zest of 1 lemon, julienned, blanched twice in boiling water, and drained

Coarse (kosher) salt

12 ounces fettuccine, homemade or commercial

1. Combine the ingredients for the vinaigrette in a small jar; cover and shake until well blended. Makes 9 tablespoons. (Any leftover tarragon vinaigrette can be used on a tossed green salad the following day.)

2. Cut the greens crosswise into ⅓-inch-wide strips. Mix them with endive, fennel, and grated lemon rind, cover and crisp in the refrigerator.

3. Combine the vermouth, white wine, and shallots in a small heavy noncorrodible saucepan, and bring to a boil over medium-high heat. Cook until the shallots are soft and the liquid has reduced to a glaze, about 10 minutes. Add the cream, 4 tablespoons of the vinaigrette, and salt and pepper to taste. Bring the mixture almost to a boil, and remove it from the heat. Cool, cover, and refrigerate until needed.

4. In a small bowl combine the tomato, 2 teaspoons of the chopped fresh tarragon, salt and pepper, and 2 tablespoons of the tarragon vinaigrette. Cover and refrigerate. (The recipe can be prepared to this point up to 5 hours in advance.)

(continued)

5. Fifteen minutes before serving, bring plenty of water to a boil in a pot. Meanwhile, reheat the creamy tarragon sauce. In a small skillet (or in a microwave) heat the tomato mixture to lukewarm. Separately, in a heavy noncorrodible skillet heat the butter and oil over high heat until sizzling. Add the scallops, and sauté for 1 minute on each side or until they are well browned. Transfer the scallops to paper toweling and keep them warm. Pour off excess fat from the skillet, deglaze the skillet with Sherry vinegar and ¼ cup of water and reduce to one-half. Return the scallops to the skillet and coat them with the skillet juices; season with salt and pepper. Top with the tomato garnish and blanched strips of lemon rind. Remove the skillet from the heat, cover it, and keep warm.

6. When the water has come to a boil, add 1 tablespoon of coarse salt and the pasta. Return to a boil, and cook the pasta until tender, but still firm to the bite. Drain it, transfer it to a warmed salad bowl, add the greens and the reheated tarragon cream sauce, and toss. Sprinkle the remaining teaspoon of fresh tarragon on top. Divide the pasta among individual warm plates. Surround with garnished scallops and serve at once.

NOTES TO THE COOK
Scallops are usually sold shucked with their coral removed. Recently, however, I've seen them sold in their shells. To open scallops, lay them on their rounded sides at room temperature. They will begin to open on their own (this will take about 20 minutes). Slide in a thin knife, then loosen the scallop from the flatter shell. Discard any dark parts plus the hard little muscle attached to the scallop. Another way to open them is to place them in a medium-hot oven. Watch them carefully. The moment they open (within minutes) place them under slow-running cool water to prevent further cooking.

Small fillets of sole or flounder can be substituted for the scallops.

A PASTA DISH FROM CATALONIA

(Fideus a Banda)

SERVES 6	*Catalan Fried Noodles with Garlic Mayonnaise*

"A dish that contains the essence of the sea," writes Catalan author Manuel Vázquez Montalbán of *fideus a banda*, a unique Catalan fishermen's preparation of toasted durum-wheat soup noodles cooked in a flavorful fish broth until crusty on top, soft and juicy underneath. A small bowl of *all-i-oli negat* (a light garlic mayonnaise) is served on the side.

A true Catalan *all-i-oli* is made without eggs. Green shoots are removed from garlic cloves, the garlic is pounded to a paste in a mortar, salt is added, pounding is continued until the garlic is reduced to a syrup, then oil is slowly added drop by drop. If the sauce breaks, the cook adds an egg yolk and starts again—thus the expression *all-i-oli negat* ("broken *all-i-oli* sauce") which differentiates this mayonnaise from the classic Catalan version.

After the *fideus* is served, it is traditional to follow with the fish and shellfish used to make the broth. In my version, I serve the shrimp at the same time as the noodles.

1 *dried ancho pepper*	18 *lightly toasted blanched almonds*
5 *tablespoons extra-virgin olive oil*	*Coarse sea salt*
1 *pound medium raw shrimp (25 to 30), shelled and deveined, shells reserved*	½ *teaspoon freshly ground white pepper*
	1 *teaspoon sweet paprika*
3 *large garlic cloves, peeled and gently crushed*	2 *pounds heads, bones, and trimmings of mixed lean white fish, washed and cut into 2-inch chunks; or ¼ cup fish glaze (see Appendix, page 343)*
1 *large onion, sliced thin*	
½ *pound fresh plum tomatoes, seeded and chopped (1½ cups)*	12 *ounces dried fidelini noodles (fideus, fideos), broken into 1-inch lengths*
Pinch of saffron threads, toasted and pulverized (see notes)	*All-i-oli Negat sauce (light garlic mayonnaise) (see recipe, page 83)*

1. Stem and seed the ancho pepper; tear it into small pieces. Soak it in a small bowl of hot water for about 15 minutes until soft; drain.

2. In a large nonstick skillet, heat 2 tablespoons of olive oil over moderately high heat. Add the shrimp shells and garlic and sauté until the shells turn pink and the oil smells

(continued)

aromatic, 3 to 4 minutes. At one-minute intervals add the onions, tomatoes, saffron, almonds, and drained ancho pepper, in this order. Cook until all the excess moisture evaporates, about 5 minutes. Scrape the mixture into a blender jar or the workbowl of a food processor. Add ¾ teaspoon of salt, the pepper and paprika, and purée until smooth.

3. Scrape the purée into a large saucepan and cook over low heat, stirring constantly, for 1 minute. Do not allow the mixture to burn. Add 2 quarts of water and the fish trimmings or fish glaze. Bring the mixture to a boil over high heat, reduce the heat, and simmer, skimming occasionally, for 25 minutes. Strain the broth. Pour it into a clean saucepan and boil until it is reduced to 5½ cups. *(The broth can be prepared up to a day in advance and refrigerated, covered.)*

4. Preheat the oven to 350° F. On a jelly-roll pan, toss the noodles in the remaining 3 tablespoons of olive oil. Bake for 3 to 5 minutes, until golden brown. Immediately transfer the noodles to a deep, heavy, ovenproof 12-inch skillet. *(The noodles can be prepared early in the day.* Set them aside at room temperature.)

5. About 20 minutes before serving, preheat the oven to 425° F. Reheat the broth to simmering. Over moderate heat, slowly warm the noodles in the skillet, stirring with chopsticks or a long fork. Increase the heat to medium-high and gradually add the hot broth, 1 cup at a time, allowing the noodles to absorb the liquid after each addition until the last cup. When the last cup of liquid has been added, cook the noodles over moderate heat until tender and still very moist, about 5 minutes. Regulate the heat to avoid burning the noodles.

6. Transfer the skillet to the middle rack of the oven and bake the noodles until crusty on top and moist and tender within, about 8 minutes. Set them aside, loosely covered with foil to keep warm. Meanwhile, skewer the shrimp.

7. Increase the oven temperature to broil. Put the shrimp on a grill and season with a pinch of salt. Broil them close to the heat source for 2 minutes. Turn, brush lightly with a little of the garlic mayonnaise and broil for 1 to 2 minutes longer, until just opaque throughout.

8. Serve the noodles right from the skillet. Arrange the shrimp on a platter. Pass a bowl of garlic mayonnaise.

NOTES TO THE COOK You can find *fideus, fideos, or fidelini* at Latin American and Spanish grocers and supermarkets carrying Ronzoni or Goya products. Another excellent brand is La Rinascente.

Before crushing your saffron threads, do as the Catalans do: gently heat them in a skillet until brittle. The saffron will not only be easier to pulverize, it will also be more potent and, some say, less acrid.

This dish can also be made with Spanish or Italian rice, in which case it comes out with a consistency something like risotto, and is called *arròs a banda*.

Garlic Mayonnaise
(All-i-oli Negat)

4 garlic cloves, peeled and halved, green
  shoot removed

1 teaspoon salt

1 cup extra-virgin olive oil

2 egg yolks

Juice of 1 lemon

Ground white pepper

In a mortar crush the garlic into a fine purée, add 1 teaspoon salt and a few drops of olive oil to make a paste. Add the egg yolks and beat until thick and smooth. Add the oil drop by drop, beating constantly, as when making a mayonnaise. When firm, stir in the lemon juice and season with salt and pepper. Scrape into a small serving dish. Keep in a cool place.

TWO COUSCOUS RECIPES

Couscous with Spiced Vegetables and Chicken Tagine with Sweet Onions

SERVES 10 TO 12

I have been preparing couscous for almost thirty years. I can do it now with one hand, blindfolded, and still dazzle my friends. This is not by way of proclaiming my proficiency, but of explaining that couscous is not at all difficult to make—certainly a lot easier than making your own pasta.

Moroccan spices and herbs used in specific combinations can create mystery and excitement, but in the end the success of a Moroccan couscous dinner depends on the choice of couscous itself. Packages of parboiled couscous that promise ease of preparation will give you nothing special, nothing memorable. High-quality couscous, whether in packages or from bins in organic food stores or bought by mail order (see Appendix, page 340), should be prepared in the traditional way for a delicate, light, and fluffy result.

(Ever since I published my *Couscous and Other Good Food from Morocco,* I have been fighting the corruption of this dish by those who advocate use of the instant grain. Therefore, imagine my outrage when I saw recipes in a well-known food magazine for "Couscous Carbonara" and "Couscous Beef Chasseur." It was like reading about the mugging of a very old friend!)

A Moroccan dinner party is a cinch. Almost everything can be prepared in advance: The broth will be better because you'll be able to remove all the fat, and the chicken *tagine* (page 165) will have time to meld its flavors. All you need to do on the day of serving is wash and trim the vegetables, and steam the couscous several times so that it will swell properly. Just before serving, as you add each vegetable to the pot, the broth takes on new dimensions of flavor, and the vegetables become plump with the aromatic broth. Don't be tempted to cook vegetables to "crisp-tender." They should be fully cooked and swollen like the couscous itself.

Serve the couscous with its "lucky seven" vegetables, its spicy sauce, and a *tagine,* or stew, of chicken with glazed onion and raisins all together. Offer as a starter a plate of ripe olives, traditionally flavored with crushed garlic and coriander, cumin, and paprika.

Moroccan food is perfect for pleasing friends, and couscous is one of those dishes you just can't stop eating. When you are sure that your guests have reached *chaban* (absolute contentment), you'll feel a sense of abundance and peace. One caveat: couscous swells when cooked, and continues to swell if more liquid is added, so don't drink too much when you eat it. . . .

For dessert simply serve a traditional winter platter of sliced oranges, perhaps showered with French imported orange flower water, a dusting of confectioners' sugar, and ground cinnamon, and a cup of very sweet green or black tea infused with plenty of spearmint for easy digestion.

2 pounds (about 5 cups) "long-cooking" couscous (see introductory notes)

2 cups whole milk

2 teaspoons salt

½ teaspoon freshly ground pepper

1 small butternut squash or 1¼-pound chunk of fresh pumpkin

2½ quarts Meaty Broth for Couscous (see below)

1 pound thin carrots, pared, cut into 1¼-inch lengths

1½ pounds small purple-topped white turnips, scrubbed and quartered

6 fresh hot red or green peppers, stemmed and slit at the pointed end

6 small firm zucchini, trimmed and cut into 1¼-inch lengths

4 small yellow squash, trimmed and cut into 1¼-inch lengths

1 red bell pepper, cored, seeded, membranes removed, and cut into 1-inch pieces

⅓ cup tomato sauce

½ cup heavy cream

6 tablespoons butter, softened to room temperature

2 tablespoons each chopped coriander and flat-leaf parsley, stemmed

Chicken Tagine with Sweet Onions (see recipe, page 165)

Hot Sauce (see recipe, page 86)

1. *The morning of the day you plan to serve the dish:* Put the couscous in a strainer and rinse it under cold running water until the grains are thoroughly soaked. Spread out the couscous in a roasting pan or wide tub and let it dry for 10 minutes. Then rake the couscous with your fingers, lifting and sifting gently to break up any lumps.

2. In the bottom of a *couscoussier* or in a stockpot, bring plenty of salted water to a boil over high heat. Set the steamer top of the *couscoussier* or a colander over the boiling water. Check for a snug fit. (See notes below.) Add one-quarter of the couscous and steam it uncovered until hot and moist. Add the remaining couscous and steam it uncovered for 20 minutes. Dump all the couscous into the roasting pan; remove the *couscoussier* from the heat, but leave the water in.

3. Spread out the couscous, using a long-pronged fork. Toss and break up any lumps while you gradually sprinkle on 1 cup of the milk and the salt and pepper. Continue stirring and sifting the grains with your fingers to break up any lumps while you sprinkle on the remaining 1 cup of milk. Let the couscous stand, tossing it occasionally and raking to break up lumps, until it is no longer tacky to the touch, 1 to 2 hours.

4. Return the couscous to the *couscoussier* or colander and steam it uncovered for 20 minutes. Dump it back into the roasting pan and gradually rake in 2 cups of cold water. Smooth it evenly and let it dry again, tossing occasionally. *(The couscous can be made to this point up to 6 hours in advance. Cover it with a kitchen towel and set it aside at room temperature.)*

5. Scrub the butternut squash or chunk of pumpkin. Halve and scoop out the pulpy core and seeds. Cut it into 2- to 3-inch chunks without peeling. In a large pot of boiling

(continued)

salted water, cook the squash until tender, about 10 minutes. Drain and let it cool completely; then peel it and set aside. *(Up to this point the recipe can be prepared many hours in advance.)*

6. In a large saucepan bring the Meaty Broth to a boil over high heat. Add the carrots, turnips, and chili peppers, reduce the heat to moderate, and simmer for 15 minutes. Lower the heat, add the zucchini, yellow squash, and red bell pepper, and cook until all the vegetables are very tender, about 20 minutes longer.

7. Meanwhile, wet your hands and toss and sift through the couscous again to break up any lumps. Return it to the *couscoussier* and steam uncovered for 20 minutes. (There will be about 4 quarts of cooked couscous.)

8. Remove the chili peppers from the vegetables. Add the tomato sauce, cream, and butternut squash. Season with additional salt and pepper to taste.

9. Dump the hot couscous into the pan or tub and toss with the butter, breaking up any lumps. Toss with 2 cups of the sauce from the vegetables.

10. To serve, spread out half the couscous on a very large, shallow serving dish. Make a well in the center and in it pile all the vegetables. Surround with the remaining couscous, covering the vegetables to form a pyramid. Moisten with some of the sauce for the vegetables. Garnish with chopped herbs, and serve with the Chicken Tagine with Sweet Onions and the Hot Sauce. Pass the remaining sauce from the vegetables in a bowl.

NOTES TO THE COOK

To effectively seal the top and bottom parts of the *couscoussier* or kettle and colander, dampen a strip of cheesecloth, and twist it into a strip the length of the circumference of the rim of the bottom part of the *couscoussier*. Tuck the cheesecloth between top and bottom. Steam rises only through the holes. The perforated top should not touch the broth below.

If instant couscous is the only type available, moisten the couscous with the broth as directed on the package. Dump onto a large serving dish. Fluff it up with a fork, then spread out and form a well in the center. Place some of the vegetables in the center. Serve the remaining broth and vegetables in a large bowl.

Hot Sauce for Couscous   MAKES ABOUT 2 CUPS

In Morocco *harissa* is a relish made simply from chili peppers crushed with salt and olive oil and sometimes a little garlic. Tunisian *harissa* also contains caraway and cumin, which softens the flavor. Imported tins are available from France and Tunisia. *Sambal oelek*, an Indonesian condiment produced in Holland, is identical to Moroccan *harissa*. It is not expensive, and once it's opened, it can be kept in the refrigerator for a long time.

2 *teaspoons* harissa *or* sambal oelek

2 *cups of Meaty Broth for Couscous (see recipe, page 87)*

3 *garlic cloves, peeled, halved, green shoots discarded, crushed with salt*

3 *tablespoons chopped parsley leaves*

3 *tablespoons chopped fresh coriander leaves*

1¼ *teaspoons ground cumin*

Combine all ingredients in a small saucepan; bring them to a boil, stirring. Set the sauce aside and serve warm.

<table>
<tr><td>M A K E S A B O U T 3½ Q U A R T S</td><td>*Meaty Broth for Couscous*</td></tr>
</table>

You will need 2 cups of this broth for the Tagine of Chicken and 2 cups for the Hot Sauce. The remainder is used to make the preceding couscous. You will use the chicken for the *tagine* after cooking it in this flavorful broth.

3 *pounds meaty lamb neck or riblets, trimmed of excess fat*

1 *pound veal neck bones or riblets, trimmed of excess fat*

10 *to 12 large chicken thighs (3½ to 4 pounds)*

3 *tablespoons olive oil*

Coarse salt and finely ground pepper

1 *large hard-stick cinnamon or 3 pieces of soft-stick cinnamon (see Appendix, page 340)*

2 *cloves*

½ *teaspoon saffron threads, toasted and pulverized to make ⅛ teaspoon*

3 *medium onions, cut lengthwise into thin strips*

2 *medium-sized carrots, sliced*

2 *red-ripe tomatoes, quartered*

6 *sprigs each fresh green coriander and flat-leaf parsley*

1. Prepare the broth in a 9-quart flameproof casserole: Combine the lamb, veal, and chicken with the oil, 2 teaspoons of salt, 1 tablespoon of pepper, spices, saffron, onions, carrots, and tomatoes. Cook the mixture over high heat, stirring, for 1 minute. Cover, reduce the heat to moderately low, and cook for 15 minutes, swirling the casserole frequently. Add the coriander and parsley sprigs and water to cover (about 4 quarts). Bring the mixture to a boil, cover tightly, reduce the heat to low, and simmer for 1 hour.

2. Remove the chicken thighs when cooked, about 45 minutes, and set them aside for the *Tagine* of Chicken with Sweet Onions on page 165. Cover the casserole and continue cooking the broth until the meat is almost falling off the bones, about 1 hour longer. When

(continued)

the broth is ready, strain it. Remove and discard all bones and vegetables. Reserve the meat for some other purpose. (*This recipe can be prepared a day in advance.* Let it cool, then cover it and refrigerate. Skim off any fat before reheating.)

Sicilian Fish Couscous

SERVES 6 TO 8

It was on the ramparts of Erice, a hill town in northwest Sicily, with Norman buildings, steep inclines, and gray cobbled medieval streets, that I first encountered the scent of Sicilian fish couscous —the scent, actually, of a perfectly balanced fish soup spiced with cinnamon, saffron and black pepper. And I detected this aroma later along the coast of the entire western half of Sicily: in the old walled quarter of Marsala, on the parklike waterfront of Mazara del Vallo, and along the southern coast as far east as Agrigento. But the place I smelled it most frequently, the place in Sicily where couscous is king, was the flat white city of Trapani, where, at the harborside, every restaurant serves its own particular version.

The easy explanation for the presence of couscous in Sicily is that it was brought by the Arabs during their conquest. If this were so, one would find it throughout the island. Since it is eaten only on the western coast, however, I believe it comes directly from Tunisia, which you can see from the heights of Erice.

There are numerous versions of this dish in Sicily, made with various combinations of fishes, cooked together in a sort of *bouillabaisse*-type stew, and enriched with ground toasted almonds. The couscous grains over which the fish and sauce are served are made as in North Africa—semolina flour and droplets of water are rolled into pellets, then steamed. But the method of steaming is quite distinctive, resulting in an entirely different texture. In Sicily the grain is covered and steamed for a long time, then plumped with a flavorful sauce; it is served moist and tender rather than dry and fluffy.

The following recipe was given to me by Vita Coppola Poma, a native of Trapani who now lives in the United States. (In her home the fish is usually served *after* the couscous, accompanied by a green salad.) Although Sicilian couscous is delicious, it sometimes looks disappointing—various fish lying on top of a platter of heavily moistened grain. You can improve the presentation by decorating the grain with steamed mussels and/or by frying the tentacles of small squid in hot oil, then using them to garnish the platter. Unlike Mrs. Poma I do not serve the fish as a separate course but on a side platter accompanying the grain, lavishly sprinkled with Italian parsley.

Both Mrs. Poma and I shun the packages of instant couscous available on supermarket shelves, not only because of the inferior taste and texture of these brands but also because of the size of the grains. She rolls her tiny pellets, half the size of commercial varieties, a true labor of love. I buy imported long-cooking couscous from large sacks in health-food stores (see Appendix, page 340, for mail-order source). Since the finer the grain the finer the Trapanese couscous, you may want to run these imported grains through a clean coffee mill before you use them.

5 to 6 pounds mixed lean white saltwater fish, as varied as possible: red snapper, rockfish, mullet, halibut, porgy, whiting, scrod, salt cod (previously soaked), croaker, yellowtail, sea bass, monkfish, or tilefish—all fish boned and cut into large chunks, rounds and steaks, fish heads, trimmings, and bones reserved (see notes)

Salt and freshly ground black pepper

½ cup extra-virgin olive oil

2 pounds small squid (see Appendix, page 349 for cleaning)

1 cup fine chopped onion

¼ teaspoon ground cinnamon

1 bay leaf

1 small carrot, sliced

¼ teaspoon cayenne pepper, or more to taste

4 cups drained canned plum tomatoes, strained through a colander, seeds discarded

¾ cup (2 handfuls) flat-leaf parsley, stemmed, not chopped

6 garlic cloves, halved, peeled, with green shoots removed

COUSCOUS

1 pound (about 2½ cups) "long-cooking" couscous (see Appendix, page 340, for mail-order source)

¼ cup extra-virgin olive oil

1½ teaspoons salt

1 teaspoon finely ground black pepper

1 teaspoon ground cinnamon

1 small red onion, chopped

2 small bay leaves

½ cup (3 ounces) toasted blanched almonds, ground fine

OPTIONAL GARNISH

6 to 12 mussels, scrubbed and debearded

Pure olive oil for frying

3 tablespoons roughly chopped flat-leaf parsley

Olive oil for frying

1. Sprinkle the cleaned fish with salt and pepper. Brush it with 1 to 2 tablespoons olive oil and keep it refrigerated. Prepare the squid as directed in the notes below.

2. Heat 6 tablespoons of olive oil in a heavy, flameproof 4-quart casserole, add the onions, and cook them over low heat until soft but not browned, about 5 minutes. Add the fish heads, trimmings, bones, cinnamon, bay leaf, sliced carrot, 1 tablespoon of salt, 2 teaspoons of black pepper, and cayenne, and sauté over medium heat for 5 minutes. Add the tomatoes and simmer, uncovered, for 15 minutes.

3. Press the contents of the casserole through the large blade of a foodmill pressing on the vegetables and fish bones to extract all their juices. Press the liquid through a finer blade. You should have about 3 cups. Reserve the liquid for cooking the fish.

4. In the workbowl of a food processor blend the parsley with the garlic and 1 cup of

(continued)

the fish sauce until smooth. Stir the mixture into the reserved sauce. *(Up to this point the dish can be prepared in advance.)*

5. About 2 hours before serving, bring plenty of water to a boil in a deep kettle or *couscoussier.* Meanwhile, place the couscous in a wide bowl and gradually stir in ¾ cup of tepid water, and ¼ cup of oil, the salt, pepper, cinnamon, chopped onion, and bay leaves; mix well to break up any lumps. When the water is boiling rapidly fasten on the steamer top and fill it with the couscous; cover with a clean kitchen cloth (a terrycloth towel, folded in two, will absorb the excess moisture). Place the lid of the pot over the towel to keep the steam from escaping. Steam the couscous for 1½ hours without disturbing it. *If necessary, add more boiling water to the kettle or* couscoussier. Check by lifting the entire steamer top. (Steam keeps the couscous from falling through the holes. Be sure that the bay leaves do not hinder the free flow of steam.)

6. After 1 hour of steaming, return the parsley-enriched fish sauce to the large casserole, add 1 quart of hot water, and bring it to a simmer. Add the squid rings and tentacles (if not using them for a garnish) and cook, partially covered, at a simmer for 35 minutes; then add the fish pieces and poach them very gently for 7 minutes (10 minutes if the fish pieces are thick). Using a slotted spoon, remove the fish to a warm platter; bone them if desired. Cover and keep warm.

7. Stir the ground toasted almonds into the fish sauce. Adjust the seasoning with salt and plenty of black pepper.

8. Dump the couscous into a heated wide serving dish. Use a long fork to break up lumps; discard the bay leaves. Gradually stir the fish sauce into the couscous, adding enough to cover the grains as they begin to swell, about 7 cups. Reserve any extra liquid to keep the fish moist. Cover the couscous with foil and a kitchen towel and set it in a warm place, for 20 minutes, or until it has absorbed all the liquid. Sicilian couscous should not be soupy, but very moist.

9. Optional garnish: Steam the mussels, remove the top shells, and slip the mussels into the couscous. Dry the tentacles and quickly fry them in ½ inch hot olive oil, 1 minute to a side (if the tentacles are large, reduce the heat slightly and cook 1 minute longer). Serve the couscous in wide soup plates. Sprinkle the 3 tablespoons fresh parsley over the fish and pass it separately.

NOTES TO THE COOK This recipe works best with Atlantic fish. If using fish from the southern California coast, choose a mixture of rock cod, ling cod, halibut, and, if available, the Mexican *totava*. To perk up the flavor, season them highly with salt and pepper, parsley, pinches of cinnamon, and red pepper before cooking. The fish can be boned, but avoid very thin fillets, which would break up in the cooking. Be sure to keep heads, tails, and trimmings for the sauce.

To effectively seal top and bottom parts of the *couscoussier,* see page 86.

CHAPTER 4 *SOUPS*

Catalan Mussel Soup

SERVES 4

Catalan food is more highly seasoned than the food in other regions of Spain, as demonstrated by this particularly rich and very satisfying soup from the coast just north of Barcelona.

The Catalans like to thicken their soups and sauces with a *picada*, a smooth paste usually made of pounded nuts, garlic, and flavorings such as spices, herbs, and wines, which gives a deeper and lustier taste than butter, cream, or flour. *Picada* has one drawback: It tends to endow food with an unappealing putty hue. To counteract this minor problem, I garnish the soup with an extra amount of freshly cooked mussels.

This soup can be prepared 1 to 2 days in advance, but the garnish should not be cooked more than 1 hour before serving.

3½ pounds (2 quarts) small fresh mussels, cleaned

1 bay leaf

1 small celery rib with leaves

Salt and freshly ground pepper

Lemon juice

4 tablespoons olive oil

1 slice of stale Italian or French bread, 3 inches in diameter, cut ½ inch thick, crust removed

¾ cup fine-chopped onion

4 large ripe tomatoes, cored, quartered and seeded, or 2 cups drained canned plum tomatoes, seeds discarded

12 toasted skinned almonds, coarse chopped

1 tablespoon roughly chopped garlic

1 inch soft-stick cinnamon, or ⅛ teaspoon ground cinnamon

Pinch of sugar

2 tablespoons roughly chopped flat-leaf parsley, stemmed

⅛ teaspoon mixed cayenne pepper and paprika

1½ tablespoons fine brandy, such as Carlos I or Cognac

GARNISH

1 pound mussels (optional)

2 tablespoons chopped flat-leaf parsley

Steps 1 through 5 can be prepared up to 1 day in advance.

1. In a wide skillet, steam open the mussels with 1 cup of water, the bay leaf, and celery, about 2 minutes. Drain the mussels, reserving the broth; discard any that do not open. Remove the mussels from the shells and season with salt, pepper, and a few drops of

lemon juice; set them aside. Strain the broth through a double layer of dampened cheese-cloth, and set aside.

2. In a large, heavy skillet or an earthenware *cazuela*, heat the olive oil over moderately high heat. Add the bread and fry it, turning once, until golden brown on both sides, about 2 minutes. Drain it on paper towels. Remove the pan from the heat.

3. Add the onion and 2 tablespoons of water to the skillet. Cook the onions over moderately low heat until softened but not browned. (Adding water at this point allows the onions to cook slowly without burning.) Add the tomatoes to the skillet and cook 15 minutes longer, stirring occasionally.

4. Meanwhile, in a blender, food processor, or mortar grind, process, or pound the almonds to a paste. Add the fried bread, garlic, cinnamon, sugar, parsley, cayenne, and paprika. Add ⅓ cup of the mussel broth and purée the mixture until smooth. Add it to the tomatoes and continue to cook for 5 minutes. Do not wash the workbowl. Process the mussels in the food processor with enough broth to make a smooth purée; stir it into the tomato mixture, and cook over low heat for 5 minutes longer to blend the flavors.

5. Push the soup through the fine blade of a foodmill; add enough mussel broth and water to make 5 cups. Adjust the seasoning with salt, pepper, cayenne, paprika, and cinnamon to taste. (*The recipe can be prepared to this point up to 1 day in advance.* Cool, cover and refrigerate.)

6. Just before serving, reheat the soup, add the brandy, and bring it to a boil; simmer for 5 minutes. Steam open the mussels for garnish, if using. Place an equal number of mussels in each individual warmed soup plate. Pour the hot soup over, sprinkle with parsley, and serve at once.

To clean mussels: Scrub each mussel under cool running water. Pull off the beard (byssus threads) that protrudes from the shells and scrape off the barnacles. Soak the mussels in a bowl of fresh cold water for 30 minutes. (Cultivated mussels raised on farms such as Great Eastern in Maine do not need soaking—if soaked they lose their flavor.) If you wish to store them after cleaning and soaking, drain them and keep refrigerated.

NOTES TO THE COOK

To cook: Rinse, steam open, remove shells, cut away any remaining beards, and use as directed above. If the mussels to be used for garnish are unusually large, remove and discard the brown-black "rubber" band around each of them.

Fresh toasted almonds give a wonderful flavor and aroma to this soup. Crack the shells, spread the unskinned almonds on a baking sheet, and slowly toast them in a preheated 275° oven for 30 minutes or until lightly browned. Remove the skins by rubbing the almonds between your fingertips.

If you are using blanched and peeled almonds, spread them on a baking sheet to toast for 10 to 15 minutes in a preheated 325° oven. After toasting they can be pounded, and stored in an airtight container for a month.

Sole Soup with Chives

SERVES 6 TO 8

"The better the wine, the better the soup," says my friend Aude Clement, who first prepared this recipe for me. She means it—she will happily choose a very fine Burgundy for the soup. Because I am less extravagant, I generally use a Mâcon Lugny.

Fresh true sole (Dover sole) is difficult to find since it must be imported from France or England. What is sold in the United States as "fillet of sole" is usually grey sole, lemon sole, or sometimes just flounder or fluke—any of which will work very well in this delicious soup.

Ask your fishmonger to save the heads and frames from 3 of any one of these fish. You will also need 2 large fillets of sole for the garnish. When sliced thin on a diagonal and whisked in at the last minute, the strips of sole will be transformed into little corkscrew shapes, which will help to thicken this very light and elegant soup. Continue the meal with a crusty Roast Leg of Lamb with Tarragon, Anchovies, and Cornichons, a gratin of potatoes, and a good red Bordeaux wine.

3 *flatfish heads and frames (sole, flounder, fluke)*

2 *bottles dry white Burgundy*

¾ *cup sliced carrots*

1 *medium onion, sliced*

Zest of ½ lemon

Herb bouquet: 2 bay leaves, 6 parsley springs, 5 thyme sprigs

1 *teaspoon black peppercorns*

1 *teaspoon coriander seeds*

1 *pound fresh fillets of flatfish, skinned*

Salt and freshly ground white pepper to taste

10 *ounces commercial crème fraîche, or 1 pint homemade crème fraîche, reduced to 1⅓ cups by draining (see note)*

¼ *cup snipped fresh chives*

1. Make the stock: Crack the fish frames into small pieces. Thoroughly wash the bones and the heads; discard the blood and gills. Place the bones in a heavy nonaluminum 4-quart saucepan with the wine and 2 cups of water, and bring just to a boil. Skim carefully, then add the carrots, onion, lemon zest, herb bouquet, and spices. Simmer, partially covered, for 30 minutes. Strain the stock through a cheesecloth-lined sieve. Squeeze the cheesecloth to extract all the fish juices; discard the remaining solids. Return the stock to the rinsed saucepan. Reduce to 5 cups.

2. Meanwhile, slice each fillet on an exaggerated diagonal, ¼ inch thick and as long as possible (cooking will cause each strip to form a "corkscrew"). Season with salt and pepper and keep refrigerated. (*Up to this point the soup can be prepared hours in advance. Cool the stock, cover, and refrigerate.*)

3. Just before serving, place the stock in a wide nonaluminum saucepan and bring it

to a vigorous boil; add the fish strips and whisk over high heat for 30 seconds. Scoop out the fish and place it in a heated soup terrine. Add the cream to the saucepan; bring the soup back to a boil, whisking constantly. Adjust the seasoning and pour over the fish. Sprinkle the soup with chives and serve at once.

To make a double-thick crème fraîche, simply drain homemade crème fraîche in a drip coffee funnel lined with a paper filter and set over a jar for about 3 hours. The whey separates through to the jar below, leaving the thickened crème fraîche in the filter.

NOTE TO
THE COOK

SERVES 4

Alsatian Watercress and Frogs'-Leg Soup

Daniel Fuchs is an Alsatian-born chef (he was personal cook to Charles de Gaulle at one point) who has lived and worked in the U.S. for more than twenty-five years. "The longer I'm away from Strasbourg," he told me, "the more I cherish my childhood food. Coq au Riesling, choucroute, Backeoffe, the luxurious freshwater fish stew, Matelote à la Strasbourgeoise, made with Riesling . . ."

There are so many things he misses: his mother's homemade noodles; the hot fritters filled with jelly that are served in Strasbourg during Lent; and perhaps most of all, nights spent catching frogs so his mother could make watercress and frogs'-leg soup.

This is an elegant soup with very little last-minute work. The soup base and the garnish are prepared ahead of time, and the egg yolk–cream liaison is added just before serving. The wine used in the cooking is the key: use an Alsatian Riesling, which has a fruity (sometimes even steely), crisp, full-bodied, deep, and complex flavor.

2 pounds fresh or frozen frogs' legs, 12 to 24 depending on size (see notes for keeping them fresh)

2 tablespoons chopped shallots

4 tablespoons unsalted butter, cut into small cubes

½ cup Alsatian Riesling (or more if needed)

4 cups well-reduced fish stock, very lightly seasoned with salt

Salt, freshly ground black pepper, and grated nutmeg to taste

2 tablespoons arrowroot

⅓ cup milk

1 large bunch watercress, or 2 small bunches, washed, shaken dry, and stemmed

3 egg yolks

½ cup crème fraîche or heavy cream

1. Drain, rinse and dry frogs' legs. In a 4-quart (nonaluminum) flameproof casserole gently sauté the shallots in half the butter. Add the frogs' legs and cook, without browning

(continued)

FISH SOUPS   95

them, for 2 minutes, stirring. Boil off any moisture expressed from the frogs' legs.

2. Deglaze with wine, add fish stock, and bring it to a boil. Add ½ teaspoon salt, ¼ teaspoon pepper, and a light sprinkling of nutmeg. Simmer, uncovered, 5 minutes, or until the frogs' legs are tender. Remove them with a slotted spoon; cool and bone them and cut the flesh into ½-inch dice. (To bone frogs' legs: slit each thigh and leg along both sides and pull out the bones.) Add the bones to the stock. Lightly season the frogs' legs with salt and pepper; set them aside. Simmer the stock and bones slowly for 15 minutes. If the stock is too thin, thicken it with arrowroot. (Blend the arrowroot with the milk, stirring until smooth; stir it into the stock.)

3. Meanwhile, blanch the watercress in boiling water for 1 minute and drain. Rinse it for an instant under cold water to stop the cooking; drain and chop it coarse. Loosen the watercress with a fork, then toss it with the reserved frogs' legs and small cubes of the remaining butter; reserve.

4. Strain the soup and return it to the rinsed-out casserole. If it is too thick, thin with a little more white wine. *(The soup can be prepared 2 to 3 hours in advance to this point.)* Set it in a cool place, partially covered.

5. About 15 minutes before serving, whisk the egg yolks and cream in a small metal bowl or a double boiler. Set the mixture over simmering water, whisking constantly until almost doubled in volume. Immediately pour into another bowl to stop the cooking, cover, and keep in a warm place.

6. Slowly reheat the soup without boiling, then gradually whisk in the egg yolk-cream mixture. Stir the soup over low heat for an instant, then add the reserved mixture of frogs' legs, watercress, and cubes of butter. Adjust the seasoning. Remove it from the heat. Ladle the soup into warmed soup bowls and serve at once.

NOTES TO
THE COOK

Order medium-small frogs' legs. They are available fresh in selected fish stores in the spring, and are available frozen year round. Legs are sold skinned, cleaned, and in pairs, usually skewered. For added flavor, rub them with fresh herbs (such as chives or tarragon) and a pinch of nutmeg and soak in milk for 1 hour before using.

In Chinese markets you can buy whole frogs. Have them skinned and cleaned, and use the chest for flavoring the stock.

To make a really strong fish stock, combine in a large pot: 5 quarts of water; 1 cup dry white wine; 5 pounds of fish heads and trimmings; 2 cut-up carrots; 1 cut up rib of celery; 1 leek, well cleaned and halved; 1 tablespoon crushed peppercorns; 1 onion, halved; 2 cloves garlic, halved; a bay leaf, 2 or 3 sprigs of parsley, and 2 sprigs of thyme. Simmer the mixture briskly, skimming, for 25 minutes. Strain the stock, then reduce it by quick boiling until you have 1 quart. Season after reducing.

A MACEDONIAN SOUP

(Fasolada)

SERVES 6

*M*acedonian White
Bean Soup

Here is a recipe for a wonderful, richly flavored bean soup from the mountains of central Greece. Unlike most *fasoladas,* which are made with tomatoes, this one is creamy-white and garnished with rings of roasted yellow peppers, squares of mildly pickled roasted red peppers, and slivers of the juicy and unique Greek Amphissa olives. (These purple-black olives are large, soft, and round, with a sweet olive oil flavor. They are excellent in stews, and, slivered, enhance many dishes in texture, flavor, and aroma.)

1 *pound dried Great Northern or navy or white kidney beans*

2 *red bell peppers, roasted, peeled, stemmed, seeded, membranes removed, and cut into ¼-inch cubes*

3 *yellow bell peppers, roasted, peeled, stemmed, seeded, membranes removed, and cut into ¼-inch thick rings*

2 *tablespoons red wine vinegar*

6 *tablespoons extra-virgin olive oil*
  Salt and freshly ground pepper

2 *medium carrots, scraped and sliced thin*

½ *cup diced celery with leaves*

1 *large onion, diced*

18 *pitted Greek black olives, preferably Amphissa, slivered*

1. Pick over the beans and soak them in water to cover in the refrigerator overnight.

2. In a small bowl combine the peppers, vinegar, and 1 tablespoon of olive oil. Add salt and pepper and toss to mix. Cover the peppers and refrigerate overnight.

3. The following day, drain the beans and put them in a deep pan; cover with cold water and slowly bring them to a boil. Meanwhile, bring 2 quarts of water to a simmer in a large heavy flameproof pot, preferably made of earthenware, as a bean pot. Boil the beans for 5 minutes and drain them in a colander. Immediately slip them into the simmering water in the bean pot. In a skillet gently sauté the carrots, celery, and onions in the remaining olive oil, stirring, for 1 to 2 minutes. Add them to the beans. Bring the mixture to a boil, reduce the heat to medium-low, and simmer for 1½ hours or until the beans are tender and the liquid reduced. If necessary, spoon off some of the liquid and reduce it by boiling in a small saucepan. Return it to the pot. (*The soup can be prepared 1 day ahead up to this point. Let it cool, then refrigerate.*)

4. Gently reheat the soup to simmering. Stir in the drained peppers, and the olives, and adjust the seasoning with salt and pepper.

(Aïgo Boullido)

Broth with Trout Fillets and Fresh Vegetables

SERVES 2 OR 3

A traditional Auvergnat recipe consisting of water, garlic, sage, olive oil, and a few slices of grilled bread is here turned into an enchanting and flavorful fish and vegetable soup. Unlike many soup recipes, it is based on water rather than stock. (Students of French provincial gastronomy will know that *aïgo boullido* means "boiled water" in Provençal. The expression is used in the Auvergne as well.) Michel Bras, who updated the recipe and taught it to me, suggested using the nongaseous bottled mineral water Volvic, which comes from his part of the Auvergne. With its natural minerals, Volvic will not only enhance the flavors of the dish but will also heighten the color of the vegetables.

2 *scallions, roots trimmed, halved lengthwise, and all but 3 inches of green shoots removed, washed and drained*

2 *Brussels sprouts, trimmed, halved, cored, and washed*

1 *medium carrot, scraped and sliced crosswise, at a slight diagonal, about ⅛ inch thick*

4 *to 6 asparagus stalks, woody bottoms trimmed, spears peeled and cut into 2-inch lengths*

2 *Bibb lettuces, split*

2 *stalks Swiss chard with leaves, root ends trimmed, stalks and leaves separated*

6 *cups water, preferably a mineral water such as Volvic or Evian*

Coarse sea salt

¼ *cup unsalted butter*

2 *garlic cloves, peeled*

1 *clove*

1 *bay leaf tied with 2 small stalks celery with leaves and 3 sprigs flat-leaf parsley*

2 *shallots, peeled and cut into ⅛-inch-thick slices*

2 *or 3 fish fillets, skinned (4 to 5 ounces each) trout, Arctic char, porgy, whiting, or small pieces of salmon trout*

Freshly ground white pepper

1½ *tablespoons French walnut oil*

1. Preheat the oven to 250° F. In a saucepan, cook the scallions, Brussels sprouts, carrot, asparagus, lettuce, and Swiss-chard stalks in 6 cups of salted mineral water until the vegetables are tender, about 8 minutes. Scoop out the vegetables, using a slotted spoon;

refresh them under cold water, drain, and place them in an 8- to 10-cup wide baking-serving dish. Add the Swiss chard leaves to the cooking liquid and boil until they are tender, about 1 minute. Remove the leaves and refresh them under cold running water. Drain them well and add to the vegetables. Place the dish in the oven to keep it warm.

2. Meanwhile, pour off all but 1¼ cups of the vegetable water (or reserve it for some other purpose). Add the butter, garlic, clove, herb bouquet, and shallots. Cover and cook the mixture over medium-low heat for 10 minutes.

3. Nestle the fish fillets in a single layer among the vegetables in the baking dish. Pour the contents of the saucepan over them and return the baking dish to the oven to cook the fish, about 10 minutes. (Note that the texture of the fish will be very smooth, owing to the low-temperature cooking.) Remove the herb bouquet and clove. Adjust the seasoning with sea salt and freshly ground white pepper. Drizzle the fish with walnut oil and serve at once.

The technique of cooking fish fillets at low temperature works best with trout, Arctic char, sea bass, salmon, and salmon trout. NOTE TO THE COOK

Creamy Chestnut Soup

SERVES 6 TO 8

Most of the chestnut soups I've tasted—even in the Auvergne, where they are an autumnal evening staple—have been filling and nutritious, but also somewhat bland. Not so this version, which I have loosely adapted from a recipe of Jean-Louis Palladin.

Jean-Louis uses as a base a rich poultry stock added to a consommé made with a great assortment of vegetables, and he garnishes the soup with quenelles of venison, crispy cubes of wild mushrooms, bits of prosciutto, fragments of chestnuts, and cubes of sweetbreads. It is, needless to say, divine! However, lacking a full kitchen staff to do all that work, I have opted to eliminate the consommé, sweetbreads, and quenelles, and instead a small amount of cream is swirled in at the end, just enough to enhance the flavor.

Chestnuts always benefit from being cooked with fennel, celery tops, and prosciutto. I prefer a chestnut soup that is very smooth and have found that pressing chestnuts through the fine blade of a foodmill or processing them in the food processor is not sufficient; the purée must be further pressed through a very fine sieve to remove every bit of fiber.

(continued)

2½ *tablespoons butter*

1 *medium onion, sliced thin*

1 *cup thin-sliced shallots*

5 *ounces prosciutto, slivered*

3¾ *pounds (6 cups) chestnuts, peeled (see note)*

Coarse salt

½ *cup sliced green celery tops*

1 *teaspoon fennel seed*

1 *bay leaf*

10 *cups rich, unsalted chicken stock, heated*

½ *cup heavy cream*

Freshly ground white pepper

¼ *cup dried cèpes, reconstituted, simmered in water to cover until tender, drained and diced*

3 *tablespoons chopped parsley*

1. In a soup kettle heat 2 tablespoons of the butter and cook the onions, shallots, and 4 ounces of the prosciutto until they are soft, about 5 minutes. Add the peeled chestnuts, ½ teaspoon of salt, the sliced celery tops, fennel seed, and bay leaf. Add 6 cups of the hot chicken stock. Bring the mixture to a boil and skim it carefully. Reduce the heat, cover, and cook slowly for about 1½ hours, or until the chestnuts are very tender but not disintegrating into the stock. Midway in the cooking, remove and reserve 16 to 18 chestnuts for the garnish.

2. Discard the bay leaf. Cool the mixture slightly, and press batches through the fine blade of a foodmill or process to a purée in the workbowl of a food processor. Then press the purée through a *tamis* or a fine wire sieve. Makes about 2 quarts of puree. (*The recipe can be prepared up to this point in advance.* Cover the purée and refrigerate or freeze it. Let it return to room temperature before continuing.)

3. Return the purée to the saucepan and heat slowly.

4. Just before serving, stir in enough hot chicken stock to reach the desired consistency. Bring it to a boil, stirring. Add the cream and adjust the seasoning with salt and pepper. Keep the soup hot while preparing the garnish. Chop the reserved chestnuts. In a nonstick skillet, gently sauté in ½ tablespoon butter the slivered prosciutto, cèpes, and chestnuts until crispy. Mix them with the parsley. Place equal amounts of garnish in individual hot soup plates. Pour over the boiling soup and serve at once.

NOTES TO
THE COOK

Lean bacon can be substituted for the prosciutto if it is blanched in simmering water for 3 minutes, rinsed, and drained.

To peel chestnuts, see page 26.

Fresh chestnuts can be frozen up to 3 months. Cooked chestnuts can be peeled, refrigerated, covered, and kept for 1 day.

Three 16-ounce jars of vacuum-packed whole unsweetened chestnuts (preferably the Minerva brand) can substitute. (See Appendix, page 340, for mail-order sources.)

Dried chestnuts are preserved in Italy during the autumn for use all winter long. An overnight soaking in water is needed before cooking them, but you will discover they are much better than the canned ones in texture as well as taste. One cup reconstituted dried chestnuts equals 1 cup fresh. (See Appendix, page 340, for mail-order source.)

SERVES 4 TO 6

Pumpkin Soup with Swiss-Chard Croûtes

This Auvergnat fall soup is served with hot crusts of toasted French bread mounded with pumpkin and Swiss-chard "debris" from the soup pot, and then gratinéed with cheese. To enhance the flavor of the pumpkin I cut it into cubes, then bake the cubes so that they cook in their own moisture and retain their natural sweetness. When simmered with the Swiss chard, the pumpkin cubes absorb its flavor too—pumpkin will, in fact, absorb the flavoring of almost anything cooked with it.

2 *pounds pumpkin or butternut squash*

4 *tablespoons butter*

2 *teaspoons sugar*

1 *medium onion, sliced thin*

2 *tablespoons sliced shallots*

1 *garlic clove, halved, green shoot removed, peeled and sliced*

3 *tablespoons (1 ounce) slivered prosciutto*

Salt and freshly ground pepper

Freshly grated nutmeg

Herb bouquet: parsley, thyme, and celery leaves

3 *large Swiss-chard leaves, washed, rolled, and shredded into ribbons (½ packed cup)*

¾ *cup milk*

½ *cup heavy cream*

12 *thin-sliced firm bread rounds, lightly toasted in the oven*

¼ *cup freshly grated cheese: Cantal, Gruyère, Cheddar, or Monterey Jack*

Garnish: 1 large Swiss-chard leaf, blanched 3 minutes, refreshed, and cut into ribbons crosswise

1. Preheat the oven to 425° F. Pare the pumpkin, halve, and discard the seeds and fibrous centers. Cut enough flesh into 1-inch cubes to make 1 quart. Shred a chunk of pumpkin on the coarsest side of a four-sided grater and set 2 tablespoons aside for a garnish. Spread the pumpkin cubes in a buttered baking pan, sprinkle with sugar, dot with 1 tablespoon of the butter, and bake 30 minutes, turning the cubes twice to develop a caramelized crust.

(continued)

2. Heat 1½ tablespoons of the butter in a heavy 3-quart saucepan over medium-low heat. Add the onions, shallots, garlic, and prosciutto, and cook about 10 minutes, stirring occasionally, until they are soft but not brown. Set the pan aside.

3. When the pumpkin has baked 30 minutes add it to the saucepan along with the caramelized juices, 1 scant teaspoon of salt, ¼ teaspoon of pepper, ⅛ teaspoon of nutmeg, and the herb bouquet. Return the pan to medium heat, stirring, for 1 minute. Add the Swiss chard and 1 quart of water. Bring the mixture to a boil and cook at a simmer for 20 minutes. Remove the pan from the heat, discard the herb bouquet, and allow the mixture to cool slightly. Transfer it in batches to a foodmill fitted with a fine blade, and press gently so that some of the "debris" is left in the mill (about ½ cup). Season the "debris" with pepper and nutmeg. Add the remaining butter and mash with a fork until well combined. (*The soup base, "debris" spread, and Swiss-chard ribbon garnish can be prepared to this point early in the day.* Cool, cover, and refrigerate.)

4. Just before serving, reheat the soup base to a simmer, stirring often. Thin with the milk and cream. Adjust the seasoning.

5. While the soup is simmering, mound about 2 teaspoons "debris" spread onto each bread round, sprinkle with cheese, and run under the broiler until the cheese is melted. Float the rounds, grated pumpkin garnish, and Swiss-chard ribbon garnish in the soup and serve at once.

CHAPTER 5 *FISH*

All fish cookbooks offer the same instructions: when you buy fish check that the eyes are clear and full, that there is no fishy odor, that the skin is taut, and that the gills are red. This would be excellent advice in an honest world. Unfortunately, today there are ways for a fish seller to shine up the eyes, eliminate the odor, firm up the skin, and rouge the gills. The one additional piece of advice the cookbooks give that will prove to be the most useful is *Find yourself a good and honorable fishmonger.*

Here is what H. F. Bruning, Jr., and C. Umberto Bullo have to say on the subject in *Venetian Cooking:*

> . . . rather than tell you how to select fish, we suggest that you select your fishmonger instead. Choose one who is fairly old—the fish business is not learned in a year or two—but not so old that he has lost the interest and desire necessary to do the job well. He should be willing to answer questions. If you want to learn about fish you must ask questions. Last, he should not be too happy. We have never met a really first-class happy fishmonger.

My own fishmonger, whom I shall here call Mr. X, has just been perfectly described. He is not a happy man; in fact, he is downright disagreeable, but he never fails to point me to his choice fish of the day. I have altered my plans for entire dinner parties right there on the sawdust floor of his shop as he has led me away from a good but not particularly tasty swordfish to an exceptional sea bass with a cobalt-colored head, shining gills, and a rainbow hue on its skin. When Mr. X says, "Grab it!" I do.

I personally prefer to buy most fish on the bone with gills intact, not only because I want the heads for stock, but also because I feel more comfortable knowing that the fish are *probably* fresher than those already filleted. Of course, I touch, smell, and examine any fish that I buy.

The best way to cook fish is usually the easiest. I see no need to adorn a good fish, unless the adornment adds depth and dimension. In summer I often grill a fish, then serve it with just the simplest addition, as in Swordfish Steaks with Anchovies and Wild Mushrooms (page 118). I have not included many grilled-fish recipes here; the techniques are well-known or fully explained elsewhere. I *have* included recipes that are, for me at least, exceptional: either because they are unusual or especially delicious, or because the approach involved will impart a certain "polish." I have a special interest in cooking fish in the oven because it is so easy: roasting at high temperature, baking and oven-poaching at medium temperature, and oven-steaming (with a pan of boiling water below) at a very low temperature. This last is a new method, taught to me by Michel Bras, that results in extraordinary succulence and texture.

I have stopped following the popular rule of "ten minutes' cooking time to the inch"—it doesn't always work. And the old rule about cooking fish until it flakes isn't valid either. Most white-fleshed fish should cook until opaque, milk-white, and fully cooked at the bone. On the other hand, monkfish is better slightly overdone, and very soft fish, such as flounder and whiting, which actually flake before they're done, should be tested at the thickest part before being removed from the fire.

WHITE-FLESHED FISH RECIPES

Porgy Baked on a Flat Plate with Herbs and Green Peppercorns

SERVES 4

Small, round fish such as porgies are usually baked in their skins, cooked *en papillote*, or else skinned, coated with a thick batter, and fried, to seal in their juices—all this lest they fall apart. Here is a recipe for small, even fillets of porgy, rockfish, ocean perch, or mullet that makes good use of the loose, firm flesh of these fish as well as their ability to stand up to strong flavors. The fillets are thickly coated with chopped fresh herbs plus a few crushed green peppercorns for piquancy, then baked on separate ovenproof plates. The coarse, flaky texture of these particular fish enables them to cook very quickly—much more quickly than the 10-minutes-per-inch rule suggested in most books.

In a good housewares department you can find attractive ovenproof porcelain plates that will work for this recipe, and even supermarkets are now stocking them. To protect your dining table, be sure to use another plate lined with a folded napkin as an underliner. Never place a hot plate on a cold or wet surface.

2 *small fillets of fish, skinned, each fillet weighing about 4 ounces*

Sea salt and freshly ground pepper

1 *tablespoon fruity extra-virgin olive oil*

1 *tablespoon green peppercorns, drained*

3 *tablespoons snipped chives*

1 *tablespoon minced fresh thyme leaves, or 1 teaspoon dried thyme*

½ *cup chopped fresh flat-leaf parsley*

1. Rinse the fish fillets, dry them, and season with salt and pepper. Brush each fillet with oil. Crush the green peppercorns and mix with the herbs. Spread an even layer of herbs over each fish fillet. Lightly brush heatproof plates with oil and place them on a baking sheet.

2. Twenty minutes before serving, heat the oven to 400° F. Place the filled heatproof plates on the baking sheet on the center rack. Bake the fish until just cooked, 3 to 5 minutes. Serve at once on folded-napkin-lined dishes.

SERVES 2	# Fillet of Flounder with Mixed Nuts and Raisins

Here is a famous Barcelona dish, light and easy to prepare, of sweet-tasting lean flounder, crunchy toasted nuts, and juicy black raisins fragrant with Cognac. The secret is the lemon butter, which not only keeps the flesh of the fish moist, but accentuates all the flavors and fragrances.

The recipe and the secret lemon butter addition were revealed to me by the late Ramón Cabau, one of Barcelona's great restaurateurs and promoters of the good life. Please don't be put off by the notion of raisins and nuts with fish—the varying textures and tastes make for a fascinating culinary experience.

This is a fast dish that requires last-minute cooking, but all the components can be prepared in advance. Moisture is retained because of the high-temperature cooking in a skillet. But be careful! A minute too long and the fish will overcook. Serve with Fried Rice perfumed with grated nutmeg, and follow with a crisp green salad.

2 tablespoons raisins

3 tablespoons Cognac

2 small flounder fillets (4 to 5 ounces each)
  Sea salt and freshly ground pepper
  Flour for dusting

2 teaspoons unsalted butter

1 teaspoon olive oil

1 tablespoon lemon butter (1 tablespoon butter blended with ¼ teaspoon grated lemon rind and 1 teaspoon lemon juice)

2 tablespoons pinenuts (pignoli), toasted and chopped coarse

2 tablespoons each almonds and hazelnuts, peeled, toasted, and chopped coarse

1 plum tomato, peeled, seeded, and cubed

1. Soak the raisins in Cognac for 10 minutes. Rinse and dry the fish; season it with salt and pepper, and dust with flour, shaking off any excess. Put the butter, olive oil, and a pinch of salt in a medium-sized nonstick skillet; heat the fat until it sizzles and just begins to brown. Add the fish and cook it until golden, turning once, about 1 to 2 minutes on each side. Transfer the fish to a heated serving dish; dot the fish with half the lemon butter, cover, and keep warm.

2. Add the mixed nuts to the skillet and brown them lightly. Stir in the raisins and the Cognac and bring it to a boil. Ignite the Cognac; when the flames die down, swirl in the remaining lemon butter and pour it over the fish. Decorate the fish with tomato cubes and serve at once.

Any sweet-tasting lean white-fleshed fish can be used, but the best choice is small sole or winter flounder. Some types of fish in this family (such as dabs and lemon sole) can be a

NOTES TO THE COOK

(continued)

little cottony in texture, and will benefit from a short soaking (30 minutes) in milk. Because of the acid in milk, fish soaked in it will take a little less time to cook. Be sure to take this into account when sautéing. Other possible substitutes are porgies, red snapper, or red drum—provided the fillets are thin. If necessary, use a wet pounder to flatten the fillets to an even thickness.

Red Snapper Baked over Fennel Stalks

SERVES 4

This is an indoor version of the famous barbecue method of grilling fish over dried aromatic stalks. The unique flavor of this dish is the result of, first, a spicy vegetable garnish; second, the baking in a very hot oven over dried fennel branches, allowing the fish to be perfumed with the wonderful scent of anise. Accompany with good crusty French bread.

1 *medium zucchini, unpeeled, trimmed and cored to remove seeds, diced fine, about 1 cup*

¼ *cup diced red bell pepper*

¼ *cup diced green bell pepper*

⅓ *cup diced young turnip*

⅓ *cup diced fennel bulb*

1 *small dried hot red pepper, stemmed*

1 *garlic clove, peeled and lightly crushed*

¼ *cup extra-virgin olive oil, preferably French*

2½ *tablespoons Noilly Prat vermouth*

1 *teaspoon minced fresh tarragon*

Juice of 1 lemon

1 *package dried fennel stalks, broken up*

4 *red snapper fillets, or substitute sea bass or rockfish, skinned (about 8 ounces each)*

Sea salt and freshly ground pepper

2 *or 3 sprigs fresh tarragon*

1. In a small saucepan of boiling salted water, cook the zucchini until tender, about ½ minute. Remove it with a skimmer, plunge it into icy water, drain, and let cool. Add the peppers, turnip, and fennel together to the same saucepan and boil until tender, 2 minutes. Drain and plunge them into icy water; drain and dry on a kitchen towel. Combine the vegetables, hot pepper, and garlic clove in a small bowl, and add all the olive oil, Noilly Prat, tarragon, and lemon juice. Cover and marinate at room temperature for about 3 hours to blend flavors.

2. Preheat the oven to 475° F. Spread the fennel stalks on the bottom of a large baking dish, preferably earthenware. Season the fish with salt and pepper and place it over the fennel in one layer. Measure out 2 tablespoons of the marinade and use to coat the fish. Bake 5 to 8 minutes or until done (the time varies with the thickness of the fish fillet). Remove the hot pepper and garlic from the vegetable mixture and discard. In a small skillet, heat the vegetable mixture to lukewarm, and season it with salt and pepper to taste.

3. Carefully transfer the fish fillets to 4 individual serving dishes, brushing away any pieces of dry fennel. Drain the vegetables and place them over the fish fillets. Save the oil for some other use. (The vegetables do not keep well.) Decorate the fish with sprigs of tarragon and serve at once.

NOTES TO THE COOK

It is important to cut the vegetables into small pieces *by hand* so that they retain their juices. Chopping them in the food processor will crush them, and then they will "water out" during the marination, and the resulting sauce will be mushy as well.

To achieve a hotter-tasting sauce, crush the hot pepper before adding to the marinade.

Long straw-colored dried fennel stalks are imported from France. You can obtain them in specialty stores, or by mail order. See Appendix, page 343.

Inspired by a recipe from Jacques Chibois.

SERVES 3 TO 4

Roast Tilefish on Potato Gratin

I have adapted this recipe from an extraordinary presentation of *dorade* (gilt-head bream) served at the Hotel Ampurdan just outside of Figueres, a Catalan city near the French frontier. If you drive by the Ampurdan you probably won't be inclined to make a special stop; it looks just like a number of other modern buildings on Route N-11. Although the hotel is very clean and comfortable, it is certainly not luxury class. The hotel restaurant is another story, for it is one of the two or three best restaurants in all of Catalonia. The kitchen continues to serve up superb executions of the recipes of its late owner and chef, Josep Mercader, the acknowledged father of the revived Catalan cuisine. This baked fish dish is a typical Mercader creation—simple, restrained, and clean-tasting, reflecting the subtlety of an art that conceals its artfulness.

(continued)

This seemingly simple dish requires great care if it is to be successful. Quality of ingredients is crucial: the fish must be supremely fresh; the black olives must be the small Niçoise type; the garlic cloves must also be small, chosen carefully from inside the head. Proportions are also important: the potatoes that line the pan are not there to provide a side dish of starch; rather, they are a crucial component. Sliced very thin and properly spaced, those under the fish will come out soft, serving as a blotter for all the delicious juices, while those along the edges will be lightly browned and just short of crisp. Serve hot with a crisp, dry white wine.

1 *pound large, firm, waxy potatoes such as red Bliss*

Fruity olive oil

Sea salt and freshly ground pepper

12 *small garlic cloves, unpeeled*

2 *fresh fillets of tilefish, with skin on, 1 inch thick, approximately 12 ounces each (see notes for substitutions)*

1½ *tablespoons chopped red bell pepper, previously roasted, stemmed, seeded, membranes removed, and peeled*

1 *plum tomato, peeled, seeded, and cut into ¼-inch dice (¼ cup)*

1 *bay leaf, broken in half*

4 *sprigs of fresh thyme*

2 *pinches of fennel seeds*

6 *Niçoise olives, unpitted*

6 *small Spanish green olives, pitted*

1. Preheat oven to 425° F.

2. Peel and slice the potatoes as thin as for potato chips (you can use a 1-mm blade of the food processor). Rinse and wipe each slice dry. Toss them with 4 tablespoons of olive oil, ½ scant teaspoon of salt and ¼ teaspoon of pepper. Cover the bottom of an oiled large baking dish (for example a 14-inch oval *le creuset*) with an even layer of potatoes. Scatter the garlic cloves on top. Bake the potatoes on the uppermost oven rack for 20 minutes. Use a flat spatula to turn the potatoes and garlic cloves every 5 minutes.

3. Generously season the fish with salt and pepper, and coat it with 2 tablespoons of oil. Scatter the red pepper, tomatoes, and herbs over the potatoes and lay the fish fillets on top, skin side up. Return the dish to the oven to bake for 10 minutes.

4. Raise the oven heat to broil. Add the olives to the pan. Baste the fish with oil and finish the cooking under the broiler for 5 minutes. Serve directly from the baking dish.

NOTE TO THE COOK *Dorade* is not available in the United States. You may substitute a white-fleshed fish that is sweet, dense, and moist, such as sea bass, red snapper, or another thick ocean fish fillet. My favorite is the violet-tinged tilefish.

Moroccan Fish Tagine with Tomato, Peppers, and Preserved Lemons

A popular Moroccan green-hued sauce used in fish stews, or *tagines,* is called *charmoula,* a balanced combination of quantities of flat-leaf parsley and fresh coriander, oil, cumin, paprika, and hot pepper. I love it for its powerful taste and the way it permeates the delicate flavor of fish, and in this dish especially it makes marvelous eating. You can make it ahead of time and keep it refrigerated for 1 or 2 days.

In Morocco fish stews are always cooked in earthenware, which is especially helpful when the stew contains tomatoes. (Tin-lined copperware and aluminum definitely alter flavor.) In this Moroccan fish *tagine,* the rich tastes of tomatoes, green peppers, and hot peppers are offset by the tart, briny flavor of preserved lemons. Traditionally this *tagine* would contain an entire fish with head intact, but I have found it easier to make with thick fillets. Serve the fish directly from the baking dish. Pass slices of anise-flavored Moroccan bread, and accompany with a light, dry red or white wine.

CHARMOULA

1 large garlic clove, crushed with 2 teaspoons salt in a blender or mortar until smooth

1½ teaspoons ground cumin seed

2 teaspoons sweet paprika

2 tablespoons coarsely chopped Italian flat-leaf parsley

2 tablespoons coarsely chopped fresh coriander leaves

¼ teaspoon crushed hot red-pepper flakes, seeds removed

2 tablespoons fresh lemon juice

2 tablespoons fruity olive oil

4 thick lean fish fillets or slices, about 8 ounces each: monkfish, red snapper, sea bass, tilefish, or other ocean fish

1 large carrot, sliced very thin

1 pound red, ripe tomatoes, cored and sliced thin

2 small green bell peppers, cored, seeded, and sliced thin

1 small green or red hot pepper, cored, seeded, and sliced thin

Sea salt and pepper

2 wedges of Preserved Lemons (page 32), rinsed and drained, pulp discarded, peel sliced thin

2 tablespoons coarsely chopped flat-leaf parsley

Sprigs of fresh coriander, for garnish

1. Early in the day, or the day before, make the *charmoula:* In a blender, combine the garlic, spices, herbs, and pepper flakes. Add the lemon juice and olive oil and blend until smooth. Scrape the mixture into a small saucepan and heat it slowly, stirring, until hot and

(continued)

aromatic, about 30 seconds; do not boil. Let it cool, then divide the spice mixture, or *charmoula,* in half.

2. Rinse the fish and pat it dry with paper towels. Rub one portion of the spice mixture into the fish and let it stand at least 1 hour, or overnight. Add ½ cup of hot water to the remaining spice mixture, cover, and refrigerate separately. *(The recipe can be prepared to this point a day ahead.)*

3. About 1½ hours before serving, preheat the oven to 300° F. Spread 2 tablespoons of reserved *charmoula* over the bottom of a shallow 2½-quart baking-serving dish (about 10 inches in diameter). Scatter the carrots on the bottom of the dish. Sprinkle with a little *charmoula.* Add half the tomatoes, bell peppers, and chili pepper; sprinkle with a little *charmoula.* Lay the fish over the vegetables and cover with the preserved lemon peel and the remaining tomatoes and peppers in a decorative pattern. Spread the remaining *charmoula* over all. Cover the dish tightly with foil and bake for 45 minutes.

4. Pour off the liquid from the fish into a small noncorrodible saucepan. Bring it to a boil over moderately high heat, and boil until it is reduced to ½ cup of thick liquid. Pour it back over the fish. *(The dish can be prepared up to 1 hour ahead to this point.)*

5. Raise the oven temperature to 500° F. Uncover the baking dish, baste with the pan juices, and bake in the top third of the oven for 10 minutes, or until a nice crust has formed over the vegetables. Sprinkle with parsley and garnish with sprigs of coriander. Serve warm.

Sicilian-Style Roast Salt Cod

In this Sicilian-inspired recipe, the cod is seared in a hot oven, then smothered with a rich and flavorful sauce, which protects the flesh from drying out. The resulting "roast" is easy and delicious. This dish is at its best with crusty bread. For a first course, I would choose an array of Sicilian vegetable dishes: Sweet and Sour Pumpkin, Pan-fried Artichokes, and Siracusan Baked Onion Slices. Finish with fresh fruit and store-bought *biscotti*.

1 *pound boneless and skinless salt cod, preferably a thick center piece (see Appendix, page 348, for notes on buying and handling salt cod)*

1 *teaspoon crumbled Greek or Sicilian oregano*

Freshly ground black pepper

6 *tablespoons fruity extra-virgin olive oil*

2 *garlic cloves, sliced thin*

1 *(32-ounce) can whole peeled tomatoes, drained, seeded, and juice reserved*

2 *tablespoons seedless golden raisins, plumped in warm water and drained dry*

2 *tablespoons pinenuts (pignoli), toasted until golden in a dry skillet*

12 *Italian salted capers, soaked and drained, or 1½ teaspoons drained capers (chop if large)*

1 *cup pitted juicy ripe olives, preferably Italian gaeta or Greek Kalamata*

¼ *teaspoon cayenne pepper*

Small pinches of sugar and baking soda, if necessary, to balance the acidity

Sea salt

1. Two days before serving, rinse the salt cod thoroughly under running water. Place it in a large bowl; cover it with cold water. Refrigerate 24 to 36 hours, changing the water four or more times.

2. Drain the cod; rinse it under cold running water. Remove and discard any bones and hard skin; cut the cod into 8 equal pieces. Fold the pieces so they are about 2 inches square and of uniform thickness; pat them dry with paper toweling. Arrange them in a single layer in lightly oiled shallow baking dish; rub with ½ teaspoon of oregano and a small amount of pepper. Sprinkle 3 tablespoons of the olive oil over the cod. *(Refrigerate the cod until you are ready to cook, up to 1 day.)*

3. Heat the remaining 3 tablespoons of olive oil in a large, heavy skillet. Add the garlic; sauté until softened but not browned, about 2 minutes. Remove the garlic from the skillet. Raise the heat, add the tomatoes, and cook, mashing, until they become scorched

(continued)

(not burned) and develop flavor, about 2 minutes. Add the reserved juices, raisins, pine-nuts, capers, olives, remaining oregano, cayenne, and salt to taste. Simmer the sauce, uncovered, for 15 minutes. Add sugar and baking soda if necessary. Makes 1⅔ cups sauce. *(Up to this point the dish can be prepared 1 day in advance.)*

4. Forty-five minutes before serving, place a rack in the highest position in the oven and a second rack in the middle; heat oven to 450° F.

5. About 25 minutes before serving, set the baking dish on the upper-middle rack of the oven and roast 8 minutes. Lower the oven heat to 375° F. Spoon the tomato sauce over the fish; bake it uncovered on the middle oven rack for 20 minutes. Serve at once.

Sea Bass Oven-Poached in Meat Stock, Agrigento Style

SERVES 4 TO 6

A whole fish cooked on the bone, with head and tail intact, makes for a spectacular presentation. But keeping a fish whole also has practical benefits. The bones not only add flavor to the flesh, but also keep it moist, and the skin of most fish has an underlying layer of fat, which will slowly seep into the flesh, giving added richness.

The method of preparation in this recipe involves neither poaching nor braising, but a type of slow cooking that is unique. The fish will definitely not be overcooked; in fact, it will still be barely pink at the bone, but its flesh will be more silky and succulent than if cooked by any other method.

Not all fish can be cooked at very low temperature, but when a variety can be prepared this way the result is sensational. (See pages 98, 129, and 131 for Michel Bras's recipes for trout and salmon.) Low-temperature fish cookery is not a new discovery: my research shows it has been used in Sicily for years, as in this specialty of Agrigento.

The use of meat stock to cook lean fish is not peculiar to Sicily; one finds similar dishes in eighteenth-century French cookbooks. Menon, in *La Cuisinière Bourgeoise*, mentions a turbot simmered in veal stock. And of course the Chinese have always combined fish and meat. A delicate meat stock doesn't mask the flavor of the fish; it enhances the flavor.

Please be sure to cook your fish *very slowly*, so that the flesh will not only absorb all the flavors of the stock, but will actually swell up—an effect you will be able to see.

The fish can be served with a light brushing of extra-virgin olive oil, fresh lemon juice, salt and pepper, and decorated with fried celery leaves. Or accompany the bass with a sauce (see page 115) made with the very best extra-virgin olive oil, balsamic vinegar, and fresh rosemary leaves.

3½- to 4-pound whole sea bass, scaled, gutted, with head, fins, and tail left on

Sea salt and freshly ground pepper

2 tablespoons green fruity olive oil

2 sprigs fresh thyme

1 sprig fresh rosemary, 2 inches long

1 small celery rib with leaves

Leaves from tender ribs of celery, about 2 handfuls

3 cups unsalted meat or chicken broth, at room temperature

½ cup dry white wine

Oil for frying

1. Rinse the fish; wipe it dry, and prick the skin many times with a thin skewer. Rub inside and out with a mixture of salt, pepper, and olive oil. Stuff the cavity with the herbs and 1 celery rib with leaves. Use loops of string to close the cavity. Cover the fish loosely with a damp towel and refrigerate until you are ready to cook.

2. Wash the celery leaves. Discard any dark-green leaves. Carefully roll them up in a kitchen towel to dry. *(Up to this point the dish can be prepared many hours in advance.)*

3. About 2¼ hours before serving, position the oven rack on the middle shelf and preheat the oven to 225° F. Place the fish in an earthenware, glass, porcelain, or enameled cast-iron shallow baking dish, preferably oval and just large enough to hold the fish (break off the tail if necessary). Avoid using a fish poacher—aluminum heats up too quickly. Pour in the stock and wine (the liquid does not have to cover the fish). Set the fish in the oven to bake, uncovered. The temperature of the cooking liquid will rise slowly to 175° F; do not hurry it. (This allows the fish to cook through evenly.) Baste the fish several times with the broth while baking. It is not necessary to turn the fish in the pan. It is cooked in about 2 hours. The flesh should still feel firm but have a little resistance when pressed; only the tail flesh should flake easily.

4. While the fish is baking, prepare the celery leaves. Heat the oil in a small nonstick skillet to the depth of ½-inch. When it is hot, drop in the celery leaves, in batches, and fry for 30 seconds or until crisp. Drain them and spread out on paper towels.

5. Transfer the fish to a heated long serving platter. Discard the string around the fish; roll back the skin, starting from the tail end, and discard. Leave the head intact. Season the flesh lightly with salt and pepper. Lightly salt the fried celery leaves and use for garnish. At the table, slide a thin-bladed knife down the backbone to detach the flesh from the bones. Lift the top fillet off the bone in two or three portions. The flesh should be just barely translucent at the bone. Snip the backbone at the base of the head and transfer it to a side dish. Serve the remaining portions.

NOTES TO
THE COOK

This dish relies on a really fresh large sea bass. If its head glistens with a bright cobalt-blue color, the fish is at its best.

On the West Coast, if North Atlantic sea bass is not available, choose a rock cod that has a similar flaky texture.

Start the long, slow cooking with a cold liquid. If too much heat is applied, the outside flesh will cook too quickly, and the flesh near the bone will be underdone. Though the oven temperature is set at 225° F, frequent opening and closing for basting keeps the actual temperature of the liquid at about 175° F.

Balsamic vinegar, fruity olive oil, and sprigs of fresh rosemary make an elegant accompaniment to a poached sea bass. The combination is truly inspired. The sweet-sour taste of the vinegar will counterbalance the strength of the rosemary, and both will be softened by the olive oil. An expensive aged balsamic vinegar is not needed to make this special sauce.

2 *tablespoons balsamic vinegar*

¼ *cup extra-virgin olive oil*

1 *4-inch sprig fresh rosemary*

Pinch of crumbled Mediterranean oregano

Freshly ground white pepper

Pinch of hot red-pepper flakes, without seeds

Sea salt to taste

Combine all the ingredients and let the sauce stand at least 2 hours. Gently heat to serve.

Inspired by a recipe from A Cookery Calendar, *edited by Cantine Lungarotti for* Le Tre Vaselle.

Mystical Salt Cod

A delicious and hearty winter dish of salt cod baked with layers of sliced potatoes and creamy onions. The young Portuguese-American woman who gave me this recipe called it Mystical Salt Cod; according to Portuguese-food authority Jean Anderson, it might bear this name because so many salt-cod dishes originated in convents.

No fish takes kindly to overcooking, but salt cod becomes especially tough and cottony if allowed to boil. Even when thin pieces of cod are brought slowly to a boil (the traditional poaching method) they can easily be overcooked and ruined. For this recipe I prefer to blanch the cod rather than poach it. Afterward, it can be left to bake slowly for a long time without damage to its tender flesh. Please use only thick pieces of salt cod for this dish.

This winter dish is excellent with a fresh green salad and a light red wine. For dessert, try the Fresh Orange Slices with Moroccan Spices.

1½ *pounds boneless, skinless salt cod*

2½ *cups milk*

Herb bouquet: 3 sprigs parsley; 1 sprig thyme; 1 bay leaf; 1 large garlic clove, halved; ½ teaspoon whole black peppercorns, cracked; all tied in cheesecloth.

1½ *pounds boiling potatoes, peeled and soaked in lightly salted water*

5 *tablespoons unsalted butter*

3 *tablespoons all-purpose flour*

½ *teaspoon freshly ground white pepper*

Coarse sea salt

Freshly grated nutmeg

½ *cup olive oil*

3 *medium-size onions, halved lengthwise, cut into thin slices*

3 *tablespoons fine breadcrumbs*

4 *tablespoons freshly grated dry Gouda, Parmesan, or Swiss cheese*

1. *One to 2 days before serving,* wash the pieces of salt cod under cool running water. Cut them into 3 or 4 pieces. Place them in a large bowl; cover with cold water. Refrigerate up to 36 hours, changing the water several times. Add 1 cup of the milk to the final soaking.

2. Drain the cod; rinse and set it aside. Place the herbs in a large saucepan half filled with cold water; slowly heat to boiling (this perfumes the water). Remove the herbs and set them aside. Place the cod in a strainer that will fit into the saucepan. Lower the pieces of cod into rapidly boiling water. Watch very carefully: when the first few bubbles begin to rise to the surface of the water indicating the water is returning to a boil, immediately remove the strainer and leave the cod to drain; cool slightly. Remove the bones and bits of hard skin; flake the cod coarse. Set it aside, loosely covered, at room temperature. Set aside

½ cup of the cooking liquid for the sauce. Save the remaining liquid to cook the potatoes in the next step.

3. Cook the potatoes with the herb bouquet in the cooking liquid until barely tender, about 15 minutes. Drain off the liquid (this can be used for a soup if desired). Return the potatoes to medium heat; shake gently to evaporate excess moisture, about 30 seconds. Set aside, off the heat, until the potatoes are cool enough to handle. Discard the herbs.

4. Meanwhile, heat the remaining milk in a small saucepan until just warmed through. Heat 4 tablespoons of the butter in a heavy 2-quart saucepan over low heat. Stir in the flour until smooth and blended; cook, stirring, until the mixture is a pale ivory color, about 2 minutes. Gradually stir in the warm milk and the ½ cup of reserved poaching liquid; increase the heat to medium. Cook, stirring constantly, until the sauce boils and thickens, then reduce the heat to low; cook, uncovered, stirring occasionally to prevent the sauce from sticking and lumping, for 10 minutes. Remove it from the heat; stir in the white pepper, salt, and grated nutmeg to taste. Keep warm, covered.

5. Set an oven rack at the upper-middle position. Preheat the oven to 400° F. Slice the cooled potatoes thin. Heat 5 tablespoons of the oil in a heavy 10-inch skillet, preferably well-seasoned cast iron, over high heat until fragrant. Toss the potatoes in hot oil to coat, then sauté them until golden brown on both sides, about 3 minutes. Drain in a colander.

6. Add the remaining oil to the skillet; heat it to hot. Add the onions and cook, stirring, until soft and golden, about 8 minutes. Remove them from the heat and drain in a colander or sieve.

7. Lightly oil a 2-quart gratin dish or other shallow baking dish. Arrange the potatoes. Spread the cod and onions on top; spoon the warm sauce over the surface. Sprinkle with breadcrumbs and cheese; dot with the remaining butter. Bake on the upper-middle rack until the top is golden brown, about 20 minutes. Let the dish stand 5 minutes before serving.

Swordfish Steaks with Anchovies and Wild Mushrooms

SERVES 2

When I make a sauce for a piece of grilled swordfish, my rule is: Keep it simple. Here my "sauce" is really a chunky spread of wild mushrooms and anchovies, which melts into the flesh of the swordfish as it is being served.

Nowadays, you can ask for swordfish that has been harpooned rather than caught in the net. The difference in flavor is quite extraordinary, and justifies the higher price. Grilled swordfish will be even tastier if marinated for an hour or so before cooking in a mixture of olive oil, seasoning, and a drop of lemon juice. If you really can get a good, hot wood fire going, I suggest cutting the swordfish very thin (½ inch), as they do in Sicily. It cooks very quickly, and will taste a good deal better than the usual inch-thick swordfish steaks. Serve with steamed potatoes and a ripe-tomato salad.

2 teaspoons crumbled dried Italian mushrooms (porcini)

2 large swordfish steaks, about ⅓ inch thick (approximately 1 pound)

3 tablespoons extra-virgin olive oil

1 tablespoon fresh lemon juice

Salt and freshly ground pepper

3 tablespoons unsalted butter

1 garlic clove, peeled and halved

¼ teaspoon dried hot-pepper flakes

2 teaspoons anchovy paste

2 teaspoons small capers, rinsed and drained (chop, if large)

¼ cup dry white wine

1. Soak the dried mushrooms in warm water to cover for 20 minutes. Drain them, reserving the liquid. Rinse the mushrooms to rid them of any sand, then chop them fine. Strain the liquid through a paper filter to remove any sand.

2. Marinate the swordfish for approximately 1 hour with 2½ tablespoons oil, the lemon juice, and a pinch each of salt and pepper. Meanwhile, heat 2 teaspoons of the butter in a small skillet, add the garlic, hot pepper, anchovy paste, capers, chopped mushrooms, and the soaking liquid. Cook over high heat, stirring, for 2 minutes or until the moisture has evaporated. Add the white wine and boil down to a glaze. Remove the skillet from the heat, discard the garlic, and swirl in the remaining butter. Taste for salt and pepper and keep hot.

3. Start a bed of hardwood coals in an outdoor grill or heat up the broiler.

4. Brush the grill with the remaining oil, and broil or grill the fish close to the heat source until it is just opaque and cooked, about 1 minute to a side. Sprinkle with salt and pepper and spread the anchovy-mushroom mixture over the fish. Serve at once.

Involtini of Swordfish with Capers

Although served throughout Sicily, these rolled-up, stuffed pieces of swordfish are truly the glory of Messina. Swordfish steaks are cut thin, then pounded, and wrapped around a stuffing made with breadcrumbs flavored with grated lemon rind, sautéed onion, pecorino cheese, and tangy Sicilian capers.

These superb roll-ups can be prepared a few hours in advance; then simply cook them for 2 to 3 minutes before serving. Be sure your broiler is very hot, or your rolls won't have an attractive color. A pinch of sugar will give them a good glaze. Serve them with an array of Sicilian dishes such as Sweet and Sour Pumpkin, Maria Sindoni's *Caponatina*, Siracusan Baked Olives, and a platter of sliced ripe tomatoes.

2¼ pounds swordfish steaks, cut ¾ inch thick, untrimmed

CAPER STUFFING

5 tablespoons olive oil

1 tablespoon minced onion

1 tablespoon minced carrot

½ tablespoon crushed garlic

2 cups (scant) fresh grated breadcrumbs, preferably Sicilian Semolina Bread (page 2)

3 heaping tablespoons salted capers, rinsed, plumped, drained, and chopped

5 tablespoons grated pecorino or Romano cheese (about 1 ounce)

1 teaspoon finely grated lemon rind

1 teaspoon finely chopped parsley leaves

Salt and pepper to taste

Fresh lemon juice to taste

12 imported bay leaves, cut into halves or quarters

1 small onion, quartered, separated into 1-inch segments

Olive oil

Pinches of granulated sugar

SALMORIGLIO SAUCE

⅓ cup extra-virgin olive oil

2½ tablespoons fresh lemon juice

1 teaspoon grated lemon rind

½ teaspoon fresh oregano or thyme leaves

¾ teaspoon salt

½ teaspoon ground pepper

¼ teaspoon sugar

1 tablespoon chopped flat-leaf parsley

Steps 1 through 5 can be done up to 3 hours in advance.

1. Cut off and discard the swordfish skin. Cut each fish steak into pieces measuring approximately 3 by 3 by ¾ inch. Cut each piece horizontally into 3 even slices, making 24 swordfish slices.

(continued)

2. Reserve and chop any trimmings for the stuffing. Place each slice between sheets of oiled waxed paper. Use a flat mallet to gently pound them. They should become about one-third larger in size. Avoid breaking the flesh. Keep the fish refrigerated between sheets of waxed paper or plastic wrap.

3. Make the caper stuffing. Place the oil, swordfish trimmings, vegetables, and garlic in a large skillet and cook 1 minute or until the vegetables are soft but not brown. Add the breadcrumbs to the skillet and mix well over low heat for 30 seconds. Scrape the mixture into a clean bowl; add the remaining stuffing ingredients and if necessary 1 to 2 tablespoons water to help bind the mixture.

4. Place the fish slices on a work surface. Evenly divide the stuffing and place a portion on each slice. Using your oiled palms, roll up one slice, press in the ends, then squeeze gently to form the shape of a stuffed grape leaf. Repeat with the remaining slices. Have ready 12 or 24 metal or bamboo skewers. Slip a small piece of bay leaf and an onion segment on either side of each roll. Thread 4 rolls using two skewers equidistant apart as illustrated below (this helps you to turn the rolls easily while broiling). If necessary, fasten any openings with toothpicks. Brush the rolls with olive oil and sprinkle lightly with granulated sugar (to develop a good color when broiled). Refrigerate until you are ready to cook, up to 3 hours.

5. Make the *salmoriglio* sauce. Combine the first 7 ingredients in a blender jar and blend until smooth and creamy. Add 2 tablespoons of hot water and blend for an instant (this makes it lighter). Makes ½ cup. Pour the sauce into a bowl. Stir in the parsley. Adjust the seasoning. (*The sauce can be made ahead and refrigerated.* Bring it to room temperature and stir before serving.)

6. Cook the swordfish rolls over hot coals or very close to a heated broiler about 1½ minutes to a side. Baste with the *salmoriglio* sauce and serve at once with the remaining sauce poured on top.

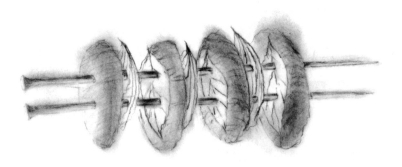

(Tunnina Ammarinata)

Tuna Smothered with Melting Onions and Fresh Mint

SERVES 4

Between all my Italian- and Sicilian-language cookbooks I count more than thirty recipes for tuna. Most of them come from the northwest side of the island, around Trapani, where tuna fishing has been a major industry since the Arab occupation. It was the Arabs who taught the Sicilians the *matanza*, the traditional and dramatic method of hunting tuna by cornering them between nets. You rarely see the *matanza* today, and tuna have nearly disappeared from Sicilian waters, but the recipes live on.

In this summer recipe from Trapani, thin tuna steaks are fried, then covered in a sweet-and-sour onion sauce, and served cold the following day. This allows the flavors to mingle and mellow. Even after several days in the refrigerator the tuna will retain good texture. The onions are cut thick in order to stand up to the dense tuna flesh.

Before dinner, I would serve slices of caciocavallo cheese with Nafplion olives, and wedges of country bread. Follow with a light first course such as Pasta with Anchovies and Toasted Bread-crumbs. If you think this won't be enough for an evening's meal, follow with a simple orange-flavored sponge cake, and glasses of chilled sweet wine, such as a California black or orange Muscat, or the rich and aromatic Sicilian Bukkuran *Moscato Passito di Pantelleria*.

3 *tablespoons extra-virgin olive oil*	4 *tablespoons vegetable oil*
3 *large brown onions, peeled and sliced into ¼-inch-thick rounds*	5 *tablespoons aged wine vinegar*
	1 *tablespoon liquid honey*
1½ *pounds fresh boneless tuna steaks, about ¾ inch thick, skinned*	8 *large mint sprigs, stemmed, leaves torn, preferably peppermint*
Coarse salt and freshly ground pepper	*Additional fresh mint sprigs for garnish*
Flour for dredging	
Coarse salt	*Freshly ground white pepper*

1. Prepare the dish one day in advance. In a heavy 10-inch skillet set over medium-high heat place the olive oil, onions, and 1 cup of water, and bring them to a boil. Cook, stirring occasionally, over medium heat until the water has evaporated and the onions are soft and golden brown, about 25 minutes.

2. Meanwhile, wash the tuna steaks, soak them 5 minutes in cold water, rinse, and dry. Season the steaks lightly with salt and pepper, dust with flour, and shake off the excess. In a second large, heavy skillet heat vegetable oil over high heat to rippling, add the tuna

(continued)

SWORDFISH AND TUNA RECIPES 121

steaks and cook them until crisp and brown, 1½ minutes to a side. Immediately remove the skillet from the heat to stop the cooking (tuna remains juicier if slightly undercooked —almost rare at the center). Transfer the tuna to a platter. Quickly pour off the oil. Add to the skillet the vinegar, ½ cup of water, and the honey, and cook, stirring, for 30 seconds or until the liquid is reduced by half. Pour it over the onions, raise the heat to high, and continue cooking until the onions are juicy, soft, and lightly caramelized. Immediately remove the skillet from the heat. Season with salt and pepper. Cool to lukewarm.

3. Season the tuna with salt and pepper; scatter torn mint sprigs over it. Pour the onions and their juices over the top and sprinkle with more torn mint leaves. Cool, cover, and refrigerate overnight.

4. To serve, remove the wilted mint leaves. Correct the seasoning with salt and pepper, and adjust the sweet-sour balance with vinegar and sugar, if necessary. Garnish with fresh mint and serve.

NOTE TO
THE COOK

If tuna flesh is dark, soak in salty water (2 tablespoons salt and 1 quart water) for 30 minutes. This allows the blood to leach out. Omit seasoning the tuna with salt in step 3.

SALMON

| SERVES 2 | *Salmon Fillet Cooked on One Side Only* |

Here is my version of the Scandinavian method of cooking salmon on one side only, a method that allows the exuding oil from the fish to fry the skin to a state of crispness. The taste of the salmon skin is delicious; grill a piece of skin over an open fire and see for yourself.

Use a heavy pan and cook the salmon very slowly so the skin can crisp and the flesh will cook evenly. (Broiling salmon skin side up cooks the fish too quickly, and all the fat stays inside.) The recipe works best with Atlantic salmon, king salmon and sockeye, which have sufficiently large fatty deposits on their bellies to act as an inner basting medium. The globules that exude during the cooking should be cut away before serving.

I garnish the fish with a sauce of cubed tomatoes, capers, lemon, chives, and sorrel, all of which create a robust counterpoint to the smooth, elegant slice of salmon. A good accompaniment would be sautéed new potatoes, and a platter of Glazed Leeks.

¾ *pound center cut of fresh Atlantic salmon fillet, skin on*

1 *tablespoon olive oil*

½ *teaspoon sea salt*

2 *teaspoons unsalted butter*

8 *small capers, rinsed, drained, and chopped (¾ teaspoon)*

3 *tablespoons sliced white part of scallion*

1 *ripe tomato, peeled, seeded, and cut into ¼-inch cubes*

3 *tablespoons cubed lemon flesh, with rind, pith, and seeds removed*

Salt and freshly ground pepper

2 *tablespoons shredded fresh sorrel*

2 *tablespoons snipped chives*

1. Cut the salmon crosswise into 2-inch-wide strips. Lightly brush them with olive oil and sprinkle with sea salt. Place the salmon, skin side down, on a heated, well-seasoned iron skillet or griddle and cook over low heat for 20 minutes *without turning*. Use a dome lid or foil to cover the salmon for the last 5 minutes to finish the cooking. (Note that the color of the salmon will not turn dull and the texture will be very juicy.) Scrape off any globules of fat and reserve.

2. Meanwhile, melt the butter in a small skillet, add the capers and scallion and cook, stirring, 1 minute. Add the tomato and lemon cubes and cook 30 seconds. Season to taste with salt and pepper. Swirl in the reserved salmon fat. Raise the heat under the large skillet to crisp the skin at the last minute. Serve the salmon, skin side down, with its warm tomato garnish, shredded sorrel, and snipped chives.

Salmon with Provençal Vegetables

SERVES 4

Coho (silver) salmon and other fish that are dense but lean are perfect for this dish. Here fillets are cut diagonally to produce strips and, though they cook quickly, they do so without loss of moisture or damage to their texture, which is played off against the crisp-tender julienned vegetables and simmered onions. All are wrapped in a foil packet and baked together at the last minute. A sprinkling of chopped black olives, red pimentos, and snipped chives make for a very attractive summer dish.

This recipe, which I have adapted from the repertoire of chef Jacques Chibois, is a good choice for the cook who likes the kitchen counter pristine. All its components can be prepared in advance and readied in their foil packets. Bring the packets to room temperature before baking (about 20 minutes) or add 2 minutes' baking time. As the packets of salmon bake in the oven, whisk a little butter into the onion sauce base.

14 *ounces boneless and skinless salmon fillet*

Sea salt and pepper

6 *tablespoons unsalted butter*

1 *medium onion, cut lengthwise into thin strips*

1 *teaspoon tamari or soy sauce*

1 *medium carrot, pared and cut into thin julienne strips*

1 *medium turnip, pared and cut into thin julienne strips*

1 *medium zucchini, pared, cored to remove seeds, and cut into thin julienne strips*

15 *oil-cured black olives, softened in hot water and pitted*

1 *tablespoon finely diced pimento*

1½ *tablespoons finely snipped chives*

1 *teaspoon olive oil*

Steps 1 through 4 can be prepared many hours in advance.

1. Cut the salmon into diagonal strips, each about 2 by ½ by ¾ inch. Season lightly with salt and pepper.

2. In a heavy saucepan, melt 2 tablespoons of the butter over medium-low heat, add the sliced onions and cook, stirring, until very soft and golden, about 10 minutes. Add ½ cup of water and 1 teaspoon of tamari sauce, and cook 5 minutes longer. Strain the onions over a small saucepan, pressing down to extract all juices. Reduce the liquid over high heat to 3 tablespoons and set aside. Reserve the cooked onions.

3. In a saucepan of boiling salted water cook the julienned vegetables until crisp-tender. Drain them and refresh under cool running water; drain and dry on a kitchen towel. Season with pepper and salt. Blanch the olives in boiling *un*salted water for

5 minutes; drain and cut into thin strips. Mix them with the pimento and chives and set aside.

4. Cut 4 sheets of parchment or foil into four 15-inch squares. Distribute the onions equally over one half of each sheet. Top onions with equal amounts of salmon and the vegetable mixture. Fold each packet and make secure seals by folding and crimping the edges. (*Up to this point the recipe can be prepared in advance.* Refrigerate the packets but remove so they can return to room temperature before cooking.)

5. Preheat the oven to 500° F. Place the foil packets side by side on a large baking sheet. Bake in the center of the oven for 5 minutes, or until the bags are puffed up. Meanwhile, reheat the reduced onion juice over low heat and whisk in the remaining butter, 1 tablespoon at a time. Whisk in 1 teaspoon olive oil (for flavor) and readjust the seasoning.

6. Have ready 4 warm serving dishes. Spoon equal amounts of sauce into the plates, then tilt the plates so the sauce evenly covers them. Open the packets and attractively arrange the salmon and vegetables and scatter the olive mixture on top.

Roast Salmon with Cabbage, Bacon, and Carrots

I like the rustic feeling of this dish. The accompanying earthy vegetables take nothing away from the elegance of the salmon.

Salmon wrapped in caul fat and roasted at a high temperature acquires an incredibly "big" taste. While the exterior turns crisp, the flavor and moisture of the fish are retained within.

¼ *pound caul fat, about 1 foot square (see notes)*

1 *tablespoon white vinegar*

2 *pounds center-cut fresh salmon, boned into 2 fillets with the skin on*

Salt and freshly ground white pepper

2 *thin slices bacon*

2 *teaspoons coarsely snipped mixed fresh herbs, such as tarragon and dill*

1 *large imported bay leaf, broken into 4 pieces*

1 *pound Savoy cabbage*

3 *tablespoons heavy cream*

1 *tablespoon chopped shallots*

½ *teaspoon green peppercorns, rinsed and drained*

1 *tablespoon chopped parsley*

2 *carrots, pared, cut into ¼-inch cubes and cooked until tender*

1 *tablespoon imported hazelnut, walnut, or fruity olive oil*

Steps 1 through 5 can be done many hours in advance.

1. Place the caul fat in a small bowl. Add the vinegar and 3 cups of cold water. Let it soak 15 minutes. Rinse it under cold running water and drain well.

2. Season the salmon fillets lightly with salt and pepper on both sides. Place the bacon on one of the fillets; sprinkle with fresh herbs. Place the other fillet on top to reassemble the fish. Set the pieces of bay leaf on top. Wrap the entire fish in caul fat and place it in a shallow medium baking dish. (*The salmon can be prepared to this point many hours in advance and kept refrigerated, uncovered.*)

3. Discard the outer leaves of cabbage. Wash and quarter the cabbage, and discard the inner core. Blanch the cabbage 1 minute; drain it and refresh under cool running water. Steam the cabbage for 10 minutes over boiling water. Drain it, refresh, and chop coarse. (This double blanching makes the cabbage lighter and easier to digest.)

4. In a wide skillet over medium-low heat combine the heavy cream, cabbage, shallots, green peppercorns, parsley, and cubed carrots; mix until well blended. Simmer 5 minutes. Season to taste with salt and freshly ground pepper. Set the mixture aside in a cool place until you are ready to reheat.

5. Thirty minutes before serving, preheat the oven to 500 ° F and remove the salmon from the refrigerator.

6. Fifteen minutes before serving, roast the salmon for 7 minutes without turning. Meanwhile, gently reheat the cabbage. Remove the salmon from the oven, tilt the pan, and drain off all the fat. Reserve 1 tablespoon. Let the salmon sit for 5 minutes. Increase the heat to broil. As soon as the fish is cool enough to handle, unwrap and peel off the caul fat and skin. (The center of the fish will be slightly undercooked.) Place the fillets, rare side up, on the baking pan. Lay the bacon slices alongside them. Brush the salmon and bacon with reserved fat and broil for 2 to 3 minutes, or until the fish is almost opaque throughout and the bacon is crisp. Divide the salmon and cabbage among warmed plates. Crumble the bacon and scatter on top. Sprinkle with hazelnut oil and serve at once.

Pork caul fat, a lacy, thin membrane often used when making country-style *pâtés*, can be purchased in Chinese, Italian, and French meat markets, or ordered from your butcher. I have kept caul fat in the freezer for as long as a year without any noticeable decay. It needs to be freshened by a brief soaking in acidulated lukewarm water (1 tablespoon of vinegar to 2 cups of water). It should be rinsed and drained before use.

NOTES TO
THE COOK

If caul fat is unavailable, wrap the salmon in 3 or 4 thin slices of bacon. The dish will not taste the same, but still will come out well.

TWO OVEN-STEAMED SALMON RECIPES
CREATED BY MICHEL BRAS

Michel Bras is an original. Virtually self-taught, he never apprenticed in a "great kitchen." For years he worked as an assistant to his mother, a good country cook who started the hotel Lou Mazuc in Laguiole, a village in the Rouerque region of the Auvergne, one of the most fascinating, underpopulated, and rustic parts of France.

In 1979 Bras and his wife, Ginette, took over the hotel, and things began to change. A dining room was created out of a renovated cheese cellar. Though his mother continued to work in the kitchen, preparing *aligot* (a potato-and-cheese dish), and other regional dishes, Bras began to delve deeply into cuisine, researching, thinking through each ingredient, creating an intellectual framework for the culinary "themes" and "messages" he wished to convey. He has a brilliant, questing scientific mind, the processes of which (tempered by his desire to nourish) are evident in his startlingly original food.

The following two recipes (which I have adapted to the American kitchen) should convey some of this quirky brilliance. In both salmon dishes the fish is cooked slowly at a very low temperature in a steamy low oven, an unorthodox yet scientifically correct way to reveal natural flavor and create a rich, moist texture, too. In the first dish the crisped fatback (reduced to crackling fiber after the fat has been cooked out of it) makes a stunning textural contrast with the fish and the soft stewed onions. The second salmon dish is a perfect example of Michel Bras's interest in what he calls "the trilogy of the main ingredient, the vegetable, and the condiment, in which each thing is there for a reason," an example, too, of his extremely sophisticated use of herbs—in this particular case, a chive infusion. Atlantic, Norwegian, or King salmon is preferred. Reduce cooking time for leaner salmon.

Oven Steamed Salmon with Cracklings

For the greens in this dish Bras uses *bocu*, a strong-flavored green that has the taste of radish and cabbage. Any strong-flavored green such as kale, collard, mustard, or turnip greens can be used. Or substitute the sweeter Swiss chard, if desired.

An interesting first course, such as the Cheese and Walnut "Terrine," can combine perfectly with this dish to make a very delicious lunch.

4½ tablespoons unsalted butter

2 medium onions, cut lengthwise into thin strips (2½ cups)

Salt and freshly ground white pepper

1 pound thin lard leaves or thin-sliced hard fatback (eight 5-by-5-by-¹⁄₁₆-inch slices)

12 large leaves of strong-flavored greens, stemmed (see suggestions above)

½ cup shelled fresh peas (about ½ pound unshelled)

1¼ pound center-cut fresh salmon fillet, cut crosswise into four 1-inch-thick portions, about 5 ounces each

1. Melt 1½ tablespoons of the butter in a 9-inch heavy skillet over medium heat. Add the onions and cook them, stirring often, until softened and golden, about 30 minutes. (The onions will have reduced to approximately ⅔ cup.) Season with salt and pepper.

2. Heat another large, heavy skillet over medium heat until hot. Rinse the lard leaves in water; shake off the excess. Add 1 slice to the skillet. Weight the lard leaf with a bacon press or a heavy cast-iron skillet, and cook until golden brown, turning it over twice, about 1 minute a side. Transfer it to paper toweling, using tongs or a spatula. Season with salt (if using salted fatback, omit the salt). Pour off the fat from the skillet. Repeat with the remaining lard leaves. (*The lard leaves can be prepared 1 day ahead.* Cool them completely. Store in an airtight container.)

3. In a medium saucepan of boiling salted water, cook the green leaves until just tender. Remove them with a slotted spoon; drain and rinse them under cool running water. Add the peas and boil for 1 minute. Drain and refresh them under cool running water. Combine the leaves and peas in a small saucepan with 2 tablespoons water and the 3 remaining tablespoons butter. Cover and finish cooking over very low heat, about 10 minutes. Add salt and pepper to taste. (*Up to this point the recipe can be prepared 1 hour in advance.*)

4. About 25 minutes before serving: Position one rack in the lower third of the oven and a second rack in the upper third. Preheat the oven to 225° F. Carefully place a skillet of boiling water on the lower oven shelf. Arrange the salmon pieces on a metal baking sheet

(continued)

and place it on the upper rack. Bake 10 minutes. Turn the salmon over and cook 1 minute longer. (Note that the color of the salmon will not turn dull and the texture will be very juicy.) Sprinkle it with salt and pepper to taste.

5. Meanwhile, reheat the onions and greens separately over low heat, stirring occasionally. Crisp the lard wafers, in the oven while the salmon cooks, or in a nonstick skillet over low heat.

6. To serve, place 1 wafer on each plate. Spoon the onion mixture over. Top each with a salmon fillet and a remaining wafer. Divide the greens among the plates.

NOTES TO THE COOK
Lard leaves, or barding strips, or paper-thin slices of fatback can be purchased at pork butchers or large supermarkets. Please note that *after frying* only the fibrous membrane remains and all the fat is discarded. Only firm white fatback, which is closest to the pigs' skin, should be used to make these wafers. Salted fatback can be substituted; soak it overnight in water, drain, pat dry, chill, and slice. But, if do you use salted fatback, *do not salt salmon or onions*.

The salmon is fully cooked; this method kills any tapeworm larvae. Be sure the oven temperature is at least 225° F for five minutes.

SERVES 4	# Oven-Steamed Salmon with *Chive Oil*

Easy and delicious, this is a very popular dish in my cooking classes.

CHIVE OIL
2½ tablespoons snipped chives
   Pinch of salt
¼ cup French peanut oil or high-quality salad oil

½ small, firm, unblemished cauliflower, broken into 12 flowerets
⅓ pound turnip greens, collards, or mustard greens, washed and stemmed

1¼ pound center-cut fresh salmon fillet, cut crosswise into four 1-inch-thick portions, about 5 ounces each, preferably Atlantic or King salmon
4 tablespoons unsalted butter
½ teaspoon coarse sea salt
1 teaspoon snipped chives

1. Make the chive oil by combining the chives, salt, and the oil in a blender jar and whirling until the mixture is smooth. Pour it into a clean jar, cover tightly, and refrigerate. It keeps up to two weeks. Return the oil to room temperature before using.

2. Bring a pot of salted water to a boil. Add the cauliflower and cook it until just tender, about 5 minutes. Remove it from the water, using a slotted spoon, and transfer it to a side dish. Add the greens to the boiling water and blanch for 2 minutes; drain and refresh under cold water. Cook the greens, covered, in a small saucepan with ¼ cup of lightly salted boiling water until they are almost tender, about 10 minutes (less for young leaves). Add the greens to the cauliflower, cover with plastic film, and set aside. (*Up to this point the recipe can be prepared in advance.*)

3. Position one rack in the lower third of the oven and a second rack in the upper third. Preheat the oven to 225° F. Carefully place a skillet of boiling water on the lower oven shelf. Arrange the salmon pieces on a metal baking sheet, and place on the upper rack. Bake for 10 minutes. Turn the salmon over and cook 1 minute longer. (Note that the color of the salmon will not turn dull and the texture will be very juicy.) Sprinkle it with salt and pepper to taste.

4. Meanwhile, in a large skillet, melt the butter over medium high heat, add the cauliflower and greens, and sauté them, tossing, until hot. Correct the seasoning and arrange the vegetables in clumps on a large serving platter. Add 3 tablespoons of water to the skillet and boil quickly to combine it with the buttery juices. Pour them over the vegetables and drizzle about 2 tablespoons of the chive oil over the juices that fall onto the platter. Place the warm salmon in the center, over the juices, and sprinkle with a mixture of coarse sea salt and chopped fresh chives.

AN UNUSUAL COULIBIAC

Fresh and Smoked Salmon with "Vesiga" in Brioche

SERVES 8 TO 10

I rarely wrap food in pastry anymore, but this *coulibiac* is too good to abandon. The ingredients for a classic *coulibiac*—brioche, cubes of fresh salmon, thin-sliced mushrooms, dill-flavored rice, hard-cooked eggs, herb-tinged crêpes, and gelatinous *vesiga* (the spine marrow of sturgeon)—probably should not be tampered with, *unless* you have found a wonderful new version that is light and delicious.

When I was making a survey of New York caterers for *New York Magazine*, I met an immigrant family from the Soviet Union, who invited me to a Russian Easter party that featured their version of *coulibiac*. It was filled with whitefish, onions, and mushrooms, and what seemed like more *vesiga* than I'd ever seen in my life. I was amazed: *vesiga* is almost unobtainable in American fishmarkets, and yet the huge amount in their *coulibiac* made it exceptionally light. In fact, as it turned out, there was no *vesiga* in the dish. The Russians had ingeniously substituted Chinese cellophane noodles (bean threads), which have the same texture—a substitution only an expert would suspect.

The addition of smoked salmon, though not traditional, adds an extra dimension, and the seasoning of black pepper and dill is perfect.

Serve with drawn butter, sour cream, or accompanied by a rich chicken broth.

1¼ *pounds brioche dough (page 333), chilled*

2 *ounces (½ package) cellophane noodles*

1 *small bunch (about ½ cup) fresh dill, snipped fine*

Salt and freshly ground pepper

3 *medium onions, roughly chopped*

8 *tablespoons unsalted butter*

12 *ounces fresh salmon, or whitefish, or a combination*

½ *pound fresh mushrooms, quartered if very large*

Juice of ½ lemon

¼ *cup raw rice*

2 *ounces smoked salmon, sliced paper-thin*

Egg glaze (1 egg beaten with 1 teaspoon cold water)

¼ *cup fine breadcrumbs*

1. One day in advance make the brioche dough.

2. The following day, cut the cellophane noodles (see note below) into 2-inch lengths. Cover them with boiling water and soak for 15 minutes; drain. Mix them with dill, ½ teaspoon salt and ¼ teaspoon pepper. Meanwhile, in a skillet over medium heat, soften the

onions in 6 tablespoons of the butter without browning. Mix with the drained noodles and set aside.

3. Skin, bone, and cube the fish; season it with salt and pepper. Set the fish aside. In another skillet, quickly sauté the mushrooms in 2 to 3 tablespoons of the butter without letting them exude their juices. Season with salt, pepper, and lemon juice. Cover the rice with cold water, bring to a boil, add salt, and cook for 10 minutes; drain well. Allow all the cooked food to cool completely.

4. About 2 hours before serving, cut the smoked salmon into 1-inch-wide strips; season it with pepper. Butter a large heavy baking sheet. Roll out the chilled dough on a floured surface to a 10-by-15-inch rectangle. Brush the entire surface with egg glaze. Make an even, narrow layer of the noodle mixture lengthwise down the middle. Arrange the fish cubes close together on top. Press so that the filling forms a compact log. Pack the mushrooms and rice on top. Lay strips of smoked salmon crosswise over the top.

5. Stretch the brioche dough gently, bring up the sides, and overlap them slightly to enclose the filling. Pinch the short ends together. Press the length of the dough to set it firmly against the filling within. Extend the short ends, brush them with glaze, fold them up, and press to seal. Turn the roll over onto the baking sheet, seam side down. Make a "chimney" for escaping steam (see notes below). Let the roll rise away from drafts for 45 minutes (it will rise very little).

6. Preheat the oven to 425° F.

7. Brush the roll with egg glaze and sprinkle evenly with breadcrumbs. Bake it on the lower-middle shelf for 15 minutes. Lower the heat to 300° F and bake 25 minutes longer.

8. Serve the *coulibiac* warm in 1-inch slices with one of the accompaniments mentioned above.

If cellophane noodles are too difficult to cut when dry, cut them after soaking. A filled brioche will often rise unevenly in the oven owing to pockets of steam building up inside. Before setting it aside for rising, make a small hole (¼ inch) in the middle of the top of the *coulibiac*. Set a thin pastry tube or foil tube in the hole to let the steam escape. If you notice any section of the *coulibiac* puffing unevenly during baking, poke a skewer into the dough to allow steam to escape.

Mussel-Celery-Root Salad with Potato Aïoli

SERVES 4 TO 6

Here's a delicious Provençal variation on that old bistro stand-by, celery-root rémoulade. Freshly cooked small mussels are tossed with shredded celery root, enrobed in an *aïoli* made with puréed potato and garlic, then left to mellow for a couple of hours. Garnish with green beans, tomatoes, and anchovies and you'll have a wonderful lunch.

I use the cooking liquor from the mussels as the medium in which to cook the potato, which in turn I use in place of egg yolks in the *aïoli*. If you make your *aïoli* by hand instead of in the food processor, you'll find that the potato can absorb a great deal of oil, and that your mayonnaise will be especially light and delicate. To make the dish even more substantial, you can serve it with fresh fennel bulbs, sliced thin and flavored with a lemony vinaigrette.

2 *pounds (about 40) fresh small mussels*

½ *cup dry white wine*

¾ *cup fruity olive oil*

   Salt and freshly ground pepper

   Bouquet garni of 3 sprigs parsley, 1 sprig thyme, bay leaf, and 3 sprigs celery

4 *garlic cloves*

1 *shallot, peeled and sliced*

1 *pinch saffron threads, crumbled*

½ *cup dry white wine*

3 *tablespoons mixed chopped herbs: chives, parsley, tarragon*

8 *to 9 tablespoons fresh lemon juice*

1 *large (about ⅓ pound) waxy potato*

1 *medium-large celery root, weighing about 1¾ pounds*

1 *large carrot*

   Cayenne pepper

½ *tablespoon Dijon mustard*

1 *scallion, sliced thin*

GARNISH

2 *or 3 scallions with 1-inch green leaves, sliced thin*

1. Pick over and discard any mussels that are cracked. Wash the mussels under running water, scrub them with a strong brush, and use a small knife to remove their beards. Soak the mussels in cold water for 15 minutes (see note below).

2. Meanwhile, in a skillet or other wide pan combine the white wine, ¼ cup of water, 1 tablespoon of the olive oil, pepper, the bouquet garni, 1 garlic clove, the shallot, and saffron. Simmer 10 minutes to blend the flavors and remove some of the wine's acidity.

Add the drained mussels, raise the heat, cover, and steam open the mussels. Remove the mussels from the skillet; discard the shells, but reserve the cooking liquor. In a mixing bowl toss the mussels with salt, pepper, 2 tablespoons of the chopped herbs, and the 2 tablespoons lemon juice, cover the bowl with plastic film and refrigerate. Makes about 1½ cups.

3. Strain the cooking liquor into a deep small saucepan. Add 2 cups of water and ½ teaspoon of salt and bring the mixture to a boil. Pare the potato, add it to the cooking liquor, and cook at a simmer until it is fork-tender. Remove the potato; drain, then crush with a fork to make ½ cup of puréed potato. Reserve 1 cup of the warm mussel broth.

4. Meanwhile, bring to a boil a pot of water with 4 tablespoons lemon juice. Peel the celery root and carrot. Separately shred the two vegetables, using the finest grating-disk attachment of a food processor. Place the celery root in a sieve; drop it into the boiling water and cook for 30 seconds. Drain, rinse, and leave it to dry on a kitchen towel.

5. Make the *aïoli:* Cut the remaining garlic cloves in half lengthwise, remove the green shoots (see notes below), and peel. Crush them with a pinch of salt in a heavy mortar or bowl until smooth. Add the warm potato purée to the bowl; pound until smooth and elastic. Add the mustard, cayenne, and 2 tablespoons lemon juice. Gradually work in the remaining olive oil. Switch to a whisk and beat in the reserved warm mussel broth, a tablespoon at a time. The *aïoli* should be very smooth and medium thick (if it breaks, place a whole egg in the workbowl of a food processor, add 2 tablespoons of the mixture, and whirl to combine; slowly add the remaining *aïoli*).

6. Mix the mussels with a few tablespoons of the potato *aïoli*, correct the seasoning, adding lemon juice to taste. In a bowl combine the celery root and carrots with the remaining *aïoli*, mixing well. Correct the seasoning. Fold in the mussels and let the mixture stand 1 hour before serving.

7. At serving time, sprinkle the dish with scallions and the remaining chopped herbs.

NOTES TO THE COOK

This recipe is best made in the fall or early winter when celery roots are young and garlic is beginning to ripen. If your garlic has sprouted, be sure to remove the shoots before making the *aïoli*. (They are said to be the cause of indigestion.)

Many mussel farms are selling these mollusks already cleaned and soaked. To repeat the soaking may result in loss of flavor. Consult your fishmonger.

When choosing mussels be sure that they are tightly closed. Avoid any that are extra-heavy, as they are probably filled with mud. If a mussel "yawns" and then refuses to close a minute or two after being tapped with another mussel, gently poke its flesh with the point of a knife. If it still doesn't shut, discard it—most likely it is dead. To clean mussels, see page 93.

(L'Eclade)

Mussels Steamed Under Pine Needles

SERVES 4

Among the oldest, most interesting and delicious ways of preparing mussels out-of-doors is *l'eclade*, a culinary tour de force of the Charente-Maritime.

The mussels, still in their shells, are arranged hinge side up on a flat wet wooden plank. Dried pine needles are piled on top and set aflame. The heat of the fire cooks the mussels, which, because of the way they are propped up, reabsorb their juices, instead of opening and pouring them out. After the fire burns out, the ashes are brushed off, and then the mussels are pulled out and eaten with one's fingers. (Be prepared with lots of napkins.) You can cook mussels this way in a fireplace equipped with a screen.

A wooden board about 18 inches square or a shallow roasting pan.

3 quarts (about 4 pounds) small mussels, cleaned and debearded

1 bucket dried pine needles or enough to cover all the mussels by about 4 to 5 inches

Thin slices of buttered French bread

1. If cooking out-of-doors, soak the wooden board in water for 15 minutes, then set it steadily on a bed of sand or in a barbecue area sheltered from any wind.

2. On the board or a shallow roasting pan, starting in the center arrange 4 mussels, hinge and pointed side up, propping them so that they support one another. Continue to place mussels in a circle, each resting slightly on the inner circle *always with the hinge side up and outward.* Top with a thick-packed dome of dried pine needles. Set the dome aflame. The flames will die out in about 5 minutes. Sweep away cinders with a piece of cardboard. Serve at once directly from the board or pan with buttered bread.

NOTES TO
THE COOK

Since the mussels are cooked in their shells there is no contamination by resinous material. Be sure the pine needles are absolutely bone dry, and do *not* substitute other dried evergreens.

Tagine of Mussels with Coriander and Spices

One variant of the Moroccan sauce *charmoula* includes tomatoes and goes beautifully with fish and shellfish, as in this very easy *tagine* of fresh mussels. In this dish the mussels are deliberately over-cooked at low temperature in earthenware to achieve a certain melding of components. When you overcook mussels they pass through stages of toughness and then become soft again. Serve with wedges of Moroccan Anise-Flavored Bread.

3 quarts (4½ pounds) fresh mussels, scrubbed and debearded

CHARMOULA WITH TOMATO

2 cloves garlic, peeled, halved, green shoot removed, and crushed with 1 teaspoon salt in a mortar or blender until a purée

⅓ cup torn-up leaves of fresh coriander

⅓ cup torn-up leaves of Italian flat-leaf parsley

¾ teaspoon ground cumin

¾ teaspoon sweet paprika

⅛ teaspoon cayenne pepper

2 teaspoons tomato paste

¼ cup fruity olive oil

2 teaspoons cider vinegar

2 tablespoons fresh lemon juice (optional)

Sea salt (optional)

1. Early in the day clean the mussels. In a large skillet combine the mussels with 1 cup of water. Cover the skillet and bring the mussels to a boil over high heat. Steam the mussels for about 3 minutes, or until they just open. Drain them, reserving the broth for some other purpose. Remove the shells and discard them.

2. To make the *charmoula,* combine the crushed garlic, herbs, and ⅓ cup of water in a blender. Blend until smooth, about 1 minute; pour the mixture into a medium noncorrodible saucepan. Stir in the cumin, paprika, cayenne, tomato paste, olive oil, vinegar, and ½ cup of water. Cook over moderate heat, partially covered, for 5 minutes.

3. Add the mussels and lemon juice to the sauce. Simmer the mixture over low heat for 20 minutes. Remove it from the heat and let it stand for about 30 minutes, so that the mussels will absorb the flavors. Just before serving, reheat gently. Adjust the seasoning, if necessary, with salt and lemon juice to taste.

Mussel Brochettes with Fennel-Seed Oil

SERVES 6

The flavors of mussels and fennel are perfectly and deliciously complementary, as in this Provençal dish, which is similar in concept to angels on horseback (oysters wrapped in bacon and grilled). Here large mussels are steamed, wrapped in bacon, then grilled over an open fire (or under the broiler). The resulting brochette is crisp on the outside and soft and juicy within. As the mussels grill, the small fennel seeds fall into the embers, burn, and release their perfume, which then permeates the mussels.

In this recipe fine, dry breadcrumbs stick firmly to the shellfish and, because no eggs are used in the coating, they do not become soggy, even if they are prepared hours in advance. Remember that the oil must be at the cool, congealing state before being applied to the mussels.

I prefer a Sicilian method of skewering. For each brochette use two thin skewers facing in the same direction, set 1 inch apart. This enables the mussels to lie flat on the grill and to be turned with ease.

I often use fennel-scented olive oil over grilled fish and to cook spinach, as well as in preparing these brochettes. Prepare the mixture at least a few hours before using. This scented oil will keep for weeks in a cool, dark place.

2 *dozen very large fresh mussels*

1 *sprig celery leaves*

1 *bay leaf*

  Freshly ground pepper and a pinch of salt

8 *strips of thin bacon*

⅓ *cup fine breadcrumbs*

¼ *cup fennel-seed oil (1 teaspoon fennel seeds, lightly crushed and macerated in ¼ cup extra-virgin olive oil)*

  Lemon quarters

1. Early in the day clean the mussels. In a large skillet, combine the mussels with the celery, bay leaf, and 1 cup of water. Cover the skillet and bring the mussels to a boil over high heat. Steam the mussels until they just open. Drain them, reserving the broth for some other purpose. Remove the shells and discard. Cut away the black-brown "rubber" band around each of them. Season lightly with pepper and a pinch of salt.

2. Cut each bacon slice crosswise into 3 equal pieces. Wrap each mussel in bacon and arrange them on skewers as directed above. Choose a shallow dish just large enough to contain all the skewers in one layer. Pour 3 tablespoons of the fennel-seed oil over them, turn to coat evenly, then cover with plastic wrap and refrigerate.

3. When the mussels are cold and the oil has congealed around them, take them out of the dish and coat them all over with the breadcrumbs. Reserve the oil. Straddle the

brochettes over a small bowl so the breadcrumbs will set. (*The recipe can be prepared up to this point many hours in advance.* Cover with plastic wrap and refrigerate.)

4. Drizzle the remaining fennel-seed oil over the brochettes and grill them over medium-hot embers or under the broiler, about 2 minutes to a side or until the bacon is crisp and brown. There is no need to baste because the bacon bastes them as they cook. Serve hot with lemon wedges.

For this dish choose large, plump mussels—small ones will dry out during the cooking. Keep the preliminary cooking time short, because the mussels will cook again when grilled. NOTE TO THE COOK

SERVES 2

Suquet of Shrimp with Toasted Almond Sauce

Suquets are fish stews popular on the Costa Brava. They can be extremely simple—prepared with anchovies, sardines, or whatever the fisherman has on hand, along with potatoes and peas—or, as in this recipe, extremely elegant.

The traditional first step in making a *suquet* is to prepare a *sofrito* of onion and tomato slowly cooked in olive oil until all their moisture has evaporated and only their intense, blended flavors remain. Then the fish is added, then a little broth, and finally a *picada* of toasted almonds, parsley, and garlic.

This is a variation on a family recipe from the town of Arenys de Mar near Barcelona. Here the Catalans make their *suquets* in a special pan whose indented bottom enables the dish to cook with a minimum amount of oil. A Chinese wok is a good substitute. To keep the flavor of the shrimp fresh, they are sautéed and tossed in a hot wok very quickly, so that the cooking will be even and the shrimps will stay moist.

If properly made, a *suquet* will contain only a small amount of liquid. Serve immediately upon completion on heated plates along with "fried" rice (recipe below) seasoned with ground white pepper and grated nutmeg. For a first course I would choose a refreshing dish like Pulled Parsley Salad with Black Olives or Smoked Salmon and Mixed Melon. Nothing could be better for dessert than a creamy vanilla ice cream topped with warm chestnut honey, and some bakery cookies.

(continued)

12 large shrimps, unshelled	Pinch of ground cinnamon
1 small piece dried chili pepper, the size of a pinkie nail	2 tablespoons Cognac
	Pinch of sugar (optional)
1 tablespoon extra-virgin olive oil	5 toasted almonds pounded to a paste
Salt and freshly ground pepper	¼ teaspoon chopped garlic
2 tablespoons fine-chopped onion	1 teaspoon chopped parsley
½ cup grated red ripe tomatoes	

1. Shell and devein the shrimp. Make a broth with the shells and 2½ cups of water. Boil them 10 minutes and strain. You should have about 1⅔ cups broth.

2. In a wok or nonstick skillet heat the chili pepper in oil until darkened, remove the pepper and discard. Add the shrimp and a pinch of salt, and sauté, tossing to sear all surfaces and firm the flesh. As soon as they are pink, remove them to a side dish, about 2 minutes.

3. Add the onions and tomatoes to the wok or skillet, reduce the heat to medium-low, and cook, stirring, for 5 minutes. Then add ¼ cup of the shrimp-shell broth, cinnamon, and Cognac, and cook at a simmer for 1 more minute. Add salt and pepper, and if necessary a pinch of sugar to balance the acidity.

4. Make a *picada* in a mortar: Pound the almonds until they are oily and smooth, add the garlic and parsley and pound until a smooth paste forms. (This can be done in a food processor, but add 2 tablespoons of the sauce with the almonds to help them form a paste.) Scrape the almond mixture into the sauce and cook 30 seconds longer, stirring. Put the shrimps in the sauce to finish their cooking. Allow the mixture to sit for 5 minutes before serving, then quickly reheat and serve hot with Fried Rice.

To Prepare Fried Rice

Fry ½ cup of rice in 1½ tablespoons olive oil in an 8-inch skillet, stirring until all the grains are coated and lightly fried, about 9 minutes. Add enough shrimp-shell broth to cover by 1 inch. And salt, nutmeg, and white pepper to taste. Stir once. Cook the rice, uncovered, over brisk heat until the liquid is absorbed and the rice is tender, about 20 minutes. Rotate and shake the skillet from time to time to cook the rice evenly.

NOTE TO THE COOK   Almonds can be toasted, pounded, and then stored in an airtight container until needed.

SQUID AND CUTTLEFISH
RECIPES

Roast Squid

Here is an Adriatic recipe that offers an unusual, delicious, and easy way to serve squid. You must buy very fresh squid with their skins on (they should be glistening pink-purple). Have your fishmonger empty the pouches, but ask him to leave on the outer mottled skin, which will help keep the flesh firm and straight during cooking.

When roasted, the squid will be tender inside and crispy outside, well glazed with a small quantity of pan juices. Serve with a green salad (as the restaurant Felidia in New York does), or use to garnish a bouillabaisse or Sicilian couscous.

8 *to 12 medium-sized squid*	*Salt and freshly ground pepper*
4 *tablespoons olive oil*	3 *garlic cloves, peeled and quartered*

1. Place the oven rack in the highest position. Preheat the oven to 425° F. Wash the squid under cold running water. Do not peel off the outer mottled skin. Remove the tentacles and reserve. Discard the entrails, thin bone, beak, and ink sac, if the fishmonger has not done this for you. Wash the body and tentacles carefully. The insides of the emptied pouches should be scraped clean with a ridged spoon (grapefruit) to be sure there are no viscera remaining. Drain dry.

2. Arrange the squid (bodies and tentacles) in a single layer, with the side fins spread out, on an oiled baking sheet. Sprinkle them with the olive oil, salt, and pepper. Scatter the garlic around the squid. Cover the pan tightly with foil and bake in the oven for 10 minutes.

3. Remove and discard the foil. Prick the squid pouches on both sides with a fork. Roast the squid, uncovered, basting once or twice with the pan juices, for 15 minutes, or until they are glazed and just tender. Serve hot.

Squid Stew with Spring Vegetables

SERVES 4

This stew of braised squid and tender spring vegetables bound with a sauce of black ink, bitter chocolate, and black Muscat wine is adapted from a recipe of the late Josep Mercader, the father of modern Catalan cuisine. Of all the squid-ink recipes in this book it is the most time-consuming. But it is also, I believe, the most rewarding on account of the harmonious quality of its sauce, the intricate play between the bitterness of the chocolate and the sweetness of the wine.

Make this dish ahead and reheat gently. Serve it in a shallow earthenware pot for a rustic presentation.

1½ to 2 pounds fresh or defrosted squid or cuttlefish, ink sacs reserved

4 cups Squid or Cuttlefish Stock (see Appendix, page 350)

⅓ cup black Muscat wine (Muscatel)

2 tablespoons olive oil

1¼ cups chopped onions

1 teaspoon chopped garlic clove

2 teaspoons chopped fresh parsley

1 large tomato, peeled, seeded, and chopped (⅓ cup)

Salt and freshly ground white pepper to taste

4 small carrots, scraped and cut into ¾-inch cubes

3 small turnips, peeled and cut into ¾-inch cubes

1 cup tiny white onions, blanched 2 minutes in boiling water, then peeled and roots trimmed

2 large artichoke bottoms, blanched in boiling water for 2 minutes, refreshed, and cubed

1 bunch asparagus, peeled and cut into ¾-inch lengths

½ cup tiny peas

FLAVORING AND THICKENING PASTE (PICADA)

1 garlic clove, peeled and sliced

10 almonds, blanched and toasted golden brown in the oven

¼ ounce grated bitter chocolate, about 1½ teaspoons

10 pinenuts (pignoli)

2 tablespoons black Muscat wine

6 drops anisette

Salt and freshly ground white pepper

2 sprigs fresh flat-leaf parsley

1 shortbread cookie, such as a Lorna Doone

Slices of oven-roasted Italian bread rounds rubbed with garlic

1. Early in the day, clean the squid or cuttlefish as directed in the Appendix, page 349. Cut the pouches and fins into bite-size pieces, rinse them and drain. Cut the tentacles

into dice. Prepare the squid stock with the squid trimmings and the diced tentacles. Cook it over medium heat for 30 minutes and strain. (Save the tentacles for salad or some other purpose.) Press the ink sacs through a strainer into a small bowl, add 1 tablespoon of the wine, cover and (for darkest color) refrigerate at least 1 hour before using.

2. Heat the olive oil and 3 tablespoons of water in a wide earthenware or enameled heavy skillet. Add the chopped onions and cook them over medium heat until soft and golden, about 10 minutes. Add the cut-up squid or cuttlefish, and cook it until the water it produces evaporates. Continue cooking until the pieces begin to turn golden, about 10 minutes. Add the remaining Muscat wine, garlic, parsley, and tomatoes, and cook over high heat, stirring, until wine evaporates, about 2 minutes. Add the strained stock and a pinch of salt, and cook, stirring frequently, for 15 minutes.

3. Add the carrots and turnips and cook 10 minutes, then add the whole onions and artichokes and continue cooking over medium-low heat 10 minutes longer. Add the asparagus and peas and cook until all the vegetables are just tender and the cooking liquid has thickened slightly, about 5 minutes longer.

4. Meanwhile combine the ingredients for the *picada* paste in a blender jar or the workbowl of a food processor. Grind them fine, then add the reserved ink and Muscat wine and whirl until very smooth. Stir the paste into the sauce and simmer for 5 minutes. Allow the dish to rest at least 30 minutes in a cool place (not the refrigerator) to allow the flavors to blend. Reheat the dish slowly and serve with warm slices of bread rounds that have been brushed with olive oil and roasted in a hot oven until golden brown, then rubbed with garlic.

NOTE TO THE COOK

As the wine, I use the California Elysium (black Muscat) by Quady, also delicious with cheese and fruit. Other Muscat wines can be substituted.

Braised Squid with Wild Greens

SERVES 4

This dish is unique to the Ionian island of Cephalonia, where in spring and early summer the women often gather bitter greens for cooking. Wild mustard, broccoli rabe, radish tops, and arugula all make good foils for the sweetness of cooked squid or cuttlefish. This dish is at its best with a slab of good (soft and not too salty) imported feta cheese, and ribbon noodles made with eggs and semolina flour, and tossed with olive oil. For a first course I would present a few small, light, and refreshing dishes (*mezethes*): Kalamata olives sprinkled with Mediterranean oregano; pickled peppers; a bowl of fresh sea urchin roe; fried rounds of zucchini with a dollop of yogurt, and a basket of crusty bread. The Caramel and Coconut Cake from Ohrid would be an ideal ending to the meal.

2 *pounds squid or cuttlefish, ink sacs reserved*

1 *can* calamares en su tinta *(see Appendix, page 339)*

6 *tablespoons olive oil*

1½ *cups thin-sliced onions*

½ *cup dry white wine*

1 *garlic clove, peeled and lightly crushed*

Salt and freshly ground pepper

1 *tablespoon lemon juice*

1 *pound (2 bunches) broccoli rabe, thick stalks discarded, leaves and buds roughly chopped, or substitute dandelion or mustard greens*

½ *pound high-quality feta cheese, cubed*

1. Early in the day, clean the squid or cuttlefish as described in the Appendix, page 349. Cut the pouches, fins, and tentacles into bite-size pieces. Rinse them and drain well; keep refrigerated. Carefully place all the long, silvery ink sacs in a small bowl; crush them with the back of a wooden spoon. Open a can of *calamares en su tinta,* spoon off the surface oil, wrap the solids in cheesecloth, and squeeze to extract the liquid. Add it to the bowl and add 1 tablespoon of water to make about 3 tablespoons of ink. Cover it and keep refrigerated at least 1 hour for best color. Place the solids in a saucepan, cover with 2 cups water, and simmer for 30 minutes. Strain and reduce to 1 cup.

2. Heat 2 tablespoons of the oil and ¼ cup of water in a 9-inch heavy skillet; add the onions and cook over medium-low heat until soft and golden, about 10 minutes. Add the squid or cuttlefish and cook until the water produced evaporates, then cook until the pieces begin to turn golden, about 8 minutes.

3. Press the ink through a sieve, add it to the wine in a cup. Add the ink, wine, garlic, and reduced stock to the skillet, and season with salt and freshly ground pepper. Simmer, covered, for 30 minutes or until the squid or cuttlefish is tender and the sauce is moderately thick. Remove the garlic. Stir in the lemon juice. (*Up to this point the dish can be prepared many hours in advance.*)

4. Gently reheat the squid or cuttlefish in a large pan. Meanwhile, heat the remaining 4 tablespoons of oil almost to smoking in a large skillet or wok. Over high heat, fry the broccoli rabe leaves and buds for 2 to 3 minutes. Fold the broccoli rabe into the squid or cuttlefish mixture, and continue to cook over low heat for about 5 minutes to blend the flavors and finish the cooking. Readjust the seasoning to taste. Divide the mixture among 4 warmed plates. Scatter cubes of feta cheese on top and serve at once.

SERVES 4 — # Basque Stuffed Squid

At Restaurant Arzak in San Sebastian, this dish is made with small cuttlefish called *chipirones*, each one about 2 inches long. In this country larger domestic squid can be substituted—look for those about 4 or 5 inches long in late spring and early summer.

Basque Stuffed Squid is most dramatic when served in an inky-black sauce that is very garlicky, rich, and flavorful. Use my tip on extracting extra ink from imported tins of *calamares en su tinta* to achieve this special color and taste. Serve with slices of bread roasted in a hot oven until golden brown with a fruity olive oil, then rubbed with garlic. Follow with rhubarb tarts decorated with unsweetened whipped cream and thin ribbons of caramel.

2 *pounds (8) small squid, cleaned and skinned (see Appendix, page 339), ink sacs reserved*

2 *or 3 cans* calamares en su tinta, *or substitute 4 grams extract of "Chipiron" (see Appendix, pages 339, 350)*

2½ *cups Squid or Cuttlefish Stock, strained and reduced to one half (see Appendix, page 350)*

½ *cup olive oil*

1½ *cups chopped onions*

2½ *teaspoons chopped garlic*

1 *small green pepper, stemmed, seeded, membranes removed, and chopped fine*

1 *2-inch stale Italian-style bread, crust removed, soaked in milk, squeezed dry and crumbled*

1 *egg, beaten*
  Salt and freshly ground white pepper
  Cayenne pepper

1 *garlic clove, peeled and left whole*

1 *small green pepper, stemmed, seeded, membranes removed, and fine-sliced*

2 *red-ripe tomatoes, peeled, seeded, and chopped fine*

12 *rounds of oven-roasted Italian bread, rubbed with garlic*

1. Early in the day, rinse and drain the squid. Leave the pouches whole, and chop the tentacles in a food processor. Refrigerate all the squid. Carefully place all the long, silvery

(continued)

ink sacs in a small bowl; crush with the back of a wooden spoon. Open the tins of *calamares en su tinta*, spoon off surface oil, wrap solids in cheesecloth and squeeze to extract liquid, and add to the bowl with 3 tablespoons of water. Cover and keep refrigerated at least 1 hour. Use the solids to make the stock.

2. About 1½ hours before serving, heat 2 tablespoons of the oil in a 9-inch heavy skillet; add half the onions, half the garlic and the chopped green pepper. Cover and cook over low heat for 5 minutes. Add the chopped tentacles, raise the heat to medium high, and sauté, tossing, until all moisture has evaporated, 4 to 5 minutes. Cool completely.

3. Meanwhile, soak the bread in milk, then squeeze out the moisture. Add the bread and beaten egg to the onion-pepper mixture, season with 1 teaspoon of salt, white pepper and cayenne, and stir well to mix. Stuff the mixture into the squid pouches and fasten the openings with toothpicks.

4. Thoroughly dry the pouches, then fry them in the remaining hot oil along with a peeled whole garlic clove in a 10-inch heavy skillet until brown on both sides (this softens the texture and enhances the flavor of the squid). Remove them to a side dish, cover, to keep moist. Remove all but 2 tablespoons of oil, add the remaining onion and garlic, the *sliced* green pepper, the chopped tomatoes, and the ink pressed through a fine sieve, and cook, stirring, until the mixture is thick and just begins to fry. Quickly stir in the stock. Add the pouches, cover with a round of oiled waxed paper and a lid, and simmer them until tender, about 45 minutes.

5. Remove the pouches to a shallow serving dish, cover, and keep hot in a warm oven. Strain the sauce; return it to the skillet and boil down to napping consistency. Adjust the seasoning. Remove the toothpicks. Pour the sauce over the squid, and garnish it with slices of bread fried in oil and rubbed with garlic. Serve at once.

FISH STEWS

Among my favorite winter dinners are fish stews. Any break in the winter weather and I rush out to purchase high-quality fish, and as many heads, bones, and trash fish as possible to make a good *fumet*. When the fish are good and fresh I can fill my winter dining room with Mediterranean light and the aromas of saffron, fennel, and garlic, a special gift to those with whom I love to eat.

SERVES 6

La Chaudrée
(New York Version)

A *chaudrée* is a creamy and sumptuous Charentaise version of bouillabaisse made with Atlantic fish cooked in dry white wine with butter, plenty of garlic, and fresh herbs. The resulting stew is more delicate but just as memorable as the Provençal specialty. The word *chaudrée* comes from *chaudière*, the pot used for the cooking.

Originally the dish was made by fishermen's wives, using a simple mixture of whatever fish could not be sold that day. But almost all the cooks I interviewed agreed that the following fish (or their equivalents) *had* to be included if the soup was to be a true *chaudrée:* delectable and tender cuttlefish (squid can be substituted); firm but very mild skate (deep-sea scallops can be substituted); fine-textured flatfish such as sole; and rich, sweet-tasting eels gathered in brackish (never fresh) water.

The following recipe was inspired by one given to me by Mireille Forgerit of the Restaurant La Gratienne in Mornac-sur-Seudre in the Charente: France's Cognac region. Knowing that many regional dishes do not travel well, I have developed this "New York version," using the fish available in many ethnic city and coastal fish markets.

Early on the day you will serve *chaudrée,* make the stock with the heads and frames of all the fish you plan to use. Allow the stock to cool down completely so that 40 minutes before serving you will be working with a *cool* stock and *cold* fish.

In assembling the *chaudrée* the fish are layered, thick pieces at the bottom, and cooked very slowly, which allows their various textures and tastes to remain distinct. The ideal vessel in which to cook and serve your New York–style *chaudrée* is an earthenware *caquelon*, a wide-mouthed, shallow baking dish with a stout handle, the kind that is often recommended as the proper vessel for a sturdy cabbage soup. Earthenware is ideal for simmering fish; it maintains a steady heat that does not damage the texture, and lengthens the cooking time, which helps to blend flavors. Lacking a *caquelon*, use a deep iron skillet.

(continued)

5½ pounds mixed fish—at least 4
varieties (see note)

1 pound (4 small) squid or cuttlefish

Sea salt

SPECIAL FISH STOCK OF THE
CHARENTE

Heads, bones, and trimmings of the
fish, with gills removed

1 small onion, halved, stuck with 1 clove

1 medium onion, sliced thin

1 medium carrot, sliced thin

1 medium leek, green part only, sliced
thin

2 small ribs celery, sliced thin

3 large shallots, peeled, sliced thin

8 gratings of fresh nutmeg

1 bottle dry white wine, such as
Muscadet

2 cups water

¼ cup white wine vinegar

Bouquet garni: 10 sprigs parsley,
5 sprigs thyme, and 2 bay leaves tied
together

½ cup unsalted AA butter, cold, cut into
¼-inch dice

⅔ cup finely sliced peeled mild garlic,
preferably elephant garlic

Bouquet garni: 5 sprigs parsley,
2 sprigs thyme, and 1 small bay leaf,
tied together

Freshly ground pepper

6 large or 12 small mussels, scrubbed

2 tablespoons heavy cream

1½ tablespoons chopped fresh Italian flat-
leaf parsley

2 tablespoons snipped fresh chives

24 rounds of French or Italian bread,
toasted and rubbed with garlic

Steps 1 and 2 can be done early in the day.

1. Cut the assembled fish and squid or cuttlefish as directed in the notes below.
Sprinkle with sea salt, place all the fish in a deep bowl, cover loosely, and keep refrigerated
until you are ready to cook.

2. Make the Fish Stock: Rinse the heads, bones, and trimmings of fish in cold water;
drain; rinse again, being sure to remove all the gills and any clumps of blood. In a large
saucepan heat all the ingredients to boiling; skim the foam from the surface. Reduce the
heat; simmer, uncovered, for 30 minutes, stirring occasionally. Strain through a sieve lined
with damp cheesecloth. Squeeze the cloth to obtain all the fish juices *but not the solids.*
Rinse out the saucepan; return the strained stock to the pan. By way of boiling, reduce to
3 cups, about 10 minutes. Cool completely before using.

3. About 4 hours before serving, heat one-quarter of the butter in a large saucepan
over medium-low heat. When the foam subsides, stir in the washed squid or cuttlefish.
Cook, stirring occasionally, to prevent sticking, until all the liquid produced has evaporated.
Sauté slowly until the squid begins to turn golden but not brown, about 20 minutes.
Transfer the squid to a side dish. Add the garlic and bouquet garni to the buttery pan
juices and cook over low heat, stirring frequently, for 10 minutes. Do this very carefully

because the garlic and the butter must not burn, but simply turn a beautiful golden color. Return the squid or cuttlefish to the pan, and stir to moisten it. (*The recipe can be prepared to this point up to 3 hours in advance.* Partially cover the pan and set it aside in a cool place.)

4. Forty-five minutes before serving, transfer the squid with the pan juices to a deep 3-quart heatproof serving dish, preferably an earthenware dish, set over a flame tamer. Reserve the garlic and the bouquet garni.

5. Arrange the thickest pieces of fish, such as skate, tilefish, monkfish, and eel on top of the squid; scatter some of the reserved garlic over the fish. Continue layering fish and garlic, saving the thinnest pieces of fish for the top layer. Pour cool stock over the fish. Sprinkle generously with pepper. Add reserved bouquet garni.

6. Heat the pan, partially covered, over very low heat. Do not allow the liquid to boil. After cooking about 20 minutes, add the mussels. Cook until the top fish turn milky white and are firm to the touch and mussels have opened, 10 to 15 minutes. (The liquid must never boil or the fish will break apart.) Ideally the temperature of the liquid should never exceed 175° F. (See page 113 for explanation of why I like to cook fish very slowly.)

7. Immediately add the remaining diced butter, the cream, and the herbs. Swirl to blend in butter and slightly thicken the juices. Season with salt and pepper to taste. Serve directly from the pan with garlic croutons.

Buying the fish: The more types of very fresh fish you use the more flavorful will be your *chaudrée*. Among the varieties recommended are skate, red snapper, monkfish, tilefish, haddock, porgy, sea robin, perch, eel, cod, weever, halibut, flounder, grouper, and any type of bass, especially sea bass. Buy the fish whole and have them gutted and scaled but not skinned. (It is easier to determine the freshness of fish when whole.) Keep the carcasses and heads for the fish stock. Rinse fish as soon as you bring them home, cut into 2-inch pieces.

Handling skate: Scrub the wings with coarse salt to remove slime. Soak in boiling water for 30 seconds. Drain and pull off all the skin. Cut the wings into strips about 1½ inches wide, cutting through the bone crosswise. Cut these strips into squares. (The faint smell of ammonia will disappear when the fish is cooked.) Soak in cold salted water in the refrigerator until ready to use.

Handling eel: Have the fishmonger kill the eel on the day it is to be served (it spoils very quickly after it is killed). Skin the eel and cut it into 2-inch pieces. Rub them with salt and pepper and let stand 1 hour before using. If you catch your own eels, kill them and skin by grasping the head in a kitchen towel and making one continuous circular slit about 1 inch below the gills. Use a pair of pliers to tug away the skin. Discard the head.

Squid and cuttlefish: See Appendix, pages 349 to 350.

NOTES TO
THE COOK

Mixed Fish Baked with Braised Leeks

SERVES 6

The combination of silky, soft leeks and assorted fresh fish is famous all along the western coast of France. What makes this recipe special is the addition of Pineau de Charentes, an apéritif from France's Cognac region made with Cognac and sweet unfermented grape juice. (Pineau goes beautifully with all seafood, ham, poultry, and desserts.) Here its strong sweet taste is balanced by a hint of green peppercorns.

I usually don't recommend the purchase of fish fillets, since they lose their flavor much faster than fish sold whole. My preference is to buy fish whole and then have the fishmonger fillet them before my eyes. (Wrap the cleaned heads and trimmings in thick airtight packages. Save for soup or stock.)

Serve with Potatoes Baked in Sea Salt and a young Muscadet.

8 medium-sized (3 pounds) leeks	1 teaspoon green peppercorns, rinsed and crushed
10 tablespoons unsalted butter	
Sea salt and freshly ground pepper	6 large sea scallops
½ cup dry white wine	6 medium-sized mussels, picked over, cleaned, and soaked ½ hour in salted icy water
½ cup Pineau de Charentes	
½ pound unskinned fillets of red snapper	
½ pound unskinned fillets of bass	1 tablespoon fresh minced herbs: parsley, tarragon, and chives
½ pound skinned fillets of sole	
½ cup crème fraîche	

1. Trim the leek root ends, then remove almost all but 1 inch of the green leaves. Cut each leek crosswise into 3 equal parts. Wash and drain. In a deep, heavy saucepan heat the butter, add the leeks, season with salt and pepper, cover, and cook over medium heat for 45 minutes to 1 hour, stirring often. The leeks and butter should just turn golden. (Leeks cooked in the microwave are sensational. Cook on high in a covered dish. Timing depends upon oven power.)

2. Add the wine and Pineau de Charentes and bring them to a boil on top of the stove. Simmer 5 minutes. (*The leeks can be prepared 1 day in advance.* Cover them when cool and refrigerate. Bring back to room temperature before proceeding.)

3. Thirty minutes before serving, preheat the oven to 425° F.

4. Spread the leeks and the cooking juices on the bottom of a deep heatproof serving dish, such as a 2½-quart soufflé dish. Curl the fish (see note below) and nestle each fillet

in the bed of leeks. Cover the dish with a circle of parchment and a lid, and set it in a water bath of boiling water. Bake 10 minutes. Meanwhile, heat the cream in a small saucepan with the green peppercorns; keep it hot.

5. Remove the dish from the oven, add the scallops and mussels, cover, and return the dish to the oven to bake 10 minutes longer, or until the fish is just cooked. The fish is cooked when milky-white and still firm to the touch. Remove cover. Pour the cream over and sprinkle on the herbs. Grasp the dish with oven mitts and swirl it to blend in the cream and herbs. Taste for seasoning and serve at once.

Sprinkle the fish with a small amount of sea salt as soon as you bring them home. Cover them loosely and keep refrigerated until you are ready to cook. **NOTES TO THE COOK**

Since fish fillets usually curl up as they cook, I suggest that you curl them yourself, then set them into a bed of cooked leeks arranged side by side. The presentation is attractive and portions are easy to lift and serve. Some fish, such as snapper and bass, are best turned skin-side out, while flat-fish fillets of sole are skinned and curled skin-side in.

Adapted from a recipe by Serge Coulons of La Rochelle.

BOUILLABAISSE

Alice Waters, of the Berkeley restaurant Chez Panisse, gave me the name of an old friend in Bandol. "Lulu makes the best bouillabaisse I've ever eaten. Of course you won't be able to send your readers to her, but still you should watch her cook."

Lulu (who has asked that I not give her full name) is the owner of an important vineyard situated on the sun-drenched slopes between Bandol and Le Castelet. A small, lively, confident woman, she has each autumn prepared a great banquet of bouillabaisse to celebrate the final day of the grape harvest. She offered to duplicate this banquet for me on a much smaller scale; I would help her cook, and then my husband and I would eat the dish with her *en famille*.

I met her in the market in Bandol, where she chose the fish and the vegetables. Back in her kitchen, with its open hearth and hanging pots, she cleaned and marinated the fish, then prepared the fish bouillon. Soon she had me working, too, making the *rouille*. I crushed garlic and salt with an olive-wood pestle against the sides of a marble mortar, added red pepper and saffron, and then, at her instruction, thickened the mixture with a slice of bread and the poached livers and roes she had removed earlier from certain of the fish. Finally, very slowly I added extra-virgin olive oil, stirring all the while.

As noon approached other members of the family turned up, each going about his task. Lulu's son, François, built a fire of olive wood and vine cuttings in a sheltered area of the garden. His wife, Paule, set the long garden table, then collected wildflower bouquets. When everything was ready, a large old copper cauldron, black on its exterior but shiny within, was filled with the fish bouillon and set over the fire.

As the bouillon began to boil, Lulu added the herbs and vegetables and a bunch of dried fennel sticks to the pot. Then at precisely defined intervals, depending on how long each ingredient would take to cook, she added sliced potatoes, crabs, and mussels, then thick slices of fish, and then thinner ones, and finally the saffron. "I feel like a painter," she said, smiling, "altering the color to suit my eye."

While the bouillabaisse cooked and Lulu skimmed the pot, an old dog slept in the sun, a proud calico cat wandered by, and we stood around sipping wine, wearing straw hats to shield us from the sun. Soon the stew was ready. We filled our bowls, the fish and mussels and crabs were set in the center of the table on a great cork platter, and we began to eat.

I must set the scene further to convey the special quality of that meal. In the foreground was the rambling old house and a spreading chestnut tree. From the edge of the lawn, vineyards spread out to carpet all the slopes and valleys around. High up in the distance stood the old walled town of Le Beausset.

The bouillabaisse ("a dish of discovery," Lulu says) was one of the very best I had ever eaten. Not only were the fish superb; so were the vegetables with which they'd been cooked. The liquid had become a harmony of fish and vegetable juices, accented with fennel and pepper, and although plenty of fine olive oil had been used there was nothing oily about the bouillon. Only its flavor was discernible in the bouillon.

During our luncheon there was much talk about bouillabaisse. "There are not enough fish in the Mediterranean to feed everyone who wants to eat this dish," François said.

"When you eat bouillabaisse you can't talk about it," protested Paule. "You're too busy picking little fishbones from between your teeth."

As we devoured this bouillabaisse I was suddenly suffused with a sense of what the dish was all about: a way of life in which fish and vegetables and herbs and smells and wine and vineyards and flowers and the sun and happy people all combine, a crystallization of all the bounty of Provence.

SERVES 8 — "Trashy" Toulon-Style Bouillabaisse

Food and wine writer Richard Olney, who lives in Provence, suggested the name for the following bouillabaisse: "I love the trashy Toulon bouillabaisse," he told me, "full of potatoes and mussels and crabs—which give it a peppery taste."

I don't bother with a first course when I serve my "trashy" Toulon-style bouillabaisse, which encompasses perfectly cooked fish, and shellfish with a good sprinkling of chopped parsley; a platter of bread rounds part-toasted golden in olive oil, rubbed with garlic, and seasoned with a mixture of fine salt, cayenne, and Mediterranean herbs; a *rouille* sauce with tomato, creamy and thick enough to spread over the croutons when they are floated on the stew; and a huge tureen of delicious broth.

After this repast I serve a simple arugula salad, dressed with lemon juice and olive oil, with an assortment of cheeses (Tomme, pecorino with peppercorns [*pepato*], and a St. André). Dessert might consist of store-bought dried Italian almond cookies to be dunked in a glass of chilled Sicilian Malvasia delle Lipari.

The morning of the day you'll serve the bouillabaisse, prepare the soup base (steps 1 through 5), make the bread rounds, make the *rouille* so the raw garlic has a chance to mellow, and marinate the chunks of fish with fennel and saffron, then wrap them in seaweed to give them the aroma and taste of Mediterranean rockfish (fish feed on seaweed near rocks), then refrigerate them until ready to cook.

With all this advance preparation, serving is easy. You must be in the kitchen the final 15 minutes, an action packed 15 minutes of fun and great aromas. When you cook the fish you will reverse the traditional method. Most cooks of bouillabaisse throw the fish into the boiling soup, then wait for the wondrous emulsion to take place. You will simply poach the fish in the simmering soup, and then just before serving, remove the fish and create the emulsion with a hard 3-minute boil.

There are three guidelines that I always follow for a successful bouillabaisse: (1) I use a fruity but light extra-virgin olive oil such as the Ligurian Ranieri for the soup and the *rouille;* (2) I choose spices and herbs carefully. I purchase saffron in thread form rather than powdered (saffron threads

(continued)

are more flavorful and less apt to be old or mixed with safflower strands or other colorings such as cochineal or marigold); and I use dried fennel sticks from Provence rather than a few drops of Pernod to flavor the soup; and (3) I use only the *freshest possible* white-fleshed fish; anything inferior is rejected. Fresh fish, fresh bones, fresh heads all smell sweet—never fishy.

Remember: Each diner need *not* be served a piece of each type of fish. If you try to do this it will take an inordinate amount of time, during which the fish will grow cool.

5 *pounds assorted lean, white-fleshed fish, such as monkfish, tilefish, sea bass, rockfish, red snapper, cod, and halibut, skinned and cut into large serving portions*

1 *cup fruity extra-virgin olive oil*

1 *package (10 grams) dried fennel sticks, bruised (see note)*

1 *tablespoon chopped dill or fresh fennel tops*

½ *teaspoon saffron threads*

1 *handful fresh seaweed, or ¼ cup reconstituted seaweed fronds, rinsed and drained (optional)*

5 *pounds heads, bones, and trimmings from non-oily, white-flesh fish (but not flatfish), or whole small "trash" fish (spot, sea robin, and mullet), cleaned, gills removed, and cut up*

4 *large garlic cloves, lightly crushed*

Coarse sea salt and freshly ground pepper

2 *medium carrots, sliced thin (1 cup)*

1 *large leek, white and 1-inch green part, sliced (1 cup)*

1 *small onion, chopped coarse (⅓ cup)*

1 *large ripe tomato, peeled, seeded, and chopped (½ cup)*

1 *celery rib*

1 *bay leaf*

2 *teaspoons tomato paste*

Pinch of cayenne pepper

6 *to 8 small boiling potatoes*

8 *small live blue crabs (in season)*

12 *large mussels, cleaned*

Snipped Italian flat-leaf parsley, for garnish

2 *French breads, cut into rounds, dried, then browned under the broiler, rubbed with ½ clove of garlic, and sprinkled with pinches of a mixture of fine salt, cayenne, and crumbled Mediterranean oregano*

Sauce rouille (recipe follows)

1. In a large bowl, combine the pieces of fish with 2 tablespoons of the olive oil, a few bruised sticks of fennel, the chopped dill, a pinch of the saffron, and the seaweed, if you have it. Let the fish stand at room temperature for 2 hours, or refrigerate, covered, for up to 6 hours. (For easier handling, make separate piles of thick and thin pieces of fish.)

2. In a large saucepan, kettle, or flameproof casserole, combine the fish heads, bones, and trimmings (or the "trash" fish) with ½ cup of the olive oil, the garlic, and half the remaining fennel sticks. Cook the mixture over low heat, stirring, until aromatic, about 5 minutes. Add ½ teaspoon of salt, a few grindings of black pepper, and 3 quarts of water. Slowly bring the mixture to a boil, reduce the heat, and simmer for 30 minutes, skimming frequently.

3. Strain the stock through a colander set over a large bowl. Discard any large fish heads and the fennel sticks. Let the stock and bones cool.

4. Working in small batches, chop the bones coarse in a food processor. Pour the stock and ground bones back into the rinsed kettle and bring them to a boil over low heat. Simmer 20 minutes longer. Strain the stock through a colander lined with several layers of dampened cheesecloth and set over a large bowl. Measure the fish stock. If there is less than 2½ quarts, add water. If there is more, boil it to reduce.

5. Heat the remaining 6 tablespoons of olive oil in a 7- to 8-quart flameproof casserole. Add the carrots, leek, onions, tomatoes, and a bundle made with the celery, bay leaf, and remaining fennel sticks. Cook the vegetables over moderate heat, stirring occasionally, until aromatic but not browned. Add the fish stock, tomato paste, cayenne, and the remaining saffron. Bring the mixture to a boil, reduce the heat, and simmer for 20 minutes. Strain the soup. (*The soup base can be prepared to this point up to a day in advance.* Let cool, then cover and refrigerate.)

6. Thirty minutes before serving, slowly reheat the soup to a simmer. Meanwhile, peel and slice the potatoes. Using tongs, wash each of the live crabs under cool running water.

7. About 15 minutes before serving, add the potatoes and crabs to the simmering soup and cook over moderate heat for 5 minutes. Add the larger pieces of fish. Cook without boiling for 3 minutes. Then add the remaining fish beginning with the medium-sized pieces of fish. Add the mussels. Cook without boiling until the mussels open and remove them, about 3 minutes. As the pieces of fish become opaque throughout and the potatoes become tender, transfer them to a large heated platter; cover them with foil to keep warm. Remove the crabs. When all the fish and shellfish have been removed, bring the soup to a rolling boil and reduce it to a good consistency, about 2 quarts. Season with additional salt and black pepper to taste. Pour the soup into a tureen. Garnish the fish and shellfish with snipped parsley. Surround it with the bread rounds. At the table, ladle the broth into soup plates and let the guests help themselves to an assortment of fish and seafood. Pass a bowl of *rouille*.

For the fish stock: I rely on an assortment of very fresh small fish, fish heads, and trimmings from easily available lean white-fleshed fish. Small fish such as whiting, porgy, spot, and sea robin can be used cut up along with miscellaneous heads, frames, and trimmings from larger fish, such as red snapper, tilefish, grouper, sea bass, etc. In different parts of the country different fish are available; consult your fishmonger for substitutes. If he doesn't have fish heads on display, ask for them—they are probably in the back of the store. Have him cut the heads in small pieces for easier handling. They should cost practically nothing and are the key to a tasty, rich fish bouillon. You can collect heads and trimmings yourself, freezing them under thick airtight wrapping and keeping them in the freezer up to a month,

(continued)

until you have built up a good variety. Be sure all blood and the gills are removed before making the stock.

Buying the fish: Remember: there is no "correct" version of this dish; each and every time it will taste different, depending on the types of *very fresh* fish you find in the market. Of course, the more varieties you use the tastier your bouillabaisse will be. Among the best choices are monkfish, wolffish, tilefish, black sea bass, halibut, black drum, red snapper, cod, grouper, porgy, lingcod, ocean perch, and rockfish.

Buy them whole and have them gutted, scaled, skinned, and cut into serving portions. Large fish should be cut into 1¼ inch chunks. There should be about 24 pieces of fish.

When buying crabs look for those that are especially lively. They should not be kept directly on ice but in a moist and cool (40° F) environment with damp shredded newspapers. Too much cold will make them lethargic. Bring them to room temperature before cooking, in order to be sure they are still alive. (Discard if there is no sign of life.) Wash the crab well under running water. They cook in about 15 minutes.

(Sauce Rouille)

MAKES ABOUT 2 ¼ CUPS

Provençal Red-Pepper Sauce

Recently I learned that the mystique that has always surrounded bouillabaisse extends to *sauce rouille* as well. Some versions contain no eggs. In others the garlic is crushed with potatoes, and many people, particularly some cooks, thicken theirs with the livers of certain fish.

In an old French cookbook, a collection of recipes of seventy doctors, a certain Dr. Vincenti of Avignon recounts a complicated tale of a fisherman who loved a girl of a higher social station. Hoping to engage her interest, he produces a truly outstanding bouillabaisse, which he then presents to her on his knees. But she rejects him, and passing by proudly on the arm of a rich man, she tells him to eat his soup alone. Then she throws at his feet, as before a dog, two hot red peppers and the liver of a fish. Hoping to find something good in this brutal rejection, he combines the things she has flung at at him and eats the resulting mixture with his fish. So, it is said, a *rouille* is like the bitter taste of bruised love, while containing, too, the invigorating force of the rupture of an affair, which helps to liberate its diner from old restraints.

4 *large cloves garlic, halved and peeled, green shoots removed*

½ *teaspoon salt*

2 *small dried hot peppers, crumbled*

Pinch of powdered saffron

3 *egg yolks*

4 *teaspoons tomato paste*

3 *slices of toasted French bread, about 3 inches in diameter, cut ½ inch thick, soaked in 3 tablespoons fish stock or water and squeezed dry*

1 *cup fruity extra-virgin olive oil*

¼ *teaspoon freshly ground pepper*

In a mortar or blender jar crush the garlic, salt, and hot peppers until smooth and pasty. Add the saffron and egg yolks, and pound or grind to a paste. Gradually stir in the tomato paste and bread and then the olive oil until the sauce is fluffy and smooth. Adjust the seasoning with pepper and additional salt. Allow it to mellow in a cool place at least 1 hour before serving; do not refrigerate.

Variation Using Fish Livers or Roe

To avoid using any polluted livers, use only those from monkfish, imported *rougets*, and Caribbean goatfish. If these are not available, substitute the fresh roe from flounder or mullet.

(continued)

Rouille is traditionally made in a stout stone mortar and pounded with an olive-wood pestle. If you have one by all means use it, but an electric blender or food processor works just as well (though the texture will be different). The sauce should be thick enough to smear on bread croutons.

CHAPTER 6

POULTRY AND GAME

THREE MOROCCAN CHICKEN TAGINES

I had just entered the kitchen of a home in a New York suburb, but from the blend of aromas that struck me I might as well have been in Fez or Rabat. Six pots containing Moroccan *tagines* or stews were bubbling away on the large range, each emitting its own special and intense bouquet. I detected the slightly bitter scent of saffron, delicate, fragrant cinnamon, rich earthy cuminseed, pungent powdered ginger, licorice-scented anise. . . . The subtle mingling of these spices, the signature of fine Moroccan cooking, was familiar. And so was the cook, Rakia, a short Berber woman with a squat nose and very dark skin.

It had been thirteen years since Rakia and I had worked in a kitchen together, back in Rabat, where she is a famous cook. Now she was visiting a Moroccan diplomat just outside New York City, and I had come to cook with her, and learn from her again. (Years ago in Rabat she had taught me many of the recipes that were included in my first cookbook.) One I will never forget, and perhaps the most difficult of all Moroccan chicken dishes, is Djej Mefenned, which involves the dazzling technique of twirling a whole chicken in sizzling fat while at the same time basting it with seasoned eggs, a procedure that results in an herbed golden cloak taking the form of the bird just before it is presented at table.

Rakia was in America to prepare several important Moroccan banquets and had brought along her strong Koutoubia cigarettes. Her laugh was still the same too—a kind of guttural snort. About sixty-five years old, she could still bend like a jackknife from the waist to pick up something from the floor. Our reunion was delightful—a mixture of sentiment and earthy Moroccan humor. In no time Rakia was cracking jokes, singing, even belly-dancing around the kitchen.

Though we were now cooking together in a modern American kitchen, her food preparation was still a labor-intensive process. Rakia grated Spanish onions and tomato halves on an old-fashioned four-sided grater, pounded garlic with salt to a smooth purée in a brass mortar, carefully hand-peeled almonds and chick-peas, and tenderly nursed each dish along as it cooked slowly to perfection.

But, be assured, her fine, time-consuming methods are not a requirement. I have adapted her recipes to the average American kitchen, and with the help of a food processor and (though not really necessary) an electric cooker with a glazed earthenware insert, you can make the same wonderful, aromatic Moroccan dishes with relatively little effort.

Moroccan food, part Arab and part Berber, is not at all like Middle Eastern. Its ingredients and cooking styles are unique; no other Arab country has such a rich and varied cuisine. To me, in culinary terms, the country doesn't even feel particularly Arab. In its South I sense a strong African influence, and in its North many sharings and borrowings from the food of Andalusia, and, in the play of sweet against spicy and the combining of meat and fruits, Catalonian Spain.

There is a truly classic quartet of great Moroccan specialties: couscous; mechoui (spit-roasted lamb scented with cumin); *bisteeya* (a flaky, layered, sweet-and-savory pigeon pie); and finally—but not least—the extraordinary and huge repertoire of traditional and regional stews that are called *tagines*. These *tagines* of meltingly tender meats cooked with assorted spices and often, too, with vegetables or fruits are the mainstay of most Moroccan meals. (Originally only meat dishes were called *tagines*, but now the term is applied to equally tender stews of fish, plain vegetables, and poultry.)

Moroccan Chicken with Eggplant-Tomato Jam

Here chicken simmers in a sauce of garlic, ginger, saffron, and black pepper until it is so tender it is falling off the bone. The chicken is then piled in the center of a dish and topped with a thick, intensely flavored "jam" made from fried eggplant that has been crushed with spices and garlic, refried with fresh tomatoes, and enriched with some of the sauce from the chicken. The remaining sauce is poured around the chicken, and the *tagine* is reheated to blend the flavors. Though delicious, this dish cannot be called "subtle."

For a first course I would serve an assortment of olives: crinkled black olives topped with a dollop of crushed red chili paste *(sambal oelek)*, "Midway" olives scented with Moroccan spices and herbs, and Greek green-cracked olives layered with thin slices of preserved lemons. Accompany the *tagine* with Moroccan bread in order to soak up the delicious sauce. For dessert, serve Paxos Cinnamon Pita. If this seems too rich, why not the Fresh Orange Slices with Moroccan Spices?

2 *pounds eggplant (about 2 large)*

Coarse (kosher) salt

Olive oil for shallow frying

3 *medium garlic cloves, crushed*

¼ *cup chopped Italian flat-leaf parsley*

¼ *cup chopped fresh coriander*

1 *teaspoon sweet paprika*

¼ *teaspoon ground cumin*

Several pinches of cayenne pepper to taste

2 *large tomatoes, peeled, seeded, and chopped (about 2 cups)*

Pinch of sugar (if needed to correct acidity)

2 *tablespoons lemon juice*

1 *tablespoon cider vinegar*

1 *chicken (about 4 pounds), preferably a free-range chicken, cut into 8 pieces, trimmed of excess fat*

1¼ *teaspoons ground ginger*

Pinch of powdered saffron

¼ *teaspoon finely ground black pepper*

½ *cup grated onion (2 small onions)*

Springs of fresh coriander and/or thin slices of lemon, for garnish (optional)

1. Trim off the top and bottom from each eggplant. With a one-holed lemon zester, remove 3 or 4 thin vertical strips of skin from each, leaving the eggplants striped; then cut them crosswise into ½-inch slices. Sprinkle the eggplant with salt and let it drain in a nonaluminum colander for at least 2 hours. Rinse and drain the eggplant; pat it dry with paper towels.

2. Heat ¼ inch of oil in a nonstick skillet over medium heat. Fry the eggplant slices in batches until golden-brown on both sides, about 4 minutes. Drain the eggplant on paper

(continued)

towels; place it on a cutting board. Strain the oil and reserve. With a potato masher, crush the eggplant with 1 of the garlic cloves, 2 tablespoons each of the parsley and coriander, the paprika, cumin, and cayenne.

3. Put 3 tablespoons of the reserved oil in a heavy skillet and reheat. Add the tomatoes, 1 teaspoon of salt, and the sugar, if necessary. Cook over moderately high heat, stirring frequently, until most of the moisture evaporates, about 5 minutes.

4. Add the mashed eggplant to the tomatoes in the skillet and cook over very low heat, stirring frequently, until most of the moisture evaporates and the mixture is very thick, about 20 minutes. Remove the skillet from the heat and stir in the lemon juice and vinegar. (*The recipe can be prepared to this point up to 3 days in advance.* Cool, cover, and refrigerate.)

5. About 2 hours before serving, trim the excess fat from the chicken. Wash the chicken; pat it dry. In a mortar, pound the remaining garlic with 1 teaspoon of salt. Blend in the ginger, saffron, and black pepper. Gradually stir in 2 tablespoons of the reserved oil and ½ cup of hot water, as if making mayonnaise.

6. In a large flameproof casserole or deep skillet, toss the chicken with the garlic-spice mixture to coat each piece. Cover the casserole and cook over low heat for 5 minutes. Add the onion, the remaining parsley and coriander, and enough water to just cover, about 2½ cups. Bring the mixture to a boil, reduce the heat to medium-low, cover, and cook for 1 hour, or until the chicken just begins to fall off the bone. Remove the chicken to a serving dish and cover it to keep moist. Skim off most of the fat, then continue cooking the pan juices, uncovered, over moderate heat until they are reduced to 1½ cups, about 15 minutes.

7. Mix half the pan juices with the eggplant purée and adjust the seasoning, adding additional salt, black pepper, and lemon juice to taste. Place the chicken in a shallow heatproof serving bowl. Pile the eggplant on top, forming a pyramid. Surround with the remaining sauce. Cover the dish loosely with foil and reheat 10 minutes in a 400° oven just before serving. Garnish the purée with thin slices of lemon and springs of coriander, if desired.

<table>
<tr><td colspan="2">SERVES 6
(as part of a Moroccan dinner)</td><td colspan="2"><h1>Moroccan Game Hens Braised and
Fried with Sautéed Almonds</h1></td></tr>
</table>

Very few *tagines* require initial browning; if there is to be browning it is invariably done *after* the lamb or poultry has been simmered and the flesh has become butter-tender and very moist. In order to accomplish this, the cooking liquid must contain quite a lot of fat. Don't be concerned by this; later it is all skimmed off.

In this recipe, the hens remain moist and silky because of the extra-slow cooking. Afterward, just before serving, their skins are crisped in sizzling butter and oil. In Morocco this type of dish is called *mhammer*, which means "reddish," the result of a generous quantity of paprika in the spicing.

Here the livers are cooked along with the hens in a mildly seasoned sauce, mashed to a paste, and then returned to the sauce, where they act as a subtle thickener. Serve the hens surrounded with wedges of Moroccan bread, and finish the meal with fresh fruit and cups of mint tea.

⅛ teaspoon powdered saffron
Coarse (kosher) salt
3 tablespoons unsalted butter, melted
3 Rock Cornish game hens (about 1 pound each), livers and necks reserved (Partridges, squab pigeons, and free-range chickens can all be substituted.)
1¼ teaspoons ground ginger
1½ teaspoons paprika, preferably medium-sweet

¼ teaspoon ground cumin seed
2 large garlic cloves peeled, halved, and green shoot removed
10 sprigs of fresh coriander, tied into a bunch
¾ cup grated onion (1 medium onion)
½ cup vegetable oil
¼ cup clarified butter
1 cup blanched almonds lightly browned in vegetable oil

Steps 1 through 6 can be done early in the day.

1. In a small bowl, mix the saffron, ¼ teaspoon of salt, and 1 tablespoon of water with the melted butter. Rub the mixture all over the skin of the hens. Set them aside at room temperature for about 2 hours.

2. In a large flameproof casserole, place each hen on its side and add the livers and necks. Sprinkle with the ginger, paprika, cumin, and 1 teaspoon of salt. Heat gently, cover, take the pot in your hands and give it a good swirl.

3. Crush the garlic to a paste with ½ teaspoon of salt. Add it to the casserole along with the coriander, onion, and enough water to just cover the hens. Cover the casserole and bring just to a boil. Reduce the heat to low and cook until the hens are very tender, about 1 hour.

4. Remove the casserole from the heat. Let the hens cool 5 minutes in the liquid,

(continued)

then carefully remove them without allowing them to break apart. Set them on a platter to cool and drain. Remove the livers from the casserole and transfer them to a work surface or a wide bowl. With a slotted spoon, remove and discard the necks and the coriander.

5. Crush the livers with a fork. Gradually work 3 tablespoons of the cooking liquid into the livers to form a smooth purée.

6. Bring the remaining cooking liquid in the casserole to a boil over high heat and boil until it is reduced to 1½ cups. Stir or whisk in the liver, and simmer until the sauce is thickened. Adjust the seasoning with salt. Add pinches of cumin and paprika to perk up the flavor. (*The recipe can be prepared to this point up to 3 hours in advance.* Set the hens and sauce aside at cool room temperature.)

7. About 20 minutes before serving, heat the oil and clarified butter in a skillet over high heat. Add the hens, in batches if necessary, and brown on all sides. (Use a splatter screen to protect yourself from the hot fat.) As the hens brown, transfer them to a deep, round serving platter, and hold them in a warm oven. The hens can be halved and browned under the broiler, but the skin will not be as crusty. Gently reheat the sauce, stirring occasionally. Serve the hens surrounded with sauce and topped with browned almonds.

Chicken Tagine with Sweet Onions

SERVES 10 TO 12
(as an accompaniment to a vegetable couscous)

For this recipe you must peel the cooked chick-peas; otherwise their skins can catch in your teeth and throat, and may impart an unpleasant taste to the dish. Remove the skins by submerging the chick-peas in a bowl of cold water and gently rubbing them between the fingers. The skins will rise to the top of the water. Discard the skins and set the chick-peas aside.

2 *cups dried chick-peas, soaked at least 12 hours, drained, or 1 twenty-ounce can cooked chick-peas, drained*

¼ *medium onion, peeled*

4 *pounds Spanish onions, peeled*

½ *teaspoon fine salt*

4 *tablespoons unsalted butter*

½ *teaspoon ground ginger*

1½ *teaspoons finely ground black pepper*

1½ *teaspoons ground cinnamon*

½ *teaspoon ras el hanout (see recipe, page 165)*

Pinch of saffron threads

¼ *cup sugar*

2 *cups Meaty Broth for Couscous or rich stock, strained (see recipe, page 87)*

1 *cup black raisins, soaked in hot water for 15 minutes, drained*

10 *to 12 large cooked chicken thighs (from Meaty Broth for Couscous)*

¼ *cup (approximately) liquid honey*

1. Cover the chick-peas with fresh cold water, add the onion quarter, and cook them over low heat for 1 hour or until tender. Discard the onion. Peel the chick-peas as directed

in the note above and reserve. (*You can prepare the chick-peas one day in advance.* Keep them in the cooking liquid in a closed jar in the refrigerator. Drain before adding to the glazed onions in step 4.)

2. Quarter and slice the Spanish onions lengthwise. Place them in a heavy-bottomed 4-quart casserole with the ½ teaspoon salt and 4 tablespoons of butter. Cover the onions and cook over moderately low heat for 10 minutes. Add the ginger, 1 teaspoon of the finely ground pepper, the *ras el hanout,* saffron, and sugar. Cover the onions and cook for 15 minutes, stirring occasionally.

3. Add the strained broth and cook the mixture, uncovered, stirring occasionally, until the onions are very soft and the sauce is reduced to about 4 cups and is very thick, about 45 minutes.

4. Preheat the oven to 450° F. Arrange the chicken thighs, skin side up, in a large, shallow ovenproof dish. Brush the skin with honey and bake the chicken until glazed, 10 to 15 minutes. Pour the onions over the chicken. Add the peeled and drained chick-peas and the raisins. (*The recipe can be prepared ahead to this point up to a day in advance.* Let the chicken cool, then cover it, and refrigerate. Bring back to room temperature before proceeding.)

5. About 30 minutes before serving, preheat the oven to 375° F. Bake the *tagine* on the highest rack of the oven, uncovered, until the *tagine* is hot and the top is slightly crusty. Serve at once.

MAKES ABOUT ⅓ CUP   *Ras el Hanout*

This Moroccan spice-and-herb mixture will keep in a tightly covered jar in a cool, dark place for up to several months.

5 *imported bay leaves*	1 *tablespoon crumbled nutmeg*
1 *tablespoon dried thyme*	1 *tablespoon whole cloves*
1 *tablespoon white peppercorns*	1 *tablespoon ground cinnamon*
¾ *teaspoon crumbled blades of mace, or* ½ *teaspoon ground mace*	

In a spice mill, grind all of the ingredients together until powdered, about 1 minute. Press them through a sieve and store in a tightly closed jar.

OTHER CHICKEN DISHES

Moroccan Fried Chicken

SERVES 4 OR 5

This is an adaptation of a popular Spanish-Moroccan dish, *criadillas*, lamb sweetbreads marinated in olive oil, garlic, and lemon juice, then cooked in a highly unorthodox way: dipped *first* in bread-crumbs, *second* in beaten eggs, and finally deep-fried. As soon as the meat hits the hot oil, a thin, lacy web of egg seals it, keeping the chicken juicy and tender, and almost grease-free. Accompany this very easy dish with Red Peppers and Preserved Lemons. The flavors mingle perfectly, making this a very fine light supper.

8 *small chicken legs with thighs (2 pounds total), each separated into 2 pieces and boned*

3 *tablespoons olive oil*

3 *tablespoons fresh lemon juice*

3 *garlic cloves, sliced thin*

1½ *tablespoons chopped parsley*

Pinch of ground ginger

Pinch of ground cinnamon

Coarse salt and freshly ground pepper

About 1 quart vegetable oil, for deep frying

3 *large eggs*

1½ *tablespoons milk*

1½ *cups fine, dry breadcrumbs*

1 *cup bite-size pieces of butter lettuce, such as Boston*

3 *lemons, cut in wedges*

Moroccan black olives, for garnish

1. Pound each chicken piece until ¼ inch thick. Trim away any fat and gristle. (Do not worry if the pieces are not all the same size.) In a bowl mix the oil, lemon juice, garlic, parsley, ginger, cinnamon, salt, and pepper. Add the chicken and let it marinate at least 1 hour at room temperature, tossing occasionally, or in the refrigerator for no more than 4 hours.

2. In a deep fryer, heat at least 4 inches of oil to 360° F.

3. In a small bowl, beat the eggs and milk until well combined. Drain the chicken pieces, but do not pat them dry; discard the marinade. Dip the moist chicken pieces in breadcrumbs and arrange them side by side on a large tray.

4. Dip 3 or 4 pieces of breaded chicken at a time (enough to fit in the fryer without crowding) into the beaten eggs and add them one at a time to the hot oil. Fry until the pieces float to the surface and turn golden brown, about 2 minutes. (Cooking time may vary because it depends on the thickness of the chicken.) Turn the chicken and fry until

166 POULTRY AND GAME

the second side is golden, 2 minutes longer. Remove the pieces with a slotted spoon and drain on paper toweling. Repeat with the remaining chicken pieces.

5. Cover a large platter with the lettuce. Arrange the chicken on top. Decorate with lemon wedges and olives. Sprinkle the chicken with coarse salt.

SERVES 2 TO 4

Game Hens Roasted in Grape Leaves

This recipe from the island of Corfu for cooking wild, dry-fleshed game birds in the autumn hunting season also works well with Cornish game hen. Here a rich-flavored, lean bird is marinated and wrapped in grape leaves, which form an impenetrable seal, keeping the oil-based marinade and the natural juices from escaping during the cooking. The bird comes out tender and juicy—pungent, too, from the taste of the leaves when roasted. I garnish with a few grape leaves fried in oil and wedges of lemon.

A good accompaniment would be Roasted Mixed Vegetables in the Style of Corfu, and a refreshing platter of watercress sprigs and orange slices dressed with a mild vinegar, and a fruity olive oil.

2 *large (1½ pounds each) fresh Rock Cornish game hens, giblets reserved for another use*

Salt and freshly ground pepper

2 *teaspoons Mediterranean oregano*

1 *tablespoon fine-minced parsley*

2 *garlic cloves, sliced thin*

2 *lemons, halved*

2 *tablespoons extra-virgin olive oil*

20 *to 24 grape leaves*

½ *cup water*

Optional vegetable oil for frying

Lemon quarters for garnish

1. Season the cavities of the birds with salt, pepper, oregano, parsley, and garlic. Rub the outside of each hen with a lemon half. Squeeze 1 lemon for its juice and mix with the olive oil. Roll the hens in the lemon-olive oil mixture. Truss the hens with string to secure the legs and wings. Wrap each hen with 3 or 4 grape leaves, and secure with string. Reserve the remaining grape leaves for the garnish. Let the birds stand at least 2 hours in the refrigerator, but no longer than 4 hours. Return to room temperature before proceeding.

2. Heat oven to 450° F. Put the hens in a shallow baking dish, breast down, and bake 35 minutes without disturbing.

3. Remove the birds from the oven; maintain oven heat. Remove, but save the crunchy grape leaves; prick the fatty skin with a fork, and return the birds to the baking

(continued)

pan, breast sides up. Rub the breasts with a lemon half (this not only enhances the flavor, but helps crisp the skin). Return them to the oven; bake until lightly browned and fully cooked, about 20 minutes. For a crispy skin, stab the lemon half with a fork and use it to baste every 5 minutes with the pan juices.

4. After the hens have cooked, let them rest 10 minutes before removing the trussing strings. Carefully spoon off any fat from the juices in pan. Add ⅓ cup of water to deglaze and set aside. Meanwhile, fry the reserved grape leaves, 1 or 2 at a time, in a skillet in hot oil until crisp and crinkly. Drain them briefly on paper toweling. Decorate a platter with all the crispy grape leaves and quarters of lemon. Place the birds on top and spoon the pan juices directly over the birds. Serve at once.

NOTES TO
THE COOK

You can find grape leaves preserved in brine in most supermarkets. If fresh grape leaves are available, by all means use them. Drop the leaves into boiling salted water to cook for 1½ minutes, then cool them quickly in a colander and drain them dry on a kitchen towel. Leaves packed in brine should be washed well and drained before use.

The bird is done when the juices run clear when pierced into the thickest part of the inside leg area.

In the summer you can spit and roast (barbecue) these birds either over an open fire or on an outdoor rotisserie. I am especially fond of the Ducane gas heated lava stone rotisserie —it has a special partition for holding the stones vertical, so that when the birds revolve, any juices that fall are caught in a pan set below. I always use these juices to make a simple pan gravy to serve with the birds.

To spit-roast, secure the birds on the rotisserie rod, rub the leaves lightly with oil, roast for about 45 minutes, remove the grape leaves, and baste with the lemon half as directed above.

To roast a small chicken in this manner, follow steps 1, 2, and 3. When the breast is nicely browned and fully cooked, remove the legs and thighs and return them to the oven to continue roasting for 5 to 10 minutes longer. Meanwhile, wrap the breast (still on the carcass) with foil and allow it to rest. Degrease the pan drippings. Place breast, legs, and thighs on garnished platter, and pour over the pan juices. Serve hot.

Paillard of Chicken with Orange and Cardamom

Chicken with Oranges is not a California creation; citrus fruit cooked with poultry has long been common in Catalonia, Morocco, and Israel. My rendition of this concept, is a sort of generalized Mediterranean dish in which the traditional combination of orange and cardamom is a gastronomic "homage" to the influence of Arab cookery throughout the region.

There is an art to pounding chicken for paillards: Use a curved tapping motion, working from the center to the outer edge to achieve even thickness. Please, don't pound too forcefully, or the paillard will tear.

For a more substantial meal, accompany this dish with Cazuela Potatoes and Winter Carrots Cooked in the Style of the Nineteenth Century.

1 *whole boneless chicken breast, skinned and halved from one 2½-pound broiler*

MARINADE
½ *cup fresh orange juice*
3 *tablespoons Cognac, previously flamed*
½ *teaspoon grated orange rind*
Pinch of grated nutmeg
Pinch of cardamom
Salt and freshly ground pepper

Wondra flour
1 *egg, beaten*
⅔ *cup fine-ground breadcrumbs, preferably from* zwieback *rusks*
2½ *tablespoons unsalted butter*
1½ *tablespoons olive oil*
10 *to 12 julienne strips of orange rind, blanched in boiling water 3 minutes to remove any bitterness*
A few mint leaves for garnish

1. Carefully trim the chicken of fat and sinews. Place the breast, skinned side down, on a sheet of plastic wrap. Cover the breast with plastic wrap and pound it with a smooth mallet to a thickness of ⅛ inch. In a bowl, combine the orange juice, Cognac, orange rind, and spices. Add the chicken and marinate it for 30 minutes at room temperature. (Over-marinating will make the flesh mushy.)

2. Drain the chicken; season it with salt and pepper, and dust it with flour, shaking off any excess. Dip the chicken into egg, then breadcrumbs. Leave it on a rack to allow the coating to set, at least 5 minutes. Put 1½ tablespoons of the butter and the olive oil in a 10-inch skillet; heat it until sizzling and just beginning to brown. Add the chicken without crowding and cook it until golden on the first side. Use a spatula to turn it over, and cook it on the second side, about 1 minute.

(continued)

3. Remove the chicken breast to a heated platter. Pour off the fat. Add the marinade to the skillet, and bring it to a boil. Add the remaining 1 tablespoon of fresh butter and swirl to combine it with pan juices. Season with salt and pepper, and pour the sauce over the chicken. Decorate with blanched orange strips and mint leaves and serve at once to prevent the flesh from drying out.

Poached Chicken Breast, Auvergne Style

SERVES 6 TO 8

Here is a version of *poule au pot,* one of the culinary gems of the French South-West. In a traditional *poule au pot,* a chicken is stuffed with liver, herbs, spices, and bread, and bound with a fresh egg, then simmered in a savory bouillon with accompanying vegetables.

In this adaptation the texture of the boned chicken breast, protected during slow poaching by a thick coating of herbal "stuffing," is positively creamy. The taste is further heightened by a layer of cabbage leaves.

The stuffing is exceptionally light because the moistened bread is mashed by hand with a fork instead of being pulverized in a food processor. Its wonderful aromatic flavor comes from the combination of Swiss chard and fresh herbs. Do *not* grind them in your food processor; instead, cut them with a knife so as not to "break" their special sweet flavor. Taste the delicious bouillon after the chicken is removed; it is a culinary miracle.

The addition of fragrant walnut oil to a finished dish is particular to some parts of the French South-West and the Auvergne. The soft, nutty scent is discernible only from a fresh can imported from France. To keep it fresh, store your opened can in the refrigerator.

Present the dish on very hot plates with plenty of crusty French bread. Follow with a sophisticated country dessert, Apple Galettes with Fried Apple Peels (page 321).

3 large chicken breasts, skinned, boned and halved

Salt and freshly ground pepper

CHICKEN AND VEGETABLE STOCK

2 or 3 raw chicken carcasses

3½ quarts water

2 leeks, split and cut into 2 inch pieces

2 carrots, pared and sliced

2 white turnips, pared and quartered

1 rib celery, sliced

1 large onion, quartered

Coarse sea salt

3 or 4 peppercorns

STUFFING

⅓ cup milk

2 cups cubed stale firm white bread (5 slices), crustless

3 ounces cured ham

2½ ounces pancetta or lean salt pork, blanched in boiling water 5 minutes, drained

½ small onion, peeled and quartered

1 large shallot, peeled

2 chicken livers, well cleaned, soaked in salty milk for 3 hours, rinsed and drained

3 chicken hearts, trimmed

3 chicken gizzards, trimmed

4 teaspoons flour

4 medium-large Swiss chard leaves, blanched 3 minutes, rinsed until water runs clear, squeezed dry

1 large egg, lightly beaten

1½ tablespoons fine-snipped fresh chives

1½ tablespoons fine-chopped fresh parsley

Salt and pepper to taste

Pinches of grated nutmeg or ground allspice, to taste

Pinch of sugar (optional)

12 large cabbage leaves from a crisp, unwithered head

3 or 4 young leeks, cleaned, trimmed, and halved lengthwise

6 young carrots, pared and sliced on the diagonal

6 small turnips, pared and quartered

Coarse salt

French walnut oil

1. Season the chicken breasts with salt and pepper, cover with plastic wrap, and refrigerate.

2. Make the chicken and vegetable stock: Chop the bones into small pieces. In a wide, deep saucepan place the bones and cover them with water. Slowly bring to a boil; remove the scum until clear. Add the flavoring vegetables, 1 teaspoon of salt, and the peppercorns, and bring the mixture to a boil. Reduce to a simmer, cover the pan partially, and cook for 1½ hours, skimming from time to time. Strain the stock, discarding the bones and vegetables. Cool, cover, and refrigerate the stock until you are ready to use it in step 6.

3. Make the stuffing: In a wide bowl, pour the milk over the bread cubes and let them stand for a few minutes. Press out and discard the milk. Leave the bread in the bowl.

(continued)

Process the chicken livers, hearts, gizzards, ham, and pancetta in the workbowl of a food processor until ground coarse. Add the onion, shallot, and flour, and process until well blended. Chop the Swiss chard fine by hand. Add the egg to the bread and mash with a fork until they are light and well combined. Mash in the meat mixture, then the Swiss chard and the herbs. Season to taste with salt and pepper, and nutmeg or allspice. Add a pinch of sugar if there is any bitter taste from the livers. Makes 2 cups. Cover and refrigerate the stuffing to mellow and firm up.

4. Blanch the cabbage leaves for 5 minutes in boiling salted water. Refresh under cold running water and drain. If the ribs are very thick, shave them off with a knife. Cool, cover, and refrigerate. (*Up to this point the recipe can be prepared in advance.*)

5. About 2 hours before serving, coat each chicken breast with ⅓ cup of the stuffing. Wrap each breast in 2 cabbage leaves, rib sides out, and tie securely with string. (If desired, wrap each cabbage roll in a 12-inch square of cheesecloth and tie with string.) Keep the rolls refrigerated.

6. About 1 hour before serving, reheat the stock in a 5-quart casserole, add the fresh vegetables, and simmer them until tender, about 20 minutes. Remove the vegetables and keep them warm in a covered dish.

7. About 30 minutes before serving, add the cabbage rolls to the simmering broth and cook them over low heat for 25 minutes.

8. Remove rolls to a work surface and let them rest 5 minutes. Reheat the vegetables in the stock. Remove strings (and cheesecloth, if used). Cut each roll into 4 slices slightly on the diagonal. Arrange the slices cut side up, on individual warm serving plates. Sprinkle the chicken with coarse salt. Surround each serving with drained vegetables; moisten with a few tablespoons of the cooking liquid, drizzle walnut oil over, and serve at once. Reserve remaining stock for some other purpose.

NOTES TO
THE COOK

Cabbage leaves: To remove the large outer leaves of a cabbage, dig out the core from the head, loosen the leaves under cool running water (the water works its way through the leaves), and carefully remove each leaf without tearing. If the head of cabbage is very tight, blanch the whole head for a few minutes in boiling water. Remove, refresh in cool running water, and peel back the needed leaves.

If desired, use the remaining cabbage as a garnish. Follow steps 4 and 5 of the recipe for Roast Salmon with Cabbage, Bacon, and Carrots (page 126). Garnish with crumbled fried bacon.

Inspired by a recipe from Michel Bras.

Chicken, Artichoke, Eggplant, and Potato Pie "Père Lathuile"

This is a modern version of a little-known nineteenth-century dish of sautéed slices of potato layered into a round cake shape, the center filled with boned chicken and artichoke bottoms. Each individual serving is decorated with strands of fried onions and curly parsley. My friend Lucien Vanel adds cubed eggplant which he calls "the cèpe of the poor."

Père Lathuile was a farmer who lived outside Paris in Barrière de Clichy. He had a little restaurant there where he served this dish, made from chickens he raised himself. In the spring of 1814, when imperial guardsmen of the Russian Czar were skirmishing with the French in the suburbs of Paris, Maréchal Adrien Moncey installed his general quarters on Lathuile's property, at which time Père Lathuile offered all his provisions and wines to Moncey's troops. "Eat, drink, my children! Nothing must be left for the enemy!" he said. And from that moment his establishment became famous. People thronged there to eat his famous cake of chicken with potatoes and artichokes. Later Manet would use the restaurant as a setting for one of his paintings.

6 chicken thighs (2 to 2¼ pounds), trimmed of excess fat

Coarse salt and freshly ground pepper

¾ pound eggplant

3 large artichokes, or 1 cup cubed blanched artichoke bottoms (see notes)

½ lemon

Olive oil or vegetable oil for frying

6 tablespoons clarified butter

4 tablespoons chopped parsley

2 teaspoons chopped fresh thyme

3 tablespoons snipped chives

1 teaspoon fine-chopped garlic

1 tablespoon lemon juice, or more to taste

5 to 6 large potatoes (see note)

GARNISH

Crisp-fried onions (see notes)

Steps 1 through 4 can be done earlier in the day.

1. Bone and skin the chicken thighs, leaving each piece whole. Season the flesh with salt and pepper. Refrigerate until you are ready to cook.

2. Meanwhile peel the eggplant and cut crosswise into ¾-inch slices. Place them in a wide bowl. Toss with 1 teaspoon coarse salt in a colander. Let stand 30 minutes.

3. Prepare the artichokes: Snap off artichoke stems and hard outer leaves. Cut off and discard the top third of each artichoke with a stainless serrated knife. Blanch the artichokes in boiling salted water for 10 minutes; drain. When cool enough to handle, remove the leaves and chokes. Place the artichokes in a bowl of water with the lemon juice, cover, and keep refrigerated.

(continued)

4. Drain and rinse the eggplant, squeeze out excess moisture, and pat dry with paper toweling. Slowly heat ½ inch of olive oil in an 8-inch nonstick skillet until hot. Add eggplant slices, one by one, and fry until golden brown on each side, about 2 minutes. Remove and repeat with the remaining slices. Drain on paper towels. Cut the eggplant into ¾-inch cubes and set them aside in a mixing bowl. Reserve the oil for frying the onions (see note).

5. About 1½ hours before serving, heat 1½ tablespoons of the clarified butter in a small skillet over medium-high heat, and working in batches, sear the chicken pieces 20 seconds to a side. Transfer to a workspace to cool down, then cut each thigh into 6 even pieces. Drain the artichokes, cut into ¾-inch cubes. Add to the skillet and cook, stirring, until just golden around the edges, 1½ minutes. Add another tablespoon butter to the skillet and, when hot, return the pieces of chicken. Toss together over high heat to combine flavors, about 2 minutes. Add to the eggplant. Add half the chopped parsley, thyme, chives, garlic, and 1 tablespoon lemon juice. Season with 1 teaspoon salt and ½ teaspoon pepper, and mix well. Set aside, covered.

6. Peel the potatoes, cut 3 of the potatoes crosswise into ⅛-inch rounds. Cut the remaining 2 or 3 potatoes lengthwise into ⅛-inch slices. Wash and pat dry (see note). Put 2 tablespoons of the clarified butter in a large nonstick skillet, set over moderate heat, and when hot add the potatoes. Cover and cook, tossing and turning the slices often so that each becomes pliable and pale golden, about 2 to 3 minutes. Transfer to a large side dish.

7. About 1 hour before serving, preheat the oven to 450° F. Butter a 9-inch straight-sided cast-iron skillet, copper *tarte tatin* pan, or a 6- or 7-cup shallow ovenproof baking dish. Cover the bottom completely with one layer of round potato slices. Then arrange the long potato slices, slightly overlapping, around the sides of the skillet and overhanging the rim. Top with a second layer of round slices. Scrape the chicken filling into the potato-lined pan. Bend the overhanging potato slices over the filling. Cover the filling with the remaining round potato slices arranged in a neat overlapping manner. Butter a small sheet of foil and place it, buttered side down, on the potatoes. Top with a heavy lid and press down so that the pie becomes compact. Bake it on the middle oven rack for 20 minutes. Remove the lid and foil, press the pie down, and continue baking 30 minutes longer, uncovered.

8. If the top layer is not sufficiently crisp, brush the potatoes with melted butter. Place the potato pie under the broiler for a minute or two to brown. Serve in the baking dish. Garnish each portion with crispy onions and the remaining chopped parsley.

NOTES TO THE COOK   One package (9½ ounces) frozen artichoke hearts may be substituted. Cut away the leaves.

In this recipe the choice of potatoes will determine the texture of the final dish. Waxy potatoes will create a crisp exterior and a meltingly tender filling. Starchy Idahos or russets will also become crisp on the outside but the interior will be creamier and absorb much of the flavorful juices from the chicken and artichokes. For me they are the potato of choice, but be sure to wash them well before using to remove their starch. Waxy potatoes need only a light rinsing before using.

Crisp-fried onions can be prepared hours in advance. Peel 3 medium onions, then cut in paper-thin slices. (I use the 1-mm slicing attachment to the food processor for even slices.) Lightly salt the rings and spread out in a single layer on a large flat baking sheet lined with paper towels. Leave to drain for several hours. Rinse the onions and pat dry with paper towels. (You can dehydrate the onions in a microwave without salting. Working in batches, spread the onions on a paper-lined dish. Cover with paper toweling. Cook on high 3 to 5 minutes, depending upon oven power.) Heat the reserved oil in a small skillet to 225° F. Fry the onions until golden brown, about 5 minutes. (You will probably have to do this in 3 or 4 batches.) Spread them out on paper towels to crisp. Makes about 2 cups.

A RECIPE FOR TURKEY

SERVES 8	*Stuffed Young Turkey, Auvergne Style*

This is not your conventional roast-turkey dinner—rather, it's a sophisticated turkey dish employing many ingredients, all found in the countryside of the Auvergne. The bird is stuffed with sautéed cèpes, prosciutto, walnuts, and white sausage (*boudin blanc*), cooked along with stuffed onions and pan juices and accompanied by sautéed salsify. Though the recipe may sound busy, it is not—it is perfectly balanced with a clean, pure taste.

Although, unfortunately, turkey toughens if it is not roasted in one continuous span, there are parts of this dish that you can prepare one day in advance: most of the turkey stuffing, the onion stuffing, the onion blanching, and the salsify.

(continued)

1 *fresh-killed turkey or wild turkey, about 12 pounds with giblets, ready to cook*

Salt and freshly ground pepper

STUFFING

8 *ounces wild mushrooms, preferably cèpes, porcini, stone, or Steinpilz, fresh or canned (1¼ cups), or substitute fresh portobello, cremini, or shiitake mushrooms*

5 *tablespoons unsalted butter*

2 *ounces prosciutto, chopped*

⅓ *cup (1½ ounces) walnuts*

4 *shallots, chopped fine*

1 *large garlic clove, chopped fine*

Salt and freshly ground pepper

¾ *pound white-meat sausage (boudins blanc, Weisswurst, or Bratwurst), pricked 3 or 4 times on each side*

3 *tablespoons chopped flat-leaf parsley*

2 *teaspoons fresh thyme leaves, or ½ teaspoon dried*

3 *tablespoons Cognac, previously flamed*

1 *cup cubed stale crustless white bread*

¼ *cup milk*

2 *eggs, lightly beaten*

5 *large sweet onions*

STUFFING FOR ABOUT 2 DOZEN ONION CUPS

3 *ounces prosciutto, diced*

1½ *tablespoons chopped shallots*

Turkey liver, gizzard, and heart, cleaned, trimmed and cut up

⅓ *cup chicken stock*

2 *teaspoons flour*

6 *medium-sized leaves of Swiss chard, stalks removed, blanched in boiling water for 3 minutes, drained, and squeezed dry (⅓ cup)*

1½ *cups (2 ounces) cubed stale crustless white bread*

⅓ *cup milk*

2 *whole eggs, lightly beaten*

2 *tablespoons roughly chopped flat-leaf parsley*

Salt, freshly ground pepper, and grated nutmeg to taste

2 *tablespoons butter, softened*

1 *tablespoon vegetable oil*

2 *cups unsalted rich poultry stock*

Sautéed Salsify (see page 281)

1. Remove the neck and giblets from the turkey cavity; save the liver, gizzard, and heart for stuffing the onions. (Use the neck to make stock). Rinse the turkey, dry it thoroughly with paper toweling, and season the cavity and skin with salt and pepper. Wrap the turkey in such a way that the breast is not covered. Refrigerate until you are ready to stuff and roast it.

2. Prepare the stuffing for the turkey. Slice thin the mushrooms and chop the stems. In an 8-inch skillet over medium-low heat, melt 3 tablespoons of the butter, add the mushrooms and prosciutto, and sauté, stirring occasionally, until they are softened and browned, about 10 minutes. Add the walnuts and brown them lightly, then stir in the

chopped shallots and garlic, and sauté, stirring, for 30 seconds. Scrape the contents of the skillet into a bowl. Season with salt and pepper. Add 2 tablespoons of the butter to the skillet, and slowly brown the sausages on all sides. Drain, cool, cut up, and put the sausages in the workbowl of a food processor, and process until they are ground coarse. In a large bowl, toss them with parsley, thyme, and mushroom-and-prosciutto mixture. Mix thoroughly, adding at the same time the flamed Cognac. (If making the stuffing one day in advance, set it aside to cool, then cover and refrigerate.) Just before stuffing the turkey, soak the bread cubes in milk 5 minutes, then squeeze gently, and toss lightly to render it fluffy. Add the bread to the stuffing and mix thoroughly, then fold in the beaten eggs. Correct the seasoning. Makes about 1 quart stuffing. Cool and set aside.

3. Peel the whole onions. Make a lengthwise slit in each onion, just halfway through. Drop the onions into boiling salted water and cook them for 15 minutes. Drain and refresh them under cool running water. Discard the thickest outer layers. Separate the layers, reserving only the 4 or 5 largest from each onion. (Use the remainder for soup or a purée, see notes below.) Place the onion cups on a work surface: season with pepper and a pinch of salt. (*Up to this point the recipe can be prepared 1 day in advance.* Cover and refrigerate.)

4. Prepare the stuffing for the onions. In a small nonstick skillet cook the prosciutto and shallots for 30 seconds, stirring; remove the skillet from the heat. Combine the liver, heart and gizzard, the stock, and flour in the workbowl of a food processor and process until they are ground fine. Chop the Swiss chard by hand. Soak the bread in milk and squeeze out excess moisture. With a fork mash the egg and bread until they are light and well combined. Mash in the liver mixture, prosciutto, chopped Swiss chard, and the parsley, mixing well. Season with salt, pepper, and nutmeg. Makes about 3 cups.

5. Four hours before serving, preheat the oven to 325° F. Place a handful of the stuffing in the neck cavity and secure it closed. Fill the main cavity with the remaining stuffing, but do not pack it in because of expansion during cooking. Tuck the wing tips behind and truss the bird if necessary (some birds come with wire locks to hold the legs tight to the body). Generously rub the bird with the softened butter and oil. Place the turkey breast side up in a V-rack in a shallow roasting pan. Roast for about 2½ hours, basting occasionally. If the turkey begins to brown too quickly, cover it loosely with foil (remove the foil during the last 30 minutes of roasting).

6. Meanwhile, fill each onion cup with a heaping tablespoon of stuffing. Roll them up jelly-roll style into football shapes. Place the onions in a buttered shallow 9-by-16-inch baking dish. Pour over ⅓ cup poultry stock, cover with foil, and bake 1 hour, basting every 20 minutes.

7. When the turkey has roasted 2½ hours, remove all the fat around it; surround with the stuffed onions and their cooking juices. Continue roasting the turkey until thoroughly cooked, about 30 minutes longer. The turkey is done when an instant meat thermometer registers 180°–185° F when inserted in the thickest part of the thigh. Remove the turkey

(continued)

from the oven; tent it with foil to keep it warm. Let it stand 20 to 30 minutes before carving. Raise the oven heat to 400° F and continue cooking the onions, basting them with the combined turkey and onion juices and allowing them to glaze on all sides, about 20 minutes. Transfer the onions to a side serving dish; cover them and keep warm. Add the remaining stock to the roasting pan, stir up all the brown bits, and pour the stock into a saucepan. Degrease, then reduce to 1½ cups over high heat. Adjust the seasoning and reserve.

8. Remove the stuffing from the turkey and moisten with ½ cup of the reserved pan juices. Carve the turkey, and surround it with stuffing, stuffed onions, and Sautéed Salsify. Pour the remaining pan juices into a sauceboat, adjust the seasoning and serve hot.

NOTES TO
THE COOK

If using a raw sausage in the stuffing, slice it thinly *before sautéing* and cook until no pink color remains. Avoid stuffing the bird until just before cooking.

A delicious onion purée to be served the following day can be made with the remaining onion. Cook the onion centers in fresh salted water until tender. Drain, cool, and squeeze them dry with your hands. Purée the onions in a food processor with a few tablespoons of heavy cream. Press them through a foodmill, if desired. (*Up to this point the onions can be prepared 1 day in advance.*) Place the purée in a saucepan and add 2 tablespoons of poultry or meat juices and reduce to about 1¼ cups. Season with salt and pepper, and thicken, if desired, with 2 teaspoons of cornstarch mixed with 1 tablespoon of cold water. Bring the mixture almost to a boil and remove it from the heat, stirring. Serve in individual small ramekins garnished with small croutons made from white bread fried in clarified butter until golden brown.

Inspired by a recipe from Michel Bras.

FOUR DUCK RECIPES

After my last book, *The Cooking of South-West France*, I thought I would never write about duck again. But in the intervening years I've acquired more good recipes both in France and Catalonia.

I've also changed my thinking about rare duck. Though I still like rare breasts, if properly and flavorfully marinated, my personal preference is for dishes in which the birds are well cooked, such as braised duck and duck *confit*. The following four recipes require long (and in some cases unattended) cooking. Happily, too, they are all better if prepared in advance.

SERVES 4 TO 6

Duck You Can Eat with a Spoon

The custom of serving duck, hare, or rabbit cooked (or "overcooked") to an extreme state of silkiness is very old in rural areas of South-West France. In the following recipe a luscious, rich concoction is made by simmering pieces of duck very slowly in wine and aromatics until the flesh is soft and succulent. The pieces are then boned, crisped under the broiler, and garnished with glacéed baby onions, crispy lardons, sautéed mushrooms, and crunchy cubes of garlic-parsleyed croutons.

The secret of obtaining the right texture for the duck is not only in the slow cooking, which prevents mushiness or stringiness, but also the slow cooling-down period in the cooking liquid, which prevents the meat from falling apart while being boned. The gradual cooking and cooling also allow the wine to infiltrate the duck flesh. The deep, full flavor of this dish derives from a balanced mixture of aromatics and the use of a good-quality wine. The sauce is thickened with the liver of the duck, enhanced with shallots, port wine, and Cognac.

In this recipe I have chosen to use a *cooked* wine marinade because it penetrates the duck flesh more quickly. Be sure you know your wine before you use it. It's a common error to think that a cooking wine can be of a lesser quality. If, in fact, it's not very good, reduction will further concentrate its poor flavor; similarly, it will concentrate an acid wine's acidity. I'm not suggesting you use a great wine here, simply a decent, sturdy one: a St. Émilion, St. Estephe, or Médoc would be ideal.

Please don't be put off by the length of this recipe, for it is really an easy step-by-step procedure, and almost all the steps can be done ahead of time.

Serve with noodles tossed in heavy cream with freshly boiled fava beans, and a good red Bordeaux. Just before serving, stir a tablespoon of the wine into the sauce for a startlingly fresh flavor. Finish with a country dessert such as Apples Baked on Cabbage Leaves as in Poitou.

(continued)

1 *duck, weighing about 4 pounds, fresh or thawed, quartered*

1 *recipe cold Cooked Marinade (see recipe, page 182)*

8 *ounces salt pork or pork belly, cut into 2-by-¼-inch strips (lardons), pork rind reserved*

1 *tablespoon olive oil*

Bouquet garni: 4 sprigs parsley, 2 sprigs thyme, 1 bay leaf, and celery leaf

3 *tablespoons dried cèpes, rinsed under running water to rid them of sand and dirt, and crumbled*

Salt and freshly ground pepper

1 *tablespoon flour*

Flour-and-water paste

DUCK-LIVER ENRICHMENT

1 *tablespoon chopped shallots*

3 *tablespoons unsalted butter*

1 *duck liver, cleaned and soaked in milky water overnight, rinsed and drained*

1 *teaspoon ruby Port wine*

1 *-inch piece orange rind*

2 *juniper berries*

Salt and freshly ground pepper

½ *teaspoon bitter cocoa, preferably Droste*

1 *tablespoon Cognac*

GARNISHES

1 *cup cubed crustless firm white bread*

4 *to 5 tablespoons clarified butter*

8 *ounces fresh mushrooms*

Salt and freshly ground pepper

8 *ounces small white boiling onions, peeled as directed in notes*

1 *teaspoon sugar*

1 *teaspoon balsamic or Sherry vinegar*

Olive oil

2 *garlic cloves, peeled*

2 *tablespoons finely chopped flat-leaf parsley*

1 *to 2 tablespoons very good red wine*

Steps 1 through 7 can be done 1 day in advance.

1. Quarter the duck, setting aside the back, neck, and wing tips. Combine the quartered duck and the cold marinade in an earthenware, stainless-steel, or glass bowl; cover and refrigerate overnight.

2. The following day, preheat the oven to 250° F. Drain all the duck pieces in a colander set over a bowl to catch the liquid. Discard the herb bouquet, orange slices, and spices. Reserve the vegetables separately. Blanch the lardons and pork rind in boiling water for 3 minutes; drain. Heat the oil in a heavy skillet over medium heat; add the blanched lardons. Fry them, turning occasionally, until light brown, about 5 minutes. Remove the lardons with a slotted spoon to a 5-quart casserole, preferably made of earthenware or enameled cast iron. Reserve the drippings in the skillet. Add the pork rind to the casserole. Deeply brown the reserved duck wing tips, back, and neck in the drippings. Add to the casserole.

4. Pat the duck skin dry with paper towels; add the duck to the pork drippings and lightly brown on the skin side only, about 2 minutes. Add the duck to the casserole along with the *fresh* bouquet garni and rinsed cèpes. Season lightly with salt and pepper. Discard all but 1 tablespoon of fat in the skillet. Add the drained vegetables from the marinade to the skillet and sauté them 2 to 3 minutes. Add the flour, stirring, and allow it to brown, about 2 minutes longer. Gradually stir in the wine marinade. Heat the mixture to boiling, scraping up brown bits that cling to the bottom and sides of the skillet. Add 1 cup of water; bring the mixture to a boil, skim once, and pour it over the contents of the casserole. Cover the casserole with a circle of waxed paper and a tight-fitting lid. Seal with the flour-and-water paste. Place the casserole in the oven and cook undisturbed for 2½ to 3 hours.

5. Meanwhile, make the liver enrichment: Over low heat soften the shallots in 1 tablespoon of the butter in a small skillet. Add the drained liver and sauté until golden on the outside and still pink in the center, about 1 minute. Add the Port wine, orange rind, juniper berries, salt, and pepper, and bring to a boil. Remove the mixture from the heat. When cool, purée in a food processor along with the remaining butter, cocoa, and Cognac. Refrigerate the enrichment until you are ready to use it.

6. Remove the casserole from the oven, uncover, and let the duck cool in the cooking liquid 2 to 3 hours.

7. Carefully transfer each duck quarter to a flat dish. Remove all the duck bones without damaging the shape or the skin. Wrap each quarter tightly in plastic film and refrigerate. Reserve the lardons. Strain the cooking juices through a fine-mesh sieve, pushing down on the vegetables to extract their juices. Skim off the fat that rises to the surface. Clean the cooking liquid by setting the saucepan partly off the heat so that only half the liquid bubbles. Simmer, skimming the fat and any impurities from the cooler side, for about 10 minutes or until reduced by half, about 1¼ cups. Cool, cover, and refrigerate the duck, lardons, and the sauce separately.

8. Make the garnishes: Completely dry out the bread cubes in a 250° F oven without coloring. In a small nonstick skillet, heat the clarified butter over medium-low heat until foaming. Fry the bread, tossing, until the cubes are golden on all sides, about 1 minute. Immediately dump them into a sieve or colander set over a dish to catch the butter. Return 2 tablespoons of the butter to the skillet and sauté the mushrooms until golden brown on all sides. Season with salt and pepper and remove them to a side dish. To the same skillet add the remaining butter, the onions, ½ cup of water, salt, and sugar. Cook over medium heat, stirring occasionally, until the water has evaporated, about 6 minutes. Reduce the heat to low; sprinkle with vinegar, and continue to cook the onions, shaking the pan occasionally, until they are tender and well browned, about 5 mintues. Remove the onions to a side dish. Crisp the reserved lardons in a little hot oil in the skillet, then drain on paper towels. Mix the lardons with the mushrooms and the onions in a skillet, sprinkle with salt if needed, and freshly ground pepper and set aside, partially covered.

(continued)

9. About 30 minutes before serving, crush the garlic with a pinch of salt in a mortar until it becomes a purée, mix with the parsley, then toss with the croutons. (To make a garlic purée without a mortar, slice the garlic thin, chop it fine, then sprinkle it with salt and crush with the side of a heavy chef's knife.) Preheat the broiler. Gently reheat the garnish. Separately reheat the sauce in a wide pan. Meanwhile, place the duck pieces, skin side up, on the broiling rack. Dab the skin with a little olive oil and run the duck under the broiler to crisp and reheat thoroughly. Cut the congealed liver enrichment into small pieces; scatter them over the sauce, and swirl over low heat until the sauce turns thick and creamy. Stir in 1 to 2 tablespoons of the wine to be served with dinner. Adjust the seasoning with salt and pepper. Do not allow the sauce to boil. Place the garnish in a deep serving bowl, cover with the sauce, and top with the reheated duck, crisp skin side up. Top with the parsleyed croutons. Serve at once.

Cooked Red-Wine Marinade

1 tablespoon vegetable oil	2 whole cloves
2 onions, sliced	3 or 4 black peppercorns
1 large carrot, sliced	¼ cup ruby Port wine
4 shallots	1½ bottles full-bodied red wine
4 garlic cloves, peeled	2 tablespoons aged red wine vinegar
Bouquet garni: 4 sprigs parsley, 2 sprigs thyme, 1 bay leaf, and 1 rib celery	2 slices orange

Up to 1 week in advance, make the cooked marinade.

In a deep, straight-sided skillet, heat the oil over low heat and cook the onions, carrots, shallots, garlic, bouquet garni, and spices until the vegetables soften and turn lightly golden. Add the Port wine, red wine, wine vinegar, and orange, and bring to a boil. Immediately lower the heat, cover, and cook slowly for 30 minutes. Remove from the heat. Cool the marinade completely before using. Keep refrigerated.

NOTES TO THE COOK

Pieces of orange rind (pared thin with a vegetable peeler) can be stored in an airtight plastic container in the freezer and used as needed.

To peel small white onions, cut an **X** in each root end. Blanch them for 2 minutes; drain. Refresh the onions under cold water until cool enough to handle. Peel the onions, leaving on enough root and stem so the onion won't fall apart.

Minorcan-Style Duck with Green Olives

Olives of all kinds and braised duck make a delicious combination. The olives from Minorca originally used for this dish have a crunchy texture and a mildly bitter flavor. Don't use the popular Spanish olive, *manzanilla;* look for a light, small, firm, cracked green olive with character, preferably packed in a light salt brine. The best is the Greek Nafplion, which has a slight tartness and a hint of bitterness. When added to the cooking liquid and brought to a boil, the olive will release some of its own oil, which will thicken the sauce, as well as flavor it spectacularly. A fortified wine like Marsala gives the sauce a subtle nutty undertone.

The duck is stuffed with a mixture of chopped raw fresh vegetables, spices, and a small quantity of chopped vanilla—an ingenious touch that gives the dish its special aroma. The flavorful moisture from the stuffing is exuded during cooking, and keeps the flesh from drying out. (In the original version, the duck is hung after it is stuffed—in effect, marinated from within.) The slow braising in a closed pot (ideally, the lid should be an earthenware dish filled with cold water, or a *doufeu*) forces rapid condensation of the pan juices. In the end the duck comes out lean, tender, moist, and flavorful, and the degreased cooking liquid is extremely savory.

(This unique and delicious recipe for braised duck with olives was given to me by Eliane Comelade-Thibaut, author of *La Cuisine Catalane,* who told me she discovered it in the archives in Mahon, on the island of Minorca.)

Normally one duck will serve two people, but because this dish is so rich and satisfying, I have found it can satisfactorily serve four. Start the meal with Grilled Onion Shoots and a Creamy Toasted Almond Sauce. Serve the duck with a gratin of potatoes and a crisp salad. A refreshing dessert would be a Quince Sorbet.

1 *five-pound duckling, fresh or thawed*

STUFFING
1¼ *cups fine-chopped onion*
1 *head garlic, halved crosswise*
1 *large rib celery, chopped*
2 *crumbled bay leaves*
2 *tablespoons roughly chopped Italian parsley*
1 *teaspoon coarse salt*
½ *teaspoon sweet paprika*
½ *teaspoon white pepper*

1 *vanilla bean, chopped*

2 *tablespoons olive oil*
½ *cup chopped peeled, seeded tomatoes*
3 *tablespoons dry Marsala, Dry Sack Sherry or Madeira*
½ *cup dry white wine*
4 *cloves*
8 *whole large shallots, peeled*
1½ *cups (7 ounces drained weight) small, light-green, cracked olives*

(continued)

1. Steps 1 through 3 can be done in the morning. Prepare the stuffing: Combine all the ingredients in a bowl, mixing well. Empty the cavity of the duck; set aside the giblets for some other purpose. Cut off the wings at the second joint; roughly chop the wings and neck and set aside. Remove the loose fat from the cavity, and around the neck and tail, and cut out the fat under the wings. Wash the duck and pat it dry. Stuff the duck and sew up the opening. Truss the duck to keep it in shape. Let it stand at room temperature for 1 hour, or refrigerate, *uncovered,* until 1 hour before cooking.

2. With the tines of a fork prick the duck skin every 1 inch. With a small paring knife make deep slits in thick, fatty areas. Place the duck in a wide skillet with 1 tablespoon of the oil. Brown the duck all over in the expressed fat and the oil. Transfer it, breast side up, to a 5- or 6-quart casserole, preferably made of earthenware or enameled cast-iron. Brown the wings and neck bones in the skillet; add to the casserole. Pour off all but 2 tablespoons of fat from the skillet, raise the heat, add the tomatoes and mash them so they lightly scorch. (This is to enhance the flavor and sweetness.) Scrape tomatoes and brown bits into casserole. Quickly deglaze the skillet with the Marsala and the white wine. Add it to the casserole. Add the cloves and shallots, cover with a circle of parchment paper or foil and a tight fitting lid. (Or an earthenware dish filled with cold water that fits snugly over the casserole.) Cook over low heat for 2¼ hours (or 25 minutes per pound of stuffed duck). Don't try to hurry the cooking by raising the temperature.

3. Remove the duck to a work surface. Let it stand at least 10 minutes. Meanwhile, strain the cooking juices, pressing duck gently to extract all the juices. Skim off the fat, then reduce to 1 cup in a saucepan. (See the notes below if the cooking juices have emulsified.) Cut the duck into quarters. Discard the backbone, wings, and stuffing. Set in a cool place. Cover the pan juices. Blanch and pit the olives, if desired. *(The recipe can be made several hours ahead of time to this point.)*

4. Ten minutes before serving, heat the broiler. In a saucepan combine the sauce and the olives, bring them to a boil and simmer to blend the flavors and thicken the sauce. Correct the seasoning, cover, and keep warm. Rub the duck skin with a dab of olive oil or rendered duck fat. Place it under a heated broiler to reheat thoroughly and crisp the skin. Place the duck in a warmed serving dish. Pour the sauce over and serve at once.

NOTES TO THE COOK Because American ducks tend to be fattier than European ones, I have included a short rendering of fat prior to braising. Whatever fat remains after the duck is fully cooked should be skimmed.

If after skimming the final cooking juices are gritty and cloudy, clean the sauce: Place the cooking juices in a small saucepan, add ½ cup of water, and bring to a boil. Set the pan half off the burner and adjust the heat so that the side over the heat slowly boils and the fat and any other impurities rise on the cooler side. By this process, with frequent skimming, you will remove in 15 minutes any remaining fat and impurities from the sauce.

The olives need to be blanched once to remove any lingering saltiness from the brine. Cover them with water, bring to a boil, and boil ½ minute. Drain, cool, and pit if desired. To pit a cracked olive, simply tap each one with a light mallet, and the pit will pop out.

Duck Legs Stuffed in Cabbage Leaves

Incredibly moist and soft-fleshed, with an herb stuffing and a sauce thickened with a puréed tart apple, these rolls should be served the day they are made, since refrigeration tends to dry them out. You can make them a few hours in advance and keep them warm in their cooking juices. (Save the duck breasts for another purpose.) Just before serving, thicken the sauce. You'll want to serve Mashed Potatoes with Olive Oil with this. For dessert, I'd serve slices of Walnut Roll—a roulade filled with ground walnuts blended with Cognac and whipped cream. If this seems too rich, why not the Sicilian Ricotta Ice Cream and some cookies.

1 large head green cabbage (3¾ pounds)
  Coarse salt and freshly ground pepper

6 duck-leg thighs

2 medium onions, chopped

2 medium-size carrots, sliced

3 garlic cloves, unpeeled, smashed
  Bouquet garni: parsley, thyme, bay leaf, celery leaf, and 2 scallions

1 cup dry white wine

3 plum tomatoes, halved, seeded, and chopped into coarse pieces

STUFFING

⅓ cup milk or cold stock

1¼ packed cups cubed stale crustless firm bread

8 ounces ground pork (15 percent fat)

2 garlic cloves, crushed to a paste in a mortar with a pinch of salt

2 chopped shallots

1 tablespoon snipped chives

1 tablespoon finely chopped parsley
  Pinch of mixed spices or grated nutmeg or ground allspice, to taste

1 large egg, lightly beaten
  Salt and freshly ground pepper

5 ounces lean salt pork, diced and blanched in boiling water for 5 minutes, drained

1 large tart green apple, such as Granny Smith
  Torn parsley leaves

1. Remove and discard the wilted outer leaves of the cabbage and dig out the core. Loosen as many leaves as possible; then slip the entire cabbage into a large pot of boiling water for 5 minutes. Remove the head and refresh it under cool running water. Carefully separate and reserve 12 large leaves.

2. Meanwhile, bring a second pot of water to a boil, add 1 teaspoon of salt and the cabbage leaves and cook for 3 minutes. Drain, refresh, and drain again. (Double-blanching the cabbage makes it more digestible.) Drain the cabbage dry in a colander.

(continued)

3. Carefully trim the duck-leg thighs of excess fat. Bone each piece. Score the skin. Remove as many tendons from the legs as possible without damaging the flesh. Season with salt and pepper and refrigerate.

4. Make duck stock: Preheat the oven to 425° F. Crack the duck bones into small pieces, place them in a heavy roasting pan, and cook them in the oven, turning once, until lightly browned, about 15 minutes. Add the onions, carrots, and garlic cloves, and continue to cook until brown, about 15 minutes. Scrape the bones and vegetables into a heavy pot. Discard the fat from the roasting pan, add 1 cup of cold water, and deglaze over moderate heat, scraping up any browned particles. Add the water and particles to the pot. Add 3 cups of water, and over medium-low heat bring the mixture to a boil. Skim it until clear. Add the bouquet garni and white wine, and simmer, uncovered, for 30 minutes. Add the tomatoes and cook another 30 minutes. Strain the cooking liquid into another saucepan; discard the bones, and press on the vegetables to extract all their juices. Degrease the liquid and reduce by boiling to 1¼ cups.

4. Make the stuffing: Pour the milk over the bread and let it stand for a few minutes, or until soft. Press out and discard the milk. With a fork mash the ground pork, garlic, shallots, herbs, and spices with the bread. Then work in the beaten egg. Add ½ teaspoon of salt and ¼ teaspoon of pepper. Refrigerate the stuffing until firm. Makes about 2 cups.

5. Slowly brown the salt pork in its own fat in a wide skillet until crisp. Remove the pork to drain, leaving the fat in the skillet. Peel, halve, and core the apple and steam it until soft. Use a fork to crush it to a smooth purée, and set it aside at room temperature. If necessary, press through a sieve. *(Up to this point the recipe can be prepared early in the day.)*

6. About 2 hours before serving, preheat the oven to 325° F. Heat the reserved fat in the skillet until sizzling, add the duck legs and brown gently for 1 to 2 minutes on their skin sides, and cook for 2 to 3 minutes. Drain the duck pieces and cut each in half. Divide the prepared stuffing into 12 equal parts and spread it over the two sides of the duck flesh. Spread out the leaves and season them with salt and pepper. Wrap each portion in a cabbage leaf and tie with kitchen string. Makes 12 rolls. Remove half the fat in the skillet and discard. Reheat the reserved fat in the skillet; add the cabbage rolls, and brown them on all sides, about 5 minutes. Remove to a work surface.

7. Arrange the rolls in one layer in a wide, heavy casserole or skillet. Add the reduced stock, and the salt pork. Cover with waxed paper to fit and a tight-fitting lid, and cook in the oven for 1 hour, turning each cabbage roll midway.

8. Transfer the rolls to a serving platter; cut away the string. Degrease the cooking liquid; reduce if necessary to about 1 cup. Beat in the puréed apple, adjust the seasoning, and pour the sauce over the cabbage. Decorate with torn pieces of flat-leaf parsley. Serve hot.

Stew of Duck Confit and Fresh Fava Beans

One of the best spring stews of the French South-West is the combination of fresh favas and duck *confit*, a variation on the original fava cassoulet, made before the discovery of America and the importation of the white bean. This is an incredibly delicious dish, and one of my favorite recipes.

Some food writers will tell you that favas and limas are interchangeable. This is not true; there is no similarity in texture or taste. California produces excellent favas, but, like a lot of wonderful things, they require a little work. For this dish you not only have to remove them from their pods but also must slip off their thick skins.

You can add other springtime vegetables, but not in such large quantities as to detract from the favas. The addition of artichokes and peas or fennel, popular around the Mediterranean, will give a certain character and distinction to the stew.

6 *pieces of duck* confit *page 268*	½ *small fennel bulb, trimmed and sliced thin*
6 *to 7 pounds fresh unshelled favas, or about 1 quart shelled beans*	½ *teaspoon sugar*
½ *cup thin-sliced shallots*	¾ *cup unsalted chicken stock, thoroughly degreased*
4 *ounces salt pork, cut into ¼-by-1-by-1-inch pieces (¾ cup), blanched in boiling water for 10 minutes, rinsed, and drained*	*Salt and freshly ground pepper*
	1 *tablespoon olive oil*
2 *small artichoke bottoms, sliced thin*	1 *tablespoon chopped fresh flat-leaf parsley*
	1 *tablespoon chopped fresh thyme*

1. Four to 5 hours before serving, remove the *confit* from the refrigerator. Meanwhile, shuck the beans and discard the pods. Drop the favas into boiling water; allow the water to return to a boil and drain the favas. Rinse them under cool running water and peel off the skins. Cool, wrap them tightly in plastic, and keep them refrigerated until you are ready to cook.

2. One to 2 hours before serving, scrape off any congealed fat from the duck confit. Place the duck in a 10-inch skillet, preferably nonstick, cover, and fry over medium heat until lightly browned and crisp, about 5 minutes. Drain the duck on paper towels. Carefully remove the duck skin and return it to the skillet to render any remaining fat. Drain the skin and throw out all but 1 tablespoon of the fat. Cover the pieces of duck and skin with foil to prevent drying out.

3. Add the shallots and drained salt pork to the skillet. Cover it and cook slowly for 5 minutes. Uncover and continue cooking until the contents are light brown around the

(continued)

edges. Add the artichoke slices, fennel, and sugar, and sauté 2 minutes, stirring. Over high heat deglaze with ¼ cup of water. Remove from the heat. (*To this point the recipe can be prepared 1½ to 2 hours ahead.* Set the skillet, uncovered, in a cool place.)

4. About 10 minutes before serving, preheat the broiler. Meanwhile, add the stock and favas to the skillet and bring the mixture to a boil. Cover tightly, reduce the heat, and cook until the favas are fully cooked, 4 to 5 minutes. Adjust the seasoning with salt and pepper. Put the duck on the broiler pan. Replace the pieces of skin, crisp side up and dab with oil. Run under the broiler to reheat the duck and crisp the skin. Arrange the pieces of duck in a deep, warm serving dish and pour over the favas. Sprinkle with fresh herbs and serve at once.

THREE FOIE GRAS RECIPES

Roast Duck Foie Gras with Port Wine and Caper Sauce

SERVES 4 TO 5
*as a first course or 3 as
a main course*

I was sitting on the terrace of a restaurant in Quercy, in South-West France, beneath the leafy branches of a giant chestnut tree, gazing out at reflections in the lazy Ouysse River. Suddenly, the idyllic calm was shattered by a series of screams: "Idiot! Fool! You don't roast it like that! You are costing me a fortune! Fool!"

There was a crash, the sound of a slap, a shriek—and then a red-faced chef, shaking with fury, appeared at the kitchen door. He breathed heavily, rolled his eyes, regained control, and then rushed back inside. A long silence ensued, lasting perhaps fifteen minutes, while a second *foie gras* (an entire *foie gras!*) was lovingly and carefully roasted for my lunch.

The dish was *foie gras bonne maman*, a whole duck *foie gras* roasted and then sauced with Port wine and capers. The chef's apprentice had initially botched the job by placing the costly liver in too hot an oven, which melted half of it away. When the second attempt finally came to the table it proved sumptuous eating—a dish of sublime and delicate taste, a perfect harmony, too, of disparate ingredients, the acid-piquant capers providing an ideal foil for the delectably rich, silky-smooth moist liver, all balanced by the sweet Port. "Worth doing twice to get it right," said the chef, restored to his normal calm state.

Understandably the chef had been upset. *Foie gras* is one of the most expensive culinary products, revered by gastronomes for its subtle flavor, buttery texture, and extraordinary fragrance. Along with caviar and truffles it is one of the great epicurean luxuries on earth.

Roasting a *foie gras* produces a special texture. The outside of the liver becomes slightly crunchy but the interior remains creamy. For roasting I prefer a perfect large lobe. (I save the smaller lobe for a quick family dinner the following day. See the next recipe, for Sautéed *Foie Gras* with Green Grapes.) Serve this dish with separate purées of celery root and carrot. It should be accompanied by a chilled rich and golden Sauternes.

1 *large lobe of a fresh domestic duck* foie gras, *"A" quality (about 1 pound), soaked, rinsed, and deveined, at room temperature*

¼ *teaspoon salt*

⅛ *teaspoon freshly ground white pepper*

¼ *pound caul fat, about 1 foot square (optional, see page 218)*

2 *tablespoons chopped shallots*

½ *cup imported red Port wine*

   Pinch of sugar

1½ *cups dark, rich veal or poultry sauce base (page 338), reduced to ½ cup*

1 *teaspoon arrowroot dissolved in 2 teaspoons water*

2 *teaspoons strained fresh lemon juice*

1½ *tablespoons small capers, drained*

1. Clean the *foie gras* as directed in the Appendix, page 339. Drain, rinse, and bring it to room temperature 1 hour before roasting. Cut away all surface fat, blood, and any green parts.

2. Thirty minutes before serving, preheat the oven to 425° F. *Foie gras* must be bone dry for roasting. Season it with the salt and white pepper. If the liver has been badly cut up after cleaning, wrap it in the caul fat before roasting. Fifteen minutes later, put the liver in a medium, oval enameled cast-iron gratin dish or ovenproof skillet. Roast it in the oven for 5 minutes. Remove the *foie gras* and reduce the oven temperature to 300° F.

3. Pour off all but 2 tablespoons of the rendered fat, reserving it for another use. Scatter the shallots around the liver. Return the liver to the still-hot oven for 10 minutes, basting with the rendered fat every 3 minutes, until the internal temperature registers 125° F on an instant-reading thermometer. (The *foie gras* will be slightly undercooked. It will finish cooking as it rests, *and* after slicing when the hot sauce is poured on top.)

4. Remove the dish from the oven. Transfer the liver to a kitchen towel and pat it gently to remove the excess fat. (If the caul fat has not melted away, remove and discard.) Cover the liver loosely with foil to keep warm.

5. Pour off the fat from the dish and reserve it for another use. (Poultry is delicious sautéed in *foie gras* fat.) Add the Port wine and sugar to the dish, and bring to a boil over high heat, scraping up any browned bits from the bottom of the pan. Continue to boil until the liquid is reduced to a syrupy glaze, 3 to 4 minutes. Add the rich, brown sauce base and bring to a boil. Cook for 1 minute. Stir in the dissolved arrowroot, and cook, stirring, for 1 minute longer. Add lemon juice to taste.

6. Slice the liver thin on the diagonal and arrange it on warm serving plates. Spoon the hot sauce over the slices (to finish the cooking) and top each portion with capers. Serve at once.

Sautéed Foie Gras with Green Grapes

SERVES 2

A classic dish with numerous presentations. In this particular recipe, the buttery-rich flavor of the *foie gras* goes beautifully with the astringent taste of the tart green-grape sauce. If your grapes are too sweet, add a few extra drops of vinegar to reestablish the proper balance of flavors. When you sauté slices of *foie gras* you have complete control over its cooking: a quick sear in a hot pan, a simple degreasing, followed by a deglazing with a little bit of acidity to offset the richness of the liver, and in minutes you have a great dish. (You'll find that sautéed domestic *foie gras* has a different texture from *foie gras* in France—a little less creamy, but still smooth and velvety.)

Sautéing can be tricky, however, if you are cooking for a lot of people, because you must slice, cook, and serve everyone within minutes. On the other hand, if your kitchen is open to your dining room the process can work out very well.

I have written this recipe for only the small lobe, on the assumption that you will use the large lobe in one of the other hot or cold *foie gras* preparations in this book. You can, of course, triple the recipe and sauté both lobes (in 2 skillets). Serve with steamed sugar-snap peas. The combination brings a wonderful crunchy quality to the smooth, velvety *foie gras*.

1 *small lobe of fresh domestic-duck* foie gras, *"A" quality, soaked and rinsed (see Appendix, page 341), about 9 ounces*

½ *teaspoon salt*

¼ *teaspoon freshly ground white pepper*

1 *tablespoon instant granulated flour, such as Wondra*

1 *tablespoon unsalted butter*

1 *tablespoon aged red wine vinegar*

1½ *cups veal or duck sauce base (page 338), reduced to ½ cup*

3 *tablespoons heavy cream*

⅔ *cup seedless green grapes, peeled*

1. Slice the *foie gras* into 6 slices of approximately equal size, just under ½ inch thick. Season both sides of each slice with half of the salt and pepper. Sprinkle each side very lightly with the instant flour. Dust off the excess.

2. Put a large, heavy, noncorrodible skillet over medium-high heat. When very hot, reduce the heat to moderate and add the butter. When the foam subsides, add the slices of *foie gras* and cook, turning once, for 30 seconds on each side. Remove the liver and drain it on paper towels if necessary.

3. Pour off the fat from the skillet. Add the vinegar and sauce base; bring to a boil over high heat, scraping up any browed bits from the bottom of the pan. Add the cream and grapes and boil to thicken slightly. Season with the remaining salt and pepper. Serve at once on individual heated plates.

<table>
<tr><td>S E R V E S   4
T O   6</td><td>Braised Duck Foie Gras with Vegetables
in the Manner of the Old Périgord</td></tr>
</table>

A whole *foie gras,* perfectly cooked until soft and smooth, nestled in a shallow serving dish, accompanied by braised cabbage and a chunky sauce made of chopped carrots, leeks, and onions, can be an understated but elegant choice for a dinner menu. Slice the liver at the table and accompany it with mashed potatoes (but not just any ordinary mashed potatoes—see page 300). Begin this autumnal meal with a Chestnut Salad with Walnuts and Pancetta. Follow with Italian Black Plums Baked in a Brioche Crust.

Danielle Delpeuch, a *foie gras* expert who gave me this recipe, told me how, when her grandfather would make a four-hour round trip to market in a horse-and-buggy, her grandmother would sometimes prepare this dish in a closed iron pot in the embers in the fireplace, moving the pot around to keep the cooking even and slow. Danielle has updated her grandmother's recipe, using an enameled cast-iron pot over gas or electric heat. Still, I would gladly make a four-hour horse-and-buggy trip knowing I was coming home to a meal like this!

1 to 1½ pounds fresh domestic-duck foie gras, "A" quality	Freshly grated nutmeg
¼ pound caul fat, about 1 foot square (see page 218)	3 medium carrots, cut into ¼-inch dice (1 cup)
1 tablespoon vinegar	1 medium onion, cut into ¼-inch dice (½ cup)
1 small head Savoy cabbage	3 medium leeks (white part only), cut into ¼-inch dice (1⅓ cups)
¼ cup rendered goose or duck fat or olive oil	1½ tablespoons chopped shallots
1¾ cups unsalted chicken stock	1 tablespoon ruby Port wine
Coarse salt and freshly ground white pepper	

1. Prepare the *foie gras* as described in the Appendix, page 342. Place the caul fat in a small bowl. Cover with cold water and the vinegar, and soak the caul for 15 minutes; rinse and drain.

2. Bring a large pot of water to a boil. Meanwhile, remove the outer leaves from the cabbage. Cut the cabbage into 8 wedges, core, and remove the thick ribs. Drop the cabbage into boiling water, cover, and quickly bring it back to a boil. Cook 3 minutes. Drain and refresh it, and repeat with fresh boiling water. Squeeze the cabbage dry in a kitchen towel.

3. Heat 1 tablespoon of the goose fat in a large skillet. Add the cabbage and cook over high heat, stirring, for 1 minute. Add 1½ cups of the chicken stock, ½ teaspoon of salt and

(continued)

THREE *FOIE GRAS* RECIPES   191

¼ teaspoon of white pepper. Cover and cook for 15 minutes. Uncover and boil over moderately high heat, stirring frequently, until the liquid evaporates and the cabbage begins to caramelize slightly, about 20 minutes. Remove the cabbage from the heat and set aside, partially covered. (*Up to this point the recipe can be prepared several hours in advance.*)

4. About 1 hour before serving, pat the *foie gras* dry. Sprinkle it with ½ teaspoon of salt, ¼ teaspoon of pepper and ⅛ teaspoon of nutmeg. Snuggle the smaller lobe into the large one. Gently press the two lobes together to form an egg shape. Wrap them in prepared caul fat.

5. In a 3-quart heavy Dutch oven over medium heat, soften the carrots, onions, leeks, and shallots in 2 tablespoons of the goose fat for 5 minutes. Midway add pinches of salt and pepper.

6. In a heavy 9-inch skillet, melt 1 tablespoon of the goose fat over moderate heat. Add the *foie gras* and cook on one side until browned, about 3 minutes. (The skillet should not be hot enough to form a crust on the *foie gras*, but when it is lightly pressed with a flat spatula, the slightest crust should just begin to form on the bottom.) Meanwhile, sprinkle the uncooked side with pinches of salt and pepper and a generous coating of nutmeg. Turn over and cook the second side until browned, about 2 minutes.

7. Pour off the fat from the skillet. Add the Port wine and gently turn the *foie gras* in the liquid to coat it and form a glaze, about 1 minute. Place the *foie gras* on top of the vegetables in the Dutch oven. Deglaze the skillet with the remaining chicken stock and pour it over the liver. Cover and braise about 30 minutes or until the internal temperature registers 130° F on an instant-reading thermometer. Remove the Dutch oven from the heat and let it stand, covered, for 10 minutes (the liver will continue to cook in its receding heat). Remove any caul fat that has not dissolved.

8. When the liver has rested 10 minutes, carefully transfer it to a heated serving dish. Tip the pan and skim off all the fat, leaving the juices behind. Surround the *foie gras* with the vegetables and the reheated cabbage. Sprinkle with the pan juices. Serve very hot.

SERVES 2	*Grilled Young Partridges with Crushed Lemon*

The faintly gamy taste of partridges and fragrant, tangy lemons make a particularly good combination, and presented on a bed of lettuce mixed with fresh mint, parsley, and thin strands of red onion, the dish is very attractive indeed.

In this recipe the breadcrumb coating protects the partridge, keeping it moist and tender. Many breaded dishes are heavy—not surprising, since the item to be breaded is usually dipped first in beaten eggs. Here the flesh is directly coated with breadcrumbs, then sprinkled with oil, then broiled *immediately*. As a result the coating remains crisp. Note that the second side of the partridge is coated only after it has been turned.

An interesting first course, such as Broiled Artichokes with Pecorino Cheese can combine with this dish to make a memorable dinner for two. Follow with a fruit sherbet surrounded with a luxurious Basil Cream.

2 *one-pound partridges, cleaned*

3 *large lemons*
   Salt and freshly ground pepper

7 *tablespoons extra-virgin olive oil*
   Pinch of cayenne

2 *tablespoons unsalted butter*

½ *cup homemade fine breadcrumbs (see note)*

1 *Bibb lettuce, washed, leaves torn into small pieces*

10 *sprigs flat-leaf parsley, stemmed*

4 *or 5 sprigs fresh spearmint, stemmed*

½ *red onion, sliced thin, soaked in ice water for 10 minutes and drained*

1. Split each partridge down its back. Cut off the wing tips at the second joint (reserve the bones for stock to use at some other time, or discard). Place each partridge with legs "knock-kneed," skin side down, on a work surface and cover with a sheet of waxed paper. Flatten it with a mallet or the flat side of a cleaver. Use a vegetable peeler to strip the rind from one-half a lemon and cut it into fine slivers. Squeeze the lemon half and reserve 1 tablespoon of the juice for the vinaigrette. Lightly season the partridges with salt and pepper, brush with 2 tablespoons of the oil and scatter the slivered rind on top. Let them stand at room temperature up to 2 hours.

2. Preheat the broiler and place the rack, lined with foil, about 6 inches from the heat source. Peel 2 of the lemons, discard the seeds, and chop the flesh to make ½ cup. Season

(continued)

with salt, pepper, and a pinch of cayenne. Scrape off the slivered lemon rind from the partridges.

3. In a 10-inch skillet over medium heat, melt the butter in 1 tablespoon of the oil, add the partridges, skin sides down, and slowly brown for 1 minute. Turn and brown on the second side. Transfer the partridges, skin side down, to the broiler rack. Off the heat combine the skillet juices and the seasoned lemon flesh. Put 3 tablespoons into the cavity of each partridge. Cover with a light breadcrumb coating (using half the amount), and sprinkle with 1 tablespoon of the oil. Immediately broil for 8 to 10 minutes.

4. Carefully turn each partridge, scatter the remaining lemon flesh over the partridge breasts, then coat them evenly with the remaining breadcrumbs. Sprinkle them with 1 tablespoon of olive oil, and run under the broiler to finish the cooking, 9 to 10 minutes. The crust should be well-browned and crisp, the flesh juicy and just cooked (not rare).

5. Cut the remaining lemon half into wedges and set them aside. Make a vinaigrette with the reserved tablespoon of lemon juice, ¼ teaspoon of salt, pinches of cayenne and black pepper and the remaining 3 to 4 tablespoons olive oil. Toss with the lettuce, herbs, and drained red-onion slices. Arrange the salad on a colorful wide platter and place the grilled partridges on top. Garnish with lemon wedges and serve at once.

NOTES TO THE COOK
To make homemade breadcrumbs, chop 2- to 3-day-old crustless bread in a food processor until fine.

Avoid substituting baby guinea hens or pheasants in this recipe—they usually don't have enough flavor to stand up to the lemon.

Pigeon "André Malraux"

SERVES 2

My husband is a great admirer of the French writer André Malraux and over the years has built up a large collection of "Malruciana." When he heard that the Paris restaurant Lasserre (Malraux's favorite) served a dish called Pigeon "André Malraux," naturally we had to try it.

It was delicious, a rare pigeon stuffed with all sorts of "riffraff" *(canaille)*. But what riffraff! In the recipe given to me by M. René Lasserre, the stuffing consists of cèpes and salsify, shallots, herbs, spices, cockscombs, and diced fresh *foie gras!* (In my home version below, the riffraff is a little less luxurious.) What's interesting about this stuffing is that it contains no bread, eggs, or flour, and what's impressive about it is its lightness and the way it keeps the birds moist from within.

Fancy restaurant recipes usually tax the home cook, but I have organized this one in such a way that nearly all the work is done in advance. All you need do is slip the stuffing into the pigeons, tie them up, brown them for a minute or two, then finish them off in the oven. The sauce is a simple deglazing of the pan without any butter or cream.

Boning a pigeon is admittedly not the simplest task one can perform, though it's harder to describe than actually to do. See notes below if you want to bone the pigeons yourself; or take the easy way— have your butcher bone them for you.

Though Malraux will certainly be immortalized for his great novels, and for his exemplary life as author, intellectual, soldier of fortune, and heroic man-of-action, gastronomes may now think of him too, as they think of Nellie Melba and Lord Sandwich, for having given his name to a wonderful dish.

A pleasant beginning to dinner could be Mixed Greens with *Confit* of Duck Gizzards. Serve the pigeon with buttered ribbon noodles. A good ending to the meal would be stemmed strawberries macerated in a fruity, sweet, and aromatic white wine such as Beaumes de Venise. Garnish with shreds of fresh mint leaves.

2 *tablespoons dried cèpes or porcini*

Salt and freshly ground pepper

2 *boned pigeons (approximately 1 pound each), with livers reserved, carcass and wings removed and reserved for stock (see notes for boning, or ask your butcher to do this for you)*

STUFFING

5½ *tablespoons unsalted butter*

⅓ *cup diced fatback, blanched 3 minutes and drained*

1 *teaspoon chopped shallots*

1 *sprig thyme*

1 *small bay leaf*

¼ *teaspoon Spiced Salt (page 259)*

1 *chicken liver, cleaned and cut into ½-inch dice*

⅓ *cup diced cèpes, fresh or canned, drained, sautéed in butter 5 minutes and drained, or substitute shiitake mushrooms, stemmed*

⅓ *cup diced cooked salsify (see note)*

2 *tablespoons Cognac*

1 *small garlic clove, peeled, chopped, crushed with salt into a purée*

1 *ounce prosciutto*

1 *tablespoon finely minced parsley*

¼ *cup dry white wine*

½ *cup reduced pigeon stock (see recipe, page 197)*

2 *tablespoons high-quality Sherry, such as Dry Sack or Tio Pepe*

GARNISH

½ *pound fresh mushrooms, preferably cèpes or shiitake, sautéed in butter*

1 *tablespoon finely minced parsley*

1. Soak the dried mushrooms in ⅔ cup of hot water with ¼ teaspoon salt for 30 minutes. Drain and rinse the mushrooms under cool running water to eliminate any grit or sand. Strain the soaking liquid through several layers of damp cheesecloth. In a small saucepan combine the soaked cèpes and their liquid and simmer for 30 minutes. Raise the heat and cook until well reduced. Use the liquid in the pigeon stock and reserve the mushrooms for the stuffing.

(continued)

2. Meanwhile season the pigeons inside and out with salt and pepper; keep them refrigerated.

3. Make the stuffing: Cut the pigeon livers into ½-inch dice. In a small skillet, melt ½ tablespoon of the butter over low heat. Add the diced fatback and sauté until golden on all sides. Transfer the diced fatback to a work surface. Raise the heat to moderately high, add the shallots, thyme, bay leaf, spiced salt, diced chicken and pigeon livers, and sauté for 30 seconds, or until the livers are just seared. Using a slotted spoon transfer the livers to the work surface. Discard the bay leaf. Add another tablespoon of the butter to the skillet and sauté the diced cèpes and salsify for 1 minute. Remove them to the work surface. Pour off the fat. Deglaze the skillet with Cognac, ignite, and when the flames go out, sprinkle the Cognac over the vegetables. Add the garlic, prosciutto, parsley, 2 tablespoons of the hard butter, and the simmered cèpes from step 1. Using a chef's knife, chop everything together until coarse but well blended. Adjust the seasoning. Makes 1 cup of stuffing. (*Up to this point the dish can be made up to 1 day in advance.* Cool, cover, and refrigerate.)

4. Forty minutes before serving, preheat the oven to 375° F. Divide the stuffing in half, stuff the pigeons, and sew them up with kitchen string. Let them stand in a cool place, but do not return them to the refrigerator.

5. Thirty minutes before serving, melt the remaining 2 tablespoons of butter over medium heat in a deep, heavy ovenproof skillet. Brown the stuffed pigeons, turning, until they are golden brown on all sides, about 2 minutes.

6. Place the skillet in the oven to roast for 18 minutes. (If you are using smaller pigeons, reduce the time to 12 minutes.) Remove the skillet from the oven. Transfer the pigeons to a work surface to rest, cover them with foil to keep warm.

7. Pour off the fat from the skillet. Add the white wine and reduced stock. Boil until reduced to about ⅓ cup. Add the sherry and reduce to ⅓ cup. Season the pan juices with salt and pepper to taste. Remove the strings from each pigeon, cut each one in half, and place on a warmed platter, and strain the pan juices over. Garnish with mushrooms sautéed in butter and sprinkled with fresh herbs. Serve at once.

NOTES TO
THE COOK

To partially bone a pigeon: Start at the tail end. Loosen the skin from both sides of the backbone with a boning knife. Use your fingers to separate skin and flesh from the rib bones and finally along the breast bone. Now switch to the neck and cut out the wishbone. Turn the bird inside out and pull out the carcass in one piece. It is not necessary to remove the bones of the leg. Turn right-side out and remove the wings at the first joint. Use any trimmings, bones, and wings for the stock.

To prepare salsify: See page 281.

The stuffing can be successfully prepared with canned salsify and canned cèpes. Drain the vegetables, dice, and sauté lightly in butter to enhance their flavor.

1 *tablespoon unsalted butter*   2 *sliced carrots*

   Pigeon bones   *Herb bouquet: parsley, bay leaf, and*

1 *sliced onion*   *sprigs of thyme*

                                            The cèpe cooking liquid

Heat the butter in a deep, heavy skillet. Add the pigeon bones and sauté them over moderate heat for 15 minutes, or until deeply browned. Add the vegetables and herbs, cèpe cooking liquid and 3 cups of water, bring to a boil, and skim. Reduce heat to low and cook at the simmer, uncovered, for 3 hours. Strain, degrease, and reduce to ½ cup. (The simmering can be done in a tightly closed container in the microwave, cook on medium for 45 minutes. Cool, strain, degrease, and reduce to ½ cup.)

SERVES 4 TO 8
Stuffed Squab with Chestnut Honey, from Badia a Coltibuono

Lorenza de' Medici, co-proprietor of the famous wine and olive oil *fattoria* Badia a Coltibuono, situated in the Chianti district of Tuscany, has written twenty cookbooks. Therefore, it didn't surprise me when, in response to my remark that her delicious chestnut honey would go well with pigeons, she came up with the following recipe.

The stuffing is a perfect blend of herbs and spices that beautifully flavors pigeon, while the skin is glazed with the bitter-flavored chestnut honey, which offsets the rather rich taste of the meat.

This is a wonderful dish to serve with a crisp green salad. Start the meal with a pasta and finish with fresh fruit and assorted cheeses—blue-veined, smooth Gorgonzola, peppercorn studded pecorino (pepato), and an extravagantly creamy Brillat-Savarin. A glass of the delicious Vin Santo di Coltibuono accompanied by almond flavored *biscotti* would be an ideal ending to the meal.

Chestnuts bloom in Tuscany in late June and July. In July, the beekeepers start making the honey, as the bees work their way through the valleys. Chestnut honey, available at fine food shops, also makes a delicious topping, when warmed, for vanilla ice cream.

(continued)

4 large squab pigeons (about 1 pound each), or substitute 4 Rock Cornish game hens (about 1¼ pounds each)

STUFFING

Livers reserved

1 cup cubed crustless dry peasant-style bread

6 to 8 black peppercorns

1 teaspoon fresh rosemary spikes (2 inch stalk)

2 tablespoons roughly chopped flat-leaf parsley leaves

3 small leaves of fresh sage

2 teaspoons fresh thyme leaves

1 small imported bay leaf

2 garlic cloves, halved and peeled, green shoot removed

12 juniper berries

1 egg, lightly beaten

¼ teaspoon fine salt

3 tablespoons unsalted butter, softened

Salt and freshly ground pepper

1 tablespoon flour

2 tablespoons chestnut honey

1 cup plus 2 tablespoons dry white wine

1. Position the rack in the middle of the oven. Preheat the oven to 400° F (350° F if using game hens). Clean the birds and the livers. Soak the bread in water until soft then squeeze dry; set aside.

2. On a wooden board, using a heavy knife or an Italian *mezzaluna* (the half-moon chopper—the indispensable utensil of any Tuscan cook), chop fine the peppercorns, herbs, garlic, and juniper berries. Then add the livers and chop them with the flavorings until well blended. (Discard one of the livers if substituting Rock Cornish hens.) Use a fork to work in the bread, then the egg, mixing well. Add ¼ teaspoon of fine salt. Makes about 1 cup stuffing.

3. Stuff each bird with ¼ cup of the mixture. Truss each securely, closing up the cavity. Rub the birds with butter, sprinkle with salt and pepper, dust with flour (to make the skin crusty), and place them on their backs in a roasting pan large enough to hold them without crowding. Combine the honey and 2 tablespoons of the white wine in a small bowl. Roast the birds ½ hour, turning and basting after 5 minutes with the honey–white wine mixture. (If using game hens, roast at 350° F for 1 hour, basting often.)

4. When the birds are cooked, remove them from the oven and allow them to rest 5 minutes before untying the strings. Do not turn off the oven. Sprinkle the birds with fine salt and pepper. Degrease the pan juices, then deglaze with the remaining white wine and ½ cup of water. Bring the liquid to a boil, and cook at a simmer for 5 minutes, stirring. Remove the pan from the heat; strain the juices and keep hot.

5. Halve the pigeons and place them cut side down on a heated platter. Return them to the oven with the door ajar to keep hot. Run the birds under a preheated broiler to crisp the skin.

Quail in Red Peppers

In this dish, from the countryside around the Spanish-Catalan city of Tarragona, the lean flesh of quail is beautifully enhanced by a rich, oily wrapping of sweet red peppers. Their cooking juices form the basis for a sauce that is cooked down, and then a *picada* (in this case, toasted almonds pounded with parsley and garlic) is added for additional thickening and flavor. Catalan cooks have a special expression for the thickness required here: they say *"xup-xup!"* to indicate how the bubbling sauce should sound when all the excess moisture has been cooked out.

When you serve this radiant and rich dish, accompany it with a platter of Mallorcan-Style Eggplant and nutmeg-scented rice—and finish with fresh fruit and the Catalan *mel i mató*, drained and molded ricotta cheese decorated with crisscrossing lines of honey on top.

8 *small quail (4 ounces each), breastbone and ribs removed and reserved (see note for boning a quail, or ask your butcher to do this)*

¼ *cup extra-virgin olive oil*

1 *teaspoon fresh thyme leaves, or ½ teaspoon dried*

1 *teaspoon chopped fresh oregano, or ¼ teaspoon dried*

1 *teaspoon minced flat-leaf parsley, plus 5 whole sprigs*

⅛ *teaspoon freshly grated nutmeg*

Coarse salt and freshly ground white pepper

8 *medium red bell peppers*

1 *medium onion, sliced*

1 *soft-stick cinnamon, crushed (see Appendix, page 340)*

2 *plum tomatoes, seeded and chopped*

PICADA

1 *garlic clove*

2 *sprigs flat-leaf parsley*

10 *lightly toasted blanched almonds*

1. Preheat the broiler. Place the quail in a large bowl, sprinkle them with olive oil, thyme, oregano, chopped parsley, nutmeg, and ¼ teaspoon each of salt and pepper. Cover the quail and let them marinate for 30 minutes.

2. Meanwhile, put the pepper under the preheated broiler, and cook, turning often, until they are blistered and somewhat blackened on all sides, but not fully cooked, about 15 minutes. Transfer them to a paper bag and let them stand until cooled. Slit the peppers open on one side and remove the membranes, stems, and seeds. Carefully pull off the skins. Spread out the opened peppers, smooth side down, on paper towels. Season them lightly with salt and pepper, turn them over and let them drain until you are ready to assemble the dish.

(continued)

3. Shake the excess marinade from each quail; reserve the marinade. Heat a large, heavy skillet. Add the quail, skin side down, and sear them over high heat for 1 to 2 minutes. Set them aside to cool. Reduce the heat to medium-high, add the reserved marinade and the quail bones, and cook, stirring frequently, until browned, about 5 minutes. Reduce the heat to moderate, add the onions and 3 tablespoons of water, and cook, stirring, until the onions are soft and golden brown, about 8 minutes. Add the cinnamon stick and tomatoes. Cook for 5 minutes, stirring. Add 2 cups of water and a pinch of salt. Bring the mixture to a boil, reduce the heat, and simmer, stirring occasionally, until the sauce is thick, about 15 minutes. Strain or pass the sauce through a foodmill, pressing down to extract as much juice and flavor as possible. In a small saucepan, reduce the cooking juices to ½ cup. Remove from the heat.

4. Fold the quail into its natural shape and place one on each opened pepper. Wrap the pepper around the quail to enclose it completely, and fasten with a toothpick. Arrange the quail-stuffed peppers in a single layer in a 10- or 11-inch baking dish.

5. In a mortar pound the garlic, parsley, and almonds until pasty. If substituting a food processor, add a few spoonfuls of the sauce to help make the mixture smooth. Slowly stir this into the reserved sauce; the sauce will be thick but will thin out during the final cooking. Season it with salt and pepper to taste. Spread the sauce over the quail and peppers. (*The recipe can be prepared to this point up to 3 hours in advance.* Cover and refrigerate. Let the quail and peppers return to room temperature before baking.)

6. About 40 minutes before serving, preheat the oven to 450° F. Finish cooking the quail on the upper oven shelf, for 15 to 20 minutes, until the quail are cooked medium. Decorate with torn parsley leaves.

NOTE TO THE COOK

To bone the quail, cut off the wings at the second joint. With kitchen shears, remove the backbone from each quail and set aside. With a cleaver gently flatten each quail, skin side down, to loosen the breastbone. Cut or pull out the wishbone, tiny rib bones, and breastbone. Leave in the thigh and leg bones.

Quail with Sage and Green Grapes

It's fashionable now to quick-sear quail so that the flesh remains rosy and all its juices are retained, but longer cooking in a covered skillet allows the bird to absorb delicious flavoring while retaining its succulence.

In this Provence-inspired dish, the quail are cooked with grapes, then the skillet is deglazed with a light vinaigrette. The quail are presented on top of a potato pancake, which absorbs the delicious juices. Start the meal with Broth with Trout Fillets and Fresh Vegetables, and finish with Roast Peaches with Black Currants.

4 *quail (4 ounces each), fresh or defrosted*	2 *to 3 tablespoons clarified butter*
3 *juniper berries*	4 *waxy potatoes*
¼ *teaspoon coriander seeds*	*Salt and freshly ground pepper*
¼ *teaspoon white peppercorns*	1 *teaspoon finely chopped shallot*
Coarse salt	½ *cup unsalted poultry broth*
4 *large leaves of fresh sage, slivered*	3 *teaspoons fresh strained lemon juice*
2 *to 3 tablespoons extra-virgin olive oil*	3 *teaspoons imported walnut or hazelnut oil*
½ *pound (½ cup) green grapes, stemmed and seeded (see note)*	

1. Rinse the quail, pat them dry with paper toweling, and set aside. Combine the juniper berries, coriander seeds, white peppercorns, and ¼ teaspoon of salt in a spice or coffee mill, and grind until fine. Stuff the cavity of each quail with a mixture of spices, sage, and 1 teaspoon of olive oil. Cover them with plastic wrap and refrigerate until you are ready to cook.

2. Peel, wash, and shred the potatoes. Wash them in several changes of water until the water is clear. Keep the potatoes in lightly salted water. Peel the grapes and wrap them airtight. *(Up to this point the recipe can be prepared 2 hours in advance.)*

3. Thirty minutes before serving, heat the clarified butter in an 8-inch seasoned or nonstick skillet until hot. Spread the potatoes in an even layer. Cover the skillet and cook 15 minutes over medium-high heat, shaking the pan often to keep the potatoes from sticking. Every 5 minutes lift the cover off to allow steam to escape. Wipe the inside of the cover dry. Tilt the skillet and spoon off any excess butter; reserve. Cover the skillet and invert it so that the potatoes rest on the lid. Return the butter to the skillet and heat; slide

(continued)

the cake back into the skillet, golden-brown side up. Continue cooking, uncovered, 15 minutes, or until the potatoes are tender and browned. Sprinkle with salt and pepper to taste.

4. Meanwhile, heat the remaining olive oil in a 9-inch skillet over medium-high heat, add the quail, and brown them evenly on all sides, about 5 minutes. Sprinkle the quail with chopped shallots and 4 tablespoons broth, and bring the liquid to a boil. Reduce the heat to medium, and cook 3 minutes, turning the quail occasionally. Add the grapes, cover tightly, and cook for 20 minutes, or until quail tests tender. Remove the quail and grapes to a dish and cover. Add the remaining poultry broth and bring it to a boil over high heat, scraping up any brown bits from the bottom. Reduce to one-half. Meanwhile, combine the lemon juice and walnut oil in a small bowl, whisk them into skillet juices, season with salt and pepper, and remove the skillet from the heat.

5. To serve, slide the potato cake onto a warm serving dish and sprinkle with salt. Place the quail and grapes on top, spoon the sauce over, and decorate with tufts of fresh sage. Serve hot.

NOTES TO THE COOK There isn't much difference in taste between the very small Mediterranean quail (genus *Coturnix*) available fresh or frozen throughout the U.S., and the farm-bred bobwhites. The latter are usually 2 ounces or so heavier. Field or wild bobwhites have much more flavor and are apt to be tougher. These birds should be cooked until the flesh is almost falling off the bones, about 1 hour.

To remove a grape pip, partially straighten a paper clip; slip the loop end into the stemmed part of the grape, and wiggle the wire in order to loosen and remove the pips.

Breast of Pheasant with Red Cabbage

Within hours of my arrival in Alsace, I found myself sitting at a long table in an enormous tent devouring garnished sauerkraut. The village I was visiting was about twenty miles south of Strasbourg, named, not surprisingly, Krautergersheim. The occasion: the town's annual *choucroute* festival, and that afternoon I saw men and women harvesting cabbages in the fields as I drove in.

There must have been five hundred people packed into that tent. There were singing and dancing and laughter and speeches, and the good food kept being thrust at us from the great vats in which it had been prepared. Heaps of steaming moist *choucroute,* slightly crunchy because the sauerkraut had been newly made, splendidly garnished with smoked sausages, chunks of country bacon, and thick-cut slabs of ham. It was my first experience in this region of France, unique in so many ways—for its food and wine, history and architecture, hospitality and warmth.

Several weeks later, on my last day in Alsace, I dined at the famous and exquisite l'Auberge de l'Ill in Illhaeusern, a quintessential French three-star restaurant situated on the bank of a serene river bordered by willows. The town of Illhaeusern is barely fifteen miles from Krautergersheim, but the experience, in terms of food, style, and ambience, might as well have been on another planet.

A feast of sauerkraut eaten in a tent, a banquet served in one of the most illustrious restaurants in the world: two poles on the Alsatian gastronomic axis, each perfect on its own terms.

Among the dishes I ate and learned from Marc Haeberlin at l'Auberge de l'Ill was this easy, elegant family-style recipe for breast of pheasant with red cabbage. It is a wonderful dish to serve with Grated Potato Cakes with Mace, and an Alsatian Pinot Noir.

1 *small firm head red cabbage (about 2 pounds)*

2 *tablespoons aged red wine vinegar, or to taste*

2 *tablespoons sugar, or to taste*

2 *teaspoons coarse salt*

2 *pheasants (about 2 pounds each), with giblets, cleaned*

6 *tablespoons heavy cream*

½ *cup clarified butter or rendered goose fat*

¾ *cup chopped onion*

1 *cup dry red wine, such as a Pinot Noir or Burgundy*

Salt and freshly ground pepper

2 *very tart medium green apples, pared, halved, cored*

¼ *cup all-purpose flour*

2 *teaspoons minced shallots*

2 *tablespoons dry white wine, preferably Alsatian Riesling*

2½ *tablespoons unsalted butter, cut into small pieces*

⅔ *cup well-reduced Pheasant Fumet (see recipe, page 205)*

Begin 1 day in advance.

1. Remove and discard tough, bruised outer cabbage leaves; wash, quarter, and core

(continued)

the cabbage. With a stainless-steel knife cut the cabbage into very thin shreds. Place the cabbage in a large bowl. Add 1 tablespoon of the vinegar, 1 tablespoon of the sugar, and the coarse salt; toss thoroughly. Refrigerate the cabbage, covered, overnight, stirring the mixture once.

2. The next day, remove the giblets from the pheasant; reserve the gizzards and hearts for the sauce and the livers for another use. Using a boning knife, remove the meat from the pheasant as follows: Cut the wings from the breast at the joint nearest the breast; reserve for the fumet. Remove and discard the breast skin. Cut around the wishbone; remove and discard. Slip the knife along the sternum and separate the breast meat from the carcass; remove and discard the tendons. Reserving the carcasses for the fumet, toss the breasts with 4 tablespoons of the cream in a small bowl. Refrigerate the breasts, covered. *(Can be done in advance to this point.)*

3. About 1¼ hours before serving, remove the pheasant breasts from the refrigerator; let them stand at room temperature. Preheat the oven to 400° F. Drain the cabbage, squeezing to extract as much liquid as possible; it should feel almost dry. Heat ½ cup of the clarified butter or the goose fat in a heavy noncorrodible 5-quart casserole over medium-high heat until it "sings." Add the onion; sauté it, stirring frequently, until softened but not browned, about 2 minutes. Add the cabbage; stir to coat it with fat. Add the red wine, ¾ cup of water, the remaining tablespoon of vinegar, and the remaining tablespoon of sugar. Increase the heat to high; heat to boiling. Cover the casserole; transfer it to the oven. Bake until the cabbage is soft but not overcooked, about 50 minutes, uncovering to stir once or twice during the cooking time.

4. Remove the casserole from the oven; taste the cabbage for seasoning. It should have a pleasant, subtle sweet-sour balance. Season with salt and pepper, then adjust the flavor balance as necessary with additional vinegar or sugar. Place the apple halves on top of the cabbage; bake, covered, an additional 10 minutes. Remove the casserole from the oven; stir to combine the apples with the cabbage. Set the dish aside, partially covered, until serving time.

5. Combine the flour, ¼ teaspoon of salt, and a pinch of pepper on a plate. Heat the remaining clarified butter in a large, nonstick skillet over high heat until hot. Pat the pheasant breasts dry; coat them with seasoned flour, shaking off the excess. Add the breasts, without crowding, to the hot butter in the skillet; sauté for 30 seconds. Reduce the heat to low; continue to sauté until the breasts are golden on the first sides, 6 to 8 minutes. Turn the breasts with a spatula. Sauté until the second sides are golden brown and the juices run pale pink, 6 to 8 minutes. Remove the breasts to a warmed serving platter; keep warm, covered loosely with foil, in the oven set at the lowest setting, while completing the sauce.

6. Pour off the fat from the skillet; discard. Replace the skillet over medium heat. Add the shallots and white wine; stir quickly and bring to a boil. Add the Pheasant Fumet;

heat to boiling. Add the remaining 2 tablespoons of cream; cook until the sauce is slightly thickened, about 2 minutes. Over high heat, whisk in the butter, all at once. When the sauce emulsifies, taste for seasoning, and pour the sauce over the breasts. Serve immediately, accompanied by the reheated red cabbage.

MAKES ⅔ CUP　　　　　　　　　　*Pheasant Fumet*

---

2 *pheasant carcasses, including necks, backs, wings, and legs, cut into 1- to 2-inch pieces with cleaver*

¼ *cup vegetable oil*

1 *medium carrot, pared, sliced thin*

1 *medium onion, sliced thin*

1 *tablespoon all-purpose flour*

¼ *cup dry white wine, preferably Alsatian Riesling*

3½ *cups water, or as needed*

1 *small fresh ripe tomato, quartered*

1 *bouquet garni: 5 parsley sprigs, 1 sprig thyme, 2 scallions, 1 medium celery leaf, and 1 bay leaf, all tied with string*

Gizzards and hearts of 2 pheasants, rinsed and trimmed

1. Rinse the pheasant pieces; drain well and dry. Heat the oil in a casserole over high heat. Add the pheasant pieces, in batches if necessary; sauté, stirring once or twice, until they start to brown. Add the carrot and onion; reduce the heat to medium-low. Cook the mixture, covered, 5 minutes. Uncover; increase the heat and sauté, stirring, until the mixture is golden brown, about 3 minutes. Sprinkle it with flour; blend well with a wooden spoon. Cook, uncovered, stirring, until the flour is browned, 2 to 3 minutes. Stir in the wine. Add the remaining ingredients and bring to a boil. Skim carefully, lower the heat and simmer, uncovered, for 1 hour, skimming occasionally.

2. Strain the mixture through a sieve; degrease. You should have about 2 cups of stock. Return it to a small saucepan and bring it to a boil. Set the pan half off the heat; simmer, uncovered, skimming off the skin that collects on the "cool" side of the pan, until the broth is reduced to ⅔ cup, about 20 minutes. Remove it from the heat. *(The fumet can be prepared in advance, cooled, covered and refrigerated up to 24 hours.*

TWO RABBIT RECIPES

Maybe we should blame it all on Beatrix Potter for her delightful stories about cuddly Peter Rabbit—how else explain the reluctance of many Americans to acknowledge this delicious meat? Rabbits, like chickens, are so versatile they can be successfully broiled, sautéed, barbecued, stewed, stir-fried, and braised. And the flavor of a packaged frozen rabbit can be a good deal better than that of an average "fresh" supermarket chicken. Rabbits have been misunderstood in the United States, which is an unfortunate prejudice, since we have such good and reasonably priced domestically raised rabbits available.

Rabbits are lean animals and thus relatively fat-free. Unlike chickens, they grow very quickly, and consequently do not need the hormones and chemicals upon which domestically raised chickens are commonly fed.

Their closely textured flesh is similar to that of veal and chicken, and thus takes well to marinades and then to slow long-simmering cooking, which can transform it into tasty stews, pâtés, and soups.

Rabbits can also be cooked quickly with great success. You can marinate choice, tender parts of the young animals (such as the saddle and hind legs), which you might also wish to lard with highly seasoned strips of fatback, in mustard and oil or crème fraîche, and then simply broil or steam them for as short a time as 10 minutes to achieve a delicious and juicy result.

It's well to differentiate between domestic and wild rabbits, the latter being real hunters' game. Domestic rabbits, as opposed to their wild counterparts, are *never* hung, but they do benefit from an overnight marinade that will develop a deeper, "gamier" flavor.

Each of the following two recipes calls for a tender rabbit, about three months old, which weighs less than 3 pounds. A mature rabbit will weigh between 4 and 5 pounds.

Stemperata of Rabbit with Capers, Green Olives, and Celery

SERVES 3 OR 4

The name of this Sicilian dish, a specialty of the city of Siracusa, derives from a Latin word that means to mix properly or regulate—from which we may infer the importance of a judicious balance of green olives, celery, capers, mint, sugar, and vinegar, to create a harmonious sweet-and-sour sauce. The Sicilian who gave me this recipe was very specific about the size of the pieces of meat, and how each vegetable was to be cut, so that everything would come out evenly cooked at the same time. The result is a tender, succulent rabbit bathed in a chunky, rich sweet-and-sour sauce, garnished with leaves of fresh mint.

Use only a very young rabbit when making this dish. It takes very little cooking time (less than 30 minutes) for a 2¼-pound cut-up rabbit to become tender, while a mature rabbit takes about 2 hours to cook to a tender stage. The strong seasoning eliminates the need for marination. Well-cooked rabbit is always *a bit* chewy—this is considered one of its charms.

This is a superb dish to serve lukewarm or cold. (The recipe can also be made with young skinless pheasant, quail, or chicken.) Serve with an assortment of Sicilian first courses. For dessert, I'd serve crisp, warm Apple Galettes: sautéed fresh apples piled on pastry rounds, and decorated with fried apple peels.

1 *small (approximately 2¼-pound) fresh or defrosted rabbit, cut into 2-inch pieces*

½ *cup extra-virgin olive oil, preferably Sicilian*

1 *medium onion, sliced thin lengthwise (¾ cup)*

1 *cup thin-sliced (¼-inch) tender celery with tops*

1 *small carrot or ½ parsnip, pared and cut into ¼-inch dice*

1 *tablespoon sugar*

6 *large green olives (Sicilian style), pitted and blanched 1 minute, drained and slivered*

4 *tablespoons plus 1½ teaspoons white wine vinegar*

1 *tablespoon drained capers, preferably salted, rinsed and drained (chop if large)*

Pinch of hot red-pepper flakes, without seeds

Salt and freshly ground pepper

2 *to 3 tablespoons poultry stock or water (optional)*

2 *or 3 aromatic fresh mint sprigs, stemmed, leaves torn*

1. Pat the rabbit dry. Heat the oil in a 12-inch noncorrodible skillet over high heat. Add the rabbit in batches (do not crowd) and quickly brown it on all sides. Transfer it to a plate.

(continued)

2. Reduce the heat to medium. Add the onion to the skillet and cook it until soft, stirring frequently, about 7 minutes. Add the celery, carrots, and sugar, and stir until the vegetables begin to caramelize, about 5 minutes. Add the olives, vinegar, capers, red-pepper flakes, salt, and 15 turns of the peppermill. Return the rabbit to the skillet. Raise the heat, boil the mixture hard, and turn the rabbit in the skillet juices, allowing the rabbit and vegetables to glaze but not burn. Adjust the heat so the liquid barely simmers. Cover the contents of the skillet with parchment paper or foil cut to fit and a tight-fitting lid. Cook until the rabbit is tender, turning once and adding stock if necessary to prevent sticking, about 25 minutes. (The rabbit will be most succulent if the heat is regulated to a slow simmer [205° F] in an electric frypan.)

3. Arrange the rabbit and the vegetables on a platter. Top with mint. Cool, loosely cover, and serve at room temperature. (You can bone the pieces *after* cooking for easier serving.)

Inspired by a recipe from Pasqualino Giudice.

Roast Rabbit Stuffed with Fennel and Salami

SERVES 3 OR 4

In central Italy this dish is called *coniglio in porchetta*, which means rabbit cooked in the manner of a suckling pig (i.e., roasted slowly over a fire). In the recipe below, which has been adapted for oven roasting, a whole tender *young* rabbit is boned and stuffed with a fresh and fragrant combination of salami, fennel, and grated lemon rind.

The stuffing and boning can be done hours in advance. The argument in favor of boning a rabbit is that the meat is easier to serve, and you end up with four nice portions from one young rabbit; unboned, it seems to provide only enough for three! (See the variation below for preparing without boning.)

The best parts of a rabbit are its saddle and hindlegs. Unless larded with fatback or wrapped in caul fat, however, these parts tend to dry out quickly. I have a special technique of stuffing and shaping a boned rabbit to keep it juicy and moist during roasting: I roll the thicker thigh and saddle portions onto the inside so that they are protected by the thinner, tougher rib and apron portions around.

On a cold night, start with a Chestnut Soup garnished with sautéed cèpes and prosciutto and lightly enriched with cream. (Make the recipe and freeze half for another dinner.) Good crusty bread and a crisp salad are all you need as an accompaniment to the rabbit.

1 *large fennel bulb with a few feathery leaves*

2 *whole large garlic cloves, peeled*

1 *ounce rindless fatback, cubed (¼ cup)*

1½ *ounces Italian salami, such as soprassata, slivered (approximately ⅓ cup)*

1½ *ounces prosciutto, slivered (approximately ⅓ cup)*

Salt and freshly ground pepper

6 *tablespoons fruity extra-virgin olive oil*

¼ *teaspoon grated lemon rind*

1 *whole young rabbit (approximately 2½ pounds), fresh or defrosted, liver saved for some other use*

1 *tablespoon strained fresh lemon juice*

Steps 1 through 4 can be done up to 1 day in advance.

1. Snip 3 teaspoons of thin, feathery leaves from the fennel bulb; reserve. Trim the bulb, cut it lengthwise into quarters, and cut away the hard core. Simmer the fennel in 2 cups of water with the garlic for 5 minutes. Transfer the fennel and garlic with a slotted spoon to a side dish; let them cool. Continue to cook the liquid until reduced to ⅓ cup. Set it aside for basting the rabbit.

2. Blanch the fatback in boiling water for 3 minutes; drain and cut it into small pieces. Place the fatback, salami, and prosciutto in a food processor; process them with the on-off motion until finely chopped. Add the fennel and garlic and process again until the mixture is chopped fine, stopping the machine and with a rubber spatula scraping down the sides of the bowl as necessary.

3. Heat 4 tablespoons of the olive oil in a medium skillet over medium-high heat. Add the fennel mixture; reduce the heat to medium. Sauté, stirring occasionally, for 5 minutes. Add the lemon rind, ½ teaspoon of pepper, and salt if necessary; mix well. Remove the skillet from the heat; let the stuffing cool. Makes about 1½ cups stuffing.

4. Wipe the insides of the rabbit with a paper towel or kitchen cloth. Use a small sharp knife to bone the rabbit in one whole piece: Place the neck end closest to you on a work surface. Cut away fatty pieces. Split the rib cage down the middle. Detach the flesh from the rib bones, working back toward the backbone along each side. Cut out the bones from the front legs. To remove the entire spinal column, carefully detach the flesh along the upper backbone, one notch of the vertebra at a time. Break off segments of loosened bone sections as you work. (Any pierced flesh can be sewn up later after stuffing.) Carefully loosen the loin meat, but keep it whole. Detach the fillets along each side of the vertebrae. At the tail end, use the point of a knife to loosen and detach all bones. Bone the upper hind legs. (A broth can be made with the bones and reduced to ½ cup to be used in step 7. See notes below.) If the back flesh is very torn up, use kitchen string to sew it together, using a zigzag pattern. Sprinkle the inside of the rabbit with the reserved chopped fennel fronds, salt, and pepper. (*The recipe can be prepared to this point up to 1 day in advance, if the rabbit is fresh, 3 to 4 hours if defrosted.* Cover and refrigerate. Let the rabbit return to room temperature before roasting.)

(continued)

5. About 1½ hours before serving: Preheat the oven to 425° F. Spread the stuffing evenly over the rabbit flesh. Roll up the rabbit, like a rug, beginning with the hind legs. It should now look like a puffed pillow with a hind leg protruding from each of its narrow ends. Sew it up to secure the closings.

6. Rub the outside of the rabbit with the remaining oil; sprinkle it with lemon juice and place the rabbit in an ovenproof skillet just large enough to hold it. Roast the rabbit for 15 minutes. Reduce the heat to 350° F and roast for about 45 minutes longer, or until the rabbit is cooked through and the juices run clear when a thigh is pricked with a fork; do not turn the rabbit while roasting. Baste it every 10 minutes with the reserved fennel liquid and pan juices.

7. Remove the rabbit from the oven; transfer it to a cutting board and wrap it in foil to keep warm. Let it stand 10 minutes before removing all the strings. Meanwhile, skim the fat from the juices and add ½ cup of water or well-reduced rabbit broth to the dish and bring it to a boil. Adjust the seasoning. Carve the rabbit into thick slices. Transfer the slices to a warmed serving platter. Serve the pan juices in a sauceboat.

Variation

To prepare the rabbit without boning: Wipe it inside and out with dampened paper toweling. Sprinkle inside with fennel leaves and salt and pepper to taste. Partially sew up the cavity, starting at the tail end of the rabbit, then place it in an ovenproof skillet just large enough to hold it. Lightly fill the cavity with one-third of the stuffing and sew the cavity up securely but do not overpack. Shape the rabbit into a semicircle; secure it with kitchen string. Rub the skin with 1 tablespoon of lemon juice and the remaining 2 tablespoons of oil. You will need an extra ounce of blanched fatback cut into 3-by-½-inch strips to lard the saddle, rump, and hind legs. With a sharp knife, pierce the thickest part of the flesh 4 or 5 times and force the lardons into the holes.

Roast until the meat is cooked through and the juices run clear when a thigh is pricked with a fork, (1¼ to 1¾ hours). Do not turn the rabbit while roasting. Baste it every 10 minutes with reserved fennel liquid. After 30 minutes, baste it lavishly with pan juices. To carve, remove the hind legs first, then the front legs. Remove the saddle in 2 pieces by cutting along both sides of the backbone and lifting the meat off. Transfer the meat and stuffing to a warmed serving platter, remove the string, and serve it hot accompanied by the pan juices.

NOTE TO THE COOK
To make a simple broth with the rabbit bones: Place bones in a sauce pan, cover with 2 cups water, and bring to a boil. Skim carefully, then reduce to a simmer and cook, partially covered, for 2 hours, skimming occasionally. Simmering can be done in a microwave in a closed container. Cook on medium for 45 minutes. Strain the liquid, degrease, and reduce to ½ cup.

A RECIPE FOR HARE

SERVES 6 TO 8   *Civet of Hare*

In 1983 I was asked by the *New York Times* to describe my most memorable bistro meal in Paris. It wasn't difficult—the memory has been with me for years, and it was a delight to share it. This is what I wrote:

"Basically my favorite bistro is l'Ami Louis. The floor is concave, as if thousands of people have trod back and forth. There are long tables, and the feeling is like a mess hall. The waiters treat you the way they treat you at Elaine's [a Manhattan restaurant where out-of-towners are often treated rudely], except the food is *wonderful*. The walls have a patina of aged dirt. To quote Gault and Millau, the kitchen is from the Paleolithic age and the toilets are Neanderthal.

"The 82-year-old chef, Antonine Magnin, has a long, white beard; he may at times appear hostile toward the customers, but he has the right attitude about food. Eat the *foie gras;* it comes out like thick slices of black bread. Then order the *civet* of hare, and out comes the whole pot. It is enough for *four* people—they give you the whole animal, and they even serve the shot in the sauce. And it's a really thick sauce—there's nothing like it. You scoop up the sauce with your bread. Then you can have potatoes béarnaise, fried in goose fat, the walnuts flown in from the Périgord. Drink Jurançon with the *foie gras,* the house Fleurie with the hare."

The recently deceased Monsieur Magnin did *not* like to share his recipes, but my friend Aude Clement, who had eaten the hare with me, knew pretty much how to make it. With her advice and a recipe in *La Bonne Cuisine de Périgord* by La Mazille, I worked up a version that is close to what I ate in Paris that memorable day.

The success of this *civet* relies on: (1) cutting the hare into only 6 pieces so that the flesh will not dry out during the cooking; (2) slow cooking, which inhibits any toughening of the flesh; (3) using plenty of salt pork, which lubricates the flesh; (4) using a good, full-bodied red wine, solid enough to hold its flavor during the long, mostly unattended cooking; (5) enriching the sauce with the hare's blood and liver (if available), which gives it its strong, delicious taste. (See the note below for substitution if blood and liver are not available.)

A sumptuous dish like this is, of course, at its best with a simple salad, mashed potatoes, and a refreshing dessert such as Frozen Lemon Parfait in a Bitters Mousse with Black-Currant Sauce.

(continued)

1½ tablespoons aged red wine vinegar

2 tablespoons red wine (from the marinade ingredients below)

1 hare, about 5 pounds, fresh or half thawed with blood and liver (see note for substitution)

MARINADE

2 bottles good red wine, preferably a full-flavored Burgundy such as a Fleurie or a Côtes-du-Rhône, at least 4 years old

1 small herb bouquet: sprigs of thyme and parsley, 1 bay leaf, and 1-inch sprig rosemary

1 medium onion, sliced

1 carrot, sliced

3 cloves

3 tablespoons olive oil

1 teaspoon crushed peppercorns

Salt and freshly ground pepper
Flour for dredging

½ pound slab salt pork with rind

1 tablespoon olive oil

1 pound onions, peeled and quartered

4 ounces (1 cup) julienne strips of prosciutto or smoked ham

1½ teaspoons sugar

4 large garlic cloves, unpeeled

5 large shallots, peeled

Pinch of quatre épices or ground allspice

1 large herb bouquet: thyme, parsley, bay leaf, celery leaf, and leek

¼ cup crumbled dried cèpes

1 tablespoon heavy cream

2 tablespoons Cognac or Armagnac

GARNISH

24 to 32 rounds of French bread toasted in the oven, rubbed lightly with crushed garlic

2 tablespoons chopped parsley

Begin 1 to 2 days in advance.

1. Place a rack over a deep bowl. Put the vinegar and 2 tablespoons of the red wine in the bottom of the bowl. Place the fresh or partially thawed hare on the rack. Let all the blood fall into the bowl below, then beat it with the wine and vinegar until they are well combined. Pour this mixture into a small container, cover it with plastic film, and keep it refrigerated. Remove and clean the liver; wrap it in plastic film and refrigerate. Remove the lungs and heart from the chest cavity and discard. Leave the kidney in place.

2. Cut the hare into 6 large pieces. Cut off the front legs and rib cage, separate the hind legs, and leave the remaining back and saddle whole. Place in a deep, nonreactive bowl. Add the ingredients for the marinade. Cover and place in the refrigerator overnight.

3. The following morning, drain the hare on a rack for about 1 hour. Meanwhile, place the wine marinade in a deep nonaluminum saucepan. Slowly bring it almost to a boil, and simmer, covered, for 30 minutes. Strain the marinade through a fine sieve,

pressing down on the solids to extract all juices. Discard the vegetables, herbs, and spices. Meanwhile, dry the hare with paper towels and rub it with a small amount of salt and pepper and flour. Cut the rind off the salt pork. Dice the salt pork; in boiling water blanch the dice and rind for 3 minutes, drain and cool. Sliver the pork rind and scatter it over the bottom of an earthenware or enameled cast-iron casserole or *daubière*, large enough to hold the hare, wine, and fresh aromatics. In a heavy noncorrodible skillet, heat the oil and slowly cook the salt pork, stirring often, until the cubes turn golden brown and a great deal of their fat has rendered out, about 10 minutes. Transfer the browned cubes to the casserole.

4. Over low heat lightly brown the hare in batches in the hot fat in the skillet. Transfer the pieces to the casserole. In the same fat lightly brown the quartered onions and the julienned prosciutto, and add them to the casserole. Pour off all the fat in the skillet. Deglaze with 1 cup of the strained wine marinade. Pour over the hare. Add the remaining marinade, sugar, garlic, shallots, mixed spices, and the large herb bouquet. The wine should just cover the pieces of hare. If necessary add water. Bring the liquid just to boil, top with a circle of parchment or waxed paper, cover tightly, and place the casserole in a preheated 300° oven to cook for 2 hours without disturbing.

5. After 2 hours, rinse the cèpes under running water, drain, and add to the casserole. Cover and cook in the oven another hour without disturbing.

6. Remove the casserole from the oven; transfer the hare to a work surface, discard the rib-cage section, remove any loose bones, cut the meat into generous serving pieces, season with salt and pepper, and cover them tightly with foil. Degrease the cooking liquid, discard the herbs, press the liquid and solids through the fine disk of a foodmill. Return the liquid to the casserole. Bring it to a boil. Set the casserole half over the heat, and cook at a slow boil, skimming on the cool side, for 20 minutes, or until reduced to 3 cups. Adjust the seasoning. Wrap up the hare and sauce separately. (*Up to this point, the dish can be prepared early in the day or one day in advance.* Refrigerate when cool.)

7. An hour and a quarter before serving, skim off any congealed fat. Return the hare and sauce to a clean casserole. Reheat slowly in a 275° F oven for 1 hour. Put the pieces of hare on a heated serving platter, cover them with foil, and keep hot. Bring the cooking liquid to a boil on the stovetop. In a food processor combine the liver, and the mixture of wine, vinegar, and blood, if using, with the cream and Cognac; purée for 1 minute. Add ¼ cup of the hot liquid to the workbowl and process to combine. Slide the casserole half off the heat. Scrape the liver mixture into the cooler part of the sauce. Stir carefully until *all* the sauce becomes thick and creamy, about 5 minutes, but do not allow it to boil. Taste the sauce, then correct the seasoning. Pour it over the hare. (There should be plenty of sauce.) Serve surrounded with toasted slices of French bread rubbed with garlic. Sprinkle with chopped parsley.

(continued)

Often hare is sold without blood and liver, both necessary to thicken the sauce of a true *civet*. That is why I suggest you defrost your hare on a rack to capture some of its liquid as it defrosts. One very fresh large chicken liver can substitute for the hare's liver. Omit any substitution for the blood.

If the sauce does not thicken to the desired creaminess, combine 2 to 3 teaspoons arrowroot with cold water, add to the sauce, and cook gently until thickened.

Hare is of the rabbit family, but while rabbit has white flesh and is very mild in flavor, hare has reddish-brown flesh and is gamy. For this recipe I use blue Scotch hare, fresh or frozen, which is now imported to the U.S. (See Appendix, page 343, for mail-order source.) American jackrabbit is in the same family, and can be cooked in the same manner.

LAMB

Every August, the town of West Tisbury on Martha's Vineyard island hosts a much-loved agricultural fair. For three days the summer people (including me) throng to it, enraptured by such country things as fiddlers' contests and exhibits of home-grown summer squash, mechanical rides for children, exotic fast food for teenagers, and stalls where, if you're an accurate pitcher, you can win yourself a funny hat.

But the real country stuff, the judging of live farm animals, takes place around back. It was there I went one morning to the exhibition of lambs and sheep, in search of knowledge about what makes a lamb taste good. Frankly, I couldn't make much sense out of the mutterings of the judges, but I did notice that the animals belonging to my summer neighbor Arnie Fischer were consistently winning blue ribbons.

Arnie is a classic Yankee farmer, and his saltwater farm is one of the prettiest on the island. His eggs are locally famous, and his forty or so breeding ewes produce numerous lambs, which are the source of utterly delicious lamb chops. I stopped to congratulate him, and when I indicated my interest in lamb, he invited me over for iced coffee. His eyes twinkled behind wire-rim spectacles, as he answered my questions.

"The best lambs are home-grown," he said firmly, "finished off well, with a nice layer of fat. I finish mine off on alfalfa, usually for six weeks." He paused, about to impart a secret. "In the fall I may run them through the oaks for a couple of weeks. Finish them up on the acorns." He nodded, eyes twinkling again. "Yep, when the acorns are good, they seem to make the lamb taste even better. No point, then, in putting on spices. What you want is to taste the meat."

With lamb, I learned, flavor is a function of feeding—the taste of the flesh of these animals is incredibly sensitive to what they eat. (And, according to some, to what they drink. I have heard experts rhapsodize about the flavors imparted by natural spring waters.) Each producer has his own preferred method of feeding. Most American lambs are finished off on grain. In New Zealand farmers raise them on highland grasses, and some may even add turnips. The delicious lambs of Provence graze on wild herbs, and in Brittany they obtain the famous *présalé* taste from grazing the salty meadows around Mont-Saint-Michel. One of the best lambs I ever ate came from the area in Morocco south of Essourira, where the animals munched *zaatar*, a wild herb similar to oregano. I spoke to one man who insisted that the best lambs in the world grazed sagebrush on the western slopes of Colorado. Leon Lianides, proprietor of the famous Coach House Restaurant in New York, prefers Kentucky lambs that have been milk fed, then finished off on Kentucky blue grass. "I'm a Greek," he says, "and we Greeks know about lamb. The animals should be raised in a region where there are clearly defined seasons. Mountain slopes are definitely the best." And he agrees with Arnie Fischer about adding other tastes. "Great lamb," he says, "has a distinct flavor and never needs a marinade." (I think he's right—*if* the lamb is great.)

When buying young tender lamb look for white fat and rosy-pink, firm-textured flesh. When buying racks inspect the rib bones—if they're pink the lamb is young, if white the lamb is more mature. Lamb, remember, is not like steak—there is no marbling within the meat. The fat of a leg, saddle, or rack of lamb is always on the outside; therefore, when you buy lamb you'll do as well with U.S. choice as with prime.

American lamb can be sensational, but it is not always consistent. Therefore, as in any meat buying, a reliable butcher is indispensable.

RECIPES USING LAMB
LEGS AND SHANKS

SERVES 4 TO 6   Roast Leg of Lamb with Tarragon, Anchovies, and Cornichons

My recipe for this flavorful and aromatic dish was inspired by an old French preparation, Gigot de Mouton à la Génoise, which appears in Menon's eighteenth-century cookbook *La Cuisine Bourgeoise*. The leg, partially boned and then stuffed, is wrapped in caul fat—which makes it partially self-basting. For a wonderful crisp crust, the lamb is additionally basted by hand. *Remember,* if you don't baste, you will be baking the lamb, not roasting it.

Serve this captivating dish with a Gratin of Melting Potatoes, and pass the sauce separately. Accompany with a good Bordeaux.

About ⅓ pound caul fat (see note)

1 leg of spring lamb, or shortened leg (shank half), about 4 pounds, leg bone intact

1 teaspoon freshly ground pepper

1½ teaspoons minced garlic

5 tablespoons unsalted butter

2 celery ribs, minced (about ¾ cup)

1 medium onion, minced (about ¾ cup)

3 ounces prosciutto or Westphalian ham, minced

1 can (1¾ or 2 ounces) flat fillets of anchovy, drained, rinsed, soaked in milk, rinsed, and mashed to a purée

2 teaspoons minced fresh tarragon, or ½ teaspoon dried

2 tablespoons finely chopped cornichons (French gherkin pickles), about 5

⅓ cup plus 1 teaspoon white wine vinegar

2 tablespoons olive oil

½ teaspoon salt

2 medium shallots, chopped

⅓ cup dry white wine

¾ cup unsalted lamb or chicken stock

1. Soak the caul fat and set it aside. Season the inside of the lamb with ½ teaspoon of the pepper and ½ teaspoon of the garlic.

2. In a medium skillet, melt the butter over moderate heat. Add the celery and onions and cook, stirring occasionally, until softened but not browned, about 10 minutes. Add the prosciutto and cook for 2 minutes. Remove the skillet from the heat. Blend in the anchovies, the remaining garlic, the tarragon, cornichons, and 1 teaspoon of the vinegar. Set the mixture aside to cool.

(continued)

RECIPES USING LAMB LEGS AND SHANKS   217

3. About 1½ hours before serving: Preheat the oven to 475° F. Stuff the leg of lamb with the anchovy mixture and press the opening shut. Spread the caul fat on a work surface. Put the stuffed leg of lamb, rounded side up, in the center and wrap it completely in the caul fat. Brush it with the olive oil and season with the salt and the remaining ½ teaspoon of pepper. Put the lamb in a roasting pan and roast, uncovered, for 15 minutes.

4. Meanwhile, in a small noncorrodible saucepan, combine the shallots, white wine, and the remaining ⅓ cup of vinegar. Bring to a boil over high heat, reduce the heat, and simmer until the liquid is reduced to ⅓ cup, about 10 minutes. Strain the shallots and reserve both shallots and liquid (see note below).

5. Reduce the oven temperature to 350° F and continue roasting the lamb, basting often with the pan juices, until the internal temperature reaches 125° F, 30 to 35 minutes. Remove the meat to a warmed platter. Cover the lamb loosely with aluminum foil and let it rest in a warm place for 20 minutes. The lamb will continue to cook as it rests. For medium-rare lamb, the internal temperature should be 135 to 140° F.

6. Degrease the pan juices. Deglaze the pan with the vinegar liquid from step 4, then add the shallots and stock; bring the mixture to a boil and reduce the heat to a simmer. Cook for 5 minutes to blend flavors. Adjust the seasoning. Slice the lamb and arrange the slices overlapping on a warmed platter. Serve the shallot sauce on the side.

NOTES TO THE COOK

Caul fat, a lacy, fatty membrane that melts as it cooks, must be ordered from a butcher shop. It is well worth looking for. When you order caul fat, buy several pounds, then freeze it in ½-pound packets. (It can be kept up to 1 year in the freezer.) Use it for cooking lamb, sausages, salmon (see page 126), and terrines. To prepare the caul fat, soak it in several changes of vinegared water (1 teaspoon of vinegar for every 1 cup of water) for 30 minutes. Drain it well and pat it dry.

Ask the butcher to partially bone the lamb for you, or do it yourself by working a thin-bladed knife around the hip end of the leg bone. Loosen the flesh around the bone until you reach the joint, then twist to remove the bone. Do not remove the shank bone.

Straining the shallots (in step 4) is important. The vinegar solution will be used to deglaze the baking pan and will brown fast. If the shallots are added at that point they will burn and make the sauce bitter.

Marinated Grilled Butterflied Leg of Lamb

Even a professionally boned and butterflied leg of lamb will be of uneven thickness, so for this dish I suggest cutting the meat into two parts. The thin part and the thick part are then grilled individually, so that each piece has a good crust and is juicy and pink inside, and no one is left with a slice that's either too rare or too well done. Tie strings around each piece so that when the meat contracts from cooking it will not buckle. And avoid pounding the flesh to even it out—this will destroy the texture. Serve the lamb surrounded with fiddlehead ferns sautéed with garlic in olive oil and finish with Rhubarb Tarts with Whipped Cream and Caramel.

5 *pound leg of lamb, boned and butterflied*

½ *cup olive oil*

⅓ *cup fresh orange juice*

2 *tablespoons lemon juice*

3 *large garlic cloves, crushed to a purée*

1½ *teaspoons fresh thyme leaves*

1 *bay leaf, crumbled*

1 *tablespoon chopped fresh parsley*

½ *teaspoon freshly ground pepper*

Coarse salt

1 *pound firm, bright dark-green fiddlehead ferns, each about 1 inch in diameter*

1. Trim the lamb of excess fat and remove all the fell (the thin membrane that covers the meat). Divide the lamb into 2 pieces, separating the thicker flesh from the thin.

2. In a large baking dish, combine all the oil, the orange and lemon juices, half the garlic purée, thyme, bay leaf, parsley, pepper, and ½ teaspoon of salt. Lay the lamb in the marinade, turning it to coat it evenly. Cover and refrigerate for 6 to 24 hours.

3. Trim away the tips of the fiddlehead ferns. Wash the ferns under running water. Rub off any brown covering. Drop them into fast-boiling salted water and cook until tender, about 5 minutes. Drain the ferns, then refresh them in icy water until cool. Drain them and place in a covered bowl and keep refrigerated until just before serving.

4. About 2 to 3 hours before serving time, remove the lamb from the marinade; reserve the marinade.

5. Light the grill or preheat the broiler. When the coals are white and hot, arrange the grill about 3 inches above the heat. Brush the grill with 1 teaspoon oil and brush each piece of lamb with the marinade. Lay the lamb on the grill and sear it for 1 minute on each side. Remove the meat and season it lightly with ½ teaspoon salt. Let it rest for 20 minutes.

6. For lamb that is less than 2 inches thick, continue grilling close to the coals. For thicker pieces, move the grill 4 to 5 inches from the heat to prevent charring before the

(continued)

lamb is done. Grill, basting frequently with the remaining marinade, until the internal temperature reaches 135 to 140° F for medium rare, about 20 to 25 minutes.

7. Meanwhile, remove the fiddlehead ferns from the refrigerator. In a large skillet toss the ferns with the remaining garlic purée, ½ teaspoon of salt, and 1 tablespoon olive oil over high heat until hot. Add pepper to taste.

8. To serve, slice the lamb crosswise on the diagonal and arrange it on a heated serving platter. Garnish with the sautéed fiddlehead ferns.

NOTES TO THE COOK

To bone leg of lamb completely: place the leg on a cutting board, round side down. Run a boning knife along the exposed shank bone. Cut along the bone, releasing the meat as you work your way to the knee joint. Follow the curves around the bone to release the flesh. Twist to lift out the bone. Spread the meat out on a work surface, rub it with seasoning, and refrigerate until 1 hour before you are ready to grill.

To crush garlic to a purée: Peel and slice it thin, then cut it crosswise, lightly sprinkle with salt, and crush the garlic pieces with the side of a heavy knife.

Barbecued Lamb Steaks with Various Sauces

I suggest you choose one of the four sauces following this recipe to accompany the dish of lamb steaks: Green Garlic-Shoot Butter; Garlic Mayonnaise with Quince and Apple; Garlic Mayonnaise with Honey; or a thick *tapenade*-style sauce made with black olives. All are delicious. I especially recommend the two garlic-mayonnaise variations, traditional in northern Catalonia, as they are unexpected and invigorating.

When you cook a leg of lamb, you normally let it rest for 20 minutes before carving, so that the meat fibers relax and the juices are reabsorbed. Even after a 20-minute rest, a large roast will still be warm when you carve it. But what about thick lamb steaks or chops? André Daguin taught me how to cook them so they are properly done: sear the steaks quickly on both sides, allow them to rest, then return them to a hot oven to finish cooking. Success with this method depends on the precise timing given in the recipe.

2 center-cut lamb steaks (1¼ pounds each), 1½ inches thick

½ teaspoon coarse salt

2½ tablespoons grapeseed or olive oil

½ teaspoon freshly ground pepper

1. Lightly sprinkle the lamb steaks with ¼ teaspoon of the salt, and rub them with 2 tablespoons of the oil. Refrigerate them until 1 hour before serving.

2. Preheat the broiler. Brush the broiler rack with the remaining ½ tablespoon of oil. Broil the steaks 3 or 4 inches from the heat, turning once, for 3 minutes on each side. Remove them from the broiler, cover loosely with a foil tent, and let them rest a minimum of 20 minutes and up to several hours at room temperature.

3. Preheat the oven to 475° F. Place the steaks on a baking sheet and bake them without turning for 8 minutes for rare, 9 to 10 minutes for medium-rare and 11 minutes for well-done.

4. To serve, immediately remove the center leg bone of each steak with a sharp, thin-bladed boning knife. Cut the lamb crosswise on the diagonal into thin slices. Season with a pinch of additional salt and pepper and pass the sauce.

Green Garlic Shoot Butter

SERVES 4

Green garlic-scented leaves spring up from unformed garlic cloves that have been planted in early winter. I have grown them in my New York apartment. Their flavor is very delicate—not at all like the unformed sprout found *within* garlic cloves. In the Charente (the Cognac region of France) they are used to flavor lamb, goat, and omelets. You may substitute Chinese chives, which are more pungent, but milder after a simple blanching.

⅓ *cup (packed) snipped green garlic shoots or Chinese chives without buds, or regular chives*

12 *sprigs of parsley*

6 *tablespoons unsalted butter, at room temperature*

Salt and freshly ground pepper to taste

1. Steam the garlic shoots and the parsley over boiling water for 1 minute. Rinse them under cold running water and squeeze dry in paper towels. Combine the herbs, butter, and salt and pepper in a food processor; purée until smooth. Pass the mixture through a fine-mesh sieve. (The butter can be made a day ahead and refrigerated, covered.)

2. Arrange lamb slices on a serving dish, dot with prepared butter, and serve at once.

Garlic Mayonnaise with Honey and Garlic Mayonnaise with Quince and/or Apple

The following two wonderful and unusual sauces, from the Catalan region of Llessui/ Pallars, are ideal with lamb, goat, or rabbit grilled over an open wood fire or under the broiler. Although these two recipes are very popular with Catalans, they may not survive the American palate.

<table>
<tr><td>S E R V E S   4</td><td>Garlic Mayonnaise
with Honey</td></tr>
</table>

2 *garlic cloves, halved and peeled, with green shoot removed*

¼ *teaspoon coarse salt*

1 *egg yolk*

½ *cup extra-virgin olive oil*

A few drops of lemon juice

2 *teaspoons hot water*

2 *tablespoons (approximately) liquid honey, preferably acacia honey*

Freshly ground white pepper to taste

1. Make a garlic purée: Slice 2 cloves of garlic; chop them roughly. Add salt and crush the garlic with the side of a heavy chef's knife to smooth purée. Or crush the sliced garlic in a mortar. Add coarse salt and continue crushing until a thin purée "ribbons" around the pestle.

2. Place the puréed garlic and egg yolk in the workbowl of a food processor. With the machine on, add the oil drop by drop until all the oil has been absorbed. Remove the bowl from the machine, and stir in the lemon juice, hot water, honey to taste, and salt and pepper. Let the mayonnaise stand at least 1 hour before serving.

<table>
<tr><td>S E R V E S   4</td><td>Garlic Mayonnaise with
Quince and/or Apple</td></tr>
</table>

1 *fragrant ripe quince and 1 Golden Delicious apple, peeled, cored, and quartered, or 2 tart green apples, peeled, cored, and quartered*

Coarse salt

¾ *teaspoon garlic purée (see recipe above)*

½ *cup extra-virgin olive oil*

Salt, pepper, sugar

1. Rinse the quince, rubbing each with a wet cloth to remove dirt and fuzz. Cut the quince into quarters, leaving skins, seeds, and cores intact. Place it in a noncorrodible heavy saucepan with 2 cups of lightly salted water. Heat to boiling and cook 30 minutes. Add the apple and continue cooking until all the fruit is tender. Transfer it with a slotted spoon to a foodmill fitted with a fine disk; purée. Return the fruit to the saucepan and cook, stirring, to reduce it to ½ cup of purée. Cool to warm.

2. Place the fruit purée in the workbowl of a food processor; add the puréed garlic. With the machine running add the oil drop by drop until all the oil has been absorbed. Stop adding oil when it begins to float on the surface of the mixture, indicating it cannot

(continued)

absorb any more. Season to taste with salt and pepper. Add sugar to taste, if necessary. Scrape the sauce into a serving bowl and let it stand 1 hour before serving.

NOTE TO
THE COOK

Quince is available in fall and early winter. If you use only apples, cook them in water with a thick slice of lemon for 10 minutes or until they are soft; drain, purée, and return the apples to the saucepan to reduce to ½ cup. A drop of lemon juice may be necessary to bring up the flavor.

Inspired by a recipe from Els Olis de Catalunya i la Seva Cuina *by Jaume Ciurana and Llorenç Torrado.*

Black-Olive Sauce   S E R V E S   4

The best olives for this sauce are black, sun-ripened, and dried on a salt bed—therefore wrinkled. I like either the rich, oily, slightly salty, and subtly bitter Greek *thassos* olives (also called *throumbes*), or the wrinkled Moroccan variety with a hint of creaminess. Here their qualities of crunchiness and meatiness contrast nicely with the soft anchovies, while their special aroma lends the sauce a perfume that is unique.

36 *wrinkled black olives, soaked 10 minutes in warm water, pitted and drained (⅔ cup)*

2 *garlic cloves, halved and peeled, green shoot removed*

½ scant *teaspoon hot red-pepper flakes, or to taste*

6 *flat fillets of anchovies, soaked in milk, rinsed, and drained*

Pinch of dry mustard

6 *tablespoons unsalted butter*

2 *teaspoons (or more) strained fresh lemon juice*

1 *tablespoon meat stock or water (optional)*

Combine the olives, garlic, ¾ cup of water, and red-pepper flakes in a small, heavy saucepan; bring them to a boil. Reduce the heat to medium and cook uncovered, stirring often to prevent burning, for 15 minutes. The contents should be a thick mass with very little moisture left in the pan. Purée the contents of the saucepan in a food processor with the anchovies, mustard, and butter. Press the mixture through a fine sieve. Add lemon juice to taste. Thin with stock or water if desired. Serve at room temperature.

"Bell-Cooked" Lamb Shanks with Lemon Potatoes, Cephalonian Style

This delicious recipe for roast lamb is from the Ionian island of Cephalonia. In the original version, an entire leg of lamb is cooked in a special pot (called a *tserepa*) made of clay and hay. The pot itself is placed in a fire until extremely hot, then removed. The meat is then added and allowed to cook, even as the pot slowly loses its heat. As a result of this reverse-heat method, the lamb obtains a unique buttery texture.

The recipe works well adapted to lamb shanks (the shank half of a partially boned leg of lamb can also be used), and an enameled cast-iron casserole makes a good substitute for the *tserepa*. Because of the very high oven temperatures at which you'll initially be working, I suggest you keep heavy padded mitts and large kitchen tongs near at hand.

4 *lamb shanks (about 1 pound each)*

3 *large cloves garlic, peeled and slivered*

1½ *teaspoons salt*

¾ *teaspoon freshly ground pepper*

½ *cup strained fresh lemon juice*

3 *tablespoons chopped fresh parsley*

1½ *teaspoons chopped fresh thyme*

1½ *teaspoons crumbled dried wild Greek oregano*

3 *tablespoons unsalted butter, melted*

5 *tablespoons extra-virgin olive oil, preferably Greek*

½ *cup chopped onion*

1½ *pounds (3 medium-size) boiling potatoes, pared, quartered lengthwise*

1. Wipe the lamb; trim away any excess fat. With a small, sharp knife, make incisions all over the surface of the shanks and insert slivers of garlic. Combine 1 teaspoon of the salt and ½ teaspoon of the pepper; rub them over the lamb.

2. Place the shanks in a large bowl; sprinkle with ¼ cup of the lemon juice. Combine 1 tablespoon of the parsley, 1 teaspoon of the thyme, and the oregano on a plate or shallow dish. Roll the lamb shanks in the herb mixture to coat; return them to the large bowl. Let them stand, loosely covered, at room temperature for 1 to 2 hours.

3. About 2¼ hours before serving, place a 4-quart enameled cast-iron casserole in a cold oven. Place the lid on a lower rack. Turn the oven to the highest setting (500° to 550° F). While the oven is heating (about 20 minutes), lift the lamb shanks from the bowl; wipe off excess moisture and coat the shanks with melted butter. Reserve the marinade. When the hottest oven temperature has been reached, use tongs to carefully place the lamb shanks in the hot casserole. Brown the shanks, uncovered, in the oven for 10 minutes.

4. Heat the marinating liquid in a small saucepan; add ¼ cup of water and bring to a boil. When the lamb shanks are browned, pour the boiling marinade carefully down

(continued)

inside the casserole. Cover tightly with a sheet of heavy-duty foil. Use heavy oven mitts to carefully remove the lid from the lower rack of the oven; place it securely over the foil-covered casserole. Reduce the oven temperature to 350° F; bake at this setting for 45 minutes.

5. Meanwhile, heat the oil in a large, heavy skillet over medium-high heat. Add the chopped onion and 2 tablespoons of water, and cook until the onions are softened but not browned and all the moisture has evaporated, about 3 minutes. Stir in the potatoes; sauté, stirring frequently to coat with oil, for 5 minutes. Add ⅓ cup of hot water, the remaining ¼ cup of lemon juice, 1½ tablespoons of the parsley, the remaining ½ teaspoon of salt, the remaining ½ teaspoon of thyme and the remaining ¼ teaspoon of pepper. Heat over high heat to boiling. Cook, covered, 25 to 30 minutes, stirring gently several times. The potatoes must not stick. Transfer them to a shallow 6-cup (about 10 by 6 inches) ovenproof serving dish. Spoon the juices over the potatoes to coat them evenly.

6. Reduce the oven temperature to 200° F; place the potatoes in the oven on the lower rack. Bake the potatoes and lamb shanks for 30 minutes.

7. Turn off the oven and allow the meat and potatoes to sit undisturbed an additional 20 minutes with the oven door shut.

8. Remove the lamb shanks and arrange them on a warmed serving platter; surround with the lemon-flavored potatoes. Sprinkle with the remaining ½ tablespoon of parsley. Degrease the lamb juices, adjust the seasoning, and pour the juices over the lamb. Serve at once.

NOTE TO THE COOK   The lamb can be marinated, covered, in the refrigerator up to 2 days. Allow about 2 hours for the chilled meat to come to room temperature before proceeding with the recipe.

THREE MOROCCAN LAMB TAGINES

The major characteristic of a Moroccan meat *tagine* is a highly seasoned sauce, gently reduced to a silken texture through long, slow, steady cooking. Fruits or vegetables are added in abundance; they are not intended merely to garnish but to become the dominant component, pushing the taste of the meat into the background flavor of the sauce.

Most *tagines* involve slow simmering of less-expensive meats. In these recipes lamb neck or shoulder or shank is cooked until it is falling off the bone. See page 4 for a simple recipe for anise-flavored bread, which I highly recommend you make and serve with the following *tagines*.

SERVES 6 | *Lamb Tagine with Melting Tomatoes and Onions*

Tagines that combine prunes (or quince, crab apples, dates, Seckel pears, apricots, raisins, or sweetened tomatoes) with lamb or chicken are among the most popular dishes in the Moroccan culinary repertoire. Sadly, many visitors to Morocco are discouraged by carelessly prepared, overly sweetened meat and fruit preparations, and consequently avoid them. When these dishes are properly made, however, they are utterly delicious.

Here is the recipe for one of my favorites of these *tagines*; I make it a day in advance, then reheat it slowly in the oven for one hour to further develop a melting texture. The lamb is cooked in a peppery sauce with saffron, onion, and ginger, then topped with a two-tiered layer of onion and tomato given depth by sugar and cinnamon. The thick onion and tomato slices are cooked together for a long time until almost all of their moisture evaporates and a charred, caramelized crust has formed on their surface. I suggest making this dish only when big red-ripe flavorful tomatoes are available.

3 pounds lamb shoulder and neck, cut into 9 or 10 pieces

1 tablespoon coarse salt

½ tablespoon finely ground black pepper

¾ tablespoon ground ginger

Pinch of powdered saffron

¼ cup grated onion (1 small)

¼ cup vegetable oil

3 pounds large Spanish onions, cut into ½-inch-thick slices

½ cup granulated sugar

2 level teaspoons ground cinnamon

2¼ pounds (3 or 4 large) red-ripe tomatoes

1. Trim the lamb of excess fat and place the meat in a medium flameproof casserole. Sprinkle the salt, pepper, ginger, saffron, grated onion, and oil over the meat and add 3

(continued)

cups of water. Bring the liquid to a boil, reduce the heat, and simmer, covered, 1½ hours (the lamb is three-quarters cooked).

2. Preheat the oven to 375° F. Arrange the onion slices in 2 layers in a large, shallow roasting pan. Strain the cooking juices from the lamb, measure, and if necessary add water to make 3 cups. Pour the 3 cups of cooking liquid over the onions; sprinkle with ¼ cup of the sugar and 1 teaspoon of the cinnamon. Bring the onions and liquid to a boil over high heat; remove from the heat. Cover the pan tightly with foil, place it on a jelly-roll pan to catch any drips, and bake in the top third of the oven for 1 hour, or until the onions are soft.

3. Meanwhile, core the tomatoes and slice each 1 inch thick. Sprinkle with 1 tablespoon of the sugar and set aside.

4. Fold back the foil, cover the onions with a neat layer of the tomato slices and sprinkle with 2 tablespoons of the sugar and the remaining cinnamon. Tightly cover the pan with foil again and bake for 20 minutes. Remove the pan from the oven, but leave the oven on.

5. Carefully pour the onion-tomato juices over the lamb in the casserole and bring to a boil. Simmer, uncovered, until the lamb is falling off the bone, about 30 minutes. Remove the lamb with a slotted spoon, correct seasoning with salt and pepper, let it cool and then discard the bones and most of the fat that surfaces. Boil the cooking juices over high heat until they are reduced to 1 cup, about 15 minutes. Meanwhile, return the onions and tomatoes to the oven and bake them uncovered for about 20 minutes, until lightly browned.

6. Increase the oven temperature to 400° F. Assemble the *tagine* in a large, shallow baking dish, preferably round. Place the lamb in one layer, and with a flat spatula carefully arrange the onion and tomato slices on top of the lamb; spoon the sauce over all.

7. Sprinkle the tomatoes with the remaining tablespoon of sugar and return the *tagine* to the oven to glaze and turn crusty (a little charring makes the tomatoes taste even better), 20 to 30 minutes. Serve hot at once. (*Or cool, cover, and refrigerate overnight. Reheat the* tagine *in a 300° oven for at least 1 hour, until hot.*)

Tagine of Lamb, Pumpkin, Chick-peas, and Raisins

One of the mistaken notions people have about Moroccan cuisine is that it is highly spicy. Many dishes are hot, but Moroccans, for the most part, actually seem to prefer sweetened foods.

To intensify the sweetness of this delicious *tagine*, a Moroccan cook will add a rich mixture of spices called *ras el hanout* (literally "top of the shop"). Just as every Indian cook has her own formula for curry powder, so each Moroccan has her recipe for *ras el hanout*. Some employ as many as a hundred spices; my formula, which follows this *tagine*, requires fewer than ten.

If I may repeat one point for emphasis, it is that *long, slow cooking* is the secret of exquisite Moroccan *tagines*. These stews are relatively easy to assemble, but the cooking must be slow to achieve the proper finish—the enticing aroma, the wonderfully intense flavor, the rich, melting texture.

This is excellent to serve with Couscous and Spiced Vegetables. Simply omit the instructions for the chicken *tagine* in that recipe.

3 *pounds lamb shanks, sawed crosswise into 1-inch pieces (ask your butcher to do this for you)*

⅓ *cup grated onion (1 small onion)*

Pinch of powdered saffron

Ground ginger

½ *teaspoon ras el hanout (see recipe below)*

3 *soft sticks of cinnamon or 1 hard stick*

6 *tablespoons unsalted butter*

Coarse salt and finely ground black pepper

½ *pound dried chick-peas, soaked overnight in water to cover, peeled before cooking as directed in notes below, or 1 cup canned chick-peas, drained and peeled as directed*

5 *large Spanish onions (about ¾ pound each), quartered and sliced lengthwise*

2 *pounds pumpkin or butternut squash— peeled, cored, and cut into 6 pieces, about 3-by-2-by-½-inch*

1 *pound carrots, peeled and cut into 2-inch lengths*

½ *pound raisins (2 cups), preferably Muscat*

¼ *cup honey, preferably orange blossom*

Ground cinnamon

Can be prepared one day in advance and slowly reheated.

1. Place the lamb in a large casserole, preferably enameled cast iron. Add the grated onion, saffron, 1 teaspoon of ginger, the *ras el hanout,* cinnamon sticks, 3 tablespoons of the butter, 1 teaspoon of the salt, ¼ teaspoon of pepper, and the *peeled* uncooked chick-

(continued)

peas (if using canned chick-peas, do not add them until step 5). Add 4 cups of water and bring the mixture to a boil. Cook over low heat, covered, for 1½ hours. Midway add the Spanish onions to the casserole.

2. Remove the lamb to a 10-inch shallow ovenproof serving dish and let it cool. Leave the broth with the onions and chick-peas in the casserole.

3. Discard the lamb bones. Season the meat with additional salt, pepper, and a sprinkling of ground ginger.

4. Skim the fat off the broth in the casserole. Add the pumpkin, carrots, and raisins. Cook for 15 minutes.

5. Preheat the oven to 425° F. Add the honey and 2 tablespoons of butter to the broth. Bring the broth to a boil and cook for 5 minutes. With a slotted spoon, remove the partially cooked pumpkin slices and set them aside. Remove the onions, carrots, raisins, and chick-peas and add them to the lamb. (If using canned and peeled chick-peas, add them at this point.) Arrange the pumpkin attractively over the meat. Discard the cinnamon sticks.

6. Boil the broth over high heat, uncovered, until reduced to 1½ cups, about 20 minutes. Adjust the seasoning with salt, pepper, and *ras el hanout* to balance sweet and spicy. Pour the sauce over the lamb and pumpkin and dot with the remaining 1 tablespoon of butter.

7. Bake uncovered in the top third of the oven until the pumpkin is slightly glazed, about 20 minutes. Serve the *tagine* hot or warm with a light dusting of ground cinnamon. (*The recipe can be made a day ahead.* Cool and refrigerate, covered. Reheat in a 325° F oven.)

NOTE TO
THE COOK

For this recipe you should peel the chick-peas; otherwise their skins may catch in your teeth and throat, and, more important, impart an unpleasant flavor to the dish. Fresh-cooked chick-peas taste better and are more easily digested when prepared this way.

To skin soaked, uncooked chick-peas: Throw the chick-peas into boiling water to which 1 teaspoon baking soda has been added, then bring the water back to a boil. Boil 5 minutes and drain. When cool enough to handle, take a handful and rub them between the palms of your hands so that the skins loosen and break off. Drop the peeled peas into a bowl of cold water, then take up another handful. Any floating skins should be discarded. Wash the peeled peas well before continuing to cook. Do not be disturbed about the baking soda —nutrients are not lost—the chick-peas are only cooked for 5 minutes. The soda is thrown out with the first water. Afterward cook the chick-peas as directed in step 1 above, or in clean water with an onion segment until tender. Uncooked peeled chickpeas should not be stored in water, but kept covered and refrigerated until ready to cook.

If using canned chick-peas, simply immerse the drained chick-peas in a bowl of cool water, then rub them with fingertips until all the skins rise to the surface.

1 *teaspoon cumin seeds*

1 *teaspoon ground ginger*

1¼ *teaspoons coriander seeds*

1½ *teaspoons black peppercorns*

¼ *teaspoon cayenne pepper*

4 *whole cloves*

6 *allspice berries*

6 *blades of soft-stick cinnamon (about 1½ teaspoons ground cinnamon)*

Combine the spices in an electric spice grinder or blender. Sieve them and bottle carefully to preserve the freshness.

Moroccan Lamb Tagine Smothered with Olives

SERVES 6

The combination of lemon and olives is so popular in Morocco that one ought to regard it as a general theme on which numerous variations, each one applicable to a specific catergory of sauce, are possible. Different-flavored olives work best with specific combinations of spices. For example, the following multi-spiced classic employs the green-cracked type of olives, more appropriate here than mellow reddish purple olives, which are used with sauces made with a combination of ginger, saffron, and olive oil. As the sauce begins to boil, the cracked olives will release some of their flesh, which in turn will thicken the sauce.

3 pounds meaty lamb neck chunks, cut into 1½-inch chunks

Pinch of powdered saffron

1 teaspoon ground ginger

1 teaspoon fine, freshly ground pepper

½ teaspoon ground cumin

½ teaspoon sweet paprika

3 garlic cloves, minced

1 teaspoon salt

2 tablespoons olive oil

¾ cup grated onions, rinsed and squeezed dry (see note)

⅔ cup minced fresh parsley

⅓ cup minced fresh coriander

1 pound cracked green olives, drained and pitted if desired

3 to 5 tablespoons strained fresh lemon juice or to taste

1 recipe Moroccan bread (page 4)

1. Trim the lamb of excess fat. With a mortar and pestle or in a blender, make a paste of the saffron, ginger, pepper, cumin, paprika, garlic, salt, and oil. In a 4- or 5-quart casserole toss the lamb with the spice paste over very low heat for 2 minutes. Stir in the onions, herbs, and 3 cups of water. Bring the mixture to a boil over high heat, reduce the heat to low, and simmer, covered, for 2 hours, or until the meat is very tender and almost falling off the bones. Remove the casserole from the heat and let it cool. (*The recipe can be prepared in advance to this point—up to 2 days.* Cool, cover, and refrigerate.) Skim off all the fat that rises to the surface.

2. In a medium saucepan, combine the olives with cold water to cover. Bring the water to a boil over high heat and cook for 30 seconds; drain.

3. About 30 minutes before serving, preheat the oven to 450° F. With a slotted spoon, remove the lamb from the casserole, cut the meat from the bones, and place the meat in a shallow ovenproof serving dish. Bake on the upper shelf of the oven for 15 to 20 minutes, or until the meat is lightly crisped.

4. Meanwhile, add the olives to the juices in the casserole. Boil over high heat until the juices are reduced to a thick gravy, about 10 minutes. Stir in lemon juice to taste. Season the juices with salt if necessary. Cover the lamb completely with olives and sauce, and serve with slices of Moroccan Bread.

NOTES TO
THE COOK

The complementary and subtle tastes of the spices can only be achieved through slow cooking. Certain spices in Moroccan cooking must be ground fine, so please don't substitute grated fresh ginger or coarse-ground black pepper. It is best to grind black peppercorns in a spice mill just before using.

The food processor does a fine job of "grating" onions. Cut up 1 or 2 onions and pulse until they are well chopped. Then dump them into a strainer and rinse under fresh water. Squeeze them dry and measure ¾ cup.

Use Greek green-cracked olives or Nafplion green olives, often sold in jars in Greek grocery stores and in many supermarkets under the labels "Peloponnese," "Krinos," or "Fantis."

BEEF
RECIPES FOR THREE BEEF STEWS

SERVES 6

Daube of Beef in the Style of Saintes

Few beef stews have as rich a flavor, as buttery a texture, and as heady an aroma as this famous dish from the Charentes region of France. Traditionally the beef, a calf's foot, and vegetables are browned in an earthenware pot (*calin*) lined with pork rind, then placed in the oven to cook very slowly so that all the gelatin in the calf's foot and in the pork rind is released. After a few hours the foot and skin are removed, cut into small pieces, then placed back in the *calin* to break down even further as the cooking proceeds. Thus the juices (they are never called a sauce in this part of France) become rich and savory.

For this *daube* you should use a fairly big red wine, one with plenty of tannin. I suggest a full-bodied Rhône wine, or a young California Cabernet Sauvignon. To achieve smoothness, the wine and Cognac are first flamed together, their flames extinguished before they die out. This may seem an

(continued)

unnecessary step, but local Charentaise cooks swear it is crucial: if the flames are allowed to go out on their own, the wine may "burn" and develop a bitter taste.

Serve this *daube* with steamed potatoes or fried bread slices rubbed with garlic. Follow with a mixed green salad and an assortment of cheeses: Chaumes, Brillat-Savarin, and Bleu d'Auvergne.

3 pounds beef top blade (ask butcher for one whole piece "chicken steak")

2 tablespoons French peanut oil, or unflavored vegetable oil

5 tablespoons unsalted butter

½ cup (5 ounces) fatback or salt pork, blanched 5 minutes, rinsed, drained, cut into lardons

½ pound fresh or salted pork rind (see note), blanched 5 minutes, cut into wide strips

1 calf's foot or 2 small pig's feet, each cut into 3 or 4 pieces and blanched 3 minutes, rinsed, drained, and dried

2 medium-sized onions, sliced thin

2 pounds carrots, pared and cut into thick slices (½ inch)

20 large shallots (½ pound), peeled

6 cups full-bodied red wine

½ cup Cognac

½ head garlic, peeled

Bouquet garni: 5 sprigs flat-leaf parsley, 2 sprigs thyme, 1 bay leaf, 3 celery leaves, and 3 leek greens, tied together with string

Salt and freshly ground pepper

12 to 16 thin slices French bread

2 tablespoons unsalted butter, softened

1 garlic clove, halved

Do steps 1 through 5 one day in advance.

1. Trim the beef of all surrounding fat, then cut it into 12 pieces of approximately equal size. Thoroughly dry the meat with paper toweling. In a heavy-bottomed skillet heat the oil over high heat, add the meat in batches, cover the skillet, and brown the beef on all sides, about 10 minutes for each batch. Drain it in a colander set over a plate to catch the drippings. Degrease the skillet, deglaze with ½ cup of water, and scrape the drippings into a small bowl.

2. Meanwhile, heat 4 tablespoons of the butter in a 7- to 9-quart earthenware or enameled cast-iron casserole. Add the lardons, the pork rind, and the calf's foot, and brown them *lightly* on all sides, about 15 minutes. Add them to the beef in the colander.

3. Cook the onions, half the carrots, and the shallots in the buttery juices in the casserole until golden, about 10 minutes. Using a slotted spoon transfer the vegetables to a side dish. Pour off the pan juices and reserve. Line the bottom of the casserole with pork rind, fat side down (the skin sticks). Top with the beef, vegetables, pork, and calf's foot. Degrease the drippings and reserved pan juices and add them to the casserole.

4. In a very deep nonaluminum saucepan heat the wine and Cognac until hot but not boiling. Remove them from the heat. Set the liquid aflame (be sure to avert your face) and

let it burn 2 minutes, then cover the saucepan to extinguish the flames. Add the liquid to the casserole. Stir to blend. Add the garlic and herbs. Slowly bring the mixture to a simmer, cover tightly, and cook over very low heat for 2½ hours.

5. Remove the beef to a deep bowl; cover it to keep it from drying. Remove the meat from the calf's foot while still warm. Chop the meat from the calf's foot, pork rind, and pork lardons with a knife until spongy and light. Spread the chopped mixture over the meat. Top with the vegetables and pour over the cooking liquid. Cool, cover, and refrigerate overnight.

6. *Four hours before serving,* remove the bowl from the refrigerator and lift off all the congealed fat. Let the meat come to room temperature, about 1½ hours. Toss the remaining carrots with the remaining butter in a skillet; cover and cook over medium heat for 2 minutes. Add to the casserole.

7. Two and a half hours before serving, preheat the oven to 300° F.

8. Cover the *daube* and set it in the oven to finish cooking, about 2 hours. Transfer the meat, the butter-glazed carrots, and all the shallots to a warm platter, and cover them with a foil tent to keep warm. Strain the remaining ingredients through a sieve, pushing down on the solids to extract as much flavor as possible. Return this sauce to the heat and bring it to a boil. Reduce it to a napping consistency. Adjust the seasoning and pour the sauce over the meat and vegetables. Serve at once with buttered and broiled slices of French bread rubbed with a cut piece of garlic.

Pork rind can be cut off either fatback or lean salt pork, or it can be purchased separately from a pork butcher. Do not use bacon rind, which is smoked. NOTE TO THE COOK

(Stifado)

Greek Beef Stew with Tomatoes and Onions

SERVES 8

I like the way Greeks entertain; they make it all so easy. First, they don't worry too much whether their dishes are hot or cold—many are served at room temperature. Second, they treat food as one of life's pleasures: you won't hear Greeks sitting around analyzing what they're eating—they're too busy enjoying it. Third, they present food nicely, scattering small dishes of uncomplicated appetizers (*mezethes*) all over the table to be shared: pieces of marinated fish; slices of fried eggplant with dollops of yogurt; store-bought pickles; herbed or spiced Greek olives; a slab of feta cheese; a bowl of shredded cabbage and carrots with capers and a lemon-oil dressing; a basket of crusty bread; and a dish of boiled greens called *horta* (see page 293). When ready for the main course, they merely add it to the assembly, leaving the plates of *mezethes* in place, unless of course they have been eaten up.

The *stifado*, or *stefatho* (onion and meat stew), presented here is adapted from a recipe given to me by Mrs. Toula Patsoulas of Detroit, who in turn learned it from her grandmother, who was from the Peloponnesus region of Greece. A large number of baby white or red onions, cooked to melting softness, smother chunks of fork-tender meat or game, which are then enrobed in a jamlike tomato sauce flavored with allspice and cinnamon. A slice of feta cheese on the plate works beautifully with this superb Greek meat stew.

In Greece, lean pieces of hare, venison, or rabbit would be the meat of choice, first marinated in vinegar and then gently stewed until fork-tender. I substitute meaty beef short ribs, which I don't marinate, but which I brown thoroughly before stewing. (Some Greek friends have told me this is incorrect, but I find it gives the stew more flavor.) By the way, the sweetened caramelized onions are not just a garnish: they make the dish special, with an incredibly intense flavor. As a general rule, by volume use about 1½ times more baby onions than *boned* meat. You can also add potatoes to stretch the dish. *Stifado* is always more luscious if prepared a day in advance, but if you do add potatoes, do so on the day you serve the dish.

After a Greek-style feast of *mezethes* and *stifado,* when everyone has eaten his fill, I clear the table, then ease the dessert into place, usually plain yogurt, drained and placed in a shallow bowl with crisscrossing lines of imported thyme-flavored Greek honey and some chopped walnuts sprinkled on as well. It's an easy and typical Greek dessert. If I want something more festive I'll make the Paxos Cinnamon Pita. Then, of course, I'll make Greek coffee and get one of the guests to read the future in the sediment.

4 to 5 pounds meaty short ribs of beef, cut into 2½-inch pieces

6 tablespoons olive oil

Coarse salt

1¼ cups chopped onions

4 garlic cloves, halved, peeled, green shoot removed, and crushed in a mortar with a pinch of salt

2¼ cups canned tomatoes packed in tomato purée and strained (see note below)

2 tablespoons whole allspice, tied in a cheesecloth bundle

1 hard or 3 soft-sticks cinnamon

2 imported bay leaves

4 pounds (60) small white boiling onions, trimmed and peeled

1 teaspoon sugar

5 tablespoons red wine vinegar

¼ teaspoon freshly ground pepper

This stew is best if started 1 day in advance so that all the fat can be removed and all the flavors are allowed to develop fully.

1. One day in advance follow steps 1 through 5. Quickly rinse the beef; let it stand in a colander to drain dry. In a large black iron skillet, heat 2 tablespoons of the oil until hot. Working in batches, brown the meat on all sides, about 2 to 3 minutes. Transfer it to a bowl and sprinkle with salt. Pour off all the fat in the pan. Add 2 cups of water to the skillet and bring it to a boil, stirring to scrape up any brown bits from the bottom of the pan, and reserve.

2. Meanwhile, in a 6-quart enameled cast-iron casserole cook the chopped onions and ¼ cup of water in 2 tablespoons of the olive oil until the water has evaporated and the onions are soft and translucent, about 10 minutes. Add the crushed garlic cloves, the strained tomatoes, the spices, and bay leaf, and bring to a simmer. Add the beef and any juices that have accumulated, plus the reserved skillet juices. Bring the contents to a rolling boil; reduce the heat until the liquid barely bubbles, cover tightly, and cook over low heat for 1 hour and 15 minutes.

3. Meanwhile, soak the small onions in very hot water to cover along with 3 table-spoons of the vinegar (this helps keep your eyes from tearing). One by one trim the onion root ends, cut an X in the root end, then peel. Boil the onions for 3 minutes and drain them (this is said to make them sweeter). Refresh them under cold water and shake them dry. Put half the onions along with 1 tablespoon of the olive oil in a 10-inch nonstick skillet and sauté until glazed on all sides. Add ½ teaspoon of the sugar and continue cooking until the onions are shiny and golden brown. Set them aside and repeat with the remaining onions, olive oil, and sugar.

4. When the meat has cooked a total of 1 hour and 15 minutes, add the onions. Cover the casserole tightly and bring it back to a boil. Lower the heat, cover, and cook 45 minutes without disturbing. From time to time, swirl the casserole to keep the meat and the onions from sticking.

5. Remove the casserole from the heat, uncover, and let it stand. Remove the fat that surfaces. Discard the bay leaf and spices. When the meat is cool enough to handle, remove

(continued)

all bones, gristle, and hard pieces of fat. Cut the meat into 1-inch pieces. (The meat and onions are *not* fully cooked at this time.) Lay a sheet of plastic film directly on the meat, onions, and liquid. Cover and refrigerate. (*Up to this point the dish can be prepared one day in advance.*)

6. The following day, about 2 hours before serving, lift off the plastic film and congealed fat; discard. Let the meat come to room temperature, about 1 hour.

7. In a wide, shallow pan slowly reheat the meat and onions to simmering. Cook, uncovered, until the sauce thickens, about 30 minutes. Add the remaining 2 tablespoons of vinegar, ¼ teaspoon of freshly ground pepper, and taste for salt. Cover and shake the pan to avoid stirring and breaking the onions. Let the casserole cook 5 minutes longer to blend flavors, then remove it from the heat and let it stand, covered, until you are ready to serve. Reheat for an instant. Serve hot along with bite-size portions of feta cheese, a platter of mountain greens dressed with olive oil, and plenty of crusty bread.

NOTES TO
THE COOK
You can substitute wild Greek onions (*volvi*) for the boiling onions. (They are available in 1-pound jars, pickled in vinegar and oil, in Greek markets or by mail order. See Appendix, page 347.) These onions will provide an extra tanginess to beef, hare, or octopus stews, but they must be soaked in several changes of water for 1 to 2 days before using, and should be dried well before being browned in oil. Add the wild onions 15 minutes before serving.

Since this is a winter dish, I specify canned tomatoes; use those packed in tomato purée. Press the contents of one 28-ounce can through a foodmill to remove the seeds before using. See Appendix (page 340) for comments on soft- and hard-stick cinnamon.

Catalan Estofat of Beef

SERVES 6

The Catalan word *estofat* means "smothered, stewed meat," and refers to a style of preparation requiring the application of slow heat to all sides of a cooking vessel so that the enclosed meat is cooked to buttery tenderness in a liquid medium, which is usually a wine. An enameled cast-iron casserole or a Crockpot can be substituted; I prefer a deep earthenware pot with greaseproof paper on top of the meat and a tight-fitting lid. The meat and its flavorings are sealed in the pot and set in a slow oven to cook for about 4 hours.

Tender beef is not a typical Catalan meat, but once in a while bull meat (*toro*) is for sale, and it was for just such a tough meat that this recipe was created. The following version of the recipe from the fine Barcelona restaurant Hostal de Sant Jordí is uniquely Catalan, with a special depth of flavor. It is made with a gelatinous cut of beef (foreshank or shin) which requires a longer pot-roasting time— extra hours for the sauce to develop body and flavor without causing the meat to disintegrate. The wine must be a strong red variety with a distinct sharpness, such as a Priorato of Tarragona. (Alternatives might be Torres's Gran Sangre de Toro, an Italian Barbera, or a good strong domestic Pinot Noir.)

The final addition of anisette and black Muscat wine will produce a rich and rounded final taste. (Yes, a lot of different bottles are involved here, but without them you won't get a truly delicious *and* different-tasting stew.)

Finally, note that unlike in other stews, the vegetables here are roasted separately and added only at the very end. Thus, while the meat and its cooking liquid meld together, the vegetables retain their separate flavors.

4½ pounds boneless beef shin, cut in 2-inch pieces (see notes)

2 bottles strong dry red wine, such as Torres Gran Sangre de Toro, an Italian Barbera or a California Pinot Noir

¼ pound pancetta or blanched salt pork, cut into lardons (¼ inch across and 1 inch long)

4 tablespoons extra-virgin olive oil

Coarse salt and freshly ground white pepper

2 large yellow onions, cut into eighths

2 large carrots, cut into 1-inch chunks

1 celery rib, cut into 1-inch chunks

8 garlic cloves, unpeeled

Herbs: ½ teaspoon oregano, ¼ teaspoon fennel seed, ½ teaspoon thyme leaves, 2 bay leaves, crumbled

Spices: 3 cloves; 2-inch piece of soft-stick cinnamon, crushed; ¼ teaspoon whole white peppercorns, lightly crushed

¼ cup flour

3 tablespoons red wine vinegar

4 tablespoons anisette, preferably Anis del Mono

3 tablespoons black Muscat or Muscatel (see note)

ROASTED VEGETABLE GARNISH

3 tablespoons olive oil

18 small white onions, peeled

18 small whole new potatoes, or 1½ pounds larger red potatoes, peeled and chunked

12 small garlic cloves, unpeeled

12 small carrots, pared and blanched 1 minute

¼ teaspoon fennel seeds

Sprigs of thyme and 2 bay leaves

Coarse and fine salt

Freshly ground white pepper

Chopped fresh parsley

Begin 2 days in advance for best results.

1. Cover the beef cubes with red wine, and keep them in a cool place or the refrigerator for 24 hours. Stir them once or twice during the marination.

(continued)

2. The next day, drain the beef, reserving the wine. Dry the meat on paper towels. Then lightly pound each piece with a mallet.

3. In a large flameproof casserole, cook the lardons in the olive oil over moderately low heat, stirring occasionally, until the fat is rendered and the lardons are lightly browned, about 15 minutes. With a slotted spoon, transfer them to a bowl. Increase the heat to high, and sauté the beef in the fat in batches, turning the pieces until browned all over, about 10 minutes. Transfer the meat to the bowl with the lardons. Season with ½ teaspoon of pepper and ¼ teaspoon of salt. Add the yellow onions, carrot chunks, celery, garlic, herbs, and spices to the casserole and brown them lightly, stirring. Pour off all but 3 tablespoons of the fat, sprinkle it with flour, stir and allow it to brown evenly. Deglaze with the vinegar, then gradually stir in the red wine. Return the meat to the casserole. Add water if the meat is not totally covered. Bring the mixture to boiling and cover it with parchment or foil cut to fit and a tight-fitting lid. Set the casserole in a 250° oven and cook until the meat is fork-tender, about 4 hours. Cooking time depends on the quality of the beef.

4. With a slotted spoon, remove the beef to a plate and cover it loosely with foil to keep moist. Strain the cooking liquid, pressing down on the vegetables to extract the juices. Skim the fat off the top of the liquid. Pour it into a large saucepan and boil it over high heat, skimming frequently, until the liquid is reduced to 2 cups, about 15 minutes. Add the anisette and Muscatel to the sauce and return it to a boil. Remove it from the heat and let cool. Pour the sauce over the meat, cover, and refrigerate overnight.

5. About 2 hours before serving, remove the meat and sauce from the refrigerator to bring them to room temperature. Meanwhile, cover the bottom of a roasting pan with olive oil and add the vegetables and herbs. Roll the vegetables to coat evenly. Roast in a 350° oven until the vegetables are glazed, crusted, and tender, about 1½ hours. Blot off the excess oil. Season with salt and pepper.

6. About 20 minutes before serving, reheat the meat and sauce in the casserole over moderately high heat. Add the vegetables, and simmer for 5 minutes to blend the flavors. Season with a good pinch of mixed coarse and fine salt and freshly ground pepper to taste. Serve garnished with chopped parsley.

NOTES TO THE COOK

There is no sense in buying an inferior Muscatel for cooking. The California black Muscat, Elysium, produced by Quadry, is delicious. You will not only find uses for it in cooking, but it is an ideal accompaniment to Gorgonzola or Saga blue cheese.

To prepare the meat: Remove all outside fat, then, using a boning knife, follow the natural lines separating the beef muscles. Cut each piece of meat crosswise into 2-inch pieces. Add the bones and tendons to the pot after adding the wine.

For a shorter cooking time, you can substitute a mix of short ribs and rump or chuck. Simmer at 325° F for about 2 hours.

TWO STEAK RECIPES

SERVES 2	*Beefsteak with Peppercorns and Raisins*

Here is my version of that old bistro favorite steak *au poivre,* in which the aggressiveness of the pepper is softened by the addition of Cognac-soaked yellow raisins to the sauce.

In the winter, without access to an outdoor grill, I prefer to sauté steak rather than grill it, especially since a home kitchen broiler never gets hot enough to sear properly. After sautéing strip (shell) steaks, I deglaze the pan with Cognac, raisins and stock to pick up all the bits and pieces, then add a small amount of cream and butter to make a quick, light sauce.

Whenever you buy steaks follow this procedure: the minute you bring them home, lightly salt them, coat them lightly with oil, then store them in the refrigerator. A light salting both tenderizes them and helps mature their flavor, and you will end up using about half as much salt as normally.

Serve the steaks with French fries. A *truc* to obtain crispy and digestible fries: soak them in lightly vinegared cold water, and shake well to dry before plunging them in medium-hot oil.

2 *boneless strip sirloin or New York beefsteaks (shell), ¾ inch thick, trimmed of fat (about 7 ounces)*	4 *teaspoons crushed mixed black and white peppercorns*
Coarse salt	¼ *cup meat stock or water*
1 *tablespoon unflavored vegetable oil*	1 *teaspoon Dijon-style mustard, preferably extra-strong*
1½ *tablespoons golden raisins*	1½ *tablespoons heavy cream*
2 *tablespoons Cognac*	1 *tablespoon unsalted butter*

1. Season steaks with salt; rub with ½ tablespoon of the oil. Cover loosely with plastic wrap and refrigerate until 30 minutes before cooking.

2. Dry the steaks with paper towels. Rinse the raisins under warm running water until soft; drain. In a small bowl macerate the raisins in Cognac for 30 minutes. Spread half the crushed peppercorns on a paper towel. Firmly press the steaks into the peppercorns. Spread the remainder on top of the meat and use your palm to press them down firmly. Let the steaks stand for 20 minutes.

3. Brush a nonstick 10-inch skillet with the remaining oil, and heat slowly until hot. Sear the steaks for 2 minutes on each side. Regulate the heat so that you don't produce too many burned peppercorns. Using a spatula carefully transfer the steaks to a cake rack set over a plate; cover with a foil tent to keep warm.

(continued)

4. Pour off the fat and any loose burnt peppercorns in the skillet. Add the raisins and Cognac and, when heated, ignite. (Be sure to avert your face.) When the flames die out, add the stock or water and bring it to a fast boil, scraping up any browned bits from the bottom of the skillet. Add the mustard and cream and any meat juices that have accumulated around the beef; bring the mixture to a boil. Add the butter and shake the skillet over medium heat until a smooth sauce forms. Adjust the seasoning and pour over the beef.

Beefsteak with Sicilian Capers

It wasn't until I went to Sicily and tasted the luscious salted capers of the islands of Pantelleria and Lipari that I understood the appeal of these extraordinary capers. They were unlike any I had tasted before—piquant, delicious, as edible as candy. Simply packed in salt, they needed only a short soaking to be revived. And their aroma is delicate—entirely different from that of capers packed in vinegar brine.

It is Sicilian capers that give this dish its highly seductive flavor and sparkle. (See Appendix, page 339, for mail-order sources.) In addition to using the whole capers, I chop up one or two, then add the pieces to the sauce for extra enrichment. Serve with golden, crisp slices of potato baked in one layer, as in the recipe for Cazuela Potatoes. For dessert, try the delicious Sicilian cheese Pepato, a pecorino-type cheese studded with black peppercorns; it is particularly excellent with the Sicilian dessert wine Malvasia delle Lipari, served chilled.

1 *boneless strip sirloin or New York beefsteak (shell) 1½ inch thick, well trimmed, at room temperature*

Salt and freshly ground pepper

3 *teaspoons vegetable oil*

4 *tablespoons unsalted butter*

2 *teaspoons minced shallots*

1½ *tablespoons red wine vinegar*

1½ *cups unsalted beef or veal stock*

2 *teaspoons tomato paste*

2 *tablespoons heavy cream*

1½ *tablespoons salted capers, soaked, drained, 3 or 4 capers chopped*

1 *teaspoon each minced parsley and tarragon*

1. Season the steak with salt and pepper; rub it with 1 teaspoon oil. Cover it loosely with plastic wrap and refrigerate until you are ready to cook.

2. In a large, heavy *sauteuse*, preferably copper, over medium-high heat sear the steak on one side in 1½ tablespoons of hot butter and 2 teaspoons oil, 2 to 3 minutes. Use a heavy spatula to press down on the meat to create a good crust. Turn and repeat on the second side for 2 to 3 minutes. Let the steak cook until it is the desired doneness, turning frequently (see the note below). Using a spatula, transfer the steak to a cake rack, cover with a foil tent, and let it rest while you prepare the sauce.

3. Pour off the fat. To the skillet juices add 2 teaspoons butter, and when it foams, add the shallots and cook over medium-low heat, stirring, for 2 minutes or until the shallots are lightly colored. Add the vinegar and boil it down to a glaze. Add the stock, the tomato paste, and the cream, and reduce by boiling to ½ cup. Add the capers and any meat juices

(continued)

that have accumulated around the beef. Off the heat swirl in the remaining butter and adjust the seasoning of the sauce. Pour it over the steak, sprinkle with herbs, and serve at once.

NOTE TO THE COOK Here is a *truc* I learned about cooking thick steaks from an article by Joël Robuchon in *La Bonne Cuisine,* a French food magazine. Contrary to general practice, Robuchon suggests turning the meat frequently, nearly constantly, so that once the surfaces are sufficiently seared the juices within will circulate, irrigating the flesh and maintaining the juicy character of the meat. For this same reason one should not serve grilled meat without allowing it first to rest.

A VEAL RECIPE

Veal Pastitsatha with Macaroni, Corfu Style   S E R V E S   5   O R   6

Having grown accustomed to the parched terrain of Crete, the beige Cyclades, and the bone-dry, sun-baked Greek mainland, I was surprised by the thick, dark forests of Corfu. Suddenly I was in a part of Greece that had the feel of Italy, a land as rich and green as Tuscany.

The food of Corfu is as unique as its landscape. It not only bears the influence of Italian cooking but lacks the elements of Turkish cooking, which is popular on the mainland. You will not find as many savory and sweet phyllo-dough confections on Corfu, or such Byzantine dishes as *iman bayildi.* you will encounter some excellent island specialties: *bourtheto* (fish simmered with puréed onions and tomatoes); *soupya* (baby squid simmered in thick tomato sauce); *psari marinata* (a marinated fish preparation reminiscent of the Venetian specialty, marinated sardines); and the following delicious recipe, *pastitsatha* (veal braised with tomatoes served with macaroni).

This may be the best of the Corfu dishes—a shoulder of veal cooked slowly with spices, garlic, wine, and vinegar, then simmered in a rich tomato and onion sauce. When it is done, the meat is sliced thick and served along with cooked pasta tubes drenched with the spicy cooking liquid.

Greek "veal," called *moshari,* is really yearling calf. To simulate its taste would require rubbing our tender milk-fed veal with vinegar, a waste of an expensive cut of meat. For this dish, choose the rosy-hued veal.

Corfiote food is spicy, while most Greek food is basically herbal. Paprika, practically unknown in the rest of the country, is used extensively on the island, and it is almost impossible to pass by the kitchen door of a restaurant there and not smell the scent of paprika cooking in oil. The blending of different peppers (black, cayenne, and paprika) is essential to obtain the deep flavor that makes this dish so good.

3 to 3½ pounds boneless veal shoulder, in one piece, rolled and tied

Salt and freshly ground black pepper

4 cloves garlic, peeled and sliced thin

⅓ cup olive oil

1 stick cinnamon

2 whole cloves

1 bay leaf

1 cup dry white or red wine

3 tablespoons wine vinegar

2 large onions, chopped fine (about 2 cups)

2 cups peeled, seeded, and chopped fresh tomatoes, or 1 (35-ounce) can drained, strained in a colander, seeds discarded

½ teaspoon sugar

Large pinch of paprika

Cayenne pepper to taste

1 pound large hollow pasta, such as ziti or penne

4 ounces unsalted butter

4 ounces grated Kefalotyri or Romano cheese (about 1 cup)

1. About 4 hours before serving, preheat the oven to 300° F.

2. Wipe the surface of the veal; rub it with 1 teaspoon of salt and ½ teaspoon of black pepper. Make small incisions all over the meat and insert thin slices of garlic, using about half of the total amount, reserve the remaining garlic.

3. Heat 3 tablespoons of olive oil in a heavy, noncorrodible 3-quart Dutch oven over medium heat. Sear the meat on all sides, about 4 minutes. Add the remaining garlic, the cinnamon, cloves, and bay leaf; reduce the heat to very low. Cook, covered, for 10 minutes, shaking the casserole 2 or 3 times to prevent sticking. Add the wine and vinegar to the casserole; increase the heat to bring the liquid quickly to a boil, then remove the casserole from the heat. Cover it tightly with heavy-duty foil; cover with a lid and bake 30 minutes.

4. Remove the casserole from the oven; carefully take off the lid and foil. Turn the meat, cover, and bake 30 minutes longer.

5. While the meat is cooking, heat the remaining 3 tablespoons of olive oil in a large, heavy skillet over medium-high heat until hot. Stir in the onions; reduce the heat to medium, and sauté the onions until softened but not browned, about 5 minutes. Stir in the tomatoes, ½ teaspoon of salt, the sugar, ⅛ teaspoon of black pepper, the paprika and cayenne. Reduce the heat to low and cook, uncovered, stirring frequently, for 20 minutes.

6. Remove the casserole from the oven; carefully remove the lid and foil. Pour the tomato sauce over the meat; replace the foil and lid. Return the casserole to the oven; bake 2 hours, or until the veal is fork-tender.

7. Heat a large, heavy saucepan of salted water over high heat to boiling.

8. Remove the casserole from the oven; increase the oven heat to 375° F. Carefully remove the lid and foil from the casserole. Remove the meat to a side dish; cover it with foil to keep warm. Remove and discard the bay leaf and cinnamon stick from the sauce.

(continued)

Let the sauce stand for a few minutes; oil will gradually rise to the surface. Carefully spoon off the oil; use a small amount to grease a wide, shallow 4-quart baking dish, discarding the remainder.

9. Cook the pasta in the boiling salted water until just tender, about 10 minutes; drain thoroughly and return it to the saucepan. Melt the butter in a small, heavy saucepan; when bubbly, add it to the cooked pasta, along with half the grated cheese. Toss the pasta to coat. Add 2 cups of the tomato sauce and toss again; turn the pasta into the prepared baking dish.

10. Untie the veal; cut it into ½-inch-thick slices. Arrange them in a single overlapping row over the pasta in the baking dish; pour the remaining sauce over all. Bake, covered with foil, for 10 minutes. Uncover and bake 10 minutes longer. Sprinkle with the remaining cheese and serve at once.

PORK
TWO ROAST PORK RECIPES

Roast Pork Stuffed with Olives in the Style of Zakinthos

SERVES 6 TO 8

On a recent trip to the Ionian Islands I was struck by the beauty of the Greek olive groves. On Zakinthos the orchards are extremely orderly, the trees well tended. When you drive through them at night and your headlights hit the branches, the sides of the road seem to come alive.

I was also moved by the deeply emotional—indeed, mystical—attachment that the people who tend these groves feel for the magnificent gnarled trees, some of which have been producing fruit since the sixteenth century. As Georgio Stroutzas, the mayor of the village of Lithakia, put it: "They are giving trees—but not in the easy way a coconut tree gives fruit on a tropical island. Here we put much hard work into them, but then they give us so much back. In the gnarled root system of an old tree you can see a symbol of the arduous struggle of man. I cannot imagine life without them."

On Zakinthos the oldest and biggest-producing trees are given names. In one Zakinthos grove belonging to Dimitri Lykouresis, I was introduced to The Holy Virgin Tree, Gardelli's Tree, The Chicken House Tree, and, with great awe, The Bank—which produces over a hundred kilos of olive oil a year.

(On the island of Paxos, in contrast the trees have been so long neglected that they have grown out of control. Their branches are so high that their olives cannot be harvested the preferable way, directly from the trees, but must be collected in nylon nets when they fall of their own accord. The result is a more acidic oil. However inferior they are commercially, these neglected trees do have a haunting beauty.)

Dimitri's wife, Maria, taught me this recipe for roast *moshari* (a yearling calf), which she stuffed with tiny black olives, crumbled cheese, and hard-boiled eggs. Dimitri had raised the calf and fed it carefully, and as a result its taste was wonderful. I have substituted pork butt, because it has so much more flavor than most commercial veal, and because, with the special chopped marinade, it ends up tasting very much like Dimitri's yearling calf!

3 *pound pork butt*	1 *teaspoon coarse salt*
MARINADE	
1 *carrot, cut up*	3 *hard-boiled eggs*
2 *onions, cut up*	10 *black Niçoise olives, pitted and chopped*
1 *garlic clove*	2 *teaspoons grated cheese (Kefalotyri or Romano)*
2 *scallions*	
1 *tablespoon chopped parsley*	*Salt and pepper to taste*
Pinch of dried rosemary	2 *teaspoons Greek oregano*
1 *teaspoon Greek oregano*	⅓ *cup fresh lemon juice*
1 *piece of soft-stick cinnamon (1 inch long)*	2 *cloves garlic, peeled and chopped*
	3 *tablespoons extra-virgin olive oil*
1 *tablespoon olive oil*	1 *fresh rosemary sprig (2 inches long)*

1. One day in advance, have the butcher butterfly the meat so that it can be stuffed and rolled into a long cylinder, with the grain of the meat running lengthwise.

2. Trim any excess fat from the butterflied pork, but leave it in one piece. Place it, fatty side down, on a work surface. Use the flat side of a mallet or cleaver to pound it to an even thickness, about 1 inch. Combine the ingredients for the marinade in the workbowl of a food processor. Process with on-off pulses until the marinade is chopped fine; rub it into the meat, roll the meat up, and marinate it overnight.

3. The following day, remove the pork from the refrigerator and bring it to room temperature. Wipe off the marinade and pat the meat dry. Preheat the oven to 500° F. Lay the pork roast fatty side down flat on a work surface. Place the eggs and olives down the center of the meat in a long row. Scatter the cheese on top. Lift the two long sides of the meat around the stuffing. Tie with string at 1-inch intervals. Rub with salt, pepper, oregano, and ¼ cup of the lemon juice. Place the pork on a roasting rack. Pour around 2 tablespoons of water and the oil. Add the rosemary sprig. Roast for 15 minutes. Lower the oven heat to 350° F. Roast for 1 hour, basting with the pan juices often.

4. Remove the meat from the oven and let it rest under a foil tent for 15 minutes. Meanwhile pour off the fat from the pan. Add 1 cup of water and bring it to a boil, scraping

(continued)

up any brown bits. Boil until reduced to half. Add the remaining lemon juice and season to taste. Pour the liquid into a small saucepan and set aside. When the meat has rested 15 minutes, remove the strings. Cut the meat against the grain at a slight angle. Reheat the pan juices and pour them over the meat.

NOTE TO
THE COOK
Top quality veal with a delicious flavor can be obtained from Summerfield Farms. See mail-order sources in the Appendix, page 351.

(La Porchetta)

Fresh Picnic Ham Roasted like a Suckling Pig

SERVES 6

There have been rainy days in the country when I craved the taste of roast suckling pig, but none was available. It was for just such an occasion that I developed the following recipe, in which I simulated the taste and texture of a Corsican suckling pig with a slowly roasted 7-pound picnic shoulder. Using my method, you will obtain rich, juicy flesh with a deep brown glaze and a crackling skin.

In order to approximate the crackling crust of a suckling pig with the skin of a tougher and much older pig, the skin is cut off in one piece, etched with a wide diamond pattern, and rubbed with oil and coarse salt. Next the pork flesh is perfumed with a marinade paste made with a collection of fresh herbs (thyme, bay leaf, rosemary, and sage) and spices (coriander seeds, black pepper, and hot red-pepper flakes), and then roasted slowly to render out its fat. During roasting, the pork skin is laid on top of the roast, making it easier to baste. Midway through cooking the skin is slipped *under* the meat so that the roast itself can develop a good brown glaze. Before serving, the skin will be crisped in a hot oven.

A picnic shoulder is a thick piece of meat with a complicated bone structure. It requires long, slow roasting (45 minutes to a pound) to cook fully. In this recipe, because the pork is not seared, all the fat is rendered out, yet the meat remains juicy and moist. Indeed, the flesh has more flavor when slightly overcooked—to 175° F internal temperature.

The rustic sauce, made with fresh tomatoes, orange and lemon juice, and fresh peppermint, is adapted from a Corsican recipe published in the French magazine *Marie Claire*.

Serve with sautéed apples, a gratin of melting potatoes, and an arugula salad. Leftover pork makes a splendid hash.

7 *pound fresh picnic ham (shoulder)*

FRESH HERB-SPICE PASTE

2 *tablespoons underlining fat of pork skin*

1 *teaspoon black peppercorns*

1½ *teaspoons coriander seeds*

½ *teaspoon red pepper flakes*

1 *bay leaf*

2 *teaspoons chopped thyme leaves*

10 *big leaves of fresh sage*

½ *teaspoon crumbled rosemary spikes*

2 *garlic cloves*

1 *tablespoon olive oil*

2 *teaspoons salt*

3 *garlic cloves, peeled, thickly sliced and soaking in water*

1½ *tablespoons olive oil*

2 *teaspoons coarse salt*

1½ *cups rich chicken or meat stock*

2 *large ripe tomatoes, peeled, seeded and chopped*

4 *tablespoons orange juice*

Juice of ½ lemon

Salt and pepper to taste

Pinch of sugar

8 *sprigs of fresh mint, preferably peppermint, shredded*

1. One to 2 days in advance, wash and dry pork. Remove the skin in one piece, trim off thick patches of fat and reserve 2 tablespoons for the Herb-Spice Paste. To make the paste: In a food processor blend the fat along with the spices, herbs, garlic, oil and salt until smooth, scraping down the sides of the bowl as necessary. With a sharp knife, make deep, diagonal slits into the pork flesh. Drain the garlic slices, mix with some of the prepared paste, and insert into the flesh. Rub the pork with the remaining paste. Do not season the pork rind. Wrap up the pork and refrigerate. Lay the skin, outer side up, on a towel-covered dish in the refrigerator to dry out.

2. About 6 hours before serving, preheat the oven to 300° F. Score the skin in a wide diamond pattern, cutting about ¼-inch deep. Rub with olive oil, then with coarse salt. Pat the meat dry if moist. Place it on a rack in a flameproof roasting pan, lay the pork skin over the meat, and roast, uncovered, without basting for 2½ hours.

3. Remove the pork from the oven; place the skin, fat side down, *under* the rack and meat. Return the meat to the oven and roast for 1½ hours longer, basting with the pan drippings every 15 to 20 minutes. Raise the oven heat to 350° F and roast 1 hour longer. (The total roasting time is 5 hours.)

4. Remove the pork to a work surface and cover loosely with foil; let it rest 15 minutes. Increase the oven heat to 400° F. Place the skin, fatty side down, on a flat dish, and return to the oven to crisp and brown, 15 minutes.

5. Meanwhile, pour off all the fat from the roasting pan, place the pan on top of the stove, add the stock, and bring it to a boil. Add the chopped tomatoes and sugar and cook for 5 minutes, stirring. Add the orange and lemon juice and cook down to half. Strain the

(continued)

sauce into a sauceboat, pressing on the tomatoes with a spoon. Adjust the seasoning with salt, pepper, and a pinch of cayenne. Keep hot. Stir in the mint leaves just before serving.

6. Slice the pork thin on the diagonal toward the bone. Arrange the slices on a warmed platter, season with salt and pepper, cover and keep warm. Cut the skin into thin strips and pass separately.

TWO PORK CHOP RECIPES

Marinated Pork Chops with Peppered Pears

SERVES 2 OR 4

In this recipe marination lends pork the taste of wild boar. The marinade itself is straightforward: a mixture of vegetables, red wine, spices, and hazelnut liqueur (which gives the sauce a wonderful flavor and aroma).

The sauce base can be made a day ahead, the compote of peppered pears early on the day you plan to serve the dish. Just before serving, simply sauté the chops and enrich the sauce with a little butter. Serve with the peppered pears and puréed chestnuts or lentils.

4 pork chops (2 pounds), about 1 inch thick
Salt and freshly ground pepper

MARINADE

½ cup fine-diced carrots

½ cup fine-diced onions

1 tablespoon fine-diced celery root or rib

⅓ cup fine-diced shallots

1 large garlic clove, peeled and slivered

1 teaspoon crushed white peppercorns

15 juniper berries

3 cups full-bodied red wine, such as a Côtes-du-Rhône

1 tablespoon olive oil

½ teaspoon coarse salt

2 tablespoons nut liqueur or brandy

1½ tablespoons olive oil

2 teaspoons clarified butter

1 tablespoon beurre manié, rolled into small balls (see notes)
Salt and freshly ground pepper

PEPPERED PEARS

1½ pounds firm pears, preferably Bartlett

3 tablespoons red or white wine vinegar

2 tablespoons liquid honey
Pinch of salt

1 teaspoon coarse-crushed white peppercorns

Begin preparation 1 to 2 days before serving.

1. Bone the pork chops, reserving the bones for the sauce. Trim and discard the excess fat. Season the pork with the pepper. In a deep glass, earthenware or stainless-steel bowl, combine the pork, the bones, and all the marinade ingredients. Cover with plastic wrap and refrigerate for 1 to 2 days.

2. Remove the chops and ribs and allow them to drain about 10 minutes. Reserve the vegetables and wine separately. Wrap the chops in plastic film and keep them refrigerated until ½ hour before cooking.

3. In a 2-quart noncorrodible heavy skillet, heat 1 tablespoon of the oil, add the well-drained bones, and brown them on all sides, for 5 minutes. Add the vegetables and brown them, stirring frequently, for 2 to 3 minutes. Tilt the skillet and spoon off the excess fat. Add the marinade and slowly bring to a boil. Simmer for 5 minutes. Add 1½ cups of water and bring the liquid back to a boil. Set the skillet half over a stove burner and adjust the heat so that the side over the heat slowly boils and the fat and any other impurities in the liquid rise on the cooler side. When the liquid is clear, partially cover the skillet and simmer over low heat for 45 minutes. Strain the liquid, then cool, cover, and chill. Remove the surface fat and, if necessary, reduce the liquid to ½ cup.

4. Meanwhile, make the pear garnish. Peel and core the pears. Cut the flesh into ¾-inch cubes. In a small, heavy noncorrodible saucepan, combine the pear flesh, wine vinegar, honey, pinch of salt, and peppercorns. Cook them covered over low heat for 30 minutes, adding a drop of water to prevent burning, if necessary. With a slotted spoon transfer the cubed pears to a serving dish. Reduce the juices by boiling to 3 tablespoons and pour over the pears. (*Up to this point the recipe can be prepared in advance.*)

5. About 30 minutes before serving: Pat the pork chops dry. Heat ½ tablespoon of the oil and the butter in a well-seasoned 10-inch heavy skillet until hot, add the chops, and cook over medium-high heat until golden brown on one side, about 8 minutes. Turn them and cook until golden brown on the second side, about 8 minutes. Transfer the chops to a rack in a warm place, cover tightly, and allow them to finish cooking in retained heat. Throw out the fat. In a small, heavy saucepan reheat the sauce base, then whisk in the *beurre manié* to thicken it. Adjust the seasoning. Place one serving of pork on each of 2 or 4 warmed serving plates and spoon the sauce over. Pass the pears separately.

I use Frangelico, a hazelnut liqueur from Italy, or Nocello, an Italian walnut liqueur, for the marinade. If neither is available, use a good Cognac.

To make a *beurre manié*, blend 1 tablespoon unsalted butter with 2 teaspoons flour until smooth. Roll into tiny balls and keep them cool until you are ready to use them. Add to the heated sauce, whisking constantly. Note that the vegetables in the marinade are cut very small so that they can give up more flavor in a shorter time.

Inspired by a recipe from Jacques Chibois.

Pan-Fried Pork Chops with Sherry Vinegar and French Cornichons

SERVES 2

Here is my version of a very old pork recipe, which has recently been revived by young French chefs and now appears on menus at chic Parisian restaurants. The lively, very aromatic sauce is quick to cook, and if you should prepare a gratin of melting potatoes as an accompaniment, you will have a fine homey dinner.

4 *loin or rib pork chops, ½ inch thick*

MARINADE

1 *garlic clove, sliced thin*

1 *teaspoon minced parsley*

1 *teaspoon minced tarragon*

1 *shallot, sliced thin*

1 *tablespoon olive oil*

1½ *tablespoons unsalted butter*

4 *or 5 French cornichons, rinsed and chopped fine (1½ tablespoons)*

2 *teaspoons vegetable oil*

Salt and pepper to taste

2 *tablespoons Sherry vinegar*

1 *teaspoon* each *minced parsley and tarragon*

1. Combine the pork chops with the marinade ingredients and let them stand at room temperature up to 2 hours, or refrigerate for longer. Bring the pork back to room temperature before continuing. With a fork crush the butter, then work in the chopped cornichons. Set the butter aside in a cool place.

2. Brush a heavy noncorrodible skillet with oil and set the skillet over medium-high heat. Wipe the chops dry and brown them for 3 minutes on each side. Transfer them to a side dish; sprinkle with salt and pepper. Throw out the fat in the skillet. Add the vinegar and 2 tablespoons of water and boil down to half. Add the prepared butter and swirl to make an emulsion. Return the pork chops to the skillet and cook over low heat, basting with the skillet juices, until the meat is thoroughly cooked, but still moist, about 3 minutes. Serve at once, sprinkled with fresh herbs.

TWO BLACK SAUSAGE RECIPES

Black Sausages with Fresh Fava Beans

"With favas you must feel modest," wrote Josep Pla, a famous Catalan intellectual and food commentator. "You must be humble before their authentic personality. Their slight bitterness comes from the dryness of the soil. They have fed generations of Mediterranean peoples long before the discovery of America. . . . Favas are both memory and sensation."

This famous Catalan dish combines my favorite sausage, *boudin noir*, with delicious, butter-tender fava beans. It is a dish of contrasting flavors and textures, creamy on account of a Catalan slow-cooking method called *obegades*, or "smothered," by which the favas cook in little moisture and thus retain their flavor. Although the beans do not stay bright green but turn gray, don't be put off: their flavor will be sensational.

What you want to achieve with this dish is a certain relationship between the components: meatiness from the sausage, perfume from the spring herbs, and a slight bitterness from the favas. You don't want to end up with greasy favas; you want the favas to absorb and mingle with the aromatics and sausage.

4 ounces salt pork, cut into ¼-inch-by-1-inch pieces, blanched in boiling water 5 minutes, rinsed, drained, and dried

1 tablespoon olive oil

¾ cup chopped onions

1 small peeled, seeded and chopped tomato

1 finely chopped garlic clove

4 pounds fresh unshelled favas, or about 3½ cups shelled beans

¾ pound Spanish- or French-style black sausages, in their natural casing

Bundle of 1 pared and quartered carrot, 3 sprigs aromatic fresh mint, 3 sprigs fresh thyme, 1 bay leaf, and 3 sprigs fresh flat-leaf parsley

2 teaspoons anisette liqueur, preferably anis del mono

1 tablespoon black Muscat wine or Muscatel

Salt and freshly ground pepper

1. Preheat the oven to 275° F. Place the salt pork, ¼ cup of water, and the olive oil in a small enameled cast-iron casserole, and cook, stirring, over low heat for 5 minutes or until some of the fat has rendered. Add the onions and cook until soft and translucent, but not brown, about 10 minutes. Remove and discard half the salt pork. Add the tomato and garlic and continue to cook 5 minutes longer.

(continued)

2. Meanwhile, shuck the beans and discard the pods. Slip off and discard the heavy skin of any large beans or those that are discolored.

3. Prick the sausages and slowly brown them in a small skillet in their expressed fat until they are crisp and light brown, 3 to 5 minutes. Drain on paper towels.

4. Add the favas to the casserole and sauté, tossing, until the beans just begin to fry in the fat. Add the carrot and herb bundle and ¾ cup of water. Bring the mixture to a boil. Place the black sausage (uncut) on top. Lay a sheet of parchment or foil cut to fit directly on top and cover tightly with a lid. Place in the oven to cook for 45 minutes without uncovering. Check to see if the beans are very tender and creamy; if not, return the casserole to the oven, cover with the paper and lid, and cook 15 minutes longer.

5. With a slotted spoon, transfer the black sausage to a work surface and cut it into ⅓-inch-thick slices. Discard the carrot and herb bouquet. With a slotted spoon, transfer the favas, black sausage, and salt pork to an ovenproof serving dish, leaving the cooking juices in the pan. Skim off the fat. If necessary, add water to make ¾ cup. Add anisette and Muscat wine and adjust the seasoning with salt and pepper. Bring the liquid to a boil and pour over the favas. Reheat just before serving.

NOTES TO THE COOK · While teaching recipes that include fava beans, I discovered that many students didn't know how to remove the pods efficiently. Simply hold the whole bean in two hands and twist in opposite directions—at about 1-inch intervals. The beans practically slip out.

Some food commentators insist you must always skin favas because their skins are bitter and tough. It is not a necessary step when making this recipe (unlike the dish of peeled favas and duck *confit* on page 187); peel only if the beans are very large and their skins are excessively tough.

Some cooks balance off the bitterness of favas with sweet herbs such as basil or mint. Please don't overdo any of these; it is the fresh taste of the fava that you want to maintain. I personally like the slightly bitter taste of fava skins; if you prefer you may add a pinch more of sugar or an extra sprinkle of sweet wine.

This dish is excellent reheated later in the day, or may be reheated the following day.

Inspired by a recipe from the late Josep Mercader.

Black Sausages with Red Beans and Chorizo

I learned this hearty peasant dish from a zany Basque chef, Madame Muruamendiaraz of the restaurant Euskalduna, in Bayonne.

The beans must cook *al-pil-pil,* which in Basque means very slowly in an earthenware pot, over very low heat. Purists say the good flavor of this dish comes from the taste of the pot. I believe the particular savor develops because the beans must be cooked very slowly to avoid breaking the pot, and thus the flavors of all the components have time to intermingle.

The special spicy edge of this dish comes from the fleshy hot peppers of Espelette, a town in the Basque region of France. The closest equivalent taste that I have found is the Thai bottled chili sauce called Sriracha, sold in oriental markets. If not available, substitute Red Devil sauce.

For best flavor, make the dish 1 to 2 days in advance. Start with a watercress salad decorated with hard-cooked egg quarters, dressed with an anchovy vinaigrette, and finish with fresh fruit.

1 *pound small red beans or red kidney beans*

¾ *pound lean salt pork*

4 *tablespoons olive oil*

2 *medium onions, sliced*

2 *cloves garlic, sliced*

1 *pound fresh chorizo sausages in natural casings, or spicy Hungarian or Italian sausages*

4 *carrots, scraped and cut into 1-inch chunks (about 16 pieces)*

3 *green Italian peppers (also called frying peppers), cored, seeded, and cut into 1-inch squares (about 24 pieces)*

Pinch of sugar

Salt and freshly ground pepper

¾ *teaspoon hot pepper sauce, or more to taste*

6 *ounces black sausage*

Red wine vinegar

Steps 1 through 5 can be done 1 day in advance.

1. One to 2 days in advance, pick over the beans, then place in a colander and rinse under cool running water until the water runs clear. Soak them in water to cover overnight.

2. Early the following day, blanch the salt pork for 5 minutes in boiling water; drain and rinse. Cut off the rind and cut it into small pieces. Cut the remaining salt pork into 8 pieces. Set it aside. Rinse and drain the beans. Place them in a deep saucepan with water to cover; slowly bring to a boil. Boil 10 minutes, skimming often.

3. Meanwhile, heat 2 tablespoons of the olive oil in a 5-quart flameproof casserole, preferably of earthenware or enameled cast iron, over medium heat. Stir in the onions and

(continued)

garlic; sauté until soft and translucent, about 10 minutes. Add the chorizo (uncut) and the salt pork and pork rind; cook 5 minutes longer, stirring occasionally.

4. Add the beans and liquid to the casserole. Bring them to a boil, skim carefully, cover, and cook over very low heat or in a preheated 275° oven for 2½ hours. To avoid drying and breaking the beans, be sure that they are always covered with the cooking liquid or enrobed in the sauce. Add boiling water if necessary.

5. Toss the carrots with 1 tablespoon of the oil in a heavy-bottomed saucepan; cover, and cook them over medium-high heat for 3 minutes, then uncover and add the green peppers, sugar, and salt, and swirl over medium-high heat for 1 to 2 minutes, or until the carrots take on a little color. Stir in the carrots and green peppers in the casserole. Continue to cook, uncovered, until the liquid is thickened, about 30 minutes. Set the casserole aside to allow the flavors to mingle. (*The recipe can be prepared up to 1 day in advance to this point.* Cool the dish quickly and refrigerate covered.)

6. About 30 minutes before serving, remove the surface fat from the beans. Stir in the hot sauce. Preheat the oven to 375° F. Heat 1 teaspoon of the olive oil in a medium skillet over medium-low heat. Prick the black sausage, add it to the skillet, and crisp it evenly, about 10 minutes. Remove from the heat and drain.

7. Remove the chorizo, salt pork, carrots, and green peppers from the beans, using a slotted spoon. Cut the black sausage and chorizo into 8 pieces each. Divide the salt pork, sausages, carrots, and green peppers among individual heatproof serving bowls. Adjust the seasoning of the beans with salt and pepper. Spoon the beans and sauce over. Bake 10 to 20 minutes, or until very hot. (The mixture can also be baked in one large serving casserole.) Serve hot with a light sprinkling of olive oil and vinegar.

NOTE TO
THE COOK

REMEMBER: There should always be enough liquid to cover the beans; add boiling water if necessary. To avoid scorching the beans, I cook them in the oven. If using an electric slow cooker with an earthenware inset, set the cooker on Simmer (about 220° F) and plan on cooking for about 10 hours.

MIXED MEATS

<table>
<tr><td>SERVES 6</td><td>**Wine Harvesters' Tourte**</td></tr>
</table>

Le Clous is the name of one of the better *winstubs* or wine pubs in Strasbourg. Rustic, heavy on atmosphere, lively, friendly, and informal, it is as likely to seat you at a table with an elegant couple as one with a working-class family in tow.

I loved the food at Le Clous: *wadele* (a form of preserved pig's knuckle that melts in the mouth, served with horseradish and light potato pancake); *jambon en croûte* (the ham soft and full of flavor, the crust delicate and crisp); and an Alsatian classic, *tourte vigneronne*, a fine, thin crust filled with pork chunks marinated in spices, bits of veal, and mushrooms, all suspended in a custard.

This *tourte* can be served as the first course of a large dinner, or as a main course with a salad for supper. The seasoning of the meats is very important: Spiced salt is the secret. (There are many versions; you'll find mine below.) In Alsace this *tourte* is baked and served on a glazed earthenware platter. A large ovenproof plate or a 10-inch porcelain quiche dish makes a good substitute.

10 *ounces boneless veal shoulder, trimmed*

10 *ounces boneless pork shoulder, trimmed*

MARINADE

1 *teaspoon spiced salt (see recipe, page 259)*

Freshly ground pepper

1 *tablespoon minced shallots*

1 *tablespoon finely chopped fresh parsley*

1 *tablespoon finely snipped fresh chives*

¼ *cup dry white wine, preferably Alsatian Riesling*

2 *tablespoons unsalted butter*

6 *ounces fresh mushrooms, wiped clean with dampened paper toweling, sliced thin*

1 *teaspoon fresh lemon juice*

Salt

Tourte *pastry (recipe on page 336)*

1 *whole egg plus 1 egg yolk*

1 *teaspoon milk*

⅓ *cup heavy cream*

1. The day before you plan to serve the *tourte*, place the meat in the freezer for 15 minutes to firm up.

2. Cut the meats into 2-inch-square chunks; cut the chunks into ¼-inch-thick strips. Combine the meat strips, 1 teaspoon spiced salt, ¼ teaspoon of pepper, the shallots, parsley, chives, and wine in a large bowl; mix well. Refrigerate, covered, overnight.

(continued)

3. The following day, heat the butter in a noncorrodible heavy medium-size skillet over medium-high heat. When the foam subsides, add the mushrooms and lemon juice; sauté, stirring, until the mushrooms are soft, about 5 minutes. Season with salt and pepper to taste. With a slotted spoon remove the mushrooms to a small bowl; let them cool to room temperature.

4. At least 2 hours before baking the *tourte*, roll out one ball of pastry dough between two sheets of waxed paper or plastic wrap to a circle 12 inches in diameter. Remove the top sheet, then flip the pastry into a 10-inch shallow baking pan. Fit the dough gently into the pan. Remove remaining sheet of paper (see note). Refrigerate until ready to fill.

5. Roll out the second ball of dough between sheets of waxed paper or plastic sheet; refrigerate until you are ready to use it.

6. Heat the oven to 400° F.

7. Drain the meats; gently press out excess liquid. Spread the meats over the pastry in the pan, leaving a 1-inch margin around the edge. Press the excess moisture out of the mushrooms; scatter on top of the meats. Season with salt.

8. Brush the 1-inch margin with a little water. Remove the top sheet of paper for the second round of dough, then flip that round onto the pan to cover the meats and mushrooms. Remove the remaining sheet of paper, then fit the edges of pastry snugly against the dampened margin around the bottom crust; press with your fingers to seal.

9. Make a small hole in the center of the *tourte* with the plain round tip of a pastry tube for escaping steam. Whisk together the egg yolk and milk; brush the *tourte* and make a decorative linear pattern on top with fork tines.

10. Bake the *tourte* in the preheated oven for 1 hour. Reduce the temperature to 350° F; bake an additional 30 minutes. Remove to a wire rack; let it rest 5 minutes. Maintain the oven temperature.

11. Whisk together the whole egg and the cream in a small bowl. Remove the tube from the crust. Cut a ring of pastry 2 inches in diameter in the center of the *tourte;* remove. Slowly and carefully pour the egg mixture into the opening, rotating the *tourte* in order to distribute the mixture evenly under the crust. Replace the pastry round. Bake for 15 minutes.

12. Cool the *tourte* on a wire rack. Serve warm.

NOTE TO
THE COOK
If the pastry dough becomes too warm for easy removal of the waxed paper, refrigerate for 5 to 10 minutes to firm it up a bit.

¼ cup coarse (kosher) salt

¼ teaspoon whole cloves

½ teaspoon ground cinnamon

½ teaspoon anise seeds

2 teaspoons freshly ground pepper

10 whole allspice berries

1 teaspoon fines herbes (dried blend available in supermarket spice sections)

¼ whole nutmeg

Process all ingredients in a food processor or electric blender until finely ground. Press through a strainer. Store the mixture, tightly covered, in a cool, dark place.

SERVES 6 TO 8 *Alsatian Backeoffe*

Here's a perfect dish to culminate a winter weekend. You marinate the meats on Friday, turn them from time to time over the weekend, and then on Sunday morning assemble them and set them in the oven to bake slowly for 3 hours. The homey appearance of *Backeoffe* and its wonderful smell are just right for a Sunday-afternoon meal.

The success of the dish depends on slow cooking, during which the potatoes and meat absorb most of the marinade. Since many people don't have the required glazed earthenware casserole that allows the proper evaporation of moisture during cooking, I have altered the recipe so that an enameled cast iron casserole can be used with great success. I simply spoon off the abundant liquid and reduce it to one-half, then return it to the casserole and continue to bake until the top layer of potatoes crisps. For an attractive presentation I add a colorful garnish of sautéed shallots, bacon bits, and parsley.

Most modern recipes for *Backeoffe* call for boneless meat, which results in a dry dish. In this version some of the meat is cooked in the traditional way—on the bone. Serve this hearty dish with a colorful salad of thinly sliced beets, sliced radishes, and slivered lettuce dressed with a horseradish dressing, and a delicious dessert, such as the Walnut Roll.

(continued)

1 *scant pound boneless beef shoulder,* trimmed of fat, cut into 1½-inch cubes

1 *scant pound meaty lamb neck,* bone in, *trimmed of fat, cut into 1½-inch cubes*

1 *scant pound lean pork butt or shoulder, trimmed of fat, cut into 1½-inch cubes*

MARINADE

2 *cups dry Alsatian white wine: Sylvaner, Tokay, or Riesling*

2 *cloves*

2 *garlic cloves, crushed*

1 *large onion, sliced thin*

1 *large carrot, pared and sliced thin*

Bouquet garni: 8 sprigs parsley, green leaves of 1 leek, 1 bay leaf, ½ bunch fresh thyme or 1 teaspoon dried thyme, all tied in cheesecloth

¼ *teaspoon lightly crushed black peppercorns*

2 *tablespoons poultry fat, preferably goose*

2 *pounds brown onions*

3½ *to 4 pounds (8 large) Eastern or Maine potatoes*

Coarse salt and freshly ground pepper

Bouquet garni: 8 sprigs parsley, 1 bay leaf, 6 sprigs fresh thyme or ½ teaspoon dried, and 1 garlic clove, halved

1 *large leek, white part only, well rinsed, cut into 2-by-⅛-inch strips*

1 *pig's foot, quartered*

Flour and water for sealing a 6- or 7-quart enameled cast iron casserole

GARNISH

6 *ounces shallots, sliced paper thin*

4 *tablespoons clarified butter*

3 *strips bacon, cut crosswise into ¼-inch strips*

3 *tablespoons chopped fresh parsley*

1. Two to 3 days before serving, place the beef, lamb, and pork in a large bowl. Pour the wine over the meats; add the remaining marinade ingredients; mix very well. Refrigerate, covered, overnight or for 2 days, turning the contents of the bowl twice a day.

2. *About 4 hours before serving:* Preheat oven to 500° F. Bring the meats and marinade to room temperature. Use rendered poultry fat to coat the bottom of the lid of a 6- or 7-quart earthenware or enameled cast-iron casserole. Peel and slice the onions thin (⅟₁₆ inch). Rinse them under running water and wring dry. Pare and slice the potatoes ⅛ inch thick; rinse off the starch and pat them dry with a terry cloth kitchen towel. In a bowl mix 2 teaspoons of coarse salt with ½ teaspoon of freshly ground pepper. Place two-thirds of the potato slices in the casserole; sprinkle them lightly with salt and pepper. Layer two-thirds of the onion slices on top of the potatoes, and season with salt and pepper.

3. Drain and season the meats; reserve the marinade. Place the meat and *fresh* bouquet garni on top of the onions. Scatter the leeks over the meat; top with the remaining sliced onions. Pour over the reserved marinade and 1 cup of water. Add the remaining potatoes in one slightly overlapping layer; sprinkle with salt and pepper. Place the pieces of pig's foot, skin side up, on top of the potatoes, spacing evenly.

4. Make a paste of flour and water. Create an airtight seal with paste and the lid. (The pieces of pig's foot will touch the inside top of the lid.) Bake the casserole for 30 minutes. Lower the oven heat to 350° F and bake 2 hours longer without disturbing.

5. Make the garnish: Cut the shallots paper-thin (you can use a food processor fitted with a 1-mm disk), rinse them under water and drain them before frying. In a 9-inch heavy skillet fry the sliced shallots in clarified butter until golden brown and crisp, 18 to 20 minutes. Remove them to drain on paper towels. Fry the bacon in the same fat until crisp. Drain well. Discard the fat. In a cleaned-out skillet, mix the shallots, bacon, parsley, and plenty of black pepper, and set aside.

6. Remove the casserole. Break the seal, uncover, and tilt to spoon off as much liquid as possible without disturbing the dish. Degrease the liquid, then quickly reduce it to about one-half. Meanwhile, carefully dig out and discard the bouquet garni. Pour the reduced liquid over the potatoes and shake the casserole for even distribution. (*The dish can wait up to 45 minutes before serving.* Partially cover and set in a warm place.)

7. Raise the oven heat to 500° F. Remove the cover and set the casserole on the upper oven shelf to crisp and brown the potatoes, 15 to 20 minutes. Meanwhile reheat the garnish in the skillet over medium heat until sizzling; scatter over the pig's foot and potatoes. Serve directly from the casserole, including in each serving a section of pig's foot, a little garnish, some of each meat, and potatoes and onions.

NOTE TO THE COOK

Rendered goose fat is available from some ethnic butchers, or by mail order (see Duck Fat in the Appendix, page 341).

If you wish to render your own poultry fat, save and freeze excess skin and fat when cooking chicken, duck, or goose. When about 2 cups' worth has been accumulated, heat the skin and fat in a small, heavy saucepan over medium heat, stirring frequently as the fat starts to liquefy. Reduce the heat to low; simmer, uncovered, about 1 hour. Strain. If not using immediately, cool, uncovered, to room temperature. Store, tightly covered, in the refrigerator up to 4 months, or freeze for longer periods.

Expatriate Ragout with Braised Pig's Knuckles and Calves' Tongues

What do you serve when a famous expatriate, the American Guru of French Food, comes to dinner? This was the problem I faced when I invited Richard Olney to my home.

I knew from his books that he appreciated simple, honest food, and disliked food that was flashy, verified when at a lunch at his home in Provence I ate perhaps the best *coq au vin* of my life.

I wanted to make something just as memorable for him incorporating my own interests, a dish that would be both sophisticated and earthy, modern yet honest.

Inspired by a dish of pig's head and truffles that I had once tasted at the restaurant Jamin in Paris, I created a ragout of succulent pig's knuckles and lean veal tongues smothered with a large assortment of fresh tender vegetables and sautéed mousserons and chanterelles. I think Richard was pleased.

An earthy Catalan Mussel Soup is a good beginning to the meal. Serve the ragout with buttered ribbon noodles, and for dessert, a wedge of Roquefort, some ripe figs, and a glass of chilled Château d'Yquem.

4 *fresh, meaty pig's knuckles, about 3½ pounds*

2 *fresh veal tongues, about 1¼ pounds each*

2½ *tablespoons olive oil*

1½ *cups chopped carrots*

½ *cup chopped onion*

1 *leek, white part only, sliced*

¾ *cup sliced shallots*

1 *pound meaty veal bones from the rib or neck*

Bouquet garni: 5 sprigs parsley, 5 sprigs coriander, leek greens, tied in a bundle

½ *cup chopped tomatoes, fresh or canned*

1 *head garlic, cut in half crosswise*

Spice and dried herb mixture (see recipe, page 264)

Salt and freshly ground pepper

VEGETABLE GARNISH

6 *tablespoons unsalted butter*

2 *cups (5 ounces) small fresh chanterelles, cleaned with a soft brush, and trimmed*

½ *cup (½ ounce) dried St. George's agaric mushrooms,* mousserons *(see Appendix, page 345 for mail-order source),* optional.

1 *cup broccoli flowerets*

2 *small zucchinis, trimmed, cored to remove seeds, and cut into 1-by-½-inch sticks*

¼ *pound tender string beans, trimmed*

Salt and freshly ground pepper

A few drops of fresh lemon juice (optional)

2 *teaspoons arrowroot*

3 *tablespoons roughly torn flat-leaf parsley*

Steps 1 through 5 can be done up to 2 days in advance.

1. Preheat the oven to 475° F. Blanch the pig's knuckles and the tongues for 10 minutes. Drain; refresh and drain again.

2. Meanwhile, heat the oil in a large (about 9-quarts) enameled cast-iron casserole, over medium-low heat. Add the carrots, onions, leek, and shallots. Cover and sweat the vegetables for 5 minutes (see note below). Remove the cover, add the veal bones, and continue cooking, stirring frequently, until the vegetables and bones begin to turn golden brown around the edges, about 10 minutes. Add the herb bouquet, tomatoes, garlic, and mixed spices and dried herbs to the casserole. Cook, stirring often, until all moisture has evaporated from the pan.

3. Arrange the drained meats in one layer over the mixture. Set in the oven, uncovered, for 30 minutes. Turn the meats once to brown them evenly. Lower the oven heat to 325° F. Cover the contents in the casserole with water, bring it to a boil on top of the stove, and skim carefully. Cover the casserole with a round of parchment or foil and a tight-fitting lid and return it to the oven to cook for 2 hours or until the meats are very tender. Remove the meats to a work surface.

4. When the meat is cool enough to handle, remove and discard the bones, gristle and fat: Cut the pork flesh and skin into 1-inch chunks. Trim the tongue, peel off the skin, and cut the flesh into 1-inch chunks. Place in a bowl and season lightly with salt.

5. Strain the liquid through a fine-mesh sieve into a medium saucepan. Skim off the fat that rises to the surface. Bring the liquid to a boil and reduce it to about 4 cups. Pour 2 cups of the liquid over the chunks of meat and set aside. Bring the remaining 2 cups to a boil. Set the pan half over the heat and boil, adjusting the heat so that the side over the heat slowly boils and the fat and any other impurities in the sauce rise on the cooler side. This process takes about 10 minutes, with occasional skimming. The resulting sauce will be clear and shiny and reduced to about 1½ cups. (*To this point the dish can be prepared up to 2 days in advance.* Cool, cover the meats and cooking liquid and the reduced sauce in separate containers and refrigerate.)

6. Prepare the garnish: Soak the *mousserons* in warm water for 30 minutes. Rinse them well; discard the soaking liquid and remove the stems with a pair of scissors. Place them in a small saucepan, cover with water, and bring to a boil. Immediately drain, refresh the mushrooms under cool running water, and drain. Heat the butter in a small, heavy saucepan and add the chanterelles and *mousserons*. Cover and cook over low heat, shaking the pan, for 2 minutes. Blanch the broccoli flowerets in boiling salted water 1½ minutes, refresh under cool running water, and drain them. Blanch the zucchini and string beans in boiling salted water for 1 minute, refresh and drain well. Add the blanched vegetables to the mushrooms, cover, and cook 3 minutes longer. Adjust the seasoning with salt, pepper, and, if desired, a few drops of lemon juice. (*To this point the garnish can be prepared 1 hour in advance.* Set aside, partially covered.)

7. Thirty minutes before serving, remove the meats and sauce from the refrigerator. Remove any surface fat from the reserved sauce. Gently reheat the meat in the cooking

(continued)

liquid over low heat. (*Do not place cold meats in hot sauce; they will become hard and stringy.*) Drain it and place in a wide (12-inch) shallow serving dish. Reheat the sauce in a small saucepan. Combine 2 tablespoons water and arrowroot, mixing until smooth. Bring the sauce to a boil; whisk in arrowroot mixture. Cook over medium-low heat until thickened, and adjust the seasoning with salt and pepper. Pour the hot sauce over the meat. Completely *cover* the meat with the vegetables. Sprinkle them with torn pieces of fresh flat-leaf parsley and serve at once.

Spice and Herb Mixture

2 teaspoons salt	2 crumbled bay leaves
1 tablespoon ground coriander	1 teaspoon thyme, crumbled
1 teaspoon ground ginger	1 inch rosemary, spikes crushed
1½ tablespoons cracked black peppercorns	2 large leaves of fresh sage, chopped, or ½ teaspoon crumbled
1½ tablespoons juniper berries	
¼ whole nutmeg, smashed	

Combine and use as directed in step 2.

NOTE TO THE COOK   To "sweat" vegetables means to cook them in a closed pot while they express their moisture. After the moisture is released the cover is removed and the vegetables are allowed to turn golden brown, which helps develop flavor and color in the sauce.

CASSOULET

A *Modern Cassoulet with Two Confits*

SERVES 12

I thought I'd pretty much had my say about cassoulet in *The Cooking of South-West France*. But when I was asked to create an especially light and modern cassoulet for a friend's birthday, I came up with the following new version. In this recipe I employ various tricks to extract the taste of fat (so I won't have to serve very much of it), and a method of double blanching the beans so diners will not become uncomfortable later in the evening.

Removing fat without removing flavor takes extra time, but to me it's worth it. Any good cassoulet recipe is long and complicated, but please don't be intimidated: many of the steps are executed in advance, some as far ahead as a week. This will not only make the final preparation easier, it will actually improve the dish, since the flavors will grow stronger and deeper on account of mellowing.

The addition of fresh pork rind to the beans makes them more flavorful and gives them a creamy coating; this step adds a little fat, but should not be ignored. The richness of the liquid that enrobes each bean is indispensable to a great rendition of the dish.

On the day you serve the cassoulet, assemble the meats and beans and crisp the duck *confit*. Then place the casserole in the oven to cook slowly; stir up the skin that forms from time to time.

Begin the meal with fresh oysters on the half shell nestled in crushed ice. Serve the cassoulet with a bitter-greens salad dressed with walnut oil and Sherry vinegar, and finish with Frozen Lemon Parfait in a Bitters Mousse with Black-Currant Sauce.

2 *pounds meaty spare ribs, trimmed of excess fat and cut into small chunks*

½ *pound pork rind with ¼-inch layer of hard fat attached*

Salt and freshly ground pepper

2 *pounds dry white beans, preferably Great Northern*

5 *springs fresh thyme*

½ *pound lean salt pork*

1 *ham hock*

8 *tablespoons fat from* confits

1 *medium carrot, pared and sliced*

1 *cup diced onions*

1 *whole large head garlic*

½ *cup crushed tomatoes, seeded*

⅓ *pound cured ham or baked ham, in one piece*

Herb bouquet: 4 sprigs parsley, 2 sprigs thyme, celery rib with leaves, and 1 bay leaf, tied together

Zest of ½ orange

16 *peppercorns*

1 *small onion stuck with 1 clove*

2 *quarts unsalted chicken or duck stock*

1 *pound fresh garlic-flavored pork sausages, preferably mildly spiced (see note if substituting 1 large garlic sausage)*

Confit *of pork (see recipe, page 269)*

Confit *of duck (see recipe, page 268)*

1½ *teaspoons chopped garlic*

1 *teaspoon chopped fresh thyme*

1 *tablespoon chopped fresh parsley*

6 *tablespoons soft white breadcrumbs*

Steps 1 through 9 can be prepared in advance.

1. *Two days before serving,* season the spare ribs and pork rind lightly with salt and pepper. Store them covered in the refrigerator overnight.

2. The following day, do steps 2 through 5. Sort the beans and rinse them under cool running water. Soak them with 2 or 3 sprigs of thyme in water to cover for 1½ hours (longer if you suspect they are over 6 months old).

(continued)

3. In a deep saucepan place the pork rind, salt pork, and ham hock, and cover with cold water. *Slowly* bring to a boil, lower the heat, and simmer for 5 minutes, skimming often. Drain, then rinse under cool running water, drain again, and pat dry with paper towels. If the pork rind is still brittle, repeat with fresh water and simmer for 10 to 12 minutes, or until it is supple. Roll up the pork rind like a rug and tie it with string. Cut the rind off the lean salt pork, and reserve the rind. Cut the salt pork into 4 even pieces and dry them with paper towels.

4. Make the pork ragout: Wipe the spare ribs dry. Heat 4 tablespoons of the rendered fat from the duck and pork *confits* in a 9-quart flameproof casserole. Add the ribs and brown them lightly on all sides, about 5 minutes. Add the carrots and onions and sauté over moderately high heat, stirring, until the onions are soft and golden, about 5 minutes. Add the ham hock and the salt pork, and allow them to brown a little around the edges, about 5 minutes. Add the rolled pork rind, salt-pork rind, head of garlic, crushed tomatoes, ham slice, herbs, orange zest, peppercorns, and the onion stuck with 1 clove. Cover with the stock, bring the mixture to a boil, skim carefully, reduce the heat, and simmer, covered, for 1½ hours.

5. After the pork ragout has cooked 1½ hours, drain the beans and place them in a heavy saucepan; cover them with water and slowly bring to a boil. Simmer 10 minutes; then, using a slotted spoon, transfer the beans to the simmering ragout. Continue cooking, covered, over low heat for 1 hour. Add ½ teaspoon of salt and cook 30 minutes longer or until the beans are tender but not splitting. Remove the casserole from the heat to cool down. Discard the whole onion, the herb bouquet, the fatty part of the salt pork, and all the bones. Separate the rinds, meats, and beans. Remove all the gristle and fatty parts from the assorted meats. Strain the cooking liquid. Separately cool, cover, and refrigerate the cooking liquid, meats, rinds, and beans.

6. Early the following day, do steps 6 through 9. Remove the cooking liquid, meats, rinds, *confits,* and beans from the refrigerator. Discard the fat that has risen to the top of the cooking liquid. Place the cooking liquid, hock's skin, and assorted rinds in a saucepan and cook at a simmer for 1 hour, or longer if they are not fork-tender. (This can be done in a microwave in a covered dish using only enough liquid to cover all the rinds. Cook on medium high for 30 minutes.) Strain, reserving liquid and solids. Measure the liquid and add enough water to make 7 cups; leave to cool and skim carefully. Scrape all the fat from the assorted pork rinds and discard it. Cut the rinds and ham hock's skin into ½-inch squares so it will easily disintegrate in the final cooking. Cut the ham hock's flesh into slivers. Dice fine the ham slice and the lean part of the salt pork, then mix all together with the meat from the ribs.

7. Prick the sausages and brown them in a teaspoon of fat in a nonstick skillet. Drain; cut them into 1-inch pieces. Pour off the fat. In the same skillet, place 2 tablespoons of the *confit* fat, and when hot sear the pieces of pork *confit* on all sides. Remove them from the heat and cut them into bite-size pieces. Set aside the skillet for later. Add the sausages and pork *confit* to the other meats, season generously with pepper, and taste for salt.

8. Carefully remove the duck skin from the *confit* in large pieces. Add 2 tablespoons of *confit* fat to the reserved skillet and heat to "rippling." Slowly crisp the duck skin on both sides. Drain it on paper towels; scrape off any unmelted fat from the skin. Carefully remove the bones from the duck and discard them. Divide the duck flesh into 12 even portions; generously season them with freshly ground pepper and gently squeeze each portion into a ball. Cover each with a piece of crisp skin. Arrange them on a plate, cover with plastic wrap to prevent drying out, and set them aside in a cool place or the refrigerator.

9. To assemble the cassoulet, spread the pork-rind squares all over the bottom of a 6- or 7-quart, wide, ovenproof serving dish—a deep ovenproof salad or pasta bowl is ideal. Cover with a layer of beans, then a layer of assorted meats (but not the duck *confit*). Combine the chopped garlic, thyme, parsley, and ½ teaspoon freshly ground pepper, and spread half of the mixture over the beans. Repeat with the meats, herbs and garlic, ending with a layer of beans. Gently reheat cooking liquid and pour just enough over the beans to cover them. Be sure there is 1 inch of "growing space" between the beans and the rim of the dish. Reserve the remaining liquid to baste the beans during the final cooking. (*The dish can be prepared many hours in advance to this point.* Set aside in a cool place, or the refrigerator.)

10. About 2¼ hours before serving, preheat the oven to 450° F. Sprinkle half the breadcrumbs over the beans, and dot them with 2 tablespoons of fat from the *confit*. Set the dish in the oven to bake 30 minutes or until a golden skin forms on top of the beans.

11. Reduce the oven temperature to 350° F. Gently stir in the skin that has formed and baste the beans with a few spoonfuls of the reserved cooking liquid. Continue to bake until another golden layer appears on the beans—in about 20 minutes. Repeat two more times: stirring, basting, and baking the dish until a skin appears on the surface. Baste once or twice, using up as much reserved liquid as necessary to keep the beans from drying out. When the dish has baked a total of 1½ hours, break up the skin, press the reserved duck *confit*, skin side up, into the top layer of beans. The crisped duck skin should be just even with the beans' surface—indicating an individual serving of duck *confit*. Sprinkle the beans and duck skin with the remaining breadcrumbs and 2 tablespoons of *confit* fat. Bake until a well-browned glaze forms on top and the *cassoulet* is bubbling hot, about 20 minutes. Serve directly from the dish.

If substituting smoked pork products, soak and parboil for 15 minutes before using. Do not marinate them in salt.

NOTES TO THE COOK

Beans may cook in a shorter period depending upon their quality and age. In step 5 be careful not to cook them to the mushy stage.

Quick Duck and
Pork Confit

I have written extensively about *confit,* the preserved meats and poultry of the French South-West, but because putting up meat for many months requires very careful preparation, many readers have asked me for a quicker version. Here is a simplified, quick *confit* recipe, one that *keeps safely only for a week.*

In order to create the *illusion* of a well-prepared, well put-up, and matured *confit,* I have increased the standard flavorings and added juniper to give the meat a slightly gamy quality. Coriander seeds heighten the taste of the meat, nutmeg gives fragrance, cloves import sharpness, peppercorns add piquancy, and the herbs impart freshness.

(Don't be put off by the amount of fat—you only cook with it, you don't eat it.)

Use the *confit* in Warm Lentil Salad (page 27); Stew of Duck Confit and Fresh Fava Beans (page 187); and A Modern Cassoulet with Two Confits (page 264).

Quick Duck Confit

2 *ducks, quartered, or 6 (1 pound) fatted duck legs (mullards) (see notes), backbone and wings reserved for making a poultry stock*

DRY MARINADE

¼ *to ⅓ cup coarse salt or 2 teaspoons coarse salt per pound of cleaned weight*

1 *tablespoon lightly cracked juniper berries*

1½ *tablespoons lightly cracked black peppercorns*

1 *teaspoon lightly cracked coriander seeds*

1½ *tablespoons roughly chopped garlic*

2 *bay leaves, crumbled*

3 *tablespoons chopped fresh thyme leaves*

1 *lightly cracked clove*

¼ *teaspoon freshly grated nutmeg*

2 *tablespoons chopped fresh parsley*

4 *cups rendered fat: any desired combination of homemade lard, goose fat, and duck fat can be used*

Begin 2 to 7 days in advance.

1. Two to 7 days before serving, trim the ducks of excess fat but leave as much skin intact as possible. Render the duck fat; cool, cover and refrigerate. Rub the duck pieces with the dry marinade. Place them in a glass, earthenware, or glazed dish, cover and refrigerate for 24 hours.

2. The following day, wipe away all the marinade and exuded juices. Place the duck pieces in a deep baking dish; add the rendered fat. (The fat should cover the meat fairly

well—more fat will render out in cooking to submerge it.) Place the dish in a cold oven; turn the heat to 275° F and leave the duck to cook about 3 hours, or until it is very tender. (If using duck quarters, remove the breasts after 2 hours if the flesh tests tender. Wrap them in foil to keep moist while the legs finish cooking.) Remove the dish from the oven and allow the duck legs to cool in the fat.

3. Transfer the duck to a deep container. Ladle fat over the duck to cover. When cold, cover with plastic wrap and refrigerate. (The *confit* keeps up to 6 days, submerged in its cooking fat in the refrigerator. Scrape off all fat before using.)

NOTE TO THE COOK

Six 1-pound fatted duck legs (mullards), and 5-pound slabs of rendered duck fat are available through mail order (see Appendix). These fatted ducks need about an extra hours' cooking time, so plan accordingly.

Quality rendered goose fat can be purchased in many German and Hungarian butcher shops during the winter months, and imported top-quality rendered goose fat is available by mail order (see Appendix, page 341). You can also freeze any unused pieces of fresh fat and skin whenever you cook a duck or goose, and then, when you have accumulated several cups' worth, render the fat (see page 261) and use as directed. Avoid using poultry or pork fat that has reached its "smoke" point or burned (i.e., drippings gathered from a roasting duck or goose). If you do not have enough rendered fat the duck can be cooked in batches. Fat used to make *confit* can be used again. Keep the fat refrigerated up to 1 month or freeze.

Quick Pork Confit

Duck and pork can cook together in the duck fat. They will each enhance the flavor of the other.

2 *pounds boneless pork shoulder or butt, cut into 6 portions, each weighing about ⅓ pound*

MARINADE
4 *teaspoons coarse salt*
12 *lightly cracked juniper berries*
2 *teaspoons lightly cracked black peppercorns*

½ *teaspoon lightly cracked coriander seeds*
2 *roughly chopped garlic cloves*
1 *bay leaf, crumbled*
1½ *tablespoons chopped fresh thyme leaves*
Pinch of freshly grated nutmeg
2 *tablespoons chopped fresh parsley*
Duck fat (see the recipe above for Quick Duck Confit)

1. Up to 7 days before serving, rub the pork with the dry marinade. Place it in a bowl, cover, and refrigerate overnight.

(continued)

2. The following day, tie each piece of pork with string to preserve a compact shape during cooking. Follow the recipe for the duck *confit*. Cook the pork fat with (or without) the duck. Remove when tender. Store as described for Quick Duck *Confit*.

CHAPTER 8 **VEGETABLES**

Roasted Autumn Vegetables in the Style of Corfu

SERVES 6

There is a type of restaurant in Greece called a *koutoukian,* usually situated at a private house with a simple garden containing eight or ten tables. *Koutoukian* food is very simple, but it is always honest.

In Corfu I visited a *koutoukian* presided over by a stout, pleasant, gray-haired woman named Sophia, who agreed to let me watch as she worked over three gas and two electric burners with fifteen or so huge pots and pans, stewing, braising, and boiling a whole slew of island specialties. She had on hand locally produced vegetables of incredible freshness, including mustard-yellow squash blossoms; slim, pointed okra; pencil-thin scallions; tiny baby artichokes; and glistening octopus, as well as such fish as sea bream, piles of whitebait, and a few *barbouni,* the delectable Mediterranean red mullet. On the counter lay a handful of fragrant herbs and a plastic jug of local olive oil, as well as large slabs of lamb, pork, and yearling veal in various unidentifiable cuts.

Sophia, in the typical manner of a Corfiote home cook, tended to combine large quantities of vegetables with small quantities of meat, and to do all her cooking with olive oil. Constantly touching, tasting, and smelling, she prepared each dish quickly, sending those that had to be casserole-roasted to the local oven first. In less than an hour she prepared stuffed tomatoes; quarters of chicken and potatoes cut into half-moon shapes seasoned with garlic, paprika, and oregano; large chunks of seasoned roasting lamb; casseroles of pork with Brussels sprouts; pork with celery, squid with tomatoes and spices, and *tourlou,* a Corfu-style vegetable mélange (called *briami* in other parts of Greece).

It was early spring when I watched Sophia cook, so her *tourlou* contained peas, artichokes, squash blossoms, and fava beans—a pastel-colored medley. In autumn, she told me, she would make the dish with tomatoes, zucchini, eggplant, and onions, all strewn with herbs and doused with fragrant olive oil.

In the following autumn version of a *tourlou,* a large, shallow baking dish is used so that the vegetables aren't overcrowded. The idea is to roast them at high heat, even char them. The combination of intense, good flavors—charred tomatoes, Greek olive oil, and the different herb accents of parsley, dill, and mint—is wonderful. Imported feta cheese, oily black olives, and crusty bread are the ideal accompaniments. This dish is perfect for a light supper served with grilled meat or poultry.

1½ *pounds ripe tomatoes, peeled, cored,*
  sliced thin, sprinkled with a pinch of
  sugar

1½ *pounds medium boiling potatoes,*
  pared, each cut into 6 wedges

1 *pound medium red or yellow onions,*
  each cut into 6 wedges

1 *pound zucchini, trimmed, rinsed, cut*
  into 1¼-inch chunks

2 *ribs celery, trimmed, stringed, and cut*
  into 1¼-inch chunks

2 *teaspoons fine-chopped garlic*

2 *teaspoons fine salt*

½ *teaspoon fine-ground pepper*

⅓ *cup fine-chopped fresh parsley*

1½ *tablespoons chopped dill*

1 *teaspoon chopped fresh mint or*
  marjoram

¼ *cup fruity extra-virgin olive oil*

1. Set an oven rack in the upper-middle position. Preheat the oven to 400° F. Oil a large baking dish (such as a 13-by-11-by-2-inch lasagna pan).

2. Spread half the tomatoes on the bottom of the dish. Scatter the potatoes, onions, zucchini, and celery on top. Lay the remaining tomatoes over the vegetables. Sprinkle with the garlic, salt, pepper, and herbs, and drizzle with the oil. Bake the dish for 30 minutes. Remove it from the oven; stir carefully to redistribute the vegetables, then bake another 30 to 40 minutes without disturbing. Serve hot or lukewarm.

Catalan Eggplant with Cheese and Honey

SERVES 6

This particular recipe is a modern version of a medieval dish. It is adapted from one of the oldest Catalan gastronomic manuscripts, *Le Libre del Coch* by Robert de Nola, published in 1520. The Catalan culinary expert Rudolf Grewe often extolls the enormous sophistication of medieval Catalan cooking. "By comparison," he told me, "what we eat in Catalonia today is more like peasants' food."

Sweetened eggplant and cheese may seem a strange combination, but the idea of adding honey to offset the mild bitterness of the eggplant works.

I like to bake and serve this dish in a shallow earthenware casserole. Serve it with grilled lamb or beef. Make it ahead and reheat just before serving.

3 small eggplants (about ½ pound each), cut in half lengthwise

Coarse (kosher) salt

⅔ cup grated Gruyère cheese

⅓ cup grated Parmesan cheese

1 whole egg

1 egg yolk

Olive oil

¼ teaspoon freshly ground white pepper

Freshly grated nutmeg

2 teaspoons honey

1. Scoop out the eggplants, leaving a thin shell. Cut the pulp into large chunks. Cook the pulp, covered, in a large saucepan of boiling salted water over moderately high heat until soft, about 10 minutes. Drain and let the pulp cool in a strainer.

2. Meanwhile, sprinkle the eggplant shells with 1 teaspoon of salt and let them drain for 20 minutes.

3. When the pulp is cool enough to handle, press out all moisture. Set aside 2 tablespoons of the Gruyère cheese. Mix together the remaining Gruyère and the Parmesan cheese. Place the pulp, cheeses, whole egg, and egg yolk in a food processor; process to a purée. Add white pepper, nutmeg, and ½ teaspoon of salt; purée until smooth.

4. Preheat the oven to 425° F. Rinse and drain the eggplant shells; pat them dry with paper towels. Slowly heat about ¼ inch of olive oil in an 8-inch nonstick skillet. When hot, add 3 shells in a single layer and slowly fry, turning once, until they collapse and the

attached pulp is tender and golden brown, about 3 minuttes on each side (be careful not to break the shells). Drain them on paper towels. Repeat with remaining shells.

5. Arrange the eggplant shells in a shallow baking dish just large enough to hold all of them in one layer. Fill each shell with eggplant purée, mounding it slightly. Sprinkle the reserved 2 tablespoons of Gruyère cheese on top and drizzle a little honey over each.

6. Bake in the upper third of the oven for 20 minutes, or until the purée is golden brown on top. (*This recipe can be made up to 4 hours ahead.* Keep it covered in a cool place. Reheat 15 minutes in a moderate oven just before serving.)

For cooking eggplants, see Frying in Olive Oil in the Appendix, page 346.

NOTE TO
THE COOK

Mallorcan-Style Eggplant

SERVES 4

These eggplant slices are crisp on the outside and creamy inside, and not greasy—the result of proper salting, soaking, and frying in olive oil.

Salting eggplant is controversial. Some food writers say you do not have to salt the vegetable if it is fresh and firm, without blemishes and dents. I always salt it, not only to remove bitter juices, but primarily to prepare it for frying. Salted slices, soaked in milk, drained, and then dusted with flour, will absorb hardly any oil during frying. One reason is because the added moisture (the milk) causes the slices to steam when they hit the hot oil, while the floured coating, which crisps, keeps the oil from entering the flesh. For more thoughts about frying in olive oil, see the Appendix, page 346.

Some eggplants will always retain a trace of bitterness, even when thoroughly salted. To remedy this, the Mallorcans dust the vegetable lightly with sugar, as in this recipe. Serve the rounds overlapping on a napkin-lined platter. They are good with grilled meats or poultry—or as a dessert.

1 *pound narrow eggplants, preferably Japanese*

2 *teaspoons coarse salt*

1 *to 2 cups milk*

Oil for deep-fat frying, preferably olive oil

Flour for dredging

Salt, pepper, and ground cinnamon

Granulated sugar (optional)

1. Peel the eggplants and cut them into ½-inch-thick rounds. Place the rounds in a colander and sprinkle them with salt. Weight them down and let them stand at least 1 hour. Rinse, place them in a bowl, cover them with milk, and let them soak until you are ready to fry. (The milk will draw out the salt.)

2. Preheat the oven to 250° F. Heat the oil in a deep fryer to 375° F. Meanwhile, drain the eggplant and pat the surfaces dry with paper towels. Season the flour with salt, pepper, and cinnamon, dredge *half* the slices in the flour, and shake off the excess in a wide sieve set over the sink. Immediately drop them, one by one, into the hot oil and fry them until crisp and brown on both sides, about 7 minutes. Drain on paper towels and place in the oven to keep warm. Repeat with the remaining slices after checking that the oil has returned to 375° F. Serve at once, sprinkle with sugar if desired.

Adapted from Luis Ripoll's Cocina de las Baleares.

CÈPES, PORCINI, AND OTHER BOLETES

SERVES 4   *Wild Mushrooms with Garlic, Herbs, and Tomatoes, Corsican Style*

This Corsican way of preparing cèpes is simple, refreshing, and unexpected. I am a great advocate of chopping garlic and parsley together, especially when the garlic is not to be fully cooked. (The parsley seems to cut the strong garlic taste.)

The original recipe calls for a wild mint unique to the Mediterranean called *nepita*. To simulate the taste of *nepita* I use a mixture of flat-leaf parsley, basil, and mint. Use the strongest-tasting mint you can find, preferably peppermint with its little round dark-green aromatic leaves. Serve hot or at room temperature with slices of grilled French bread.

1 *pound fresh cèpes or other boletes, cleaned and trimmed*	2 *sprigs fresh flat-leaf parsley*
3 *tablespoons extra-virgin olive oil*	5 *fresh basil leaves, shredded*
Salt and freshly ground pepper	1 *small ripe tomato, peeled, seeded, and cut into ¼-inch dice (see note)*
2 *garlic cloves, halved and peeled, green sprout removed*	2 *sprigs fresh aromatic mint leaves, slivered*
	Salt and freshly ground pepper

1. Wipe the mushrooms with a damp cloth. Separate the stems from the caps. Slice the stems into 1-inch strips. If the mushroom caps are large, cut these in half. In a 10- or 11-inch skillet heat the oil; add the mushrooms, and cook them, covered, over medium heat, shaking the skillet often, until the mushrooms express their moisture, about 5 minutes. Uncover and cook until the skillet juices have evaporated.

2. Meanwhile, chop the garlic cloves and parsley together. Add them to the mushrooms and continue cooking until the mushrooms are tender. Add the basil, tomato, and mint, and season with pinches of salt and pepper.

NOTE TO THE COOK

If your tomato is very ripe, don't bother to place it over a gas flame or drop it into boiling water to remove its skin. Simply slit the top with a small knife, then use a vegetable peeler to roll back the skin. Halve the tomato, remove the seeds, and dice.

Michel Bras's Cèpe Tarts with Walnut Cream

MAKES 8 TARTS

This is a signature dish of my friend Michel Bras, who works in Laguiole, a small town in the Aveyron, an almost savage rural area in the high pasturelands of the Aubrac Mountains of France. Michel finds almost all his ingredients in the local countryside: crayfish and trout in the streams, lambs and calves on the farms; mushrooms and nuts, apples, raspberries, and wild herbs . . .

His achievement is to have raised peasant cooking to a new and extraordinary level. A perfect example are his irresistible tarts of wild mushrooms with a creamy walnut filling, a dish that conveys to me the essence of the forest.

Michel's wife, Ginette, who acts as sommelier in his restaurant Lou-Mazuc, suggested I accompany these tarts with a 1971 Gaillac "Premières Côtes" of Robert Plageoles. This is a curious wine, called a *vin de voile,* on account of the way its vines are trained to grow low on very soft sandy soil, so low that they spread themselves over the earth almost like a sheet. I found this tawny-colored wine smooth, fragrant, and rather sweet—excellent with the tart. Since *vins de voile* are virtually unobtainable in this country, my suggestion would be to serve the nearest equivalent, a fine dry Sherry such as Tío Pepe.

I suggest you serve these tarts as a separate course so that their taste, texture, and aroma can be fully appreciated.

FILLING

2¼ *pounds small cèpes, porcini, Steinpilz, stone, boletes, or Italian brown mushrooms, fresh or canned*

2 *ounces shelled walnut meats*

1 *large egg*

2 *ounces prosciutto, diced fine*

1⅓ *packed cups cubed fried bread, soaked for 10 minutes in ⅓ cup milk or water and squeezed dry*

1 *large shallot, chopped and sauteed in 1 teaspoon butter until soft*

½ *cup heavy cream, chilled*

Salt and freshly ground pepper

2 *tablespoons unsalted butter, melted*

1 *garlic clove, crushed*

8 *4- or 4½-inch flan rings or tart molds lined with pastry, chilled (see Pastry for Tarts, page 337)*

1 *to 2 tablespoons French walnut oil*

1. Trim fresh cèpes' stems and wipe the caps with a damp paper towel. Blanch the cèpes for 5 minutes in 3 quarts of boiling water with 3 tablespoons of coarse salt added; drain and press until thoroughly dry in kitchen toweling. If using canned cèpes, drain, and dry thoroughly.

2. Use the grating blade of a food processor to grate the walnuts; this will make ⅔ cup. Place the egg, prosciutto, bread, walnuts, and shallots in the workbowl of the food processor fitted with the metal blade and grind to a smooth paste, scraping down the insides of the workbowl from time to time. Scrape the mixture into a wide soup bowl, cover, and refrigerate for 45 minutes. Using a dinner fork gradually work in small amounts of the cold heavy cream into walnut mixture. Each portion of cream must be blended in before the next is added. Season to taste with salt and pepper.

3. Preheat the oven to 400° F. Spread a thin, even layer of the walnut mixture on the dough. Cut the cèpes vertically into very thin slices; fan the slices slightly and place on top of the filling. Brush the surface with a little melted butter mixed with crushed garlic, salt and pepper. Bake on the middle oven shelf for 30 minutes. Sprinkle mushrooms with a few drops of walnut oil. Serve hot.

Try to choose mushrooms with very small, firm heads.

NOTES TO THE COOK

In this recipe the fresh mushrooms are first blanched in salted water, a method that preserves their moisture during the baking of the tart. The addition of salt raises the temperature of the water so that there is a quick and efficient seal. After removing the mushrooms from the water, a quick refreshing under cool running water will eliminate the salt.

If you use flan rings, place them on a dark-finish baking sheet for a crispy crust. See Appendix for mail order for flan rings, (page 343).

If using tartlet molds, cool on a wire rack for five minutes before turning out.

Baked Mushrooms with Green-cracked Olives

SERVES 4 TO 6

Greek green-cracked olives are large, dark, and sharp, with a hint of bitterness and a slightly smoky flavor that mingles well with dried wild mushrooms. These easy-to-make stuffed mushrooms make a good first course, or can be served with grilled poultry or meat.

⅓ cup crumbled (¾ ounce) dried imported Boletus edulis (porcini, cèpes, or Steinpilz)

Salt and freshly ground pepper

15 to 20 (about ¾ pound) fresh, firm cultivated mushrooms

1 tablespoon olive oil

4 tablespoons unsalted butter

4 tablespoons chopped flat-leaf parsley

¼ teaspoon Mediterranean oregano, crumbled

Juice of ½ lemon

15 Greek green-cracked olives, pitted and chopped fine (⅓ cup)

1. Preheat the oven to 325° F. Cover the dried mushrooms with warm water containing a pinch of salt and soak for 20 minutes. Wipe the fresh mushroom caps; remove the stems, trim off the ends, and chop the stems fine to make 1 cup. Place the mushroom caps in an oiled shallow baking dish. Season half the butter with pinches of salt and pepper, and divide it evenly among the caps. Bake them for 10 minutes.

2. When the dried mushrooms have soaked for 20 minutes, strain the soaking liquid through several layers of cheesecloth. Rinse the dried mushrooms under cool running water to eliminate any grit or sand, then chop them fine.

3. In a medium skillet, slowly cook the dried mushrooms, their soaking liquid, and the chopped stems until all the liquid has evaporated and the mushrooms are tender. Allow to cool to lukewarm. With a fork work in the remaining butter, parsley, oregano, lemon juice, and chopped olives. Season to taste with salt and pepper.

4. Raise the oven heat to 400° F. Stuff each mushroom with the olive-mushroom mixture and return them to the oven to bake 10 minutes longer. Serve hot or lukewarm. (The recipe can be prepared in advance and reheated.)

Sautéed Salsify

SERVES 8

2 pounds firm salsify, or 2 (14-ounce) jars
  or cans cooked salsify (see note)

1 lemon

4 tablespoons unsalted butter

Salt and freshly ground pepper

2 tablespoons fine-chopped parsley

1. Prepare the salsify: Separate the greens (if attached) from the roots. Separately cook the salsify greens (if available) in boiling salted water until tender, and set them aside. If using fresh black salsify, wash it well in several changes of water; using a stainless-steel knife, peel it and cut it into 2-inch pieces. If using white salsify do not peel until after cooking. Immediately drop the pieces into water with a little lemon juice added (in the proportion of 1 tablespoon of lemon juice to 2 cups of water) to keep them from darkening. Cook the salsify in plenty of boiling salted water with the juice of ½ lemon until just tender, 8 to 10 minutes. Drain it well and dry on a kitchen towel. Makes about 2 cups. If using canned salsify, drain, rinse, and allow to dry on a kitchen towel.

2. Just before serving, melt the butter in a medium skillet over moderate heat. Add the salsify and cook until golden brown on all sides, about 3 minutes. Add the green tips, if available, and salt and pepper to taste. Sprinkle with lemon juice and chopped parsley.

NOTE TO THE COOK

Salsify is a cold-weather root vegetable that is beginning to appear more frequently in our markets. Since it is one of the few vegetables that takes well to canning, a can or jar imported from Belgium or France can be substituted. Simply drain the salsify and sauté in butter until golden.

There are two types of salsify: white and black. Black salsify, also called *scorzonera*, is the more flavorful variety but the less digestible. Either can be used in this recipe.

Grilled Onion Shoots with Catalan Almond Sauce

SERVES 4

Calcots (cultivated shoots of stored onions, resembling fat bulbous scallions) are a specialty of the town of Valls in the Spanish-Catalan province of Tarragona. Here, from November to March, their mass preparation and consumption at outdoor festivals has become a gastronomic cult. At these festivals thousands of *calcots* are laid out over fires of vine cuttings on huge iron grids. Diners devouring the onions wear special bibs, as the process is fairly messy—one holds the shoot in one hand, while using the other to pull off the blackened exterior from the root end. Then the tender, smooth interior is dipped into *salbitxada* sauce (a variation of the famous sauce *romesco*) and eaten along with frequent swigs of earthy red wine drunk directly from the spout of a Catalan *porron*.

In the last ten years this very old regional specialty has grown so popular that people from Barcelona will frequently drive up to Valls on a Sunday just to eat it. A typical serving at a farmhouse restaurant is about three dozen *calcots,* followed by grilled sausages, lamb chops, and a second sauce of *all-i-oli* (see page 83).

The following recipe has been adapted for preparation of leeks in a home oven. If you wish to grill your leeks out-of-doors, use grapevine cuttings and spread the leeks out in one layer on netting or a fine grid to cook. (Grapevine cuttings impart a wonderful aroma and delicious flavor to the leeks.) Grill thick asparagus (if available) and fat radishes along with the lamb chops and sausages for an entire meal. Smear the *salbitxada* sauce directly on the lamb during the grilling for a crusty finish. The *salbitxada* sauce keeps for a week in the refrigerator. It is delicious simply spread on grilled bread, or as an accompaniment to hard-boiled eggs or grilled shrimp or fish. A sherbet would be the best way to finish this meal.

SALBITXADA SAUCE

1 *small red bell pepper*

2 *plum tomatoes*

4 *large garlic cloves, unpeeled*

10 *hazelnuts (filberts)*

½ *cup (2¼ ounces) blanched almonds*

½ *tablespoon pinenuts* (pignoli)

½ *small dried ancho pepper (see note), stemmed and seeded*

2 *sprigs parsley*

1 *to 3 fresh mint leaves (optional)*

1½ *tablespoons red wine vinegar*

4 *tablespoons extra-virgin olive oil*

Salt and freshly ground pepper

16 *thin leeks (4 leeks to a pound)*

Oil

1. Preheat the oven to 350° F. Put the bell pepper, whole tomatoes, garlic, hazelnuts, and almonds in separate piles on a jelly-roll pan and set in the oven. Remove the nuts

when golden brown. Remove the peppers and tomatoes when the skins are blistery, and the garlic when it is soft, about 30 minutes. Let the ingredients cool. Peel and core the tomatoes. Peel, core, and seed the pepper. Peel the garlic. Rub off the skins of the hazelnuts.

2. Meanwhile, combine the ancho pepper with ¼ cup of water in a small saucepan. Cook over moderately high heat for 10 minutes. Reduce the heat, and simmer until 1½ tablespoons of water are left, about 10 minutes.

3. In a food processor, combine the nuts with 3 tablespoons of water. Grind them to a smooth paste. Add the parsley, mint, ancho pepper with its liquid, the tomatoes, garlic, and bell pepper. Process until they are very smooth. With the machine on, add the vinegar. Gradually add the oil, drop by drop, in a slow, steady stream. Season the sauce with salt and pepper. Let it stand at room temperature for at least 3 hours before serving to allow the flavors to ripen. Stir the sauce before serving. Makes about 1¼ cups.

4. One hour before serving, preheat the oven to 475° F.

5. Trim all but 1 inch of green leaves from the leeks. Do not remove the tough outer leaves; discard the roots. Beginning about 1 inch from the base, split the leeks lengthwise, using a thin, sharp knife. Wash the leeks thoroughly; if they are very sandy, let them stand in a bowl of cold water for 10 minutes.

6. Drain the leeks and pat them dry. Arrange them in one layer on a lightly oiled baking sheet. Lightly brush each leek with oil. Set the sheet on the upper oven shelf to bake 30 to 45 minutes, turning them midway. Set the leeks aside to steam for 10 minutes. Serve warm with the sauce.

The best substitutes for *calcots* are thin leeks, not fat scallions.

NOTES TO THE COOK

The *ancho* pepper (a dried *poblano*) is a wonderful substitute for the two popular mildly spicy peppers (*romesco* and *nyores*) that are traditionally used in this recipe. The *romesco* is a burnished red pepper that is fleshy, aromatic, and flavorful, but it is nearly impossible to find, even at the market in Tarragona. Thus, most Catalan cooks settle for the less-expensive and milder *nyora*, which looks and sounds (when shaken) like a Mexican *cascabel*, but for which a *cascabel* is much too strong a substitute.

G*lazed Leeks*　　　　SERVES 4

The easy cooking method described below produces a mellow-tasting leek with a shiny coating, attractive and wonderful enough to accompany any main course, including roast pork, grilled lamb, and roast salmon fillets.

　　When caramelizing vegetables one usually swirls the pan as butter, sugar, and vegetable juices combine to create a thick glaze. However, if this procedure is applied to leeks, they lose their attractive shape. So I blanch them first, drain them, and then quickly bake them in the oven in melted butter with a dusting of sugar so they will not shrivel or dry out.

12 *tender young leeks*	1¼ *teaspoons granulated sugar*
5 *tablespoons unsalted butter, melted*	*Grated nutmeg*
Fine salt	

　　1. Trim all but 1 inch of green leaves from the leeks. Remove any remaining tough outer leaves; discard the roots. Beginning about 1 inch from the base, split each leek lengthwise, using a thin, sharp knife. Wash them thoroughly; if they are very sandy, then let them stand in a bowl of cold water about 10 minutes. Tie them in bundles of 3 or 4.

　　2. Blanch the bundles of leeks by cooking in plenty of boiling salted water for 5 minutes. Drain them, refresh with cold water, and drain again. Untie the bundles and press each leek between two kitchen towels to remove moisture. Remove any outer skins that have become puffy and misshapen. Arrange the leeks side by side in a buttered shallow baking dish. Brush each leek with melted butter. Sprinkle with salt, sugar, and grated nutmeg. (*Up to this point the recipe can be prepared 2 hours in advance.* Cover the leeks loosely with plastic wrap and let them stand at room temperature.)

　　3. Preheat the oven to 425° F. Bake the leeks on an upper oven shelf until glazed and browned, about 10 to 15 minutes.

Red Kidney Bean Purée

This is a rich, wonderful accompaniment to wild game. The rustic flavor of red kidney beans is enhanced by the addition of red wine and spices. You will notice that I enrich the dish with a small amount of butter (not cream) to retain the deep red color of the beans.

½ *pound red kidney beans, washed and picked over*

1½ *cups full-bodied red wine*

1 *soft-stick cinnamon, or a pinch of ground cinnamon (see Appendix, page 340, for types of cinnamon)*

1 *onion stuck with 1 clove*

Herb bouquet with parsley, bay leaf, and pinch of thyme

¼ *teaspoon crushed red-pepper flakes*

Salt and freshly ground pepper

4 *tablespoons unsalted butter*

A few drops of balsamic vinegar

1. Soak the beans in cold water overnight, or use the quick method following package directions.

2. Heat the wine in a saucepan with spices, onions, herbs, and peppers, and 2 cups of water. Bring the liquid to a boil and keep it at a simmer. Meanwhile drain the beans, cover them with cold water, and bring them to a boil. Boil hard for 5 minutes and drain. Immediately add the beans to the simmering wine, cover, and cook over medium low heat 1 to 1½ hours. Add boiling water if necessary to keep the beans covered. (Season with 1 teaspoon of salt only when the beans are tender.)

3. Drain the beans, reserving ½ cup of the cooking liquid. Discard the cinnamon stick, bouquet, and onion. Purée the beans in a food processor; then press them and the ½ cup of cooking liquid through the fine blade of a foodmill. Return the beans to the saucepan and cook, stirring with a wooden spoon, over low heat until the purée becomes thick enough to come away from the sides of the pan.

4. Gradually beat in the butter. Correct the seasoning. (*The beans can be prepared one day in advance.* Reheat them slowly in a double boiler or in a covered glass dish in the microwave.)

Winter Carrots Cooked in the Style of the Nineteenth Century

I found this technique for cooking carrots in an old French cookbook, where it is called the "original" *carottes à la Vichy*. While several commentators insist the carrots must be cooked in real Vichy water, others simply state they should be cooked with butter, salt, sugar, and water until the water evaporates and they begin to glaze. Here the carrots are cooked under a soup bowl of cold water, which increases the speed of condensation. As a result they steam in their own moisture and glaze in their natural sugars.

1 *pound large winter carrots, pared*	*Pinch of salt*
3 *tablespoons water*	*Pinch of sugar (optional)*
¼ *cup unsalted butter*	

Cut the carrots into 2-inch chunks and halve each lengthwise. With a vegetable peeler or a small paring knife hollow out the hard centers and discard them (or use in a stock). Place the carrots in an enameled cast-iron saucepan just large enough to hold them in one layer. Add the water, butter, and a pinch of salt. Cover the pan with a porcelain or earthenware soup bowl filled with water. Cook over low heat for at least 30 minutes, replacing the water in the bowl if it evaporates. (The slower the cooking, the sweeter the carrots will be.) Once, during this time, remove the bowl and shake the carrots to keep them from sticking. Five minutes before serving, sprinkle them with a pinch of sugar if desired.

NOTE TO THE COOK   This recipe works equally well with small, tender carrots. Trim and pare the carrots, then cut them diagonally into 1-inch pieces. Check for tenderness after 20 minutes.

Carrots Sautéed with Bacon

Here is a superb recipe that blends poultry fat and bacon, using both as flavor enhancers. But don't be alarmed: the two are blended and their tastes imparted to the carrots, then the fat is discarded, leaving a savory residue in the bottom of the skillet. A simple deglazing with water, *while the skillet is still very hot,* creates a delicious emulsion.

¾ *pound fresh garden carrots, trimmed and pared*

2 *teaspoons rendered duck or goose fat, or substitute butter*

2 *thin slices bacon, cut into 1-inch squares*

Salt and freshly ground pepper

1 *teaspoon chopped fresh parsley*

1. Cut the carrots on the diagonal into thin slices. Heat the fat in a 10-inch skillet. Add the carrots and bacon and sauté until the bacon is crisp and the carrots are tender and begin to caramelize in the skillet, about 5 minutes.

2. Pour off all the fat from the skillet. Season the carrots with salt and pepper. Remove the carrots and bacon to a dish lined with paper towels. Raise the heat under the skillet, add ⅓ cup of water, and bring it to a fast boil. Swirl to deglaze and make a small "sauce." Transfer the carrots and bacon to a heated serving dish. Sprinkle with salt and pepper to taste. Pour over the contents of the skillet and garnish with parsley.

Inspired by a recipe from Jacques Chibois.

SPRING VEGETABLE RECIPES

Garlic Custard

SERVES 6

A lot of recipes for garlic custard call for cooking the cloves until soft and creamy—good, of course, but not taking complete advantage of their full flavor potential. In this recipe, the garlic cloves are cooked until they begin to caramelize in their cooking juices. The result is a gentle, rich custard with a heady aroma, and utterly delicious. Serve with roasted meats or poultry.

½ *pound (4 large fresh) garlic heads with unpeeled cloves separated*

1 *cup chicken stock*

1 *teaspoon butter*

2 *pinches of sugar*

½ *teaspoon wine vinegar*

½ *teaspoon salt*

¼ *teaspoon finely ground white pepper*

2 *eggs at room temperature, lightly beaten*

1 *egg yolk, at room temperature, lightly beaten*

⅔ *cup cream, warmed*

1 *cup milk, warmed*

1. Preheat the oven to 300° F.

2. Cover the garlic with cold water; bring it to a boil, cook 2 minutes, and drain. Repeat; peel the garlic. Slowly simmer it in the stock with the butter, sugar, vinegar, salt, and pepper for 30 minutes or until the liquid is reduced to a golden glaze. Crush the garlic with a fork to make a purée. Combine it with the remaining ingredients and press them through a sieve. Ladle the mixture into six ⅓-cup buttered porcelain ramekins.

3. Place the ramekins in a baking pan and set it on the middle shelf of the oven. Add boiling water to the pan and bake until the custards test firm, about 30 minutes. When the custards are done they just puff lightly and barely shiver when lightly prodded with two fingers. Since different shaped molds and cups require different cooking times, you may need to cook them 5 minutes longer. If the custards are not set, turn off the heat and let them stand in the oven 5 to 10 minutes longer. Remove the pan from the oven and let the molds stand in the water 10 minutes longer before turning them out. (The custards can be prepared up to 2 hours ahead to this point. They can be reheated in a warm oven for 5 minutes before unmolding.)

NOTES TO THE COOK To turn out all the molds onto a single warmed serving platter: Place a wide spatula over the first mold; with the spatula holding the custard in place, invert the mold over the serving dish. Slip the spatula from underneath, leaving the custard and mold in place. Lift off the mold. Repeat with the remaining molds.

If using metal molds you will need to line the baking pan with 2 or 3 layers of newspaper for insulation. Cut a slit through the center of the paper so it won't bulge when wet. If using glass molds, lower the oven temperature by 25 degrees.

It is a good idea to fill a baking pan with boiling water directly on the oven shelf. Place the baking pan on the middle oven rack. Remove one of the filled molds. Fill the pan with sufficient boiling water to rise halfway up the sides of the molds. Return filled mold.

To prepare 4 larger portions, use ½-cup molds and bake for 45 minutes.

Inspired by a recipe from Jean-Louis Palladin.

SERVES 8 | # Asparagus with Black Morels

The stunning combination of asparagus and morels makes for an elegant, easy-to-prepare, and marvelous spring vegetable dish. Though excellent with fresh morels, this dish is even better when made with dried morels, which have a deeper flavor.

The milk-and-water soaking liquid, a very important step in the recipe, makes the morels more succulent, but be sure to strain it through several layers of cheesecloth before using. The perfume of the sauce becomes intoxicatingly intense if they are prepared in advance and allowed to stand a few hours. Serve alone before or after a main course, so that the extraordinary flavor and aroma can be appreciated.

2 *ounces dried dark morels, stemmed, and halved if large*	1 *cup heavy (whipping) cream or crème fraîche*
½ *cup milk*	½ *cup chicken stock*
2 *tablespoons unsalted butter*	5 *dozen asparagus spears*
1 *tablespoon lemon juice, or more to taste*	1 *tablespoon fine Port or Sherry*
Salt and freshly ground white pepper	12 *sprigs Italian parsley*

1. In a bowl, soak the morels in the milk and 1¼ cups of warm water until softened, about 30 minutes. Scoop up the morels, squeeze the liquid back into the bowl, and set the morels aside. Strain the soaking liquid through cheesecloth and reserve it. Rinse the morels thoroughly under running water to remove any sand. Combine the soaking liquid and

(continued)

morels in a skillet and bring the liquid almost to a boil. Simmer 5 minutes or until the liquid has been reabsorbed by the morels. Add the butter, ½ cup of water, the lemon juice, and salt and pepper to taste, and cook, partially covered, 5 to 10 minutes, or until the morels are tender and the liquid in the skillet has once again evaporated. Add half the cream and the stock; bring back to a boil and remove from the heat. (Do not worry about the abundant amount of sauce, the morels will absorb most of it.) Makes about 2 cups sauce.

2. Wash the asparagus under running water, break off the bottom portion of each, and peel the spears, using a paring knife or a swivel-bladed peeler. Cook the asparagus until just tender in boiling salted water (time depends upon the thickness and age of the asparagus). Drain it on a kitchen cloth, cover, and set it aside. *(The dish can be prepared several hours in advance to this point.)*

3. Just before serving, reheat the morels and sauce in the skillet, add Port or Sherry and the remaining cream. Adjust the seasoning with salt, pepper, and a few drops of lemon juice. Reheat the asparagus in a microwave or arrange the stalks on a flat plate and reheat over simmering water. Pour the sauce over the asparagus, strew with torn bits of flat-leaf parsley, and serve.

Spring Vegetables in the Style of Laguiole

There is no precise way to execute the following recipe; the fun is in playing around with it. It's a vegetable ragout without pretension made with tender young spring vegetables and a piece of cured pork. This is one of my favorite vegetable recipes.

In springtime, choose whatever produce is young and fresh in the market: Swiss chard, young leeks, carrots, turnips, radishes, cabbages, Brussels sprouts, broccoli, celery, snow peas, zucchini, asparagus, shallots, scallions, or whatever. Cook the vegetables first in *pure mountain water* (Evian or Volvic), which contains minerals that will bring out their natural flavors. Then sauté them with pancetta, along with a nut of butter and some fresh herbs.

This dish will always come out well if you use a *small quantity* of each vegetable, so that no single flavor dominates. I suggest the following ingredients, which may be changed so long as there are representatives from each of the three groupings:

Group 1: spinach, Swiss chard leaves and stalks, a few cabbage leaves, a few Brussels sprout leaves, celery ribs, asparagus, snow peas, zucchini

Group 2: garlic, young leeks, shallots, scallions

Group 3: carrots, turnips, radishes, beets

Count about 1 cup of mixed vegetables per serving.

2 *quarts bottled spring water, preferably Volvic or Evian*

Coarse salt

GROUP 1, FOR EXAMPLE

4 *asparagus, trimmed of thick stalks and pared*

⅛ *pound snow peas, halved crosswise*

4 *Swiss chard, leaves and stalks separated*

3 *Brussels sprouts, halved and cored*

GROUP 2, FOR EXAMPLE

4 *thin scallions, trimmed*

4 *shallots, peeled and halved*

GROUP 3, FOR EXAMPLE

2 *small carrots, pared and cut on the diagonal into ¼-inch slices*

2 *baby turnips, cut into halves (see note)*

3 *radishes, cut in fourths*

¼ *pound pancetta, cut into ⅛-inch thick slices, or substitute lean salt pork (see note)*

2 *tablespoons unsalted butter*

Coarse salt and freshly ground pepper

1 *tablespoon mixed chopped fresh herbs: tarragon, chives, parsley, chervil*

1. In a deep saucepan bring the 2 quarts of water and 2 teaspoons of salt to a rolling boil. Cook the vegetables in each of the groups separately until tender—about 2 to 3

(continued)

minutes, depending on the size and type of vegetable. *Use the same water for all.* Use a slotted spoon to remove the vegetables to a colander and refresh under cool running water; drain. Reserve ½ cup cooking liquid for the sauce; the remainder should be reserved for soup or stock.

2. Cook the pancetta in a 12-inch skillet over moderate heat until just crisp, turning occasionally, about 10 minutes. Discard the fat in the skillet. Stir ½ cup of the reserved cooking liquid into the skillet, scraping up any brown bits. Boil until reduced to ¼ cup. Add the butter and shake the skillet until the mixture thickens and forms an emulsion. Immediately add the vegetables and allow them to roll in the pan juices to reheat and glaze, about 2 minutes. Season with pepper and taste for salt. Remove the pancetta if desired. Divide the vegetables among 4 shallow bowls. Sprinkle with herbs and serve hot.

NOTES TO
THE COOK

If the pancetta is very salty, soak in water for 2 to 3 hours; drain and rinse. If substituting lean salt pork, cut the piece in half, then blanch it for 3 minutes in boiling water; drain and rinse.

If tender turnips (i.e., ones that do not require thick paring) are difficult to find in your region, you can substitute the heavier white turnips available everywhere, but they must be peeled thick, cut into small pieces, and blanched separately in boiling salted water for 2 minutes. Then cook with the rest of the vegetables in Group 3 as described above.

Inspired by a recipe from Michel Bras.

(Horta)

SERVES 4

Greek Greens

Here is another healthful vegetable dish. *Horta,* or greens (bitter, pungent, tangy, and sharp), are boiled until tender, cooled to room temperature, and dressed with a fine Greek olive oil and fresh lemon juice. This goes beautifully with simple fried fish and roasted meats.

Greeks usually cook such cultivated greens as Swiss chard, dandelion greens, mustard greens, garden arugula, and home-grown purslane individually. In late winter and spring they hand pick wild greens in the fields or mountains, then usually cook them together.

If the greens are unusually bitter, add a few soaked currants to the dressing.

2 *pounds young fresh greens (Swiss chard tops, dandelion greens, kale, mustard greens, arugula, or purslane, etc.)*

Coarse (kosher) salt

2 *tablespoons fresh lemon juice, or more to taste*

4 *to 5 tablespoons extra-virgin olive oil, or more to taste, preferably Greek*

Remove hard stems. Discard old, yellowed or thick leaves. Wash the greens well until the water is clear. If the leaves are very large cut them crosswise in half. In a large nonaluminum pot bring plenty of water to a boil. Add a pinch of salt and the greens. Cook them uncovered for 10 to 20 minutes, or until the greens are just tender. Do not overcook. Leave them to drain in a colander until cool. Press down with a spatula to extract excess moisture. Place in an earthenware or glass serving dish. Use a fork to loosen the leaves. In a small bowl whisk together lemon juice and olive oil until combined. Add salt and pepper to taste. Immediately pour over the greens. Serve them warm or at room temperature.

Turnip Stew as Prepared in Zakinthos

SERVES 4

In this simple Greek recipe, spring turnips are stewed with spring garlic, fragrant Greek olive oil, and juicy tomatoes. This dish is not heavy because the turnips are first cooked in a small amount of water, then simply stewed (not fried) in the oil over low heat, so that, in the words of a Greek friend, "the turnips co-exist with the olive oil."

It is important to be generous with the oil; it is not merely a flavoring, but a major part of the sauce. The turnips are delicious served as an accompaniment to grilled meats or fish. On Zakinthos they are often served as a main course during Lent.

2 *pounds (12) young white turnips with stems and leaves, or substitute 1½ pounds purple topped turnips and ½ pound mustard greens*

1 *tablespoon crushed garlic*

½ *teaspoon fine salt*

⅓ *cup extra-virgin olive oil, preferably Greek* agoureleo *(see note)*

1 *cup strained tomatoes (see note)*

Freshly ground pepper

1. Trim, peel, and halve the turnips. Cut the stems and leaves crosswise into 1-inch pieces. Combine the turnips, stems, leaves, and 1¼ cups of water in a deep saucepan. Bring the turnips to a boil, cover, and cook until they are almost fully cooked, about 15 minutes. Pour off any remaining liquid. Add the garlic, salt, and oil to the vegetables, cover, and cook gently for 1 minute, shaking the pot to avoid burning. Add the strained tomatoes, cover, and cook the mixture over medium-low heat for 20 minutes, or until the turnips have absorbed most of the tomato sauce. Set them aside, covered, until you are ready to reheat. *(It is preferable to make this dish at least 4 to 5 hours in advance.)*

2. Gently reheat the turnips until just warm. Sprinkle them with freshly ground black pepper and serve.

NOTES TO THE COOK
Greek olive oil at its best (early-harvest extra-virgin) is the equal of high-quality Italian oils, and, with the damaging freeze a few years ago in the Italian groves, you may well be tasting Greek oil, without knowing it, in many bottles marked "Italian."

In the spring when luscious tomatoes are out of season, substitute those packed in cans. Drain, then press enough tomatoes through a foodmill to make 1 cup.

SUMMER VEGETABLE RECIPES

SERVES 4

Summer Carrots and New Onions with Butter Vinaigrette

In this recipe young, tender vegetables are simply boiled to retain their texture and flavor, then enrobed in a gentle vinegar-oil dressing, lightened with *un*melted butter, and sprinkled with fresh herbs. You will make this simple dish often to serve with grilled fish, poultry, or meats.

1 *pound young carrots, scrubbed and trimmed*

16 *new onions, with ½-inch green stem*

2 *tablespoons red wine vinegar*

Coarse salt

Freshly ground white pepper

3 *tablespoons fruity extra-virgin olive oil*

3 *tablespoons unsalted butter, cold and cut into small pieces*

2 *tablespoons snipped chives or tarragon*

Cook the vegetables together in boiling salted water until just tender. Drain them and keep warm. Beat the vinegar, ½ teaspoon of salt, and ⅓ teaspoon of pepper in a small noncorrodible saucepan until the salt is dissolved. Over very low heat, whisk in the olive oil and then the butter, bit by bit. Pour over the vegetables, sprinkle with herbs, and serve at once.

Zucchini with Thyme and Black Olives

SERVES 3 TO 4

Here is a simple recipe to serve with grilled fish or chicken. Please be sure the zucchini slices are dry so they will brown nicely on a film of oil, and so that they will leave some of their flavor in the skillet for the deglazing.

1 *pound (3) firm zucchini, washed, dried, and cut into ½-inch rounds*

Coarse salt

4 *teaspoons unsalted butter*

1½ *teaspoons chopped fresh thyme*

Freshly ground white pepper

Lemon juice to taste

½ *tablespoon extra-virgin olive oil*

3 *juicy black olives, preferably Niçoise, pitted, slivered, and blanched 1 minute in boiling water and drained*

1. Toss the zucchini slices with salt and set them out in one layer on a baking sheet lined with a paper towel. Let them stand at room temperature for 2 hours.

2. On a flat work surface crush the butter and fresh thyme with a fork until well combined. Season with salt and pepper and a few drops of lemon juice. Set the butter aside.

3. Rinse and dry the zucchini slices. Brush a heavy skillet with olive oil; set it over medium-high heat until hot. Add the zucchini slices without crowding and reduce the heat to medium. Slowly brown the rounds on each side. Remove them to paper toweling. When all the zucchini slices have been browned, immediately add 2 tablespoons of water to the skillet. Bring it to a boil, add the thyme butter, and swirl to form an emulsion. Put the zucchini in a serving dish, pour the pan juices over, and top with slivered olives. Serve hot.

296   VEGETABLES

André Guillot's Lettuce Mousse

André Guillot is a legend: for more than sixty years this short, bespectacled Burgundian with thinning hair and a melodic voice has thought passionately and deeply about the preparation of food. He is always generous in his explanations of his culinary theories and full of anecdotes and aphorisms, too. "There are only two cuisines; good and bad," he told me once. "The categories *grande cuisine* and *cuisine simple* are not significant." I found him, as Fredy Girardet, Switzerland's best-known chef, said, "a well of knowledge." Nevertheless, Guillot is modest and won't even call himself a chef. "I am just a cook," he protests.

Fifteen years ago Guillot settled in Menton, in the south of France, where he studies and writes. Though he no longer gives his famous cooking course for chefs, it is a measure of his importance that there exists in France an Association of the Friends of André Guillot composed of people who honor his work and inspiration. Among the most famous members are Marc Meneau, Gérard Vie, Émile Jung, and Richard Olney. I am proud to be a member, myself.

Here is one of Guillot's simplest dishes, a lovely lettuce mousse. As most of his recipes are quite demanding, intended for professional chefs, it is a pleasure to present one here that can be made in a home kitchen.

This mousse makes an unusual and delicious accompaniment to any roast. Serve in individual ramekins with tiny cubes of fried bread.

3 *pounds Romaine lettuce, or 8 heads Boston lettuce*

¾ *cup heavy (whipping) cream*

3 *tablespoons unsalted butter*

Salt and freshly ground pepper

1 *cup small croutons made from white bread fried in butter until golden*

1. Core each head of lettuce. Cut the thick central stems from each leaf. Wash each leaf carefully in several changes of cool water. Shake them dry.

2. In a large kettle, bring plenty of salted water to a boil. Add the lettuce in thirds to avoid lowering the water temperature, and cook it at a high boil, uncovered, for 5 to 7 minutes. Drain and chill the lettuce under cool running water. Drain very well by taking one handful of leaves at a time and squeezing to extract as much water as possible. When it is cool, put it in a towel and squeeze to remove the remaining water.

3. Purée the lettuce in a food processor with the cream. Reduce over high heat until the mixture begins to pull away from the sides of the pan and thickens. Add the butter and adjust the seasoning. Makes 1¾ cups purée. Serve in small ramekins garnished with fried croutons.

Little white summer potatoes are so full of flavor that the less one does to them the better. I simply clean them with a wet cloth, then sauté them in a skillet just large enough to allow them to roll around in butter. I then cover the pan and let them cook, shaking often, until they are tender. With the addition of a spoonful of chopped fresh herbs, a nut of fresh butter, and pinches of salt and pepper, they achieve a kind of culinary perfection.

Summer, however, is only one season; during the rest of the year my potato preparations can occasionally become quite elaborate. Here is a sampling of my potato recipes, each one in some way very special.

Gratin of Potatoes in the Style of the Auvergne

SERVES 6 TO 8

In *The Cooking of South-West France,* I give a recipe for a rustic dish called *le gatis*—a mixture of Cantal and Roquefort cheeses served melting hot in a crust of brioche. After the book was published, a friend sent this recipe from the Auvergne, which joins these two cheeses with a potato gratin. You can substitute Monterey Jack for the hard-to-find Cantal, but do use a good blue-veined cheese—real Roquefort or Bleu d'Auvergne. This gratin goes well with grilled or roasted beef.

3 *pounds Red Bliss potatoes*	*Salt and freshly ground white pepper*
4 *cups whole milk*	¼ *teaspoon freshly grated nutmeg*
Coarse salt	¼ *teaspoon ground red pepper*
3½ *ounces Roquefort or other blue-veined cheese*	½ *clove garlic, crushed*
	2 *tablespoons butter*
½ *cup heavy cream*	
¼ *cup (1 ounce) shredded Cantal or Monterey Jack cheese*	

1. Pare, wash, and slice the potatoes thin, to ¹⁄₁₆ inch; you can use the food processor fitted with a thin (2 mm) slicing disk. (Do not wash or dry them after slicing.) Rinse a large, heavy pot with cold water, but do not dry it inside (this helps prevent the milk and starchy potatoes from scorching). Place the potatoes in the pot and cover with 3 cups of the milk. Add ¼ teaspoon of salt. Cover the pot, bring it to a boil, reduce heat to low and cook, stirring occasionally, until the potatoes are just cooked, about 15 minutes. Remove the pot from the heat.

2. Meanwhile, in a wide mixing bowl, crush the blue cheese with the heavy cream until smooth and pliable. Add the remaining milk, the shredded Cantal, a pinch of salt, the white pepper, nutmeg, and red pepper.

3. Rub a wide 3-quart baking dish with garlic. Using a slotted spoon transfer layers of potatoes to the dish, alternating with the prepared cheese mixture, and ending with the potatoes. If the milk remaining in the pot is not thick, reduce it, and spread it over the potatoes in an even layer; dot with butter. (*To this point the dish can be prepared up to 3 hours before serving.* Cover loosely and set it aside in a cool place.)

4. Two hours before serving, preheat the oven to 400° F. Place the dish on a flat baking sheet to catch any overspill and set it in the oven to bake for 1½ hours, or until the gratin is bubbling and brown and the liquid is nearly absorbed. Serve directly from the baking dish.

If not serving at once, reduce the oven heat to 200° F. The cooked gratin can hold 1 hour.

The potatoes can be peeled 2 to 3 hours in advance and kept covered in salted water in the refrigerator. Do not slice them until you are ready to assemble and bake the dish.

Mashed Potatoes with Olive Oil

Mashed potatoes can be watery, lumpy, and tasteless, the way they always are in school dining halls. Or they can be . . . celestial. The famous French chef Joël Robuchon always makes his just before serving, using as much as 2 cups of butter for every 2 pounds of potatoes!

I certainly like to eat celestial mashed potatoes, but prefer not to consume so large a quantity of saturated fat. After experimenting a bit, I've come up with the following recipe, which combines olive oil and milk with a last-minute addition of only 2 tablespoons of butter. The result is a convincing *illusion* of butter, but without anywhere near the amount used by Robuchon. You won't, in fact, taste the olive oil in this recipe; it is there to add richness and to heighten the natural flavor of the potatoes.

2 *pounds Idaho potatoes*	*Freshly ground white pepper to taste*
Coarse salt	*Pinch of freshly grated nutmeg*
⅓ *cup light extra-virgin olive oil*	2 *tablespoons unsalted butter, softened*
¾ *to 1 cup whole milk, heated*	

1. Peel the potatoes and carefully remove all discolored parts. Leave them whole (or they will be watery). Place them in a deep saucepan and cover with about 3 quarts of water. Add 2 tablespoons of salt. Cover the pot and bring it to a boil. Reduce the heat to *just below* the boil and cook for 45 minutes or until the potatoes test tender when pierced with a thin skewer. Drain well, return them to the saucepan, and cover with a kitchen towel and a lid. Let them stand until dry, about 5 minutes. Cut the potatoes into small pieces and press them through a ricer or the fine blade of a foodmill. Return the potatoes to the pan, beat vigorously with a wooden spoon until light and fluffy, adding the olive oil, by spoonfuls, and then gradually work in the heated milk. (The slower and longer you beat with a wooden spoon, the more milk the potatoes will absorb, and the lighter and fluffier your mashed potatoes will be.) Cover with a piece of plastic film to prevent crusting. Keep the potatoes hot in a double boiler for up to 2 hours.

2. Just before serving, combine pepper, a pinch of salt, and nutmeg with the softened butter, and beat it into the potatoes. Serve very hot.

NOTE TO
THE COOK

To reheat cold mashed potatoes: Lightly coat the inside of the upper pot of a double boiler with butter. Add the potatoes and 2 to 3 tablespoons of warm milk. Use a wooden spoon to incorporate the milk. Heat until the potatoes are steaming hot.

Cazuela Potatoes

Here is a lighter, crisper version of the classic French potato gratin, made with a lot less butter and cream, and with the potato slices arranged in a single layer thin as a crêpe. This dish is easy to make and goes well with a steak. As a variation, halve the amount of potatoes and alternate with thin slices of peeled celery root.

An authentic shallow glazed earthenware dish (*cazuela*) is not really a requirement; tin-lined copper, or enameled cast-iron gratin pans can substitute. Still, for me glazed clay is the dish of choice. Nothing else quite provides the proper evaporation of moisture and the slow, even cooking necessary to produce a golden, crisp round of potatoes. (See Appendix, page 339, for mail-order source and for instructions on seasoning and cleaning *cazuelas*.)

¾ *pound waxy potatoes, peeled*	1 *tablespoon heavy cream*
1 *clove garlic, peeled and halved*	*A pinch of mixed fine and coarse salt*
4 *tablespoons unsalted butter, melted*	*Freshly ground white pepper*
2 *tablespoons whole milk*	

Preheat the oven to 375° F. Peel the potatoes and cut them into thin slices. Rinse them in cold water; pat them dry between kitchen toweling. Rub a cut garlic clove inside a shallow 16-inch round or oval baking dish, preferably earthenware, tinned copper, or enameled cast iron, and brush with butter. Toss the potatoes with butter for an even coating. Arrange the potato slices in rows, overlapping, *in one layer* and brush with any remaining butter. Bake for 30 minutes or until the edges are just beginning to brown. Raise the oven temperature to 450° F. Mix the milk and cream; sprinkle them over the potatoes and return the dish to the oven to bake until the moisture is absorbed and the potatoes turn golden brown and crisp, about 15 minutes. Just before serving, sprinkle them with salt and pepper.

The milk and cream are added near the end just to keep the potatoes moist; they will be very quickly absorbed and thus will not separate.

NOTE TO
THE COOK

Grated Potato Cakes with Mace

SERVES 6

Crisp-brown on the outside and meltingly tender within, these little cakes are good with most meats and poultry. The flavor of the mace should almost be subliminal. Don't worry about the amount of butter; most of it is drained off during the second half of the baking.

2 *pounds waxy potatoes*

8 *tablespoons clarified butter, warm*

Fine salt and freshly ground white pepper

Pinch of ground mace

Coarse salt

1. Preheat the oven to 475° F.

2. Peel the potatoes; grate them coarsely, wash in several waters, and squeeze them in small batches with your hands to express excess moisture; makes 4 cups. Immediately unravel; toss them with warm clarified butter, season with 1 teaspoon salt, ⅓ teaspoon white pepper, and a pinch of ground mace, and firmly put the potatoes into 6 buttered ½-cup ramekins without pressing down on them. Bake them on the middle oven shelf for 30 minutes.

3. Cool the ramekins on a cake rack for 5 minutes. Invert each ramekin onto the cake rack and place the rack on a rimmed heavy baking sheet or jelly-roll pan. When cool enough to handle, carefully lift off the ramekins. Brush the cakes with expressed butter. Return the cakes to the oven, and bake until well browned, about 25 minutes. Carefully slide the cakes onto a warm serving dish. Sprinkle with a mixture of coarse *and* fine salt.

S E R V E S   4

Potatoes Baked in Sea Salt in a Clay Pot

Of all the potato dishes I know this is the easiest. Small new potatoes (or *primes*, as they are called on the Ile de Ré on the Charentais coast), are washed, dried carefully, and then placed in a closed pot on a small bed of sea salt. As cooking proceeds a reaction takes place; the salt gets hot, and begins to release an aromatic steam that penetrates the flesh of the potatoes. In effect the potatoes cook in the steam of sea water, which preserves their flavor and keeps them moist.

Traditionally this three-hundred-year-old dish is cooked in a *diable Charentais,* an unglazed earthenware pot-bellied utensil with a fitted cover. If, by rare chance, you happen to have one, allow it to heat up slowly over a flame tamer for about 10 minutes. Then raise the heat and cook, shaking the pot often, until the potatoes are done. (By the way, the *diable* is never washed; when bought its insides are rubbed with garlic, which the Charentais believe inhibits rancidity and strengthens the pot.) Lacking a true *diable* please do *not* substitute the sort of unglazed pot that is soaked. Instead use an enameled cast-iron cocotte.

Though the sea salt can be mixed with coarse (kosher) salt with excellent results, one should ideally use salt farmed on the flats of the Ile de Ré. The first skimming of this salt is called the *fleur de sel*, an immaculate rosy-white crystal with a powerful, "aggressive" taste, nicknamed "white gold" on account of its wonderful flavor. Gourmets come to the Ile de Ré from all over the world to taste this salt on fresh fish. The potatoes are wonderful served with fresh sardines that have been rolled in sea salt and grilled over thick grapevine cuttings.

On the Ile de Ré, the home cook will accompany these potatoes with a spread made from a whole head of garlic that has been cooked in hot coals, then peeled, the pulp removed, and kneaded with a little fresh butter and white cheese.

1½ pounds small new potatoes

1½ cups sea or coarse (kosher) salt

1. Preheat the oven to 450° F. Wash and dry the potatoes. Spread salt in an even layer on the bottom of an enameled cast-iron cocotte and arrange the potatoes on top side by side. Cover and bake 45 minutes to 1 hour.

2. Remove the pot from the oven. Set the cover askew and let the pot stand 5 minutes. Remove the potatoes and brush off the salt. Serve hot with or without butter.

Cool the salt, scrape it into a jar, and keep to use the next time you wish to cook potatoes this way. Always add some fresh salt for each batch.   NOTE TO THE COOK

Gratin of Melting Potatoes

This is a rich, wonderful gratin, but it takes time. The potatoes are sliced as if for potato chips, layered with scallions, thyme, and garlic, simmered in light cream until swollen, then baked in the oven until meltingly tender. These soft-as-silk potatoes are a variation of the classic *gratin dauphinois*, but with one major difference in procedure: in this version the paper-thin potato slices were *washed*.

2½ *pounds russet potatoes*

4 *tablespoons finely chopped scallions*

1 *teaspoon minced garlic*

1 *teaspoon chopped fresh thyme*

1¼ *teaspoons fine salt*

Freshly ground white pepper

Grated nutmeg

2 *tablespoons unsalted butter*

2 *cups half-and-half, or light cream*

1. Preheat the oven to 300° F.

2. Peel the potatoes, slice them paper-thin; rinse them under cold running water. Shake off the excess water and drain them well. Combine scallions, garlic, thyme, salt, pepper, and grated nutmeg in a small bowl; mix well.

3. Butter a 10-inch flameproof baking-serving dish. Place a layer of raw sliced potatoes on the bottom; sprinkle with some of the scallion mixture. Repeat for four more layers, finishing off with a layer of potatoes. (The level of the potatoes should not rise higher than three-quarters the height of the pan.) Pour in just enough half-and-half to cover the potatoes. Cover the pan and set over very low heat for 20 minutes. Then remove the cover and place the dish on the middle rack of the oven. Dot with the remaining butter, and bake for 2 to 2½ hours without disturbing. (The gratin can wait up another hour in a 200° F oven.)

CHAPTER 9 *DESSERTS*

A ROULADE, A CAKE, AND TWO GREEK SWEETS

Walnut Roll

SERVES 8

In 1959, very early in my career, I went to see James Beard. I had served a year's apprenticeship under Dione Lucas and was looking for a job. Mr. Beard asked me to cook for him. I did, and apparently he was satisfied, for shortly thereafter he kindly recommended me as caterer for a luncheon that Mrs. Joshua Logan was giving for 150 people in her Connecticut home. I was a little scared; I'd never cooked for so many people before. But Beard calmed my fears: "Don't worry. Call her up, discuss the menu, then just follow your recipes."

I phoned Mrs. Logan, and she asked for a lunch of Quiche Lorraine, Boeuf Bourguignon, Fish in Aspic, and for dessert "a delicious cake"—a rather extraordinary menu, it seems to me now, especially for a lunch in May. In any case, I studied the menu carefully and assured myself I could bring it off. I did remain a little worried about the cake, as desserts were not my strong point, so I went back to Beard for advice. He gave me this recipe for a walnut roll. "It's easy," he said, "and it always works. You can triple it, quadruple it, multiply it as many times as you like. It will freeze. It will keep for days. It's delicious." I took his advice, and made fifteen rolls for the party.

When I got off the train at Stamford station with my walnut rolls, there wasn't anyone there to meet me. I was getting worried when a man with a chauffeur's cap tentatively approached. "Are you Mrs. Wolfert?" he asked, and when I nodded, he shook his head. Apparently he had questioned every mature woman who had gotten off the train, and finally, desperate, had come up to me, though, as he told me, "you seem so young."

At the house Mrs. Logan took one look at me, became very upset, and took to her bed. Her words, according to her cooks, were: "Why have they done this to me? Sent a child to cook the lunch!"

Undaunted, I sent up a portion of the walnut roll, which restored Mrs. Logan's confidence. The lunch went well, all the dishes were a success, and when I departed Mrs. Logan told me she was very pleased.

Years later, when I found the recipe for this dessert in *The House & Garden Cookbook*, it brought back memories of my first professional culinary foray. Since then I have prepared the walnut roll in various forms, turning it into a yule log with meringue mushrooms for Christmas and a birthday cake for my children. It has been my favorite cake for twenty-eight years, so how could I not include it?

5 *egg yolks*

½ *cup sugar*

   Pinch of salt

1¼ *cups (5 ounces) fine-ground walnuts*

½ *teaspoon baking powder*

5 *egg whites, at room temperature*

WALNUT FILLING

½ *cup hot milk*

1½ *cups (6 ounces) ground walnuts*

¼ *pound (1 stick) unsalted butter*

⅔ *cup sugar*

2 *tablespoons Cognac*

1 *cup heavy cream, whipped*

½ *cup confectioners' sugar*

1. Preheat the oven to 375° F. Dot a jelly roll pan (11 by 17 inches) with butter, and line with waxed paper, leaving about 1 to 2 inches of paper hanging at each end. Butter the paper.

2. Beat the egg yolks, gradually adding the sugar and a pinch of salt. When they are light, add the walnuts and baking powder, mixing well with a large wire whisk. Beat the egg whites until they are stiff. Use a spatula to fold the egg whites into the yolk mixture. Spread evenly in the prepared pan. Bake 15 minutes or until a cake tester comes out clean. Cover the cake with a damp kitchen cloth and place it in the refrigerator for 30 minutes.

3. Meanwhile, prepare the filling: Pour the milk over the walnuts and allow the mixture to cool. In a mixing bowl, cream the butter, gradually adding the sugar. Cream until light and fluffy. Beat in the nut mixture and Cognac. Fold in the whipped cream.

4. Sprinkle the top of the cake with confectioners' sugar. Spread a 20-inch long sheet of waxed paper over the cake. Grip the ends of the jelly roll pan, holding all the waxed paper ends firmly, and quickly invert the cake and pan. Remove the pan, and peel the paper from the cake. Use a spatula to spread the filling on it. Use the second sheet of waxed paper to help roll it up like a jelly roll. Cover the roll with foil and refrigerate until firm. Dust the top with confectioners' sugar just before serving.

Use a nut grinder or the grating blade of a food processor to grind the walnuts.

The roll can be frozen up to 2 weeks.

NOTES TO
THE COOK

Caramel and Coconut Cake from Ohrid

SERVES 8 TO 10

Ohrid is tucked away in the south-west corner of Yugoslavia, close to the Albanian and Greek frontiers. There is a Hansel and Gretel charm about the old town, the overhanging upper floors of the houses embracing the visitor as he walks the narrow, stone-paved streets.

Many of the desserts of this part of Yugoslavia reflect the influence of Greece and Albania, though they are usually less sweet. I especially like this cake made with walnuts and coconut and frosted with caramel; it resembles the Greek walnut cake *karidopita*.

Bake the cake the day before serving, so the lemon syrup can be completely absorbed and the cake can mellow.

1½ cups all-purpose flour, sifted

1⅓ cups (about 5½ ounces) fine-ground walnuts

2 ounces (⅔ cup) unsweetened shredded coconut

1 teaspoon baking powder

½ teaspoon ground cinnamon

¼ cup unsalted butter, softened

½ cup granulated sugar

4 eggs, separated

½ cup coarsely chopped walnuts

SYRUP

¾ cup sugar

1 tablespoon lemon juice

CARAMEL FROSTING

Makes about 1½ cups, enough to frost top and sides of 9-by-5-inch cake

1½ cups (packed) light-brown sugar

¼ cup milk

Pinch of salt

6 tablespoons butter

½ teaspoon pure vanilla extract

Begin 1 day in advance.

1. Preheat the oven to 325° F. Line a 9-by-5-by-2½-inch loaf pan with kitchen parchment, or grease it well with oil.

2. Combine the flour, ground walnuts, coconut, baking powder, and cinnamon in a large bowl; stir and set aside.

3. Beat the butter in a large bowl until creamy; gradually beat in the ½ cup of sugar until the mixture is light and fluffy. Add the egg yolks, one at a time, beating until the mixture is very light.

4. Separately beat the whites until stiff but not dry; fold them into the egg-yolk mixture. Fold the dry ingredients into the egg mixture just until blended. Scrape the batter into the prepared pan; sprinkle it with the ½ cup of chopped nuts. Bake until a cake tester

inserted in the center of the cake is withdrawn clean, about 1 hour. Cool the cake 1 hour in the pan.

5. Make the syrup by combining the sugar, ⅔ cup of water, and the lemon juice in a small saucepan. Bring the mixture to a boil and simmer 5 minutes. Pierce the cake, still in the pan, with a skewer in a dozen places. Pour the hot syrup over the cake. Cover it with foil and let it stand at room temperature overnight to allow the syrup to permeate the cake.

6. The following day, turn the cake out of the pan; cut it into 2 even horizontal layers. Set the top layer on a flat plate, walnut side up. Invert the bottom layer; place it on top of the first.

7. Make the frosting: Heat the brown sugar, milk, and salt in a small saucepan over medium heat, stirring until the sugar dissolves. Increase the heat to high; heat the syrup to boiling. Boil it to the soft-ball stage (235° F on a candy thermometer). Remove the pan from the heat; stir in the butter, and set the frosting aside until cool, about 10 minutes. Stir in the vanilla. Beat the mixture until light and creamy and just beginning to hold its shape, about 5 minutes. Frost the sides and top of the cake immediately with caramel frosting. Serve at room temperature.

According to Yugoslav cooks, the rule for a successful cake is: "Hot syrup on a cold cake or cold syrup on a hot cake." This same rule applies when preparing stuffed filo desserts that are to be soaked in sugar syrup.

NOTE TO
THE COOK

TWO SWEETS FROM THE
ISLAND OF PAXOS

When I first visited the Ionian island of Paxos I thought: "This is the paradise of my dreams." Unfortunately tourism has changed the island, as it has all of Greece, but the people there still remain kind and open-hearted.

On Paxos you have no need to beware of Greeks bearing gifts. If you take a house on the island, even for a week—preferably a house with a garden filled with trees bearing plums, lemons, hazelnuts, guavas and tangerines—a neighboring woman will most likely arrive on your doorstep with a welcoming basket of flowers and fresh eggs.

Two desserts on Paxos were particularly memorable: a tender almond-butter cookie flavored with ouzo, sold in a little store in Loggos; and a cinnamon-custard *pita* so flat it can be rolled into a cone.

Paxos Cinnamon Pita

SERVES 8 TO 10

These square farina-filled pastries are a specialty of Elena's Pastry Shop in the town of Gaios on Paxos.

1 *egg plus 1 egg yolk, at room temperature*

¼ *cup granulated sugar*

1½ *cups milk*

¼ *cup regular (not quick-cooking) farina*
   Pinch of salt

2 *teaspoons fresh lemon juice*

½ *teaspoon pure vanilla extract*

½ *teaspoon ground cinnamon, plus additional for dusting*

8 *to 10 sheets filo dough, thawed if frozen*

½ *cup unsalted butter, melted, or ½ butter and ½ vegetable oil*

Confectioners' sugar

1. Beat the egg and egg yolk in a medium bowl until frothy; beat in the sugar until the mixture is thick and foamy, about 3 minutes. Set the mixture aside.

2. Heat the milk in a heavy, medium saucepan over medium heat until it is hot but not boiling. Remove it from the heat; whisk a small amount of the hot milk into the egg mixture. Pour the eggs into the hot milk, stirring constantly.

3. Return the saucepan to medium-low heat; cook the egg-milk mixture, stirring continuously, until heated through, about 3 minutes. Do not allow the mixture to boil.

Gradually sprinkle in the farina, stirring constantly; stir in the salt. Reduce the heat to very low; cook, stirring constantly, until the mixture is thick and smooth, about 5 minutes. Do not allow the mixture to boil or burn. Remove it from the heat; let it cool to room temperature, stirring often to prevent a skin from forming. Stir in the lemon juice, vanilla, and ½ teaspoon of cinnamon.

4. Preheat the oven to 350° F. Unroll one sheet of filo, keeping the remaining sheets carefully covered with plastic wrap. On a work surface place the unrolled sheet with one narrow end facing you. Brush the entire surface lightly with melted butter or a mixture of oil and butter.

5. Place 3 tablespoons of the cooled farina mixture on the lower third of the filo sheet. Using a thin, flexible spatula, spread the mixture into a wide rectangle approximately 10 by 5 inches, barely covering the lower third of the filo sheet. Fold the right and left sides of the filo in toward the center so that the edges just meet; lightly brush the folded sides with butter. Fold the lower third up; brush it lightly with butter. Fold the upper third down to form an envelope; brush each layer lightly with butter. Lightly brush the top and bottom of the filo package; place it on an ungreased large baking sheet. Repeat with the remaining sheets of filo until all the farina is used, being sure to keep unused filo sheets covered.

6. Bake the packages until golden brown, about 15 minutes. Serve warm, lightly dusted with confectioners' sugar and cinnamon.

Unbaked pastries can be stored, tightly wrapped, in the freezer up to 2 weeks. Do not thaw them before baking; bake in a 350° oven until golden brown, about 35 to 45 minutes. NOTE TO THE COOK

Greek Butter-Almond Cookies

I like these cookies so much I served them on my wedding day. Make them a few days in advance, as they improve with age. They will keep several weeks if stored in a tight tin box.

½ cup cake flour

1⅓ cups all-purpose flour with a low gluten content

1¼ teaspoons baking powder

1 cup plus 2 tablespoons clarified butter, chilled (see notes)

7 tablespoons confectioners' sugar, plus additional for dredging

1 egg yolk

1 tablespoon ouzo

½ teaspoon pure vanilla extract

¼ teaspoon pure almond extract

¾ cup almond meal (see notes)

Sifted confectioners' sugar

1. Sift the cake flour with the all-purpose flour and baking powder into a small bowl or onto a sheet of waxed paper. Resift the mixture twice; reserve.

2. Beat the chilled clarified butter in a medium bowl at medium speed until very light and fluffy, at least 5 minutes. (The more you beat the lighter the cookie.) Gradually beat in the 7 tablespoons of confectioners' sugar; beat 2 minutes. Add the egg yolk; beat 2 minutes. Add the ouzo, vanilla, and almond extract; beat 1 minute. Carefully fold in the flour mixture with a rubber spatula, stirring always in the same direction, then gently fold in the almond meal. The dough will be quite soft. Refrigerate, wrapped in plastic, until the dough is cold enough to shape into small balls, about 45 minutes.

3. Heat the oven to 350° F.

4. Shape the dough into small round cakes about 1 inch in diameter and ½ inch high. Place on an ungreased baking sheet about ½ inch apart. Bake 12 to 15 minutes; the color should be pale, not brown. Place the baking sheet with the cookies on a wire rack; immediately sift confectioners' sugar generously over the cookies. Cool for 5 minutes before removing them from the baking sheet. Roll the cookies in additional confectioners' sugar to coat them. Store the cooled cookies in airtight tins at least 2 days (to mellow) or up to several weeks before serving.

NOTES TO THE COOK   Only almond meal, a preparation of finely ground almonds, yields a light cookie. It is available in specialty food stores and some supermarkets, or can be ordered by mail (see Appendix, page 339). Blanched almond meal is preferable, but unblanched can be used; 8

ounces will be enough for several batches of cookies. Please do *not* use a blender or metal blade of a food processor to grind almonds into meal, as this will produce a heavy, greasy texture. Keep unused almond meal in the freezer.

You will need 10 ounces of unsalted AA butter to make enough clarified butter for this recipe. Melt the butter in a small saucepan over low heat without stirring. Lift off and discard the foamy top. Pour the butter into a cup and refrigerate it for 2 to 3 hours or until congealed. Measure 1 cup plus 2 tablespoons for this recipe and cut it into cubes. Discard the milky sediment at the bottom of the cup. Store any remaining clarified butter in the refrigerator and use for some other purpose.

FRESH FRUIT, TARTS, AND
A FRUIT FLAN

Roast Peaches with Black Currants

SERVES 6

Whenever I eat this wonderful dessert I wish the peach season weren't so short. I actually prefer cooked peaches to raw, perhaps because heat accentuates their delicate flavor. This recipe should only be made with fresh fruit; frozen or canned peaches won't do. And it really should be eaten soon after it comes out of the oven, though it will hold a while in a low oven with the door slightly ajar.

6 *large yellow peaches, firm, ripe, and unblemished*

Sugar syrup: 1¼ cups sugar, 4 cups water, juice of 1 lemon

7 *tablespoons unsalted butter, at room temperature*

6 *tablespoons superfine sugar*

2 *egg yolks*

¼ *teaspoon pure vanilla extract*

¼ *cup black currant jelly, or strained jam*

2 *tablespoons strained fresh lemon juice, or more to taste*

Unsweetened whipped cream

1. Wash the peaches. With the tip of a small knife make a very light crisscross through the skin on the *round* side of each peach. Drop them into boiling water, leave about 30 seconds, then immerse in cold water to peel easily.

2. Combine the sugar, water, and lemon juice in a heavy saucepan, bring to a boil, and simmer 5 minutes. Poach 3 peaches at a time: slip them into the syrup, cover with a circle of parchment or a small clean cloth (to keep them submerged) and poach them uncovered for 5 minutes. Turn off the heat; leave the peaches in the syrup for a few minutes. Cut each peach in half; remove the pits. Drain, cut side down, on a cake rack over paper toweling.

3. Cream the butter and sugar until fluffy with electric beaters or a wooden spoon. *Do not use a food processor.* Gently work in the egg yolks, one by one, then flavor the mixture with the vanilla. Makes about 1 cup. Cover the mixture and keep it refrigerated until you are ready to assemble the dish. Gently heat the jelly; add enough lemon juice to make it taste tart, and set it aside. *(Up to this point the recipe can be prepared early in the day.)*

4. About 40 minutes before serving, preheat the oven to 500° F.

5. Pat the peaches dry with paper toweling. Arrange them cut side down in a buttered shallow 12-inch baking dish, preferably a porcelain quiche dish. Scatter the butter-egg yolk

mixture between the fruit. Bake the peaches on the middle shelf of the oven for 8 minutes or until the butter mixture begins to set. Drizzle the jelly over the peaches and return the dish to the hot oven to finish "roasting," about 3 minutes. Remove the peaches from the oven and let them stand until just warm, about 15 minutes. Serve them with a bowl of whipped cream.

Use the cooking syrup for compote, sangria, or sherbets.

SERVES 6   # Fresh Orange Slices with Moroccan Spices

The famous spice mixture *ras el hanout* (literally "top of the shop") includes any spice the cook wishes to add, so long as the final blend is harmonious. There is no one standard mixture; in fact, in this book I offer one blend for savories, and another (below) for sweets. This particular sweet blend works well with fresh sautéed fruits or even an apple tart. I add a little cayenne because I feel it heightens the sweet flavor of orange.

10 *juicy seedless oranges*	6 *sprigs fresh mint*
2 *tablespoons orangeflower water*	½ *pound pitted dates*
8 *tablespoons granulated sugar*	*Pinches of* ras el hanout *(see recipe, page 316)*
2 *limes*	
1 *lemon*	*Confectioners' sugar*

1. Pare the oranges until free of all membrane and separate them into segments. Squeeze the juice from the parings of the oranges over the sections to keep them juicy. Put them into a serving bowl. Add the orangeflower water and a tablespoon of the sugar and refrigerate the oranges for an hour or longer.

2. Meanwhile, using a vegetable peeler, remove the zest from the limes and lemon. Cut it into very thin strips. Blanch the strips in boiling water for 1 minute, drain and run them under cold water. Place the remaining sugar and 1 cup of water in a small saucepan. Heat, stirring, until the sugar dissolves. Continue to boil ½ minute, then add the zest. Lower the heat, stir once, and simmer very slowly until the zest is very soft, about 5

(continued)

minutes. The syrup must not caramelize. Spread the strips over an oiled cookie rack to dry. Use a fork to separate any tangled strips.

3. Just before serving, shred the mint leaves and chop the dates. Scatter mint, dates, and pinches of *ras el hanout* over the oranges. Decorate with candied zest and a dusting of confectioners' sugar.

Inspired by a recipe by Jean-Louis Palladin.

Ras el Hanout

¾ *teaspoon freshly ground nutmeg*

¼ *teaspoon ground cloves*

1 *teaspoon freshly ground black pepper*

1 *teaspoon freshly ground white pepper*

1¾ *teaspoons ground cinnamon*

2 *teaspoons ground cardamom*

¼ *teaspoon cayenne pepper*

Combine all ingredients in a spice mill and grind them until fine. Press through a sieve. Bottle the mixture tightly to preserve the freshness.

SERVES 6

Apples Baked on Cabbage Leaves as in Poitou

When I first heard about this dish, called *grimolles*, I recalled a famous nonsense line of the eighteenth-century satirical dramatist Samuel Foote: "So she went into the garden to cut a cabbage leaf to make an apple pie . . ."

In this unusual, sophisticated-earthy dessert the cabbage leaves, used in place of a pie crust, act as a conductor for even cooking. A skillet is first lined with the leaves; a mixture of apples and thick batter, flavored with lemon rind, Cognac, and cinnamon, is baked on top. The slightly burnt cabbage, which can be eaten or not as you wish, imparts a marvelous smoky flavor to the fruit. I guarantee you that this will be a memorable closing to a meal. Serve very warm for best results. It is excellent with vanilla ice cream, unsweetened crème fraîche, or whipped cream.

¾ cup (3½ ounces) all-purpose flour

2 whole eggs

¼ cup heavy cream, at room temperature

½ cup milk, at room temperature

Pinch of salt

2 dashes of ground cinnamon

2 teaspoons grated lemon rind

1 tablespoon Cognac

3 to 4 tablespoons sugar

4 tablespoons unsalted butter, melted and divided

1 pound flavorful apples

About 6 large cabbage leaves

1 tablespoon light brown sugar

Confectioners' sugar

1. At least 2 hours before serving (so the batter has time to sit), place the flour in a medium bowl. With a wooden spoon make a well in the center, and add one by one the eggs, stirring until well combined. Then slowly add the cream and milk; mix until absolutely smooth. If the mixture is not smooth, strain it. Flavor with salt, cinnamon, lemon rind, and Cognac. Sweeten with sugar (the amount depends upon the sweetness of the apples). Stir in half the butter.

2. Peel, core, and quarter the apples. Cut them into ⅛-inch thick slices and fold them into the batter. Cover it and let stand at room temperature.

3. One hour before serving, preheat the oven to 425° F. Wilt and soften the cabbage leaves one at a time in a heated nonstick skillet. Spread the cabbage leaves out, rib side down, in a 12-inch well-seasoned cast-iron black skillet, or black pizza pan, or round griddle. Flatten them out to cover the pan without overlapping more than is necessary. Spread the apple batter over the cabbage in a thin, even layer. Sprinkle the brown sugar and remaining melted butter on top. Bake on the middle shelf of the oven until golden brown, about 40 minutes. (The center should still be slightly supple.) Remove the cake from the oven; dust with confectioners' sugar and serve hot from the skillet, or slide it out onto a large serving plate.

Italian Black Plums Baked in a Brioche Crust

SERVES 6 TO 8

A pie crust made of brioche creates quite a different effect from the usual firm sugar crust or flaky pastry used for fruit tarts. People are enchanted by the rustic look of ragged edges of brioche hanging over the rim of an earthenware pie plate, and brioche tarts are delicious, especially when the pastry can absorb some of the fruit juices during baking.

I've tried all sorts of fruits with brioche-based crusts, including peaches and gooseberries and black cherries. I've also tried lining the crusts with pastry cream and spreading the fresh fruits on top before baking. All these variations are wonderful, but this tart of Italian black plums is my favorite.

Flour
¾ *pound brioche dough (page 333)*
Egg glaze (1 egg mixed with 1 teaspoon cream or milk)
1½ *pounds firm Italian black prune plums*

⅓ *cup sugar cookies, such as Lorna Doone, crumbled in the food processor*
Pinch of ground cinnamon
¾ *cup sugar (more if the plums are very sour)*
Confectioners' sugar

1. Sprinkle about 2 tablespoons of flour on a work space. Roll out the dough to make a 13-inch circle. Line a buttered 10-inch porcelain, glass, or earthenware quiche or pie dish with the dough. Fold the excess over the rim for a rustic look or trim neatly with a sharp knife or a pair of scissors.

2. Prick all over the bottom with a fork. Let the dough rest 1 hour in a cool place, out of the refrigerator. Brush the bottom with egg glaze.

3. Preheat the oven to 400° F. Split the plums and remove the pits. Spread the crumbled cookies, and a pinch of cinnamon, on the bottom of the tart. Arrange the plums, cut side up, slightly overlapping or side by side, pressing them together. Sprinkle with sugar. Lightly glaze the rim with egg. Bake on the lower-middle shelf for 15 minutes. (If the crust browns too fast, cover the edges loosely with foil.) Lower the oven heat to 300° F and continue baking 30 minutes longer.

4. Serve at room temperature with a good dusting of confectioners' sugar.

<table>
<tr><td>SERVES 6</td><td></td></tr>
</table>

Rhubarb Tarts with Whipped Cream and Caramel

This refreshing dessert tart makes an ideal ending to a hearty meal, and served with a small dollop of whipped cream it becomes truly luxurious. I use either fresh or frozen rhubarb with equal success.

2½ to 2¾ pounds crisp, tender fresh rhubarb, or 2 (15-ounce) packages frozen cut rhubarb

1⅓ cups granulated sugar plus more if necessary

Pinch of salt

6 well-chilled, unbaked 4-inch tart shells (see Pastry for Tarts, page 337, or use puff pastry)

2 teaspoons grated orange rind

½ cup heavy (whipping) cream

¼ teaspoon pure anise extract

½ teaspoon pure vanilla extract

Confectioners' sugar

CARAMEL SAUCE

¼ cup sugar

1½ tablespoons light corn syrup

⅓ cup heavy cream, at room temperature

1 tablespoon unsalted butter, at room temperature

1. Preheat the oven to 450° F.

2. If using fresh rhubarb, trim the ends and scrape the stalks; discard strings. Cut the rhubarb into 1-inch lengths. Toss the fresh or frozen rhubarb with the sugar and a pinch of salt; spread it out in one layer on an aluminum-foil-lined heavy jelly-roll pan, and bake 15 to 20 minutes or until the rhubarb is lightly caramelized. Scrape it into a strainer set over a small, heavy-bottomed saucepan and let it drain for 20 minutes.

3. Meanwhile, lower the oven heat to 350° F. Prick the bottoms of the tartlet shells all over with the tines of a fork to prevent puffing. Line the shells with foil, fill with beans or rice, and place them on a parchment-lined baking sheet. Bake for 15 minutes.

4. Reduce the rhubarb juices to a few tablespoons. Stir in the orange rind. Remove the foil and weights; spread the orange-rind glaze on the bottom of each pastry shell and return the shells to the oven to bake another 10 minutes. Remove and cool them on cake racks.

5. Beat the cream until soft mounds form. Beat in the flavorings and 2 teaspoons of confectioners' sugar. Keep chilled. Meanwhile, taste the rhubarb, and if necessary, add sugar.

6. Make the caramel. Heat the sugar and corn syrup in a small, deep saucepan, preferably copper, and cook over low heat until the sugar has dissolved and the mixture

(continued)

begins to change color. Bring it to a boil and continue to cook, swirling the pan, until the mixture turns a rich golden brown. Remove it from the heat to stop the cooking; add the cream and butter (be very careful to avoid getting spattered). Return the pan to the stove and cook, stirring, until the caramel is smooth. Pour into a bowl to stop the cooking. Makes ½ cup. *(Up to this point the recipe can be prepared hours in advance.)*

7. When you are ready to serve, dust the pastry edges with confectioners' sugar, divide the rhubarb among the 6 tarts, add a dollop of whipped cream, and decorate with criss-crossing lines of warm caramel. (Use only enough to make an attractive design; reserve the remainder in a closed jar in the refrigerator. Save for some other purpose.)

NOTE TO
THE COOK
If the caramel is not easy to pour in a thin stream, stir in a little water, heat to blend and cool before using.

Apple Galettes with Fried Apple Peels

When Alain Senderens saluted New York ("the Big Apple") with a fabulous assortment of apple desserts, he sprinkled them with crunchy fried apple peels dusted with confectioners' sugar. I have borrowed this decoration for these *galettes* of rich short-crust pastry and apples sautéed with butter and flavored with a bitter-orange marmalade.

1 *recipe Rich Short-Crust Pastry (see recipe, page 322)*

6 *large tart green apples (Granny Smiths, Pippins, or Greenings)*

2 *tablespoons lemon juice*

⅓ *cup clarified butter*

3 *tablespoons safflower oil*

4 *tablespoons unsalted butter*

5 *tablespoons imported Seville orange marmalade*

2 *tablespoons Cognac*

Confectioners' sugar

1. Make the pastries.

2. Peel the apples so that the peelings are thick. Cut the peelings into ¼- by 2-inch strips. Cut 3 of the peeled apples into medium slices and place in a bowl. Sprinkle with some of the lemon juice; toss them and set aside. Rub the remaining apples with lemon juice, wrap in plastic and reserve for another use.

3. Heat the clarified butter and oil until sizzling in a small skillet. Working in batches, fry the peelings 2 to 3 minutes or until browned. Once the right temperature is reached, very little fat is absorbed and the browning can be controlled properly. When the peels are well-browned around the edges, use a slotted spoon to transfer them to a paper-towel-lined baking sheet to drain. They will crisp as they dry. They can be made hours in advance, but do not refrigerate. If they lose their crunchiness, simply place them in a slow oven to crisp, about 30 minutes. Pour off the fat from the skillet and discard.

4. Melt 2 tablespoons of the butter in a 10-inch skillet. Add the apple slices and sauté them, turning often, for 1 minute or until they are barely soft. Push the apples to one side of the skillet, add the marmalade, Cognac, and remaining butter, and mix with the pan juices. Fold in the apple slices and cook over high heat, turning the apple slices constantly until they are well-caramelized, about 3 minutes. Cool them completely on a side plate.

5. About 1 hour before serving, arrange overlapping apple slices in a pinwheel fashion on the baked rounds.

6. Just before serving, top with the reserved fried apple peelings, and lavishly dust with confectioners' sugar.

Rich Short-Crust Pastry

This marvelous pastry is so fragile that its dough must be rolled through sheets of plastic wrap, lest it absorb additional flour.

1 *cup (4½ ounces) pastry flour*

¼ *cup confectioners' sugar*

Pinch of salt

5 *tablespoons unsalted butter, at room temperature*

1 *egg yolk*

1 *tablespoon heavy cream*

1 *teaspoon pure vanilla extract*

1. Sift the flour, confectioners' sugar, and salt onto a work surface. Make a well in the center of the flour mixture. Place the remaining ingredients in the center. Quickly work the butter, egg yolk, and liquid with the tips of the fingers of one hand to just blend, about 30 seconds. Use a long chef's knife or long spatula to gradually flip and chop the flour into the butter-egg mixture. The butter must not become oily. Chop until the mixture has the consistency of coarse crumbs, about 1 minute. Use a plastic bag such as a large-size Baggie to gather the dough into a single mass, and press gently to form a smooth ball. The dough should not be sticky. If it is too dry, sprinkle with a teaspoon of water; if too moist dust lightly with flour. Flatten the dough slightly before wrapping it tightly. Refrigerate at least 1 hour, better overnight.

2. Roll out the chilled dough to ⅛-inch thickness between sheets of plastic wrap or directly in the plastic bag. If using the bag cut it and remove.

3. Cut the dough into six 4-inch circles, using a 4-inch cookie cutter or a glass with a 4-inch diameter base. Cut carefully around the form with a small sharp knife lightly dipped in flour. Prick the dough all over. Place the circles on a parchment-paper-lined baking sheet. Chill for at least 30 minutes.

4. Preheat the oven to 325° F. Place the sheet in the oven on the center shelf, and bake for 10 minutes, or until lightly golden. Cool on the paper on a cake rack. Gently glide them off the paper when cool. Handle carefully; once the galettes are baked, they are extremely fragile.

Red and Green Grape Flan

She was talking about the light. *"Regard! Magnifique!* So luminous! It is like Provence, *n'est-ce pas?* Painters come here and try to capture it. But the light here is ineffable. So almost always they must fail."

I was sitting in her garden. Vivaldi was playing on the phonograph inside the house, and the music wafted to us out on the lawn. Madame Cocuard, a charming, vivacious woman, grape grower and owner of this fine manor near the town of Saintes in the Charente, had just fed me a good home-cooked meal culminating in a simple rustic dessert, a mixed-grape flan flavored with vanilla, orange rind, and reduced Cognac.

Now we were sitting outside talking and sipping coffee. She wanted me to understand her region. The light, the luminosity, was its glory, she said—the exhilarating, dancing light and the incredible sparkling blue of the sky.

But already I was in love with the place, perhaps because at first it *did* remind me of Provence. Though it is situated north of Bordeaux on France's Atlantic coast, the climate was balmy, Mediterranean, and, with their red-tiled roofs, the houses in the coastal towns looked Provençal. The colors of the vegetation, the aroma of garlic issuing from the kitchens—these, too, brought back memories of the South. The Charentais enjoy the notion that their country is nearly Mediterranean. *"Nous sommes midi moins le quart,"* they say, playing on the words, which mean "We are three-quarters *midi* (Provençal)," and also referring to their geographical position in France vis-à-vis the hands of a clock.

Still, the region has its own distinctive quality, particularly evident in the interior (called, simply, the Charente, as opposed to the coastal Charente-Maritime). Here the stony ground is carpeted with vineyards, bearing the *ugni blanc* grapes used in Cognac production. The rolling hills are dotted with chestnuts, and are sites, too, for windmills and megaliths built by Stone Age man. The valleys of the Saintonge are often shrouded in mists, conjuring up romantic fantasies. There are great oak forests inhabited by wolves, closed medieval towns that seem almost Moorish, and old castle keeps overlooking the lazy, limpid, looping Charente River, which François I called the most beautiful in his kingdom.

Lined by grassy banks and fairytale châteaux bearing notched and conical towers, the Charente River meanders through the imposing historical city of Angoulême, then down through the town of Cognac, where, in late summer, one can smell the fumes of brandy in the streets. Here the roofs are black from a fungus caused by "the angel's share," the part that evaporates as the Cognac matures in barrels.

In the following recipe the Cognac, used to flavor a delicate custard enrobing ripe, flavorful grapes, is cooked down to intensify its taste. The cooked-off part, as the Charentaise say, goes "to the angels."

(continued)

4 cups 1¾ pounds ripe, flavorful assorted
  grapes
⅛ cup Cognac
1¼ cups milk
¾ cup all-purpose flour
3 tablespoons granulated sugar

3 large eggs
  Pinch of salt
⅓ teaspoon pure lemon extract, or more
  to taste
1 tablespoon unsalted butter
  Confectioners' sugar

1. Preheat the oven to 400° F. Stem, wash, and dry the grapes. Seed them if desired: partially straighten a paper clip; slip the loop end into the stemmed part of the grape, and wiggle the wire in order to loosen and remove the pips from each grape.

2. In a small saucepan heat the Cognac, and allow it to reduce slowly to one-half. Add the milk and heat to lukewarm; set aside. Meanwhile, in a mixing bowl combine the flour and sugar. Add the eggs, one at a time, stirring well with a wooden spoon (always in one direction) until the mixture is smooth and creamy. Gradually stir in the milk and Cognac, salt and lemon extract. The mixture should be absolutely smooth. Butter a 10-to 11-inch shallow baking dish, preferably porcelain or earthenware. Spread the grapes out in an even layer in the dish. Pour the batter over the grapes, and bake in the oven until lightly puffed and golden brown, 45 minutes. Serve warm or at room temperature and generously dusted with confectioners' sugar.

ICED DESSERTS

Quince Sorbet

The inspiration for this recipe comes from L'Arsenal in Strasbourg, a not-so-humble little bistro on a crooked little street in a working class–student neighborhood. Everybody in Strasbourg who cares about good food knows this wonderful place.

When I arrived one afternoon, the restaurant was jammed; students, painters, bank directors, the prefect of police—and not a tourist in sight. On the menu there was a drawing of a goose with its head stuck into a *Kugelhopf,* and the slogan: "An Alsatian hears nothing, sees nothing, does nothing, but he eats very well!" I can testify that the last part of this slogan is absolutely correct.

Apple and pear sorbets are usually made by liquefying their pulp after cooking. In this recipe I use only the cooking liquor obtained after long slow cooking of the quinces. The result is a lighter-textured sorbet.

Quinces vary greatly in flavor and fragrance after simmering; some will turn a beautiful orange red while others will turn amber-gold. To perk up flavor I add Cognac or *eau de vie* and lemon juice.

To serve, fluff the sorbet up in a food processor, pile into tall glasses, and accompany with thin, crisp cookies.

2½ *pounds (4 large) fragrant, lemon-yellow quinces*

½ *vanilla bean, split*

⅔ *to ¾ cup granulated sugar*

½ *cup heavy (whipping) cream*

3 *tablespoons Cognac or* eau de vie

Strained lemon juice to taste

1. One day before serving, wash the quinces and rub each with a wet cloth to remove dirt and fuzz. Cut each quince into eighths without removing peel or core, and place in a large noncorrodible saucepan. Add the vanilla bean and 1 quart of water and bring to a boil. Reduce heat and cook, partially covered, until the quinces are soft and have turned a lovely pink or amber color, about 1 hour. Strain the liquid through several layers of cheesecloth and a sieve, pressing on the pulp to extract as much liquid and flavor as possible. You should have about 3 cups of liquid. If you have less, add cold water to make up the difference. Discard the pulp. Add the sugar and continue cooking for 10 minutes, stirring often. Taste for sugar (this depends upon ripeness and the cultivar used). Allow to cool to room temperature.

2. Whip the cream until foamy but not stiff. Gradually stir in the quince liquid and add Cognac, or *eau de vie,* and lemon juice to taste. Transfer the mixture to ice cream freezer; freeze according to manufacturer's directions. Pack into freezer container; store overnight, tightly closed.

Frozen Lemon Parfait in a Bitters Mousse with Black Currant Sauce

Adapted from a recipe by Michel Bras, this dessert dish is a perfect example of his interest in playing off the different qualities of a recipe's components. In this case the bitterness of the outer mousse, which is flavored with Angostura bitters, is balanced by the inner sweet-and-sour creamy lemon parfait. The two confections are then brought into harmony by the sauce of acidic berries. When they are combined the sensation is dazzling—all the tastes explode together in the mouth.

FROZEN LEMON PARFAIT

½ cup water

½ cup superfine sugar

3 large egg whites, at room temperature
Pinch of salt

2 pinches of cream of tartar

1 cup heavy (whipping) cream, well chilled

1 teaspoon pure lemon extract (see note)

BLACK CURRANT SAUCE

2 tablespoons red wine

1½ tablespoons sugar

1¼ teaspoons grated lemon peel

1½ cups (½ pound) black currants, stemmed, or 1 (1-pound) jar black currants in syrup, drained or see notes for other substitutions

BITTERS MOUSSE

4 tablespoons unsalted butter, melted and cooled

1 teaspoon unflavored gelatin

2 tablespoons Angostura bitters

5 whole eggs, separated, at room temperature

7½ tablespoons granulated sugar

THE LEMON PARFAIT

1. Line a 5-cup capacity mold with enough plastic wrap to overhang the edges.

2. In a small, heavy saucepan, preferably unlined copper, cook the water, 6 tablespoons of the sugar, and pinch of cream of tartar over low heat, stirring, until the sugar dissolves. With a small wet brush, wash down the inside of the pan to the syrup. Boil, without stirring, until a candy thermometer registers 234° F. Remove the pan immediately from the heat. Place in icy water to stop the cooking. Meanwhile, start beating the egg whites with an electric beater. Beat them until frothy, add a pinch each of salt and cream of tartar, and 1 teaspoon of the sugar. Continue beating until soft peaks form, then gradually add the remaining sugar. Beat until the whites are shiny and stiff.

3. Gently reheat the sugar syrup. With the mixer running, gradually add the hot syrup in a slow, steady stream onto the beaten whites. When all the syrup has been

incorporated, continue to beat 5 to 7 minutes longer, slowly reducing the speed as the mixture becomes cold and thick. Set it aside covered with a damp cloth until completely cold.

4. In a chilled bowl using chilled beaters whip the heavy cream until soft mounds form. Add the lemon extract and continue to beat until the cream forms soft peaks. Gradually fold the cream into the cold meringue (it will stiffen further). Scoop the mixture into the prepared mold. Cover it securely and set it in the freezer for 3 hours. (Can be prepared up to 1 week ahead.)

THE BLACK CURRANT SAUCE

Cook the wine, sugar, and lemon peel in a small, heavy saucepan over low heat, swirling occasionally, until the sugar dissolves. Increase the heat and boil until the mixture is reduced by half. Add half of the currants. Purée the mixture in a processor. Strain it through a fine sieve into a bowl. Stir in the remaining currants and thin the sauce with cold water if desired. Set aside. (*The sauce can be prepared 1 day ahead, covered with plastic and refrigerated.* Bring it to room temperature before serving.)

THE BITTERS MOUSSE

Make the bitters mousse when the lemon parfait has chilled at least 3 hours.

1. Line a 10- or 11-cup loaf pan with enough plastic wrap to overhang edges.

2. Melt the butter in a heavy, small saucepan over low heat. Cool it to room temperature (the butter should be liquid) and set aside. In another small saucepan combine the gelatin and bitters. Set in a pan of simmering water and stir to dissolve. Remove it from the heat and cool it slightly. Using an electric mixer, beat the yolks until pale yellow and a slowly dissolving ribbon forms when the beaters are lifted. Stir the syrupy gelatin mixture into the beaten eggs; set aside, stirring occasionally, until mixture mounds when dropped from a spoon.

3. Using clean dry beaters and a dry bowl slowly beat the egg whites until they begin to froth. Raise the speed to medium and "tighten" by adding 2 tablespoons of the sugar. Continue beating for 1 minute. Then add the remaining sugar in a steady stream, beating continuously on medium speed until the whites are stiff, thick, and glossy, about 2 minutes. (The whites should feel smooth and silky.) Use a large wire whisk to fold in one-fourth of whites into the egg-yolk mixture to lighten. Gently fold in remaining whites. Very delicately fold in the *cool but liquid* butter (the mixture will slightly deflate at this point).

4. Pour half of the mousse into the prepared mold and tap lightly on the work space to even the mousse. Unwrap the lemon parfait and place it in the center. Cover with the remaining bitters mousse. Cover with plastic wrap and refreeze overnight.

(continued)

5. One-half hour before serving, transfer the mold to the refrigerator. To serve, invert the dessert onto a chilled platter. Cut it into ¾-inch-thick slices. Place them on individual plates and surround each slice with 1 to 1½ tablespoons of black currant sauce.

NOTES TO
THE COOK For the lemon parfait, use a 5-cup foil mold, obtainable at supermarkets. For the assembled dish use a large bread mold (9 by 3 by 4 inches).

Pure lemon extract can be found where high quality baking supplies are available, or through mail order, see Appendix, page 343.

If fresh or jarred currants are unavailable, substitute one 12-ounce jar of black currant preserves. Cook with the wine and lemon zest, but omit the sugar. Press the mixture through a sieve.

Fresh or preserved elderberries can be substituted for the black currants.

Fresh Citrus Sherbet with Basil Cream

SERVES 4

At first I was a little wary of basil cream with fruit sherbet. But when I tasted this combination at the Royal Gray Restaurant in Cannes, where it is served on a black dish, the presentation was so sensational and the taste so fresh and extraordinary I became an instant convert. If you own black plates, by all means use them. Just imagine a pool of green sauce on the plate, covered by scoops of sherbet, topped in turn with sections of fresh fruit and fresh mint leaves.

I like this iced dessert so much I sometimes make the basil cream sauce, then use it under store-bought sherbet (tangerine, clementine, or orange). Be sure to use the appropriate fruit as a garnish.

ORANGE SHERBET

1½ *cups freshly squeezed orange juice, strained*

3 *to 4 tablespoons fresh lemon juice, strained, plus 3 or 4 drops*

4 *to 5 tablespoons superfine sugar, depending on the sweetness of the oranges*

SWEET BASIL CREAM

5 *medium-large sprigs fresh basil*

1 *cup minus 2 tablespoons heavy (whipping) cream*

1 *teaspoon superfine sugar*

1 *teaspoon arrowroot*

GARNISH

Fresh small mint or basil leaves and fresh fruit sections

1. To make the orange sherbet: In a food processor or blender combine the orange juice, 3 or 4 tablespoons of lemon juice, and sugar, and whirl them for 10 seconds. Taste

for sweetness and add more sugar if necessary. Freeze the mixture in an ice-cream maker until firm. (If sorbet is made 1 day in advance, it will crystallize: whirl in a food processor to "fluff" it and refreeze.)

2. Take the basil leaves off the stalks and shred them coarse, then set them aside. Roughly chop the stalks and combine them with the cream and sugar in a medium saucepan. Bring the cream to a boil over moderate heat and simmer it slowly for 5 minutes. Strain the cream and discard the stalks.

3. Return the cream to the pan; add the leaves and the arrowroot mixed with 1 tablespoon of cold water, until smooth. Whisk the cream over low heat until thick, but do not allow it to boil or overcook. Immediately cool the pan and its contents in a large bowl of ice water (this quick change of temperature keeps the color and taste of the basil), and keep stirring until cool. Purée the mixture in a food processor or blender, then strain it through a fine sieve. Add drops of lemon juice to taste. Makes ⅔ cup. (*Up to this point the recipe can be prepared in advance.* Refrigerate the basil cream sauce. Return it to room temperature before serving.)

4. To serve, divide the basil cream among 4 individual plates. Place 2 scoops of sherbet on top of each and decorate with mint leaves and fruit sections. Serve at once.

Inspired by a recipe from Jacques Chibois.

Grand Marnier Parfait Filled with Fresh Berries

This is a simplified variation on a recipe included in my *The Cooking of South-West France*. There I molded a mint parfait around a chocolate mousse.

Here a parfait is filled with fresh berries, and surrounded with a light custard cream. The parfait is best if made 1 day in advance.

⅔ cup plus 1½ tablespoons superfine
    sugar

7 large egg yolks

1½ cups heavy cream, well chilled

3½ tablespoons Grand Marnier

FILLING

1 *pint* small *strawberries, blueberries, or*
    raspberries

Crème Anglaise (see recipe, page 331)

1. Two days in advance, choose one 10-cup or 12-cup mold, and one 2-cup mold, both preferably stainless steel. Place the molds in the freezer to completely chill them.

2. The following day, combine the ⅔ cup of sugar and ⅓ cup of water in a small, heavy-bottomed saucepan. Bring the mixture to a boil over medium-high heat. Stir until the sugar is completely dissolved. Remove the pan from the heat for an instant.

3. Meanwhile, place the egg yolks in a mixing bowl of a heavy-duty electric mixer. Beat them at medium speed until thick, about 3 minutes. Decrease the mixer speed to medium-low and slowly add the hot syrup in a thin, steady stream. Set the bowl over a saucepan filled with barely simmering water and cook the mixture, stirring until it thickens. When the mixture holds its shape, it is ready to be removed from the heat. Return the bowl to the mixer and beat on medium-high speed for 2 minutes. Reduce the speed to low and continue to beat until the mixture has expanded and will form a slowly descending ribbon when the beaters are lifted, about 15 minutes. (The slower the beating the lighter the parfait.) Set the mixture in the refrigerator to chill. When cold, stir in 2½ tablespoons of the Grand Marnier.

4. Place the whipping cream in a cold mixing bowl and whisk until it begins to thicken, then add 1½ tablespoons of sugar. Whip until soft peaks form. Do not overbeat (this would create crystals in the parfait).

5. *The egg yolk mixture and the cream must be the same temperature before combining.* Carefully fold one-fourth of the whipped cream into the egg mixture to lighten it. Gradually and gently fold the remaining whipped cream into the egg mixture until they are thoroughly blended. Carefully spoon the parfait mixture into the chilled large mold; cover it with plastic wrap and return it to the freezer until the mixture is very cold and thick. Then place

the smaller mold in the center of the parfait, pressing down until the parfait mixture rises up around the mold but does not overflow into it. Leave the smaller container in place. Cover them with plastic wrap and freeze overnight.

6. Three to 4 hours before serving, gently rinse the berries, then hull them. Cut the larger ones into small pieces. In a bowl mix the berries, the remaining 1½ tablespoons of sugar and 1 tablespoon of Grand Marnier. Let the berries macerate. If substituting blueberries, crush them slightly in order to create a "sauce."

7. Just before serving, pour a small amount of very hot water into the small mold pressed into the parfait, and quickly and carefully lift the mold out. Fill the cavity with fresh berries. Cover with a plate to keep the berries in place. Cover the mold all around with a warm towel, immediately invert it and unmold onto a chilled serving plate. Serve the Crème Anglaise in a sauceboat. Pass a bowl with extra berries, if desired.

Crème Anglaise

2 *cups milk*

1 *vanilla bean, or 1 scant tablespoon pure*
  vanilla extract

5 *large egg yolks*

6 *tablespoons superfine sugar*

  Pinch of salt

In a heavy saucepan scald the milk with the vanilla bean; set the milk aside, covered. (If using vanilla extract, add when cold.) In a mixing bowl whisk the yolks and sugar together until thick and pale yellow, but not to the ribbon stage. Whisk in a pinch of salt. Add the hot milk to the yolks, whisking constantly. Pour the mixture into the washed-out saucepan, set it over low heat, and cook, stirring, until the mixture thickens, the back of a wooden spoon is well coated, and the mixture registers about 165° F on a candy thermometer. The mixture must not be allowed to boil. Immediately remove it from the heat. Strain at once into a chilled bowl. Cool the mixture down quickly, stirring often. Flavor it with vanilla extract, if using. When it is cold, cover it and refrigerate until you are ready to serve.

Sicilian Ricotta Ice Cream

Here is a subtle frozen dessert (not really a *gelato*) that is perfect after a rich and well-seasoned Sicilian dinner.

Begin making the ice cream mixture 2 to 3 days in advance so the flavor of the ricotta cheese will have a chance to ripen. Though in Sicily it is served simply on a cone, you might want to decorate individual portions of the ice cream with candied fruit or chopped pistachios, or serve it with fresh figs or pears.

2 *fifteen-ounce packages part-skim ricotta cheese, strained*

1 *cup (scant) confectioners' sugar*

¾ *cup well-chilled heavy (whipping) cream*

1 *tablespoon pure vanilla extract*

2 *tablespoons dark rum*

1. Beat the ricotta until fluffy using an electric mixer. Gradually beat in the confectioners' sugar. Place in a bowl, cover the ricotta, and refrigerate for 2 days so that the cheese will ripen in flavor.

2. Whisk 1 cup of cold water into the cheese. Beat the cream in another bowl until soft peaks form. Flavor with vanilla and rum. Fold the whipped cream into the cheese and refrigerate until the mixture is well chilled. Process the mixture in an ice cream maker according to the manufacturer's directions. Keep the ice cream frozen for several hours to mellow the flavors. If it is frozen solid, soften it slightly in the refrigerator before serving.

RECIPES FOR THREE DOUGHS

B*rioche*

For a lot of people (myself included) brioche was always that dry, tasteless, fluted muffin "thing" that came in the croissant basket when you ordered coffee in France, the roll you were stuck with after you ate up all the croissants.

But we were mistaken—brioche is truly one of the great breads, a superbly rich, light confection. When properly made in its traditional muffin form, as at a bakery near the railway station in Tours, which turns out nothing else, it can be as sublime in its bready ways as the lightest, most buttery croissant.

Several years ago I took a course in pastry making at Gaston Lenôtre's baking school outside Paris. Many of my fellow students were professional bakers, and they were all very admiring of Lenôtre's brioche. I listened to them discuss it in the canteen and I heard many of them say that, despite the admonitions of our teacher that the finest grade of butter must be employed, they planned to continue to mix in some margarine in their bake shops "because the public will never know."

It's regrettable when professionals take that point of view—that *they* can tell the difference, but *others* cannot—and it has encouraged, in my opinion, a general decline in the culinary arts. Those "things" in the croissant basket that too many of us have taken for brioche are often the result of just such an attitude, and have led to an underestimation of the grandeur of this dough.

Brioche, essentially an egg-butter-flour-yeast combination, must be handled and allowed to rise in special ways. It's very interesting to find bakers who make excellent brioche but who follow totally different methods. The great Lenôtre, for example, uses the traditional first rise in warm air and second rise in cold, and his brioche is superb.

Jean-Claude Szurdak, a New York–based French-born pastry chef, also bakes outstanding brioche while taking just the opposite approach. He has adapted a technique he learned at the age of fourteen when he apprenticed to an eighty-seven-year-old master *patissier* who worked at the time for Escoffier.

Each afternoon the fourteen-year-old Jean-Claude and the man old enough to be his great-grandfather would go down to the cellar of the bakery (where it was quite cold) to prepare the yeast-flour-milk mixture for brioche, known as the *levain*. While the yeast was "working up," they would beat together a mixture of flour, eggs, and butter until it became a smooth, light, elastic dough. They would then spread this dough out on a work table, place the very soft *levain* in its center, and, with the help of a dough scraper and an intricate series of foldings, enclose it securely in the dough.

They then left the dough to rise in the cellar for a long while, on the old man's theory that a long, slow rise developed a better-structured crumb and a tastier brioche. The risen dough was then "knocked down" and left overnight to ripen in the same cold cellar room. Finally, it was shaped and brought upstairs to the warm, humid baking room for its final rise before going to the oven. In the words of Jean-Claude, the dough then "exploded" into a light, spongy cake with all the attributes of a perfect brioche: a hairline crust, an even crumb, and a delicious, even egg and buttery flavor.

As I explained in *The Cooking of South-West France*, I developed my own system for making brioche after a good deal of experimentation with proportions, rising times, and temperatures. I have found that the smaller amount of yeast I used the more flavorful was my brioche. I also discovered that, for various reasons, one could not simply double the amounts of the ingredients and obtain fine results. For this reason I worked up two different formulas for the cook who requires a greater or lesser amount of dough. In fact I've found that each of my recipes yields a dough rather different from the other, each suitable for a specific use. For example, the soft, spongy quality that one likes in an individual brioche roll is better obtained from the 1¼-pound formula than from the recipe for ¾ pound. On the other hand, the ¾-pound formula yields a somewhat firmer crust, perfect for wrapping up a small sausage or as a shell for a fruit tart.

Though both doughs take about twenty-four hours to develop, the actual working time is only fifteen minutes. Basically the procedure one follows is simple: Create a spongy yeast mixture and let it rise; knead it with flour, butter, and eggs in a food processor, and then let this dough rise until it almost triples in bulk; rupture the expanded mass to redistribute the yeast cells; ripen it overnight in the refrigerator; shape; allow a final rise; and finally bake the pastry.

Formula for a ¾-pound brioche dough made in a food processor

1 *teaspoon active dry yeast*	2 *eggs, at room temperature*
2 *tablespoons milk, scalded, then cooled to warm*	½ *teaspoon salt*
2 *tablespoons sugar*	7 *tablespoons unsalted butter, cut into 7 pieces, at room temperature*
5¼ *ounces (about 1 cup) unbleached all-purpose flour or bread flour*	*Egg glaze (1 whole egg mixed with a pinch of salt and 1 teaspoon milk)*

Begin at least one day in advance.

1. *Making the sponge:* In a small bowl, dissolve the yeast in the warm milk with a pinch of sugar. Scrape the mixture into the workbowl of a food processor fitted with the metal blade. Add ¼ cup of the flour and 1 egg. Process on and off to combine. Sprinkle the remaining flour over the mixture; do not mix in. Cover and let the sponge and flour stand 1½ to 2 hours at room temperature in the workbowl.

2. *Kneading the dough:* Add the 2 tablespoons of sugar, the salt, and remaining egg to the workbowl. Process 20 seconds. With the machine on, quickly add the butter, tablespoon by tablespoon, through the feed tube. When all the butter has been incorporated into the dough, process it 30 seconds longer. (If the processor stalls [this happens when the butter is added too quickly] wait 3 minutes and continue.)

3. *The first rise:* Scrape the resulting "cream," into a lightly greased 6-cup bowl, and sprinkle the top lightly with flour to prevent a crust from forming. Cover it airtight with

plastic wrap. Let it rise at room temperature about 3 to 4 hours in summer, 5 to 6 hours in winter, or until it is light, spongy, and tripled in bulk. Refrigerate the dough, covered, until somewhat firm, about 20 minutes.

4. *Deflating and redistributing the yeast cells:* Using a plastic scraper, deflate the dough by stirring it down. Turn it out onto a lightly floured board. With floured hands and a plastic scraper, spread the dough into a 9-by-5-inch rectangle, then gently fold it into thirds. Turn the dough 90 degrees, gently spread it out, and fold into it thirds again. (Gentle but firm handling of the dough at this point helps build an even crumb.) Lightly dust the dough with flour, wrap it in plastic wrap, weight it down with a heavy object, and let it ripen in the refrigerator overnight or for at least 8 hours. Use as directed in the recipe.

If using all-purpose flour, check that the gluten (protein) content is at least 12 percent. NOTES TO
     The dough will keep 3 days in the refrigerator if well wrapped and weighted down, or it THE COOK
can be shaped and frozen for 1 week. To defrost, thaw it overnight in the refrigerator, shape
if necessary, brush it with egg glaze, bring it to room temperature, let it rise, brush it again
with egg glaze, and bake. (The dough doesn't freeze well for longer than 1 week.)
     Baked brioche that is well wrapped keeps many weeks in the freezer.

*Formula for a 1¼-pound brioche dough
made in a food processor*

1½ teaspoons dry yeast	3 eggs, at room temperature
3 tablespoons milk, scalded and cooled to warm	3 to 4 tablespoons sugar
	¾ teaspoon salt
8 ounces (about 1⅔ cups or 227 grams) unbleached all-purpose flour or bread flour	10 tablespoons (1¼ stick) unsalted butter, melted but not hot
4 tablespoons scalded milk, cooled to warm	

Make the dough as described above with the following changes: Use ⅓ cup of the flour, 1 egg, 3 tablespoons of milk, and the yeast to make the sponge.
     Add the remaining eggs to the workbowl when you are ready to knead the dough. Process it for 15 seconds, then pour in the melted butter in a steady stream through the feed tube. Process 20 seconds longer. If the machine stalls (this happens when the butter is added too quickly), let the machine rest for 3 minutes. Meanwhile, check that the blade is not clogged. Rising, deflating, and ripening in the refrigerator are the same as described above.

Many large, uneven holes will form in brioche if you use more yeast than called for in the NOTES ON
recipe or allow the dough to rise too fast in too warm a place. BAKING
                                                                   BRIOCHE
                                                    (continued)

Sometimes during the final rising or baking of brioche, cracks may appear on the surface of the dough. This occurs because a crust was allowed to form on the dough during the final rise. To prevent cracks, brush the dough with egg glaze before allowing it to rise, then let the brioche rise in a place with some humidity—in a turned-off oven, for instance, with a pan of hot water on a rack beneath the dough.

A damp brioche means that you didn't bake it long enough. Check your oven, or next time bake the brioche a little longer at a slightly reduced temperature. A trussing needle inserted into the center of a brioche should come out clean when it is done.

Even though a brioche dough is rich in eggs and butter (a deterrent to making the dough too gassy), it will fall flat while baking if left to rise too long just before baking.

An exceptionally rich and especially delicious brioche can be made by substituting an equal amount of melted, and clarified *beurre noisette* for one-quarter of the butter in the dough. Be sure that the browned butter is at the same temperature (room temperature) as the fresh butter when adding it to the dough.

An old wives' notion is to include 20 percent *old* butter in the dough. If you do this, the legend goes, your brioche will be more highly "perfumed."

Heavily buttered molds give a truly golden color and richer taste to brioche.

Pastry for Wine Harvesters' Tourte

Here is a recipe for a two-crusted pie—perfect for savory fillings. I use a combination of lard and butter for flavor and flakiness.

11 *ounces (about 3 cups less 2 tablespoons) all-purpose flour*	4 *tablespoons leaf lard, chilled, cut into pieces*
¾ *teaspoon salt*	5 *to 6 tablespoons ice-cold water*
12 *tablespoons unsalted butter, cold, cut into pieces*	

1. *Make the pastry 1 day in advance.* Place the flour and salt in the workbowl of a food processor fitted with the metal blade. Sift the flour by turning the processor on and off once. Scatter the butter and lard over the flour, and process with 4 or 5 short pulses, or until the mixture resembles cornmeal. Add water, 1 tablespoon at a time, mixing well after each addition. Gather the dough into a ball, pushing any loose crumbs into the ball with the heel of your hand.

2. Lightly flour a work surface. Break the dough into walnut-sized nuggets. One at a time, place each nugget on the work surface; smear it across by pressing away from you with the heel of your hand. Set aside. When all the nuggets of dough have been treated in this manner, scrape the dough into a ball with a pastry scraper. Divide it in half; flatten each into a 1-inch-thick round. Dust the rounds lightly with flour; wrap them in waxed paper or plastic wrap and refrigerate overnight. Use as directed in the recipe.

TO MAKE 6 OR 8
UNBAKED TART SHELLS

Pastry for Tarts

This is the essential recipe for Michel Bras's Cèpe Tarts with Walnut Cream on page 278, and for the Rhubarb Tarts with Whipped Cream and Caramel on page 319. For a light, crisp, and tender crust, have all the ingredients cold and handle the dough as little as possible. To make the tart shells extra-thin, I roll out the dough between sheets of plastic film.

1⅓ cups (170 grams) all-purpose flour   *3½ ounces unsalted butter, chilled and cubed*
Pinch of salt   *2 to 4 tablespoons ice-cold water*

1. *Make the pastry 1 day in advance.* Place the flour and a pinch of salt in the workbowl of a food processor. Sift by turning on and off once. Scatter the butter over the flour, process with 4 or 5 short pulses, or until the mixture resembles cornmeal.

2. Dump the mixture onto a work surface covered with a sheet of plastic film. Gather it into a dough. It should not be too crumbly; if it is, sprinkle it with droplets of icy water —just enough to mass the dough together; it will not be smooth. Wrap it tightly and chill overnight.

3. Place the dough between sheets of plastic film and roll it out to make a large rectangle. Lift off the top sheet and fold the pastry dough into thirds. Turn the dough one-quarter and repeat the rolling and folding. Chill the dough for 20 minutes, then cut it into 6 or 8 equal pieces. Roll out each portion between plastic film to a paper-thin round, remove the top sheet, and fit the dough into a mold or flan ring. Remove the second piece of plastic film. If necessary, patch with odd pieces of dough. Keep the rolled and molded dough chilled and covered with plastic film to prevent drying. Repeat with the remaining pieces of dough. Use as directed in the recipe.

Use six or eight 4- or 4½-inch-wide tartlet molds or flan rings. If you use flan rings, place them on a dark-finish baking sheet for a crisp crust. Flan rings are available through mail order (see page 343). The dough can also be used to make one 12-inch tart shell.

NOTE TO
THE COOK

A SAUCE BASE

(Jus brun de veau, jus brun de canard)

Dark, Rich Veal or Poultry Sauce Base

MAKES
ABOUT 2 CUPS

I use this sauce base in several recipes (i.e., Roast Duck *Foie Gras* with Port Wine and Caper Sauce, page 188 and Sautéed *Foie Gras* with Green Grapes, page 190) to provide "background" flavoring.

Here I carefully brown the bones for a meatier flavor and a darker color, but to offset any possible bitterness I do not reduce the stock to a *demiglace*.

3½ *pounds meaty veal or duck bones, cut into 1-inch pieces*	*Bouquet garni: 8 parsley sprigs, 1 bay leaf, 1 sprig celery leaves, 1 sprig thyme*
1½ *tablespoons vegetable oil or duck fat*	1 *small tomato, roughly chopped*
2 *medium carrots, cut up*	2 *garlic cloves, unpeeled*
2 *small onions, cut up*	¼ *whole nutmeg*
1 *large shallot, sliced*	1 *clove*
1 *medium leek (white part only), sliced thick*	8 *black peppercorns*
5 *medium cultivated mushrooms*	¾ *teaspoon coarse salt*

1. Preheat the oven to 425° F. Place the bones in a greased shallow roasting pan, and roast, turning once or twice, until the bones are browned, about 15 minutes. Add the carrots, onions, shallots, and leeks and roast for 15 minutes longer.

2. Transfer the bones and vegetables to a stockpot. Add 2 to 2½ quarts of cold water to cover, and bring the liquid to a boil over moderate heat.

3. Pour out the excess grease from the roasting pan. Place the pan over high heat, pour in 1 cup of water, and bring to a boil, scraping up all the browned bits from the bottom of the pan. Add this liquid to the stockpot, and bring it back to a boil. Skim carefully then add the mushrooms, herbs, tomato, garlic, spices, and salt. Cook, skimming frequently, for 4 hours. Do not stir.

4. Strain the stock through several thicknesses of dampened cheesecloth. Chill, degrease carefully, and place the stock in a heavy saucepan. Bring it to a boil. Set the saucepan half over the heat. Cook at a slow boil, skimming, for 30 minutes, or until the stock is reduced to 2 cups.

ALMONDS

MAIL ORDER: Almond Exchange, Dean & Deluca

Whole almonds, blanched almonds, and almond meal from blanched or unblanched almonds.

To blanch almonds: Drop them into boiling water, immediately remove the pan from the heat, and allow the almonds to sit 1 to 2 minutes. Drain off the water, then one by one push the skins off the nuts with your fingers.

To toast almonds for Catalan dishes: Blanch the almonds and remove their skins. Spread them out on a jelly-roll pan and toast in a 325° F oven until golden brown, about 10 to 15 minutes. Allow the nuts to cool completely before packing them airtight in jars. Store them in a cool place up to 1 month.

ANCHO PEPPERS

MAIL ORDER: Dean & Deluca

The *ancho* pepper (a dried *poblano*) is a wonderful substitute for the two popular mildly spicy peppers (*romesco* and *nyores*) that are traditionally used in Catalan dishes.

ANCHOVIES

MAIL ORDER: Todaro Brothers

Salted, or in jars, imported from Sicily.

BLACK INK (SEE CALAMARES EN SU TINTA)

BOTTARGA

MAIL ORDER: Todaro Brothers

CALAMARES EN SU TINTA

Calamares en su tinta are available in supermarkets in 4-ounce cans; Goya is a particularly good brand. To extract ink from canned *calamares en su tinta:* First carefully open all the cans you are going to use. (One 4-ounce can will yield approximately 3 tablespoons liquid.) Put the contents into cheesecloth, gather up the ends, then twist them over a bowl. Skim off the oil, then mix the extracted liquid with wine or water as directed in the recipes. Save the solids to make a stock. See SQUID AND CUTTLEFISH below for more information.

CALF'S LIVER, BABY

MAIL ORDER: Summerfield Farms

CAPERS, SALTED

MAIL ORDER: Todaro Brothers, Dean & Deluca, Balducci's

CAZUELA

MAIL ORDER: Williams-Sonoma

The authentic shallow, glazed earthenware dish called a *cazuela* (*cassola* in Catalan) is not a requirement when preparing Catalan or Moroccan food, but I am convinced that foods cooked in it taste better. It's an extremely handsome cooking vessel, and you can use it to good advantage for all kinds of food preparation.

If you do buy a *cazuela,* it is essential that you season and "cure" it. *Cazuelas* are fragile—they inevitably do break—but proper curing will harden them to the point that they can be used directly over a gas flame. If you (1) *never* put a hot *cazuela* on a cold surface; (2) never pour hot liquid into a cold *cazuela;* and (3) are certain that, when using it over an open flame, you start the flame very low and only gradually increase the heat, you will enjoy your *cazuela* for a long time.

To cure: Soak the entire dish in water to cover for 12 hours. Drain and wipe dry. Rub the unglazed bottom with a cut clove of garlic. Fill the dish with water to ½ inch below the rim, then add ½ cup of vinegar. Place the dish on a flame tamer over low heat and slowly bring the water to a boil. Let the liquid boil down until only about ½ cup remains. Cool slowly and wash. Your *cazuela* is now ready for use—the garlic has created a seal.

To clean, soak in sudsy water and scrub with a soft brush to remove any hardened food.

Dealing with a cracked *cazuela* (a tip from my friend Rosa Rajkovic): "Submerge the dish in milk in a wide pan, bring slowly to a boil, and cook 1 hour. The crack welds itself together, and the dish is as strong as new."

CÈPES

MAIL ORDER: Dean & Deluca, Balducci's, Zingerman's

Dried, and fresh in season. Canned from France, and Germany.

CHESTNUT HONEY

MAIL ORDER: Balducci's, Dean & Deluca

CHESTNUT KNIFE

MAIL ORDER: Fred Bridge

CHESTNUTS

MAIL ORDER: Dean & Deluca, Balducci's Williams-Sonoma

Vacuum-packed, and dried.

CINNAMON

MAIL ORDER: Spice House, Dean & Deluca

There are two major varieties of cinnamon: the delicate and fragile, soft-stick type found in Latin American markets, which is "true" cinnamon from Sri Lanka; and the thick "quill" cinnamon, really *Cinnamomum cassia,* which is robust, aromatic, and smooth.

True cinnamon has a sweet, pleasant aroma, and best of all, its flavor does not get stronger as it cooks. For all the Catalan dishes you will want to use this variety. If for some reason you cannot find it, substitute a small fragment of the second type or a judicious pinch of ground cinnamon. The second type is excellent in Moroccan *tagines,* German game dishes, and Indian curries.

COUSCOUS

MAIL ORDER: Dean & Deluca, Kalustyan

The best-tasting couscous is sold loose, and can be obtained in health food stores and fine food stores. Boxed couscous indicating that the couscous can be cooked "the traditional way" as well as "instantly," is acceptable.

COUSCOUSSIER

MAIL ORDER: Dean & Deluca

CUTTLEFISH AND SQUID (SEE SQUID AND CUTTLEFISH)

DUCK CONFIT

MAIL ORDER: D'Artagnan

Precooked, wrapped in Kriovac, and perishable.

DUCK FAT

MAIL ORDER: D'Artagnan

Available in five-pound slabs. Goose fat imported from France comes in jars. Many German and Hungarian butcher shops sell rendered goose fat around Christmastime.

DUCK FOIE GRAS

MAIL ORDER: D'Artagnan

For years fresh *foie gras* was unobtainable in America, except in cans, or in the *mi-cuit* (half-cooked) state. Now, finally, there is a small but excellent American production of duck *foie gras* (no goose available at this time), and it has become possible to indulge.

If our American duck *foie gras* is carefully chosen, well seasoned, and well cooked, it can equal the best duck *foie gras* in France —and I write this on the authority of some of the greatest French chefs. But in order to prepare *foie gras* well you must first know how to buy it. Selecting the proper raw livers is not easy, for you must be able to spot whether the livers are too fatty. Just as important is to know how to cook them so they won't fall apart or dissolve. Because of these difficulties, because proper handling of *foie gras* requires a great deal of experience, and because experimentation with it can turn

out to be an incredibly expensive hobby, I asked two French friends, both experts, to teach me how to choose, prepare, and cook *foie gras*.

Ariane Daguin, proprietor of the mail-order source d'Artagnan, learned the art at her father's knee—Gascon chef André Daguin is the most knowledgeable man I know on the subject. She now chooses *foie gras* for many of the top restaurants and fine food outlets in New York, produces a line of cooked *foie gras* terrines and galantines, and will sell specially chosen domestic *foie gras* directly to you, shipping by overnight express.

Danielle Delpeuch teaches the preparation of *foie gras* throughout the United States. She has raised geese in her native Périgord, and is an expert on the cooking of livers of both ducks and geese.

If you decide to cook your own *foie gras* you must be prepared to splurge. (At the time of publication domestic raw duck *foie gras* runs approximately $40.00 per pound.) But if you like it you will have a whole lifetime of adventurous cooking and eating ahead of you, because *foie gras* goes with almost everything, whether the flavors are salty, sweet, or acidic.

To choose a good liver takes knowledge and experience. Even in the French southwest, many people are insecure about selecting *foie gras*. To quote André Daguin: "It's much easier to cook *foie gras* than to know how to buy it." A perfect *foie gras* should smell sweet and have a creamy color and a firm but "giving" texture. Most cooks, including me, always buy from a trustworthy source.

Raw top grade *foie gras* (known as "A" or "prime" liver) varies considerably in quality even though any given piece is good enough to be used in terrines, mousses, or sautés. (A few may have some extra blood, and thus won't be suitable for braising, roasting or poaching in goose fat.) On the average an A-grade duck *foie gras* will weigh approximately 1½ pounds and will be creamy in color with few surface blood spills.

Smaller livers, or B's, are not as readily available, but when they are they are mostly used in rillettes, sauces, *foie gras* butters, stuffings, and pâtés by restaurants and small charcuteries. (Some chefs use them in sautés and terrines as well.) B's often have thick, dark, bloody veins throughout the flesh and need very careful cleaning.

At present, American *foie gras* is sold only vacuum-packed in heavy plastic wrap, giving it a refrigerator shelf life of about 10 days, if unopened. *Never* store any *foie gras* in the freezer.

1 *Separate the lobes of the* foie gras *by pulling them apart gently. Set aside any small extra pieces.*

2 *First remove the large vein running lengthwise down the inside of the small lobe.*

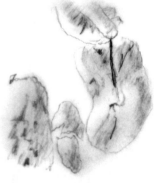

3 *To devein the larger lobe, grasp the end of any large veins you see and pull gently but firmly to remove them.*

4 *Slit the liver as necessary to get at the remaining network of larger veins (shown in the diagram above) and pull them out.*

5 *Trim off any greenish parts or large blood spots from both lobes.*

6 *For sautéing, the liver can be sliced as shown without bothering to remove the veins.*

Preparation and Cooking

A *foie gras* is made up of two lobes, one small and one large. All livers should first be rinsed and scraped of any exposed green parts and exposed fat. Then use a porcelain dish or wooden board to keep the liver completely submerged for *3 hours* in icy, lightly salted milk or water. Rinse it in clear, tepid water, drain, and dry it on a kitchen towel.

For cold terrines: You will need to order your liver a week in advance so you can prepare it as described below, marinate it, cook it, and allow it to "ripen" at least a few days before serving.

For hot preparations: Choose firm and not too bloody or blemished livers. Remove only the larger veins because to remove the rest will mar the *foie gras*.

To devein a *foie gras* (see illustrations on page 342): Let the liver come to room temperature. Place it smooth side down on a work-surface covered with a kitchen towel, with the smaller lobe to your right. Separate the two lobes by pulling gently at points A and B with your hands. If the surface membrane begins to peel, remove it.

Start on the smaller lobe. Pare off any bloody parts with a seesaw motion so that as little as possible of the liver is lost. With the inner part facing you, gently bend the smaller lobe lengthwise so you can see veins C to D to E. With your fingers or a small knife loosen the exposed veins and pull them out firmly but gently, without breaking up the flesh. Cut away any greenish parts. Set the small lobe aside.

The larger lobe has a more complicated network of veins. Begin by slitting the liver from F to G and pulling out veins F_1 and F_2. From G to H to I to J, bend the lobe gently or slit it with a knife if necessary so that you

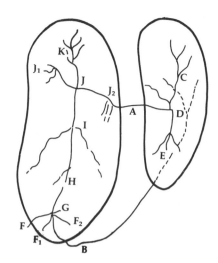

can reach the veins. Pull them out. At J, where the vein separates into three major parts, cut carefully and pull out veins J_1 and J_2. If the vein toward K is not excessively thick, leave it in place. Trim off any greenish parts or visible blood spots.

DUCK GIZZARDS

MAIL ORDER: D'Artagnan

Fresh and preserved *confit* of gizzards is packed in Kriovac in 2-pound bags.

EARTHENWARE BOWLS FOR CASSOULET

MAIL ORDER: Fred Bridge

Six-, 9-, and 12-quart white glazed bowls.

FAVA BEANS

Write for the nearest outlet: Freida's Finest Produce

FENNEL BRANCHES

MAIL ORDER: Dean & Deluca, St. Remy

Dried stalks imported from France.

FISH GLAZE

MAIL ORDER: Dean & Deluca

FLAN RINGS

MAIL ORDER: Fred Bridge

Four-inch, or 4½-inch flan rings are ideal for Michel Bras's Cèpe Tarts with Walnut Cream.

GAME BIRDS

MAIL ORDER: D'Artagnan

Pheasants, partridges, quails, guinea hens, etc.

HARE

MAIL ORDER: D'Artagnan

Fresh or frozen, imported from Scotland.

LEMON EXTRACT, PURE

MAIL ORDER: Dean & Deluca

LENTILLES DE PUY

MAIL ORDER: Balducci's

LENTILS (very small brown lentils)

MESCLUN

MAIL ORDER: Cook's Garden

Mesclun comes from the Provençal *mescla,* meaning a mix—in this case, a mix of greens. Not only lettuces are used but also some herbs, and sometimes flowering buds as well.

If you have trouble finding the youngest greens, you can grow *mesclun* yourself, even in a windowbox. Kits are available at the sources mentioned above. Each kit contains enough seeds for more than 6 dozen servings, and includes a collection of ten differ-ent kinds of green seeds imported from France: *cos ballon, palla rossa,* oak leaf let-tuce, arugula, lambs' lettuce, chervil, *blande du Cazard,* wild greens, *pancalière chicorée frisée,* and *escarole de Bordeaux. Mesclun* grows best at 70 degrees, the temperature of a heated home. Pick when plants are just 2 to 3 inches tall, just a few weeks after plant-ing. When harvesting, cut just above the soil; more will grow from the same plant.

MORELS, DRIED

MAIL ORDER: Dean & Deluca, Green River Trout Farm, American Spoon Foods

These strange and wonderful spring mush-rooms are the cook's prize. Conical, multi-wrinkled and hollow inside, they are usually no more than 2 inches tall yet they exude a powerful fragrant aroma of maple or wal-nuts. Their taste is both nutty and meaty, woodsy and musty, which makes them one of the most sought after mushrooms. And one of the few types that are fool-proof-safe for the experienced gatherer.

Morels are delicious in cream or wine sauces, or served with beef, veal or chicken, as well as vegetables. Chop them up and mix them in stuffings for birds and vegeta-bles. Sausage meat, chopped vegetables and shellfish mousse can all be stuffed inside their hollow caps. Or serve them simply sautéed in butter and with a simple roast chicken. To extend their flavor try serving them in sauces or in rice pilafs or pastas. For a more intense flavor experience a quick sauté in butter is best.

Morels appear in all colors—brown, blond, gray or black. The darker the color the deeper the flavor. If you find fresh mo-rels in the woods or at your local store, they should be damp to the touch, and show no sign of deterioration. If necessary, store them for 1 to 2 days in the refrigerator between sheets of paper towels to keep away any other refrigerator odors. When ready to use wash quickly under running water so that any hidden sand is washed away. Cut away the thick part of the stem. If the morels are large cut them lengthwise or crosswise to clean out the centers.

Dried morels, when reconstituted, also make excellent eating. Morels do not lose their taste when dried—they actually become more intense in flavor and aroma. Dried French morels have a smoky aroma while American ones are earthy and meaty. Their texture is not as fluffy, but they are firmer and therefore easier to stuff.

To reconstitute dried morels: Soak them in cool milky warm water until swollen to their original size and weight. Gently squeeze out the excess liquid by hand directly over the bowl. Once they are reconstituted they look and smell almost the same as the fresh variety. Save the rehydration liquid to use when cooking.

To learn more about fresh morels in your area contact your local mycological society. And remember: Never eat a wild mushroom unless it has been positively identified as edible. Morels must not be eaten raw; they are toxic though not fatal. Five minutes cooking time removes their toxicity.

MOUSSERONS
MAIL ORDER: Rycoff

In Europe St. George's mushrooms *(mousserons)* are called *Tricholama georgii, Tricholoma gambosum,* or *Tricholoma graveolens.* This is similar in appearance to the fairy-ring mushrooms, *Marasmius oreades.* Unless you know wild mushrooms, it is best to substitute the excellent ⅞-ounce packets of dried *mousserons* imported from France.

To use the dried *mousserons,* soak for 30 minutes in warm water, rinse and drain, then blanch for one minute—exactly as if they were fresh. There are a few important things to remember about these mushrooms: The stalks are always removed, because they are too tough to eat, and *the soaking water must be discarded and the mushrooms blanched before they are used.*

OLIVE OIL

ITALIAN OLIVE OIL
MAIL ORDER: Balducci's, Corti Brothers, Dean & Deluca, Todaro Brothers, Wally's Liquors

FRENCH OLIVE OIL
MAIL ORDER: Dean & Deluca

GREEK OLIVE OIL
MAIL ORDER: Peloponnese Products, Aegean Trader

Early Harvest *(Agoureleo)* Olive Oil.

CATALAN OLIVE OIL
MAIL ORDER: Dean & Deluca

SPANISH OLIVE OIL
MAIL ORDER: Dean & Deluca, Wally's Liquors, Zingerman's

I use many kinds of olive oils—generally, the less-expensive Colavita for cooking and the more costly extra-virgin olive oil when I am going to eat the oil raw on salads, etc.

Choosing an olive oil is a matter of personal taste. I look for those oils with a true taste of olives, a definite fragrance, and a low amount of greasiness. There are literally dozens of varieties on the market, and price doesn't necessarily indicate quality.

Below are my current suggestions, which may not be right for you. Note, too, that oils, like wine, change from year to year and labels cannot always be trusted. Several years ago, when the Tuscan groves were badly hit by frost, many oils bearing famous Tuscan names were actually blends of oils bought from Greek and Sicilian producers.

There are so many delicious Italian oils on the market it's difficult to mention them all. I highly recommend the Tuscan Castello di Ama for its perfect balance of flavor and aroma—delicious enough to use like a condiment! Though Tuscan oils receive a great deal of attention in the press, many people find them too peppery. Olive oil from Umbria is richer than Tuscan; I recommend Lungarotti for its clean and fruity taste, and the unfiltered Trevi for its earthiness.

The best French olive oils are, unfortunately, difficult to find. The delicate, light l'Olivier brand is excellent.

Greek oils are not well known here, yet they can be extraordinary. I particularly like the oil made from olives that were picked young, which is prized for its subtlety and fruitiness. I recommend the brand Peloponnese.

Catalan oils have a robust and nutty flavor and are light enough to use for all dishes. I especially like Lerida EV.

Three Spanish olive oils that are excellent: Nuñez de Prado from Baena, Almazara from Murcia, and Talcual EV from Valencia.

As a general all-purpose oil for cooking, I recommend the light, flavorful, and readily available Colavita extra-virgin olive oil.

Frying in Olive Oil

Pan-frying in olive oil is *not* an extravagance. I choose one that is inexpensive and readily available in Middle Eastern stores. Always heat the oil slowly so that it reaches the desired temperature evenly. Fry in olive oil that heats to 375° F without smoking; unfortunately a few brands smoke at lower temperatures. Foods cooked in sufficient *hot* olive oil absorb little of the oil, and the oil can be used again after cleaning. To clean olive oil after frying: simmer a slice of lemon or potato in the oil for 2 to 3 minutes, then strain the oil through cheesecloth. You can reuse this oil once or twice provided it has not been overheated. If desired, you can perfume used oil by adding a stick of cinnamon just before frying.

For almost all frying I use a nonstick skillet, which holds olive oil at a steady heat better than thin, deep fryers, or cast-iron. I add only a few slices of food at a time, so that the oil temperature does not lower. And I use a spatter screen, essential with any kind of frying. With a spatter screen you won't be afraid to fry at the proper temperature, and as a result your food will be less greasy.

OLIVES, GREEK

MAIL ORDER: Peloponnese Products, Aegean Trader

Olives are black, green, or violet depending on when they are picked. They are then manipulated by different methods of curing, then preserved in oil or a vinegar or salt brine. It is their unique taste, texture, and degree of oiliness that makes each type distinct. Some olives are bitter, others pungent, juicy, meaty, or sour.

The texture of a good olive should be firm, not pulpy or mushy, and its flavor should not be overwhelmed by brine or curing. It should be neither too salty nor too bitter. It should capture and impart the great fresh aromas of the tree.

Our domestic olives tend to be bland; the Spaniards, who produce many marvelous olives, only send us their manzanillas and gordalis (Queens), and from France we have the excellent Nyons, Niçoise, and Picholine. But only the Greeks, through companies such as Peloponnese, are exporting seven different kinds: Kalamata, *thassos (throumbes)*, Amfissa, Nafplion, green-cracked, Atalanti (also known as Royal), and the ordinary green table olives sometimes called Ionian Green—each of which has a different taste, and, in cooking, a special use.

Don't store olives in the refrigerator; when they're cold they're not as good to eat. Keep them at room temperature covered with oil, except for wrinkled, dried black olives, which should be kept in a cool cupboard in a tightly closed jar, and should be rinsed before using.

Occasionally when you purchase olives you will see a lacy white substance clinging to them, or a dense brine. These are perfectly harmless: The flesh of the cracked olives has merely clouded the brine. When using only a few olives from a bottle they should be removed with a pair of wooden tongs or a spoon; *never* use your fingers lest you introduce bacteria into the brine.

ORANGEFLOWER WATER

MAIL ORDER: Dean & Deluca, Kalustyan

OREGANO (GREEK)

MAIL ORDER: Peloponnese Products, Aegean Trader, The Spice House

PASTA

MAIL ORDER: Balducci's, Dean & Deluca, Todaro Brothers, Zingerman's

My friend Lidia Bastianich, says top-grade pasta will hold its *al dente* state for a while, even if you overcook it by a minute or two, while inferior pasta will go limp soon after it is drained.

There is no big secret to cooking pasta properly. Simply cook the best quality you can find in *plenty* of boiling *salted* water (adding the salt just before you add the pasta), drain it fast (a deep pot with a slotted inset is an excellent investment), then transfer it very quickly to a heated wide bowl for serving with whatever sauce you choose.

PASTA CON LE SARDE SEASONING BASE

MAIL ORDER: Todaro Brothers

PEPPERS

To prepare peppers, grill them under the broiler or over a gas flame, turning them until the skins are completely blackened, or bake them in a hot oven until the skins are blistered and they collapse. Place in a plastic bag or in a covered dish for a minimum of 10 minutes (this enables the skin to separate from the flesh.) Remove when cool, stem, seed, and slip off the skins. Avoid rinsing under water, or they will lose flavor. Scrape off any remaining seeds. Cut the pepper flesh into strips or small pieces and set them aside.

SAFFRON

MAIL ORDER: The Spice House, Dean & Deluca, Balducci's

Saffron threads should be brittle and lightly toasted before being pulverized, lest they lose some of their potency and turn bitter. To toast, place the threads on a plate set over a pan of boiling water, or wrap them in parchment paper and dry in a warm oven. After 10 minutes, pulverize the threads in a mortar. Avoid safflower threads from Mexico, Egypt, and Greece, which have a similar color and form but no flavor.

If you are lucky enough to find Kashmiri saffron, which costs four times the price of Spanish saffron, use half the amount called for in a recipe, because it has a more powerful taste and aroma.

SALSIFY

MAIL ORDER: Dean & Deluca

Canned salsify from Belgium.

SALT COD

You will find whole sides of salt cod with the bone and skin, boneless fillets, and boxed choice sections in most Spanish, Portuguese, Greek, and Italian groceries and fish markets, and in large supermarkets.

A Portuguese friend who is a true aficionado of salt cod insists that the bone-in slab tastes better. But even she admits that boneless and skinless fillets are easier to handle. If you do buy salt cod with the bone in, you must soak it longer and remove the bones and skin before frying or after poaching.

Buy 4 to 5 ounces per person (1 pound of dried boneless and skinless salt cod yields about 1½ pounds salt-free soaked fish). Look for ivory-colored flesh with a faint tinge of green or yellow; salt cod doesn't need to be snowy white (in fact, a white color sometimes means the fish has been treated or is too heavily salted).

A well-soaked (refreshed) piece of salt cod will actually require salt in the final dish. Because there are so many different methods of salt-curing there is no hard rule for refreshing the fish. Therefore, think of the following instructions as general rules to be adapted as you see fit. Your fishmonger can advise you, and boxes of salt cod often contain instructions, too.

First, place the cod in a colander in a bowl filled with cold water; change this water 3 or 4 times, or until it no longer has a salty taste. You can add a cup of milk during the final soaking to help draw out excess salt.

Boneless and skinless fillets, shredded into flakes and soaked in many changes of water, will be ready in as little as 2 hours, while cut-up pieces take 18 hours, and small fillets about 24. Larger pieces of cod require a much longer soaking time, about 36 hours in several changes of water.

Once your piece of cod has swelled from its soaking, it is ready to be poached, fried, casserole-cooked, roasted, braised, baked, or sauced in any number of different ways. Salt cod can even be cooked directly in a flavorful sauce, as long as the liquid does not boil (boiling toughens the flesh). However, once salt cod has been poached or fried, it can simmer gently in a sauce for a long time without damage to its tender and succulent flesh.

When you serve salt cod, you'll find that red wine goes better with it than white.

It is best to use enameled or glazed dishes when cooking salt cod. Metals tend to discolor it.

SEA URCHINS

MAIL ORDER: Caspian Caviars

Fresh sea urchins and sea-urchin roe from Maine are available from November to

April. The roes vary in size, but the largest are usually available in January. Though they are very inexpensive (about 1 dollar for 4 to 8 sea urchins), their shelf life is so brief that they must be shipped "next day air."

SEMOLINA FLOUR

MAIL ORDER: Balducci's, Dean & Deluca, Todaro Brothers, Baker's Catalogue

SMOKED SALMON

MAIL ORDER: Dean & Deluca, Balducci's, Petrossian Boutique

When purchasing smoked salmon, buy from a shop that specializes in first-quality smoked products. Salmon should be moist with a glistening sheen, firm and full of good flavor so it will stand up to whatever you plan to serve with it. Since a side of salmon has a refrigerator life of about 10 days and is easy to slice, consider investing in a full side. As you use up your piece, simply fold over the skin to keep the remainder moist.

A. J. McClane, author of *The Encyclopedia of Fish Cookery* (Holt, Rinehart, Winston) describes how he developed a modern version of the airless Greek amphora to keep smoked salmon fresh:

"Leftover pieces [of salmon] can be preserved for long periods of time in screw-top jars by cutting them into thin slices, as you normally would do for serving, and covering the slices with cottonseed, peanut, or olive oil. They should be stored in the refrigerator. The fish will not absorb the oil and the airproof medium retards the growth of spoilage bacteria through oxidation. I have kept smoked salmon this way in perfect condition for 6 months."

Freezing is not suggested; salmon dries out even when it is wrapped airtight.

SPICES

MAIL ORDER: Aphrodisia Products, The Spice House, Kalustyan

SQUID AND CUTTLEFISH

Squid and cuttlefish (which may be used interchangeably in the recipes on pages 44, 65, 141, 142, 144, and 145) are, like the giant octopus, among the five hundred or so species of cephalopods. These creatures squirt ink as a defense against predators, blackening the water around them, and then slip away. Their ink, which has some protein value, has a thickening effect on sauces, and, because of its saline content, enhances flavor, too. It also has a strong cosmetic effect, giving a fascinating black sheen to pasta, rice, and other dishes.

Squid is at its best in the warmer months, when it is succulent, tender, and full of flavor. In America we have two main types of edible squid: one found around Monterey, California, and the other around Nantucket. Both varieties are often available at urban fish stores.

When you buy fresh squid look for good sheen and a firm body, a mottled, pink skin; and an ivory pouch underneath. (If the pouch is yellow or the squid smells fishy it's been out of the water too long.) Ask your fishmonger to clean your squid for you; if you wish to clean them yourself, follow the instructions below.

As for large cuttlefish (the ink of which is particularly abundant, and the flesh of which is chewier and sweeter than that of squid), they are available frozen if specially ordered. (Imported frozen cuttlefish tend to be very large; one can serve four people.) Allow them to thaw in the refrigerator for 24 hours.

To clean squid

Wash them under cool running water. Peel off the outer mottled skin. Pull the head and viscera from the body. (If the transparent quill bone comes out easily the squid is very fresh.) Collect the thin, elongated ink sacs and set them aside in a small cup. Remove the tentacles by cutting just below the eyes, then turn the head over and press out the tough round beak. Discard the beak, the viscera, and the transparent quill bone. Wash the inside of the body carefully. Leave the pouch whole for stuffing or cut it into bite-size pieces. Store the pouch and tentacles in a small amount of icy water until you are ready to use them.

To clean cuttlefish

Rinse well, then separate the body from the head by gently pulling them apart. Cuttlefish have large ink sacs, but they can be very sandy. Wrap all the ink sacs in cheesecloth, place them in a cup, press down hard with a spatula, and leave them to soak in wine or water for at least 1 hour. Discard the emptied sacs. Cut the body open on one side of the wide, flat bone. Discard bone and viscera. Rub both sides of the opened pouch with coarse salt, rinse well, then peel off skin. Cut cuttlefish into lengthwise strips or bite-size pieces. Cut away the beak and the eyes from the head and discard. Cut the tentacles into bite-size portions.

Squid or Cuttlefish Ink

Crush ink sacs in a bowl with a fork or spoon, add a tablespoon of water or wine and let stand at least one hour. The liquid will become thick and very black. Strain before using.

One pound of baby squid (about 8) will supply about ¼ teaspoon ink. One 1-pound large cuttlefish with one ink sac will supply about ½ teaspoon.

A good alternative to canned *calamares en su tinta* are the new, innovative packets from Spain sold under the name of "Chipiron," available in some fine food markets. Call Specialty Foods in Los Angeles: Telephone 213-395-1783, for nearest supplier. These glycine packets (4 grams or about ½ teaspoon) contain an extract of all sorts of cephalopods (squid, octopus, cuttlefish, etc.). Use very sparingly, as the extract is considerably more potent than the ink in canned *calamares en su tinta*. One packet will suffice for the *Catalan Black Rice* on page 65, and *Basque Stuffed Squid* on page 145. For the remaining recipes in this book, use no more than a few drops to flavor and color the dishes.

Squid and Cuttlefish Stock

Use the peeled skin of squid and cuttlefish as well as the squeezed solids from cans of *calamares en su tinta* (optional; see above). Place 6 cups of water, ½ white of leek, sliced thin; 1 small carrot, sliced; and an herb bouquet in a medium saucepan. Add the peeled skin, and the solids if using them. Bring to a boil and skim. Reduce the heat and simmer, covered, for 30 minutes. Strain the stock and reserve.

TERRINE MOLDS FOR FOIE GRAS
MAIL ORDER: Dean & Deluca, Fred Bridge

TOMATOES
No matter how beautiful or luscious a to-

mato may look, if it doesn't smell like a tomato, it won't taste like one.

In winter Israeli tomatoes can be delicious (but are not always). Hothouse tomatoes are expensive, and generally tasteless. If you buy fresh tomatoes for cooking and they have little taste, broil or bake them until soft to concentrate their flavor before using in these recipes. Often green-tinged tomatoes will give an off taste to a sauce, but are excellent in Spanish-style salads.

Canned tomatoes should be pressed through a foodmill or squeezed gently in a colander set over a bowl to remove seeds and catch the juices. The flesh then may be chopped as desired. (If seeds are left in, and the sauce is puréed in a food processor or blender, it will have a bitter taste.)

Fresh Italian plum tomatoes are good raw. They are easily peeled with a vegetable peeler after a notch is made at the stem end. Halve, squeeze out the little bit of juice that they have, then cube and use for garnish.

When I want to peel very ripe tomatoes I never drop them into boiling water, but simply use a paring knife to remove the skin. Even a little bit of boiling water can "cook" them.

One of my favorite late summer salads consists of thin-sliced vine-ripened tomatoes laid out on a flat plate and sprinkled with sea salt and fruity olive oil. I never spoil the delicious fresh taste of good tomatoes with pepper or vinegar.

VEAL

MAIL ORDER: Summerfield Farms

WALNUT OIL

MAIL ORDER: Balducci's, Dean & Deluca

Imported from France. Store in the refrigerator after opening.

ADDRESSES OF MAIL-ORDER SOURCES

American Spoon Foods, Inc.
411 East Lake Street
Petoskey, Mich. 49770

Almond Growers Exchange
1802 C Street
Sacramento, Ca. 95814

Aphrodisia Products, Inc.
282 Bleecker Street
New York, N.Y. 10014

Baker's Catalogue
P.O. Box 876
Norwich, Vt. 05055

Balducci's
42-25 12th Street
Long Island City, N.Y. 11101

Fred Bridge and Company
212 East 52nd Street
New York, N.Y. 10022

California Sunshine
144 King Street
San Francisco, Ca. 94107

Caspian Caviars
Highland Mill
Camden, Maine 04843

Cook's Garden
P.O. Box 535
Londonderry, Vt. 05148

Corti Brothers
5770 Freeport Blvd.
Sacramento, Ca. 95822

D'Artagnan
399-419 St. Paul Avenue
Jersey City, N.J. 07306

Dean & Deluca
560 Broadway
New York, N.Y. 10012

Frieda's Finest Produce Specialties, Inc.
P.O. Box 58488
Los Angeles, Ca. 90058

Green River Trout Farm
RR #1, Box 267
Mancelona, Mich. 49659

Kalustyan
123 Lexington Avenue
New York, N.Y. 10016

Peloponnese Products
Agean Trader
2227 Poplar Street
Oakland, Ca. 94607

Petrossian Boutique
182 W. 58th Street
New York, N.Y. 10019

Rycoff Importers
P.O. Box 21467
Los Angeles, Ca. 90021

Williams-Sonoma
P.O. Box 7456
San Francisco, Ca. 94120-7456

The Spice House
1031 North Old World Street
Milwaukee, Wis. 53203

St. Rémy
818 Lexington Avenue
New York, N.Y. 10021

Summerfield Farms
Route 1, Box 43
Boyce, Va. 22620

Todaro Brothers
557 Second Avenue
New York, N.Y. 10016

Wally's Liquors
2107 Westwood Blvd.
Los Angeles, Ca. 90025

Zingerman's
422 Detroit Street
P.O. Box 1868
Ann Arbor, Mi. 48106

AGULLO, FERRAN. *Llibre de la Cuina Catalana* (Barcelona, 1933).

BENKIRANE, FETTOUMA. *La Nouvelle Cuisine Marocaine*, Paris: J. P. Taillender, 1979.

BRUNING, JR., H. F. AND CAV. UMBERTO BULLO. *Venetian Cooking*, New York: Macmillan, 1973.

CIURANA, JAUME/TORRADO, LLORENÇ. *Els Olis de Catalunya i la Seva Cuina*, Barcelona: Servei central de la generalitat dept. de la presidencia, 1981.

CHANTILES, VILMA LIACOURAS. *The Food of Greece*, New York: Atheneum, 1975.

COMELADE-THIBAUT, ELIANE. *La Cuisine Catalane*, Tome II. Paris: Éditions Lanore, 1978.

CONSOLI, ELEONORA. *Sicilia—La Cucina del Sole*, Catania: Tringale Editore, 1986.

CORIA, GIUSEPPE. *Profumi di Sicilia*, Palermo: Vito Cavalloto Editore, 1981.

CORRENTI, PINO. *Il Libro d'Oro della Cucina e dei Vini di Sicilia*, Milan: Editore Mursia, 1976.

COULONS, SERGE. *La Cuisine du Terroir—Poitou, Charentes, Vendée*, Paris: Editions Menges, 1982.

COURTINE, ROBERT. *Zola à Table*, Paris: Éditions Robert Laffont, 1978.

D'ALBA, TOMMASO. *La Cucina Siciliana di Derivazione Araba*, Palermo: Vittorietti, Sp. A. Editore, 1980.

DAVIDSON, ALAN. *Mediterranean Seafood*, London: Penguin, 1972.

DOMÈNECH, IGNASI. *La Teca*, Barcelona: Edicions Marc 80, no date.

———. *Apats*, Barcelona: Quintila i Cardona Ed., no date.

GIRODOT-CANTEL, HELENE. *Les Recettes de la Table Charentaise*, Paris: Éditions Castiella, 1985.

GOSETTI DELLE SARDE, ANNA. *Le Ricette Regionale Italiane*, Milan: 1967.

GREWE, RUDOLF. *Llibre de Sent Sovi*, Barcelona: Editorial Barcino, 1979.

GRUENAIS-VANVERTS, MONIQUE A. *La Cuisine de Provence Lubéron*, Denoël, 1982.

GUILLOT, ANDRÉ. *La Vraie Cuisine Légère*, Paris: Flammarion, 1981.

LA MAZILLE. *La Bonne Cuisine en Périgord*, Paris: Flammarion, 1929.

LLADONOSA I GIRO, JOSEP. *La Cuina Medieval Catalana*, Barcelona: Édicions Laia, 1980.

———. *La Cuina que Torna*, Barcelona: Edicions Laia, 1979.

MENON. *La Cuisinière Bourgeoise*, Paris, 1803

MONTALBÁN, MANUEL VAZQUÉZ, *L'Art del Menjar a Catalonya*, Barcelona: Edicions 62, 1977.

OLIVER, FIAMETTA DI NAPOLI. *La Grande Cucina Siciliana*, Milano: Moizzi Editore, 1976.

PARADISSIS, CHRISSA. *The Best Book of Greek Cookery*, Athens: Efstathiadis & Sons, 1976.

PLA, JOSEP. *El Que Hem Menjat,* Barcelona, Edicions Destino, 1972.

POLI, FRANÇOIS. *Tutta a Cucina Corsa,* France: Éditions du Rocher, 1983.

POMAR, ANNA. *La Cucina Tradizionale Siciliana,* Roma: Anthropos, 1984.

RIPOLL, LUÍS. *Cocina de la Baleares.* 3rd ed. Palma de Mallorca, Luis Ripoll, 1984.

SALAMAN, RENA. *Greek Food,* Great Britain: Fontana Paperbacks, 1983.

70 MÉDECINS DE FRANCE. *Le Trésor de la Cuisine du Bassin Méditerranéen,* no city, no date. Les Laboratoires du Dr. Zizine.

Salmon *(cont.)*
    smoked, about, 348
    smoked, with mixed melon, 38
Salsify, Sautéed, 281
Salt Cod
    about, 348
    esqueixada, 40
    fritters, 42
    mystical, 116
    Sicilian-style, roast, 111
Salt, Spiced, 259
Samfaina. *See* Mediterranean Caviar
Sardines, Smelts, and Small Mackerel a la
    Planxa, 45
Sardines and Wild Fennel, Pasta with, 67
Sauce
    balsamic vinegar and rosemary, 115
    base for, dark rich, veal or duck, 338
    black olive for lamb, 224
    charmoula with tomato, 137
    crème Anglaise, 331
    garlic mayonnaise with honey for lamb,
        222
    garlic mayonnaise with quince and/or
        apple, 223
    green garlic shoot butter for lamb, 222
    hot, for couscous, 86
    pepper (two), for jellied terrine, 60
    Provençal, red-pepper (rouille), 157
    salbitxada, 282
    tomato, homemade, for jellied terrine, 60
Sausages. *See* Black Sausages
Scallops, Sautéed, and Mixed Greens,
    Warm Pasta with, 78
Scandinavian Salmon Fillet Cooked on One
    Side Only, 123
Sea Bass, Oven-Poached in Meat Stock,
    Agrigento Style, 113
Sea Urchins, about, 348
Sea Urchins and Sautéed Artichokes,
    Linguine with, 75
Seafood. *See* Name of Seafood
Semolina Bread, Sicilian, 2
Seven-Day Preserved Lemons, 32
Sherbet, Fresh Citrus with Basil Cream,
    328
Short Crust Pastry, Rich, 322
Shrimp, Suquet of, with Toasted Almond
    Sauce, 139
Shrimps a la Planxa, 45
Sicilian
    artichokes, broiled, with pecorino cheese,
        17
    artichokes, pan-fried, 16
    beefsteak with capers, 243
    bread, Pasqualino's crunchy, 3
    bread salad, spicy, Island of Lipari, 10
    bread, semolina, 2
    caponatina, Maria Sindoni's, 11
    fish couscous, 88

Sicilian *(cont.)*
    linguine with sea urchins and sautéed
        artichokes, 75
    marmalade of spring greens, 19
    olives, Siracusan baked, 15
    onion slices, Siracusan baked, 13
    pasta with anchovies and toasted
        breadcrumbs, 70
    pasta with fried eggplant, tomatoes, and
        toasted ricotta salata cheese, 73
    pasta with squid in its ink, 77
    pasta with wild fennel and sardines, 67
    pumpkin, sweet and sour, 14
    rabbit, stemperata of, with capers, green
        olives, and celery, 207
    ricotta ice cream, 332
    sea bass, oven-poached in meat stock,
        Agrigento style, 113
    spaghetti with tuna caviar and smoked
        herring, 71
    -style roast salt cod, 111
    swordfish with capers, involtini of, 119
    tuna smothered with melting onions and
        fresh mint, 121
Siracusan baked olives, 15
Siracusan baked onion slices, 13
Smelts, Gypsy-Style Small Fish with
    Currants, 33
Smelts, Sardines and Small Mackerel a la
    Planxa, 45
Smoked Salmon
    about, 348
    and fresh salmon, with "vesiga" in
        Brioche, 132
    with mixed melon, 38
Smoked Tongue Salad with Spring Greens,
    51
Snapper. *See* Red Snapper
Sole Soup with Chives, 94
Sorbet, Quince, 325
Soup, 92–102. *See also* Stock
    broth with trout fillets and fresh
        vegetables, 98
    chestnut, creamy, 99
    meaty broth for couscous, 87
    mussel, Catalan, 92
    pumpkin with Swiss-chard croûtes, 101
    sole with chives, 94
    watercress and frogs'-leg, Alsatian, 95
    white bean, Macedonian, 97
South-West France. *See* French
Spaghetti with Tuna Caviar and Smoked
    Herring, 71
Spanish. *See also* Catalan
    duck with green olives, Minorcan style,
        183
    eggplant, Mallorcan style, 276
    fillet of flounder with mixed nuts and
        raisins, Barcelona, 105
    stuffed squid, Basque, 145

Spanish *(cont.)*
    suquet of shrimp with toasted almond
        sauce, 139
Spice and Herb Mixture, 264
Spiced Salt, 259
Spices, Moroccan, Ras el Hanout, 165, 231;
    for Sweets, 316
Spicy Eggplant and Tomato Salad, 30
Spread, Marmalade of Spring Greens, 19
Spread, Mediterranean Caviar, 18
Spring Vegetable(s), 288–94
    asparagus with black morels, 289
    garlic custard, 288
    Greek greens, 293
    squid stew with, 142
    in the style of Laguiole, 291
    turnip stew as prepared in Zakinthos,
        294
Squab Stuffed with Chestnut Honey, from
    Badia a Coltibuono, 197
Squid and Cuttlefish
    about 349; ink, 350
    Basque stuffed, 145
    braised with wild greens, 144
    and its ink, pasta with, 77. *See also* Black
        Rice
    a la planxa, fresh young, 44
    roast, 141
    stew with spring vegetables, 142
    stock, 350
Steak. *See* Beef
Stemperata of Rabbit with Capers, Green
    Olives, and Celery, 207
Stew. *See also* Bouillabaisse, Tagine
    beef, Catalan estofat of, 238
    beef, Greek, with tomatoes and onions,
        236
    beef, daube of, in the style of Saintes,
        233
    of duck confit and fresh fava beans, 187
    expatriate ragout with braised pig's
        knuckles and calves' tongues, 262
    squid with spring vegetables, 142
    suquet of shrimp with toasted almond
        sauce, 139
    turnip as prepared in Zakinthos, 294
Stifado, 236
Stock
    fish, special, of the Charente, 148
    pheasant fumet, 205
    pigeon, 197
    squid and cuttlefish, 350
Summer Vegetable(s), 295–97
    carrots and new onions with butter
        vinaigrette, 295
    lettuce mousse, André Guillot's, 297
    zucchini with thyme and black olives,
        296
Suquet of Shrimp with Toasted Almond
    Sauce, 139

FOR THE BEST IN PAPERBACKS, LOOK FOR THE

In every corner of the world, on every subject under the sun, Penguin represents quality and variety—the very best in publishing today.

For complete information about books available from Penguin—including Puffins, Penguin Classics, and Arkana—and how to order them, write to us at the appropriate address below. Please note that for copyright reasons the selection of books varies from country to country.

In the United Kingdom: Please write to *Dept. JC, Penguin Books Ltd, FREEPOST, West Drayton, Middlesex UB7 0BR.*

If you have any difficulty in obtaining a title,.please send your order with the correct money, plus ten percent for postage and packaging, to *P.O. Box No. 11, West Drayton, Middlesex UB7 0BR*

In the United States: Please write to *Consumer Sales, Penguin USA, P.O. Box 999, Dept. 17109, Bergenfield, New Jersey 07621-0120.* VISA and MasterCard holders call 1-800-253-6476 to order all Penguin titles

In Canada: Please write to *Penguin Books Canada Ltd, 10 Alcorn Avenue, Suite 300, Toronto, Ontario M4V 3B2*

In Australia: Please write to *Penguin Books Australia Ltd, P.O. Box 257, Ringwood, Victoria 3134*

In New Zealand: Please write to *Penguin Books (NZ) Ltd, Private Bag 102902, North Shore Mail Centre, Auckland 10*

In India: Please write to *Penguin Books India Pvt Ltd, 706 Eros Apartments, 56 Nehru Place, New Delhi 110 019*

In the Netherlands: Please write to *Penguin Books Netherlands bv, Postbus 3507, NL-1001 AH Amsterdam*

In Germany: Please write to *Penguin Books Deutschland GmbH, Metzlerstrasse 26, 60594 Frankfurt am Main*

In Spain: Please write to *Penguin Books S. A., Bravo Murillo 19, 1° B, 28015 Madrid*

In Italy: Please write to *Penguin Italia s.r.l., Via Felice Casati 20, I-20124 Milano*

In France: Please write to *Penguin France S. A., 17 rue Lejeune, F–31000 Toulouse*

In Japan: Please write to *Penguin Books Japan, Ishikiribashi Building, 2–5–4, Suido, Bunkyo-ku, Tokyo 112*

In Greece: Please write to *Penguin Hellas Ltd, Dimocritou 3, GR–106 71 Athens*

In South Africa: Please write to *Longman Penguin Southern Africa (Pty) Ltd, Private Bag X08, Bertsham 2013*